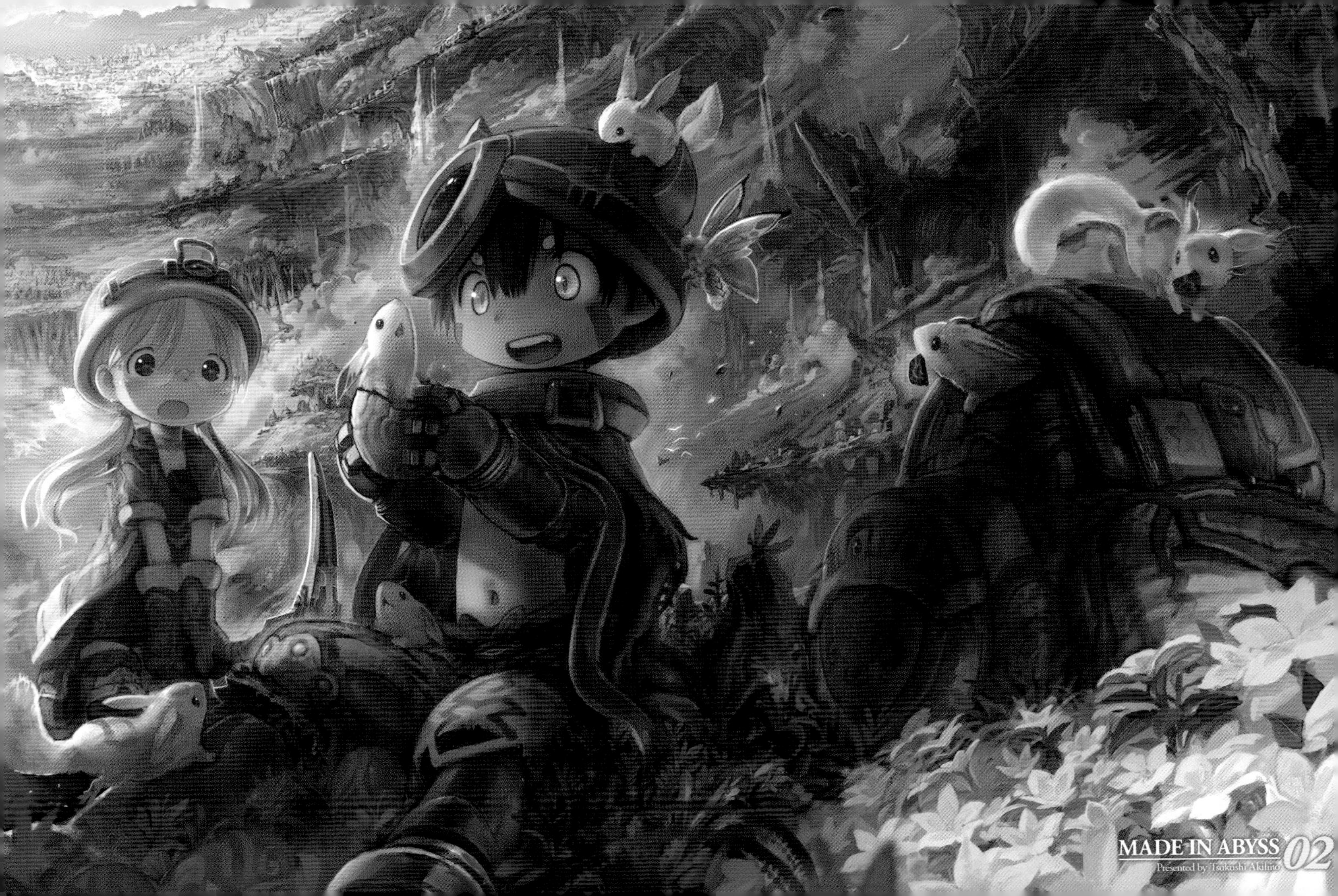
MADE IN ABYSS 02
Presented by Tsukushi Akihito

WHISTLES

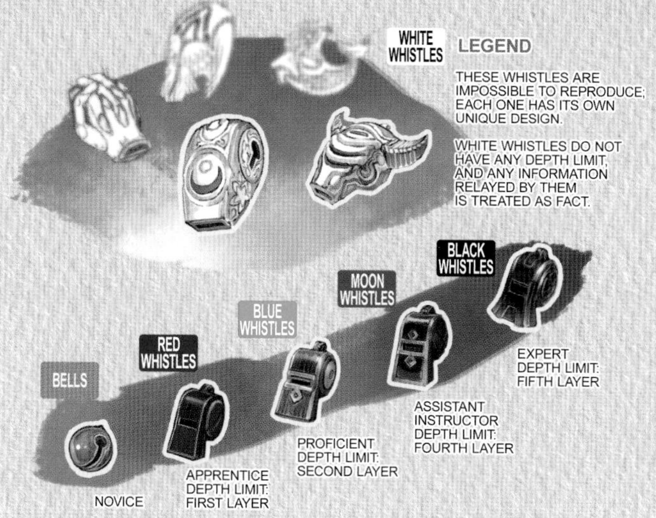
WHITE WHISTLES
LEGEND
THESE WHISTLES ARE IMPOSSIBLE TO REPRODUCE; EACH ONE HAS ITS OWN UNIQUE DESIGN.
WHITE WHISTLES DO NOT HAVE ANY DEPTH LIMIT, AND ANY INFORMATION RELAYED BY THEM IS TREATED AS FACT.
BLACK WHISTLES
EXPERT DEPTH LIMIT: FIFTH LAYER
MOON WHISTLES
ASSISTANT INSTRUCTOR DEPTH LIMIT: FOURTH LAYER
BLUE WHISTLES
PROFICIENT DEPTH LIMIT: SECOND LAYER
RED WHISTLES
APPRENTICE DEPTH LIMIT: FIRST LAYER
BELLS
NOVICE

CHARACTERS & CLASS

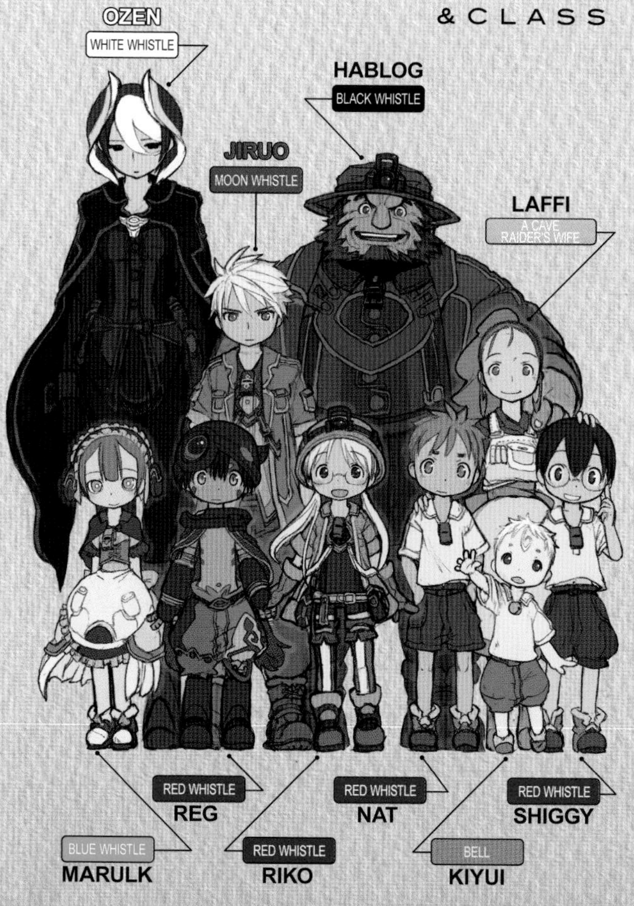
OZEN
WHITE WHISTLE
HABLOG
BLACK WHISTLE
JIRUO
MOON WHISTLE
LAFFI
A CAVE RAIDER'S WIFE
RED WHISTLE
REG
RED WHISTLE
NAT
RED WHISTLE
SHIGGY
BLUE WHISTLE
MARULK
RED WHISTLE
RIKO
BELL
KIYUI

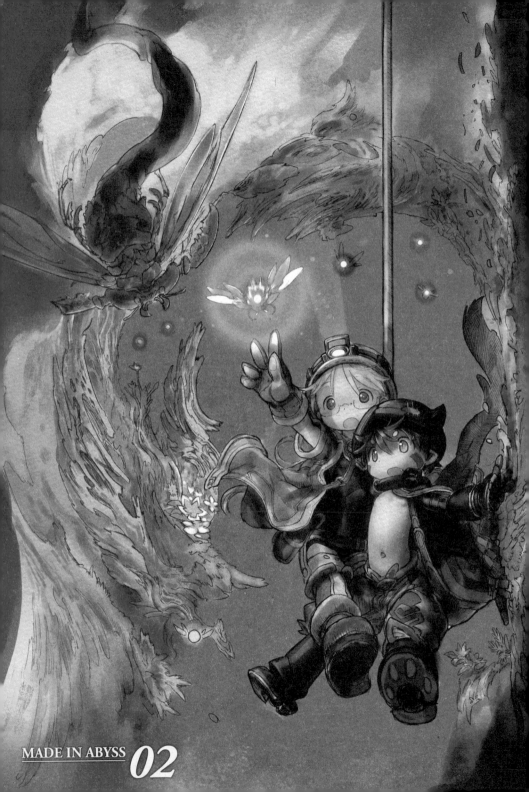

MADE IN ABYSS *02*

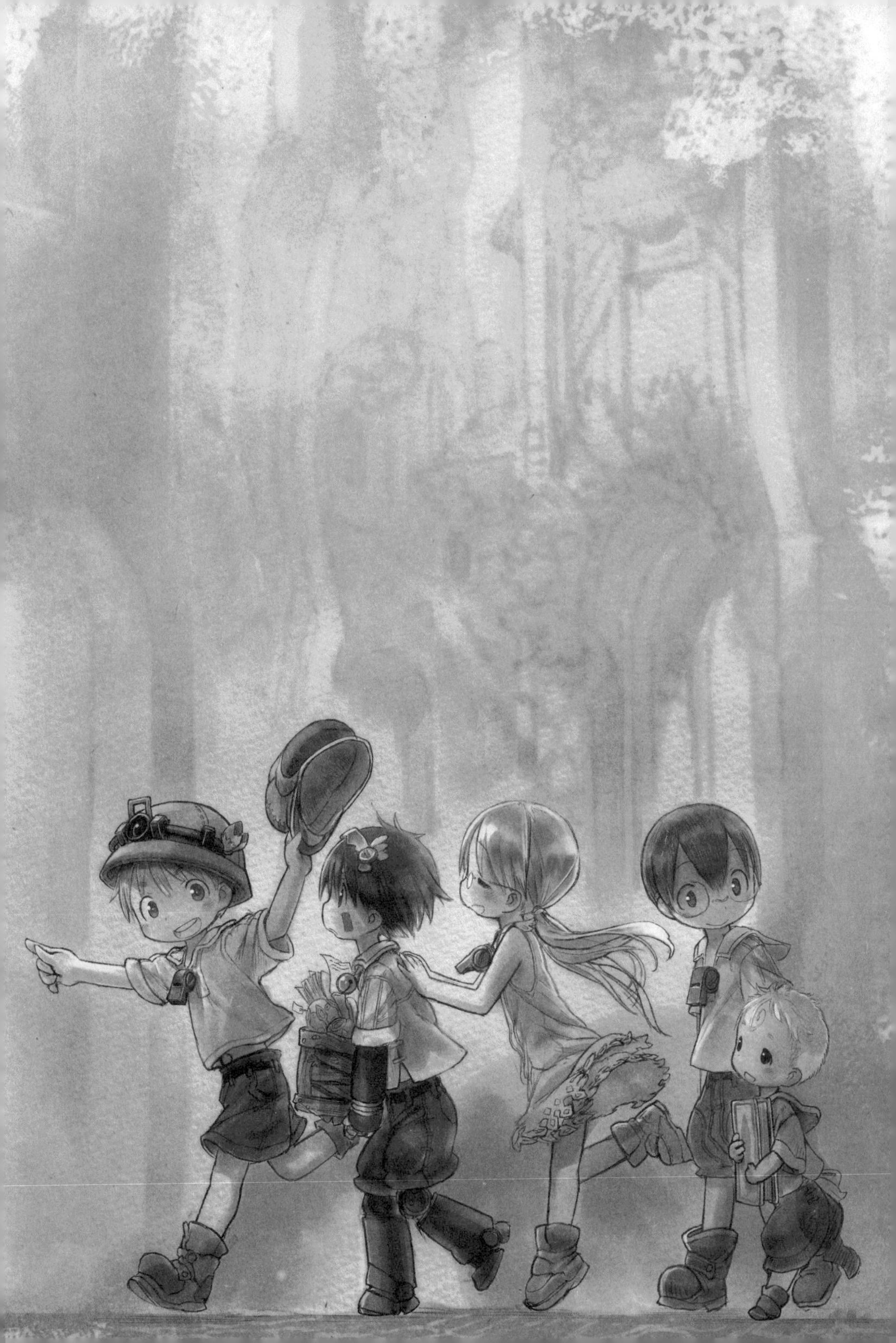

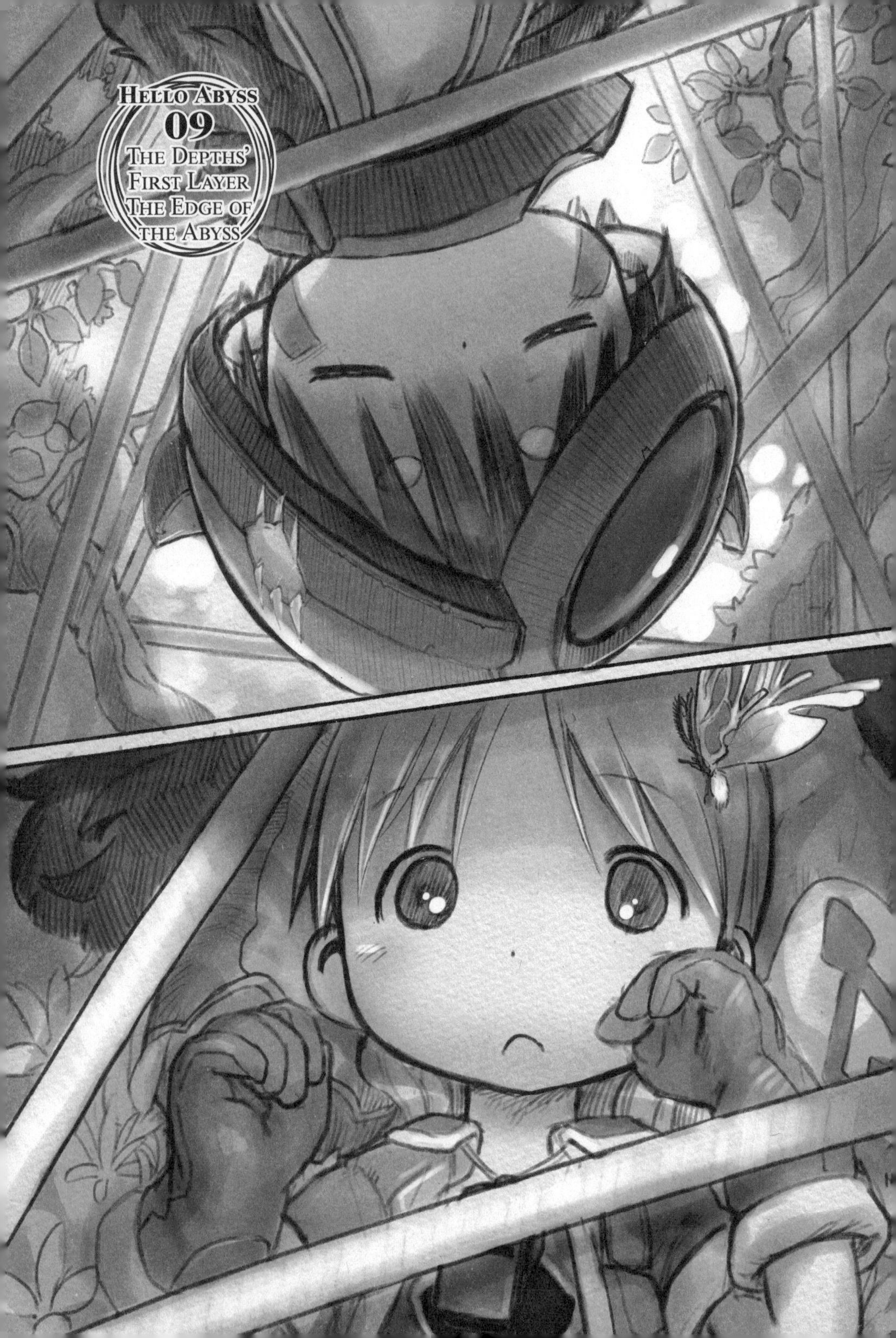
HELLO ABYSS
09
THE DEPTHS' FIRST LAYER
THE EDGE OF THE ABYSS

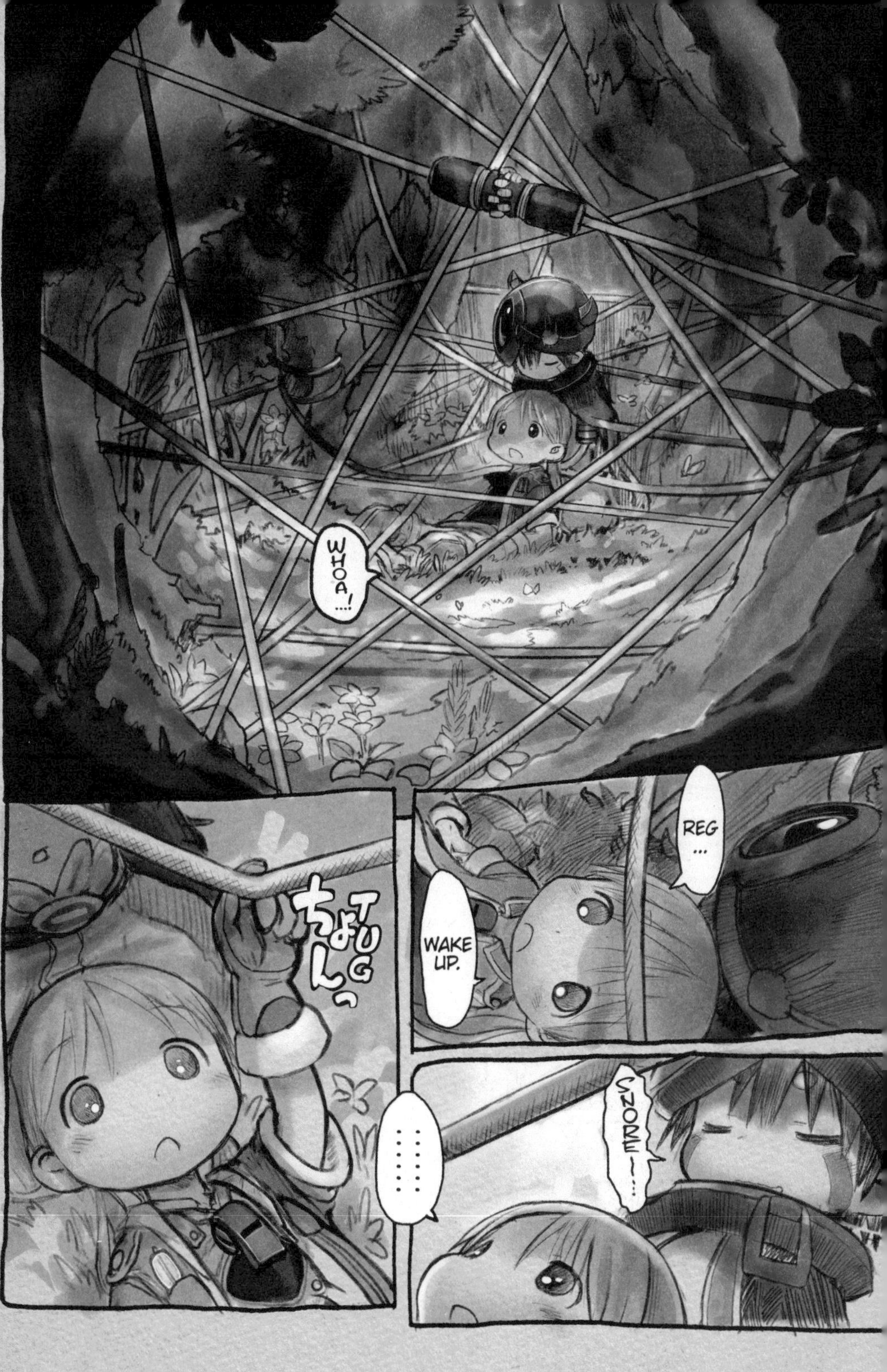
WHOA! ...!
REG ...
WAKE UP.
SNORE!...
TUG
ちょん
......

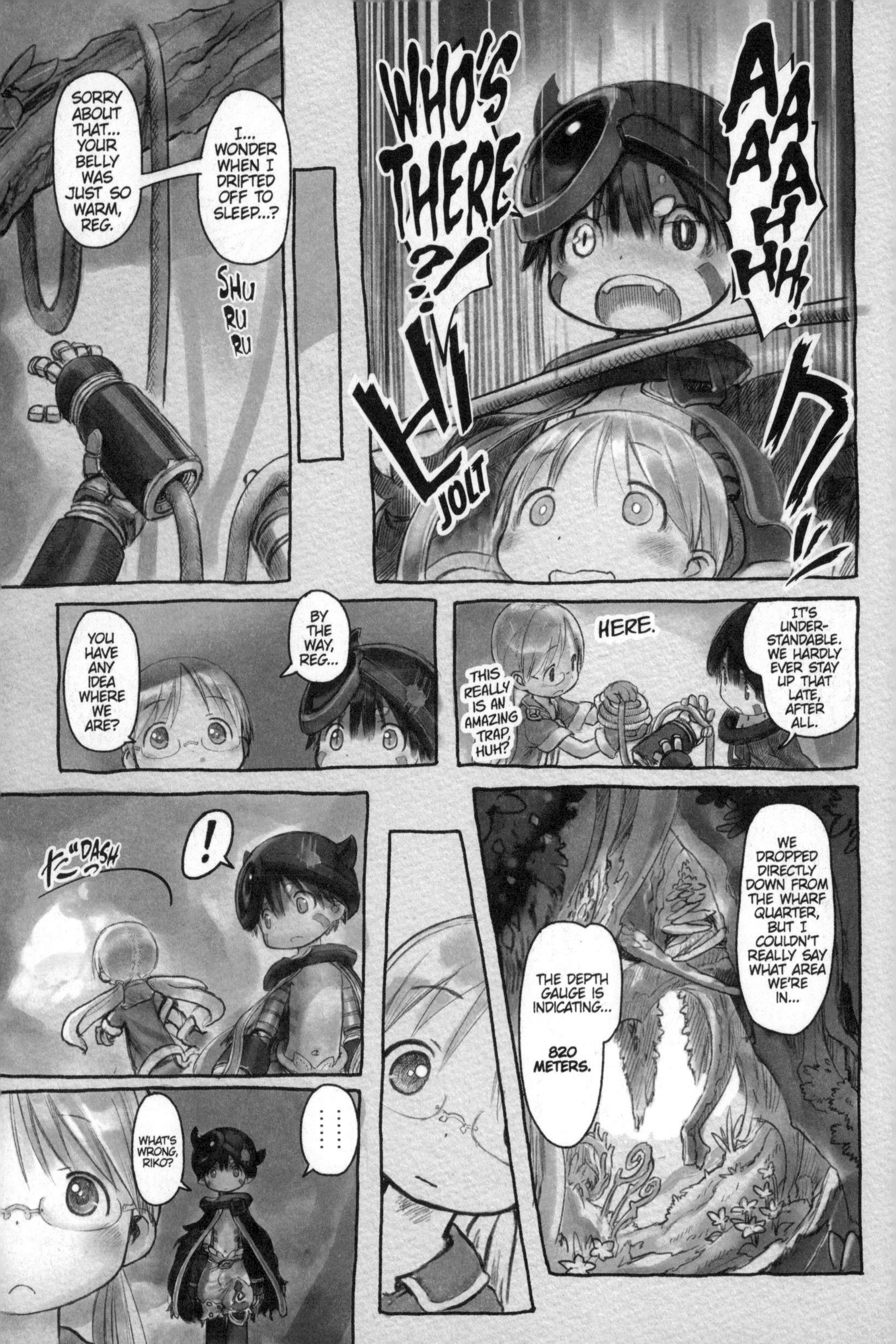

AAAAHHHH!!
WHO'S THERE?!!
JOLT
I... WONDER WHEN I DRIFTED OFF TO SLEEP...?
SORRY ABOUT THAT... YOUR BELLY WAS JUST SO WARM, REG.
SHURURU
IT'S UNDER-STANDABLE. WE HARDLY EVER STAY UP THAT LATE, AFTER ALL.
HERE.
THIS REALLY IS AN AMAZING TRAP, HUH?
BY THE WAY, REG...
YOU HAVE ANY IDEA WHERE WE ARE?
WE DROPPED DIRECTLY DOWN FROM THE WHARF QUARTER, BUT I COULDN'T REALLY SAY WHAT AREA WE'RE IN...
THE DEPTH GAUGE IS INDICATING...
820 METERS.
!
DASH
......
WHAT'S WRONG, RIKO?

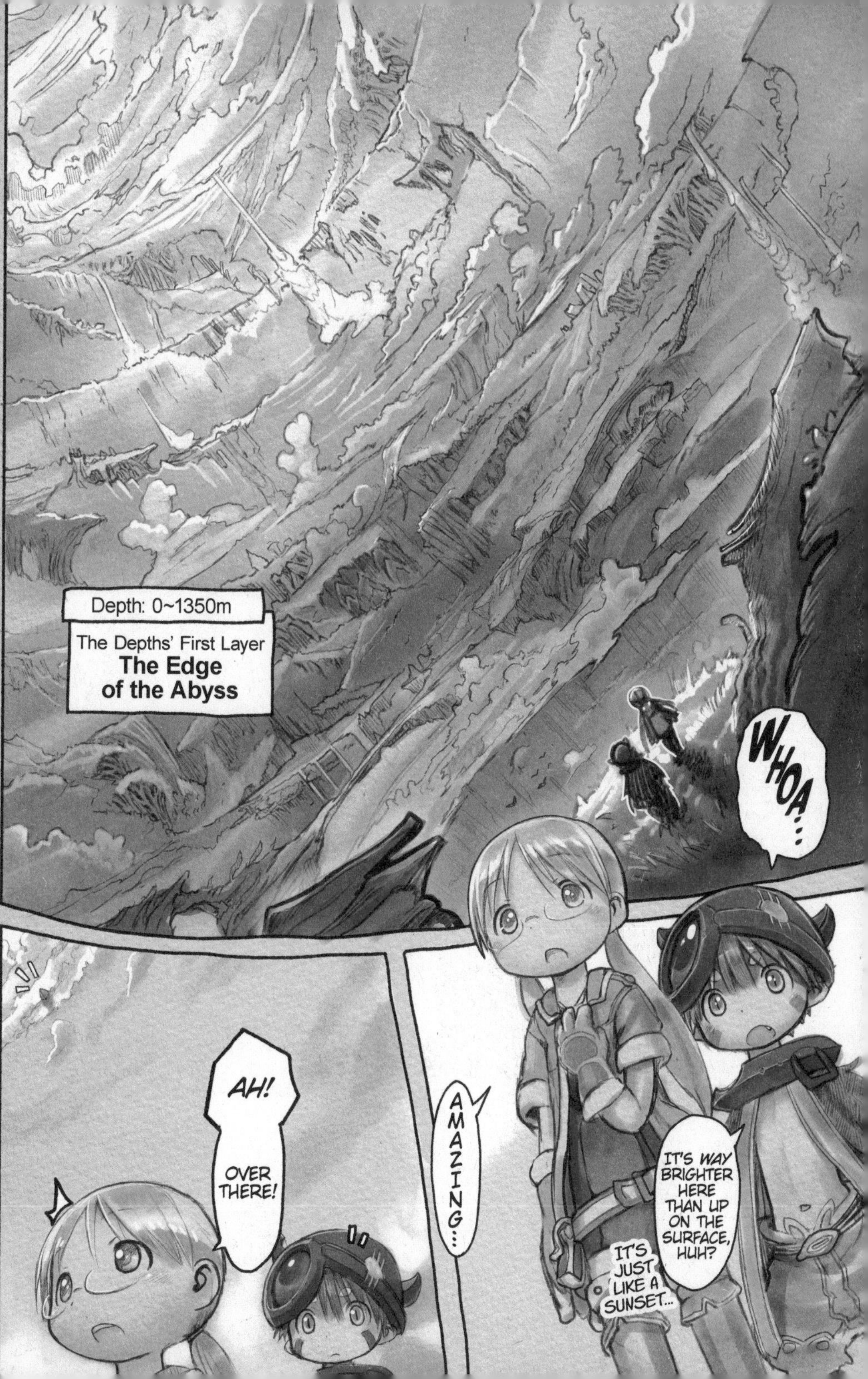
Depth: 0~1350m
The Depths' First Layer
The Edge of the Abyss
WHOA...
AMAZING...
IT'S WAY BRIGHTER HERE THAN UP ON THE SURFACE, HUH?
IT'S JUST LIKE A SUNSET...
AH!
OVER THERE!

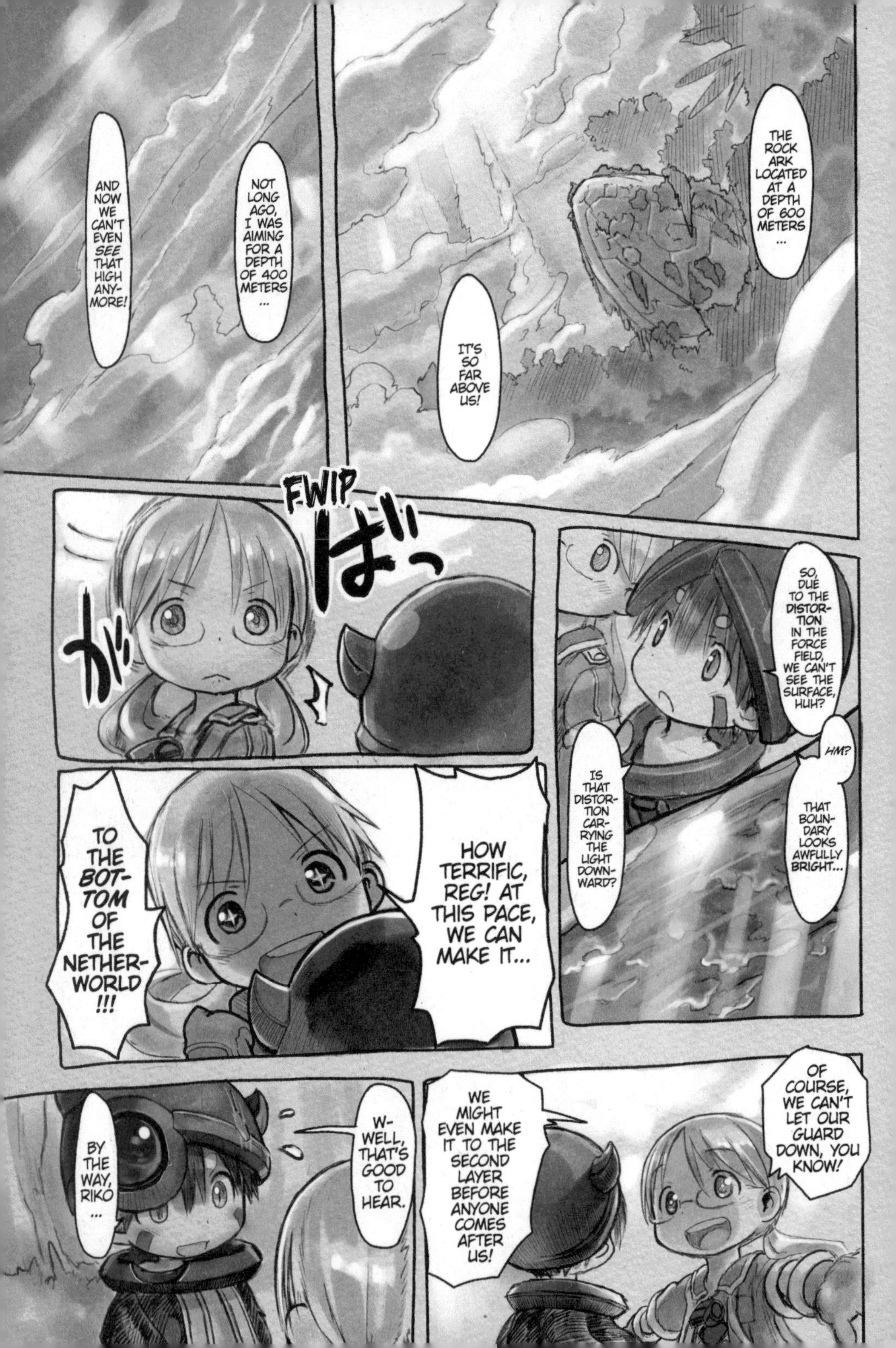
THE ROCK ARK LOCATED AT A DEPTH OF 600 METERS ...
IT'S SO FAR ABOVE US!
NOT LONG AGO, I WAS AIMING FOR A DEPTH OF 400 METERS ...
AND NOW WE CAN'T EVEN SEE THAT HIGH ANYMORE!
SO, DUE TO THE DISTORTION IN THE FORCE FIELD, WE CAN'T SEE THE SURFACE, HUH?
HM?
THAT BOUNDARY LOOKS AWFULLY BRIGHT...
IS THAT DISTORTION CARRYING THE LIGHT DOWNWARD?
FWIP
HOW TERRIFIC, REG! AT THIS PACE, WE CAN MAKE IT...
TO THE BOTTOM OF THE NETHERWORLD!!!
OF COURSE, WE CAN'T LET OUR GUARD DOWN, YOU KNOW!
WE MIGHT EVEN MAKE IT TO THE SECOND LAYER BEFORE ANYONE COMES AFTER US!
W-WELL, THAT'S GOOD TO HEAR.
BY THE WAY, RIKO ...

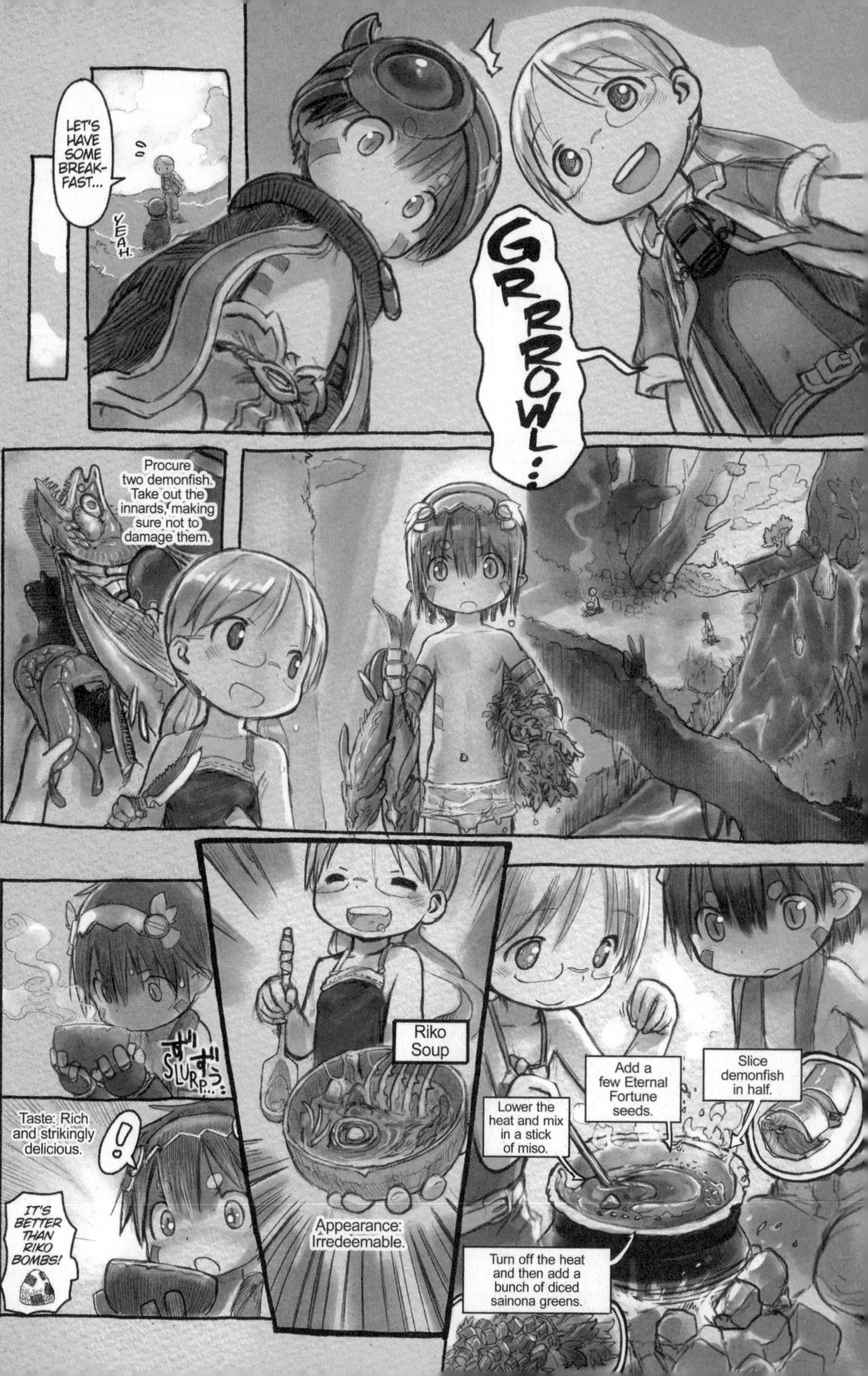

!
GRRROWL...
LET'S HAVE SOME BREAK-FAST...
YEAH.
Procure two demonfish. Take out the innards, making sure not to damage them.
Slice demonfish in half.
Add a few Eternal Fortune seeds.
Lower the heat and mix in a stick of miso.
Turn off the heat and then add a bunch of diced sainona greens.
Riko Soup
Appearance: Irredeemable.
ずず SLURP... ずずぅ
!
Taste: Rich and strikingly delicious.
IT'S BETTER THAN RIKO BOMBS!

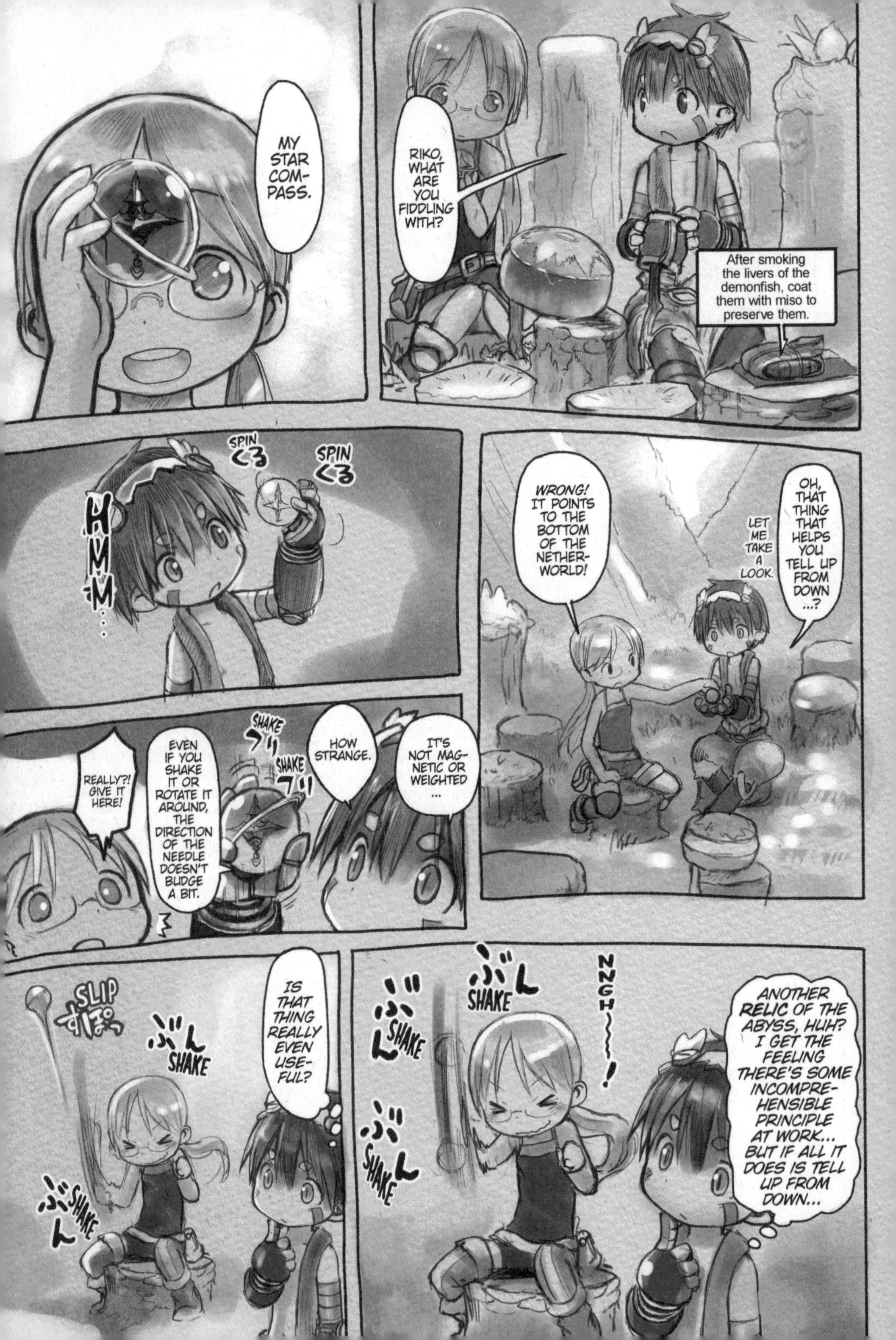
RIKO, WHAT ARE YOU FIDDLING WITH?
After smoking the livers of the demonfish, coat them with miso to preserve them.
MY STAR COMPASS.
OH, THAT THING THAT HELPS YOU TELL UP FROM DOWN ...?
LET ME TAKE A LOOK.
WRONG! IT POINTS TO THE BOTTOM OF THE NETHER-WORLD!
SPIN くる
SPIN くる
HMM...
IT'S NOT MAGNETIC OR WEIGHTED ...
HOW STRANGE.
SHAKE ブリ
SHAKE ブリ
EVEN IF YOU SHAKE IT OR ROTATE IT AROUND, THE DIRECTION OF THE NEEDLE DOESN'T BUDGE A BIT.
REALLY?! GIVE IT HERE!
ANOTHER RELIC OF THE ABYSS, HUH? I GET THE FEELING THERE'S SOME INCOMPRE-HENSIBLE PRINCIPLE AT WORK... BUT IF ALL IT DOES IS TELL UP FROM DOWN...
NNGH~~~!
ぶん SHAKE
ぶん SHAKE
ぶん SHAKE
IS THAT THING REALLY EVEN USE-FUL?
ぶん SHAKE
SLIP すぽっ
ぶん SHAKE

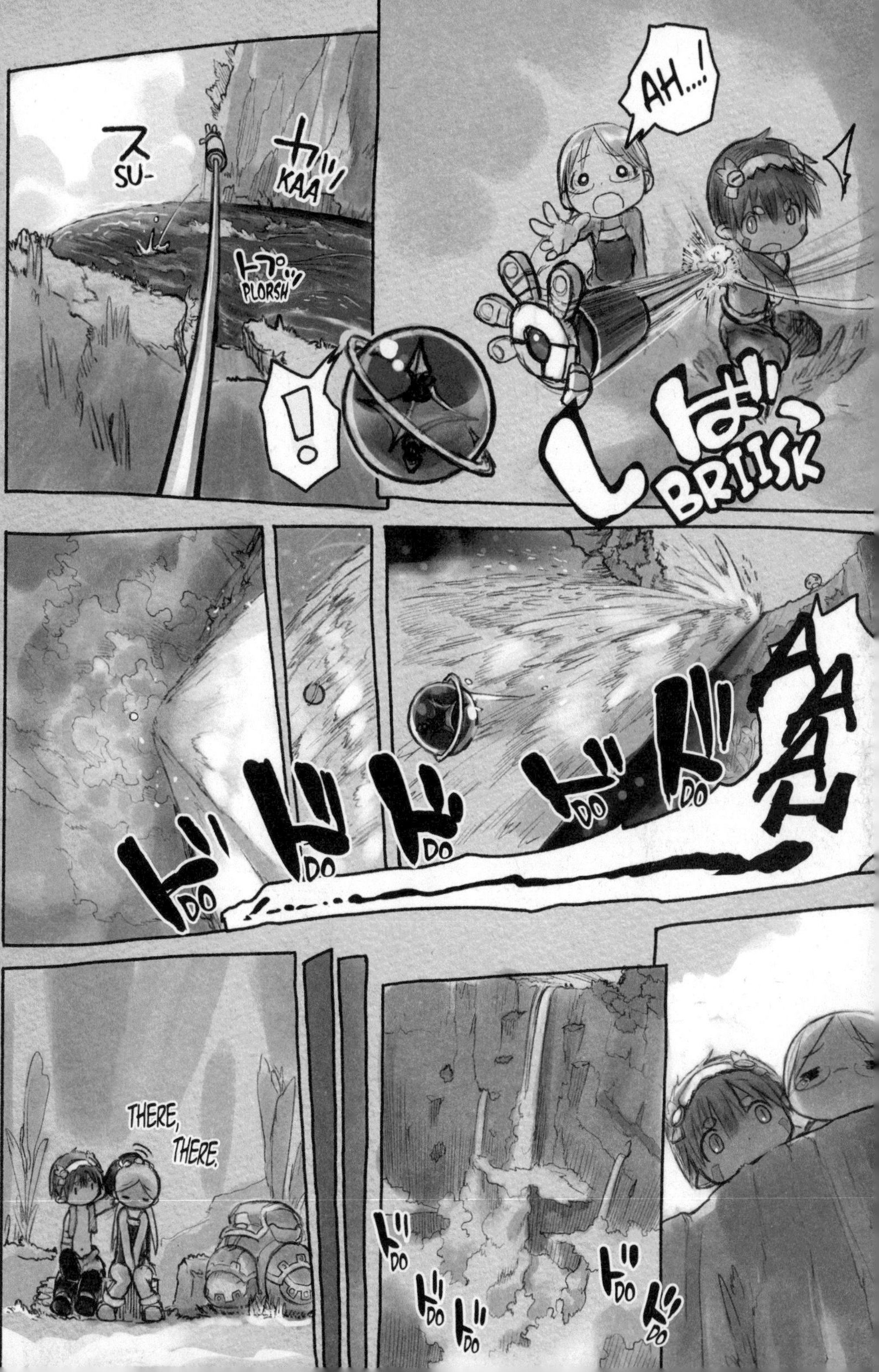
AH...!
しばっ
BRIISK
ス
SU-
カッ
KAA
トプッ
PLORSH
ドドドドド
DO DO DO DO DO
ドドドドドド
DO DO DO DO DO DO
THERE, THERE.

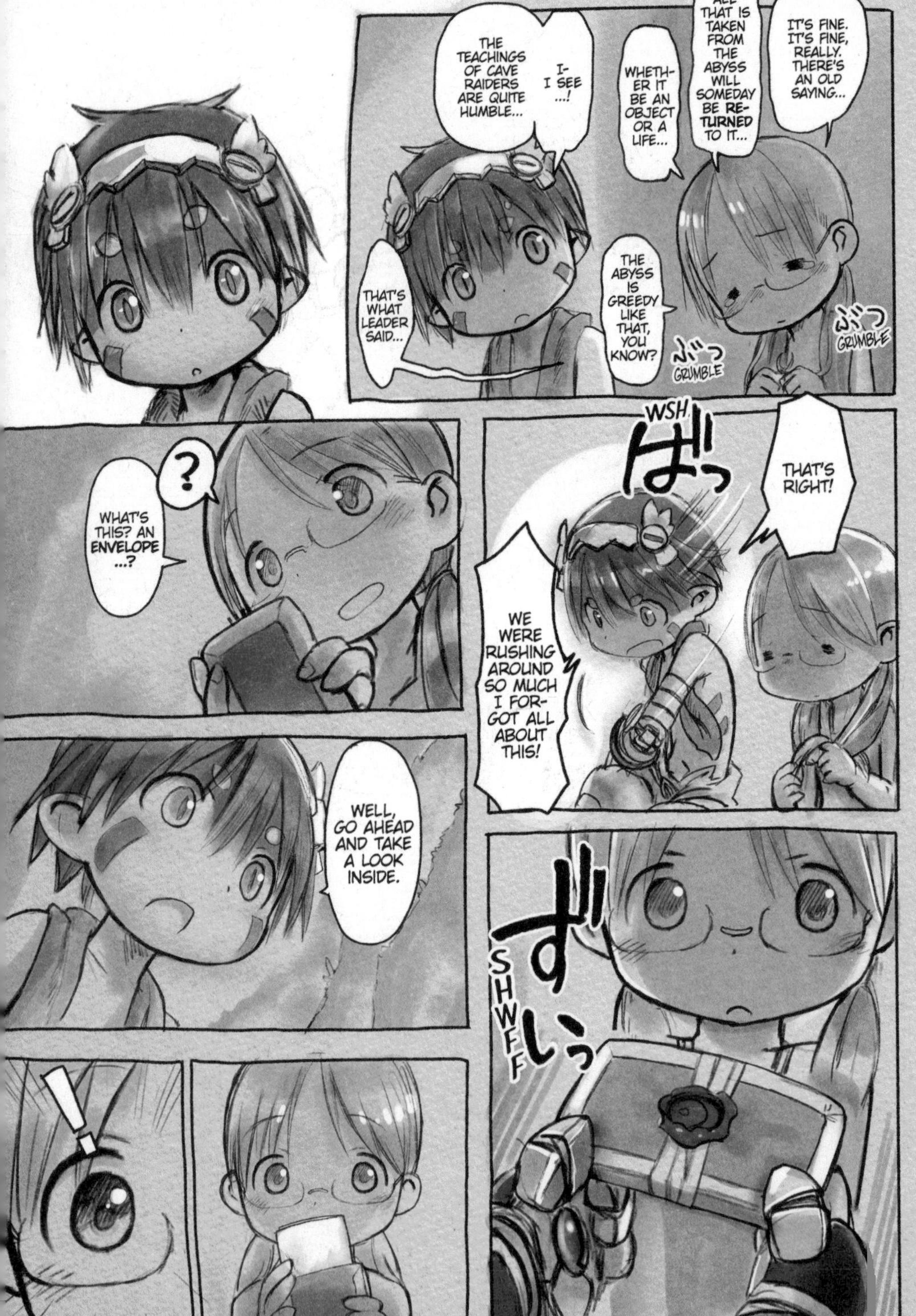
IT'S FINE. IT'S FINE, REALLY. THERE'S AN OLD SAYING...
ALL THAT IS TAKEN FROM THE ABYSS WILL SOMEDAY BE RE-TURNED TO IT...
WHETH-ER IT BE AN OBJECT OR A LIFE...
I- I SEE ...!
THE TEACHINGS OF CAVE RAIDERS ARE QUITE HUMBLE...
ぶつ GRUMBLE
THE ABYSS IS GREEDY LIKE THAT, YOU KNOW?
ぶつ GRUMBLE
THAT'S WHAT LEADER SAID...
WSH ばっ
THAT'S RIGHT!
WE WERE RUSHING AROUND SO MUCH I FOR-GOT ALL ABOUT THIS!
?
WHAT'S THIS? AN ENVELOPE ...?
ずいっ SHWFF
WELL, GO AHEAD AND TAKE A LOOK INSIDE.
!

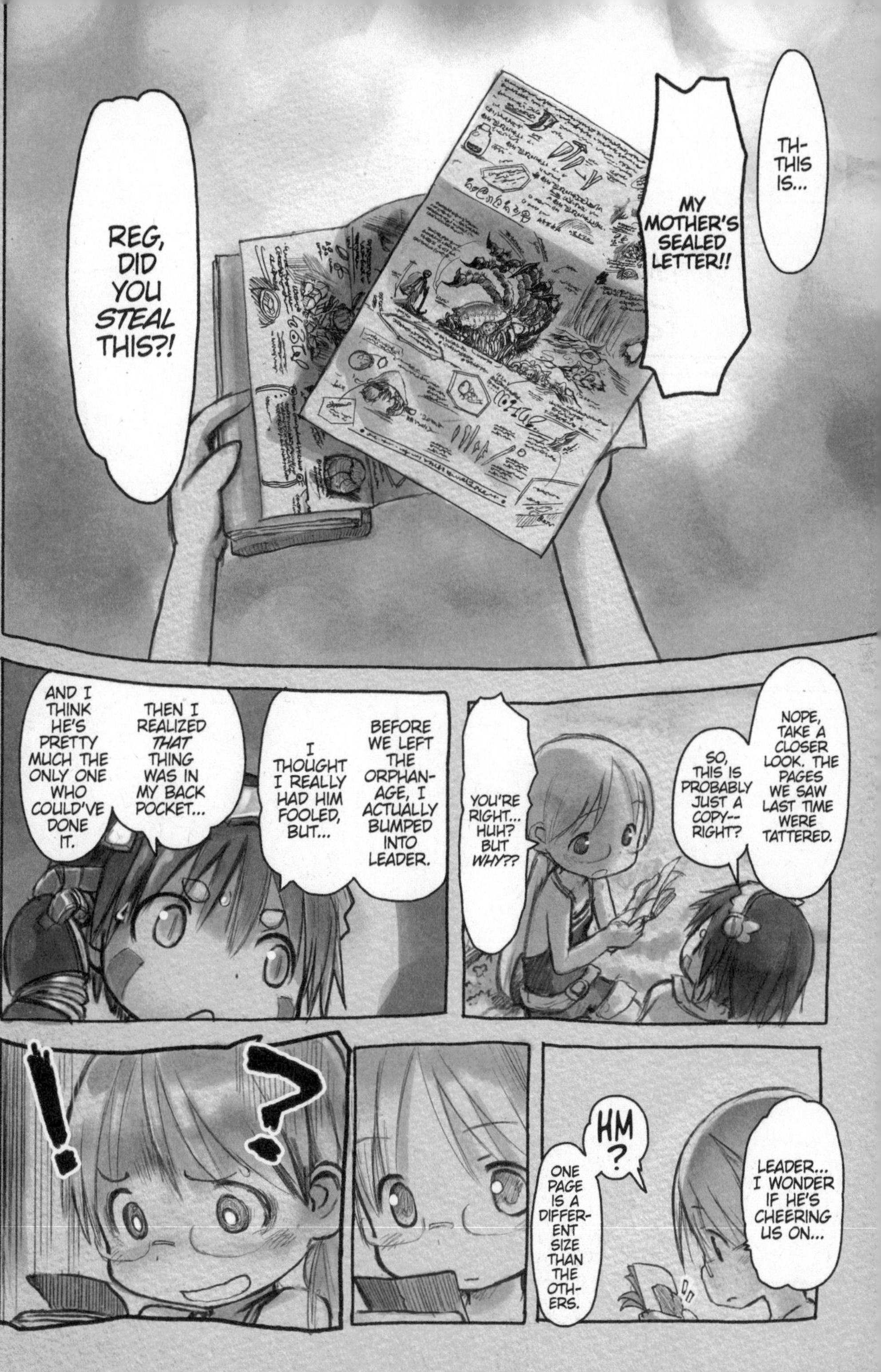
TH- THIS IS...
MY MOTHER'S SEALED LETTER!!
REG, DID YOU *STEAL* THIS?!
NOPE, TAKE A CLOSER LOOK. THE PAGES WE SAW LAST TIME WERE TATTERED.
SO, THIS IS PROBABLY JUST A COPY--RIGHT?
YOU'RE RIGHT... HUH? BUT *WHY*??
BEFORE WE LEFT THE ORPHAN-AGE, I ACTUALLY BUMPED INTO LEADER.
I THOUGHT I REALLY HAD HIM FOOLED, BUT...
THEN I REALIZED *THAT* THING WAS IN MY BACK POCKET...
AND I THINK HE'S PRETTY MUCH THE ONLY ONE WHO COULD'VE DONE IT.
LEADER... I WONDER IF HE'S CHEERING US ON...
HM?
ONE PAGE IS A DIFFER-ENT SIZE THAN THE OTH-ERS.
!?

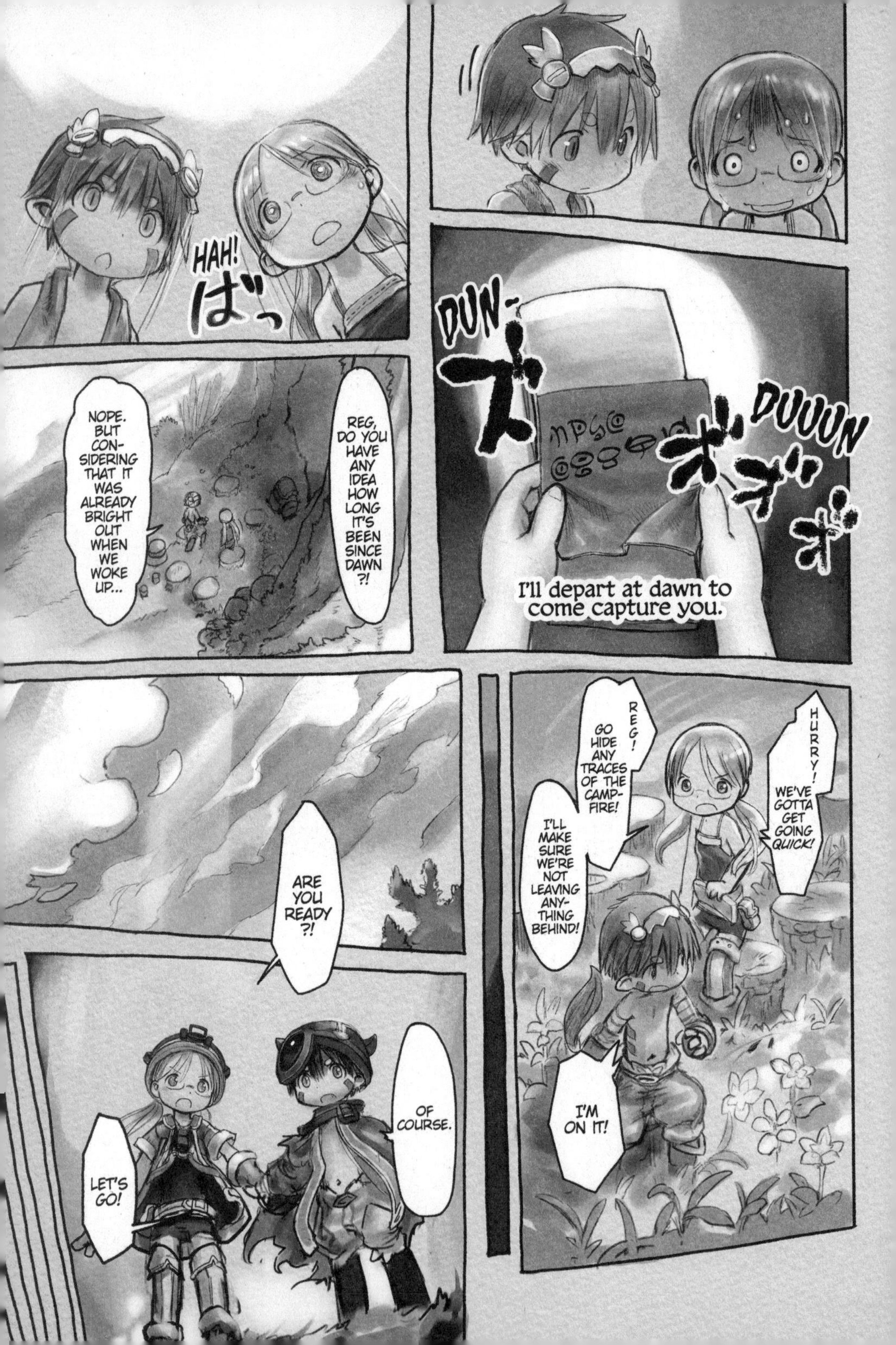
HAH!
ばっ
DUN-
ズ
DUUUN
オ゛オ゛オ゛
I'll depart at dawn to come capture you.
REG, DO YOU HAVE ANY IDEA HOW LONG IT'S BEEN SINCE DAWN?!
NOPE. BUT CONSIDERING THAT IT WAS ALREADY BRIGHT OUT WHEN WE WOKE UP...
HURRY! WE'VE GOTTA GET GOING QUICK!
REG! GO HIDE ANY TRACES OF THE CAMPFIRE!
I'LL MAKE SURE WE'RE NOT LEAVING ANYTHING BEHIND!
I'M ON IT!
ARE YOU READY?!
OF COURSE.
LET'S GO!

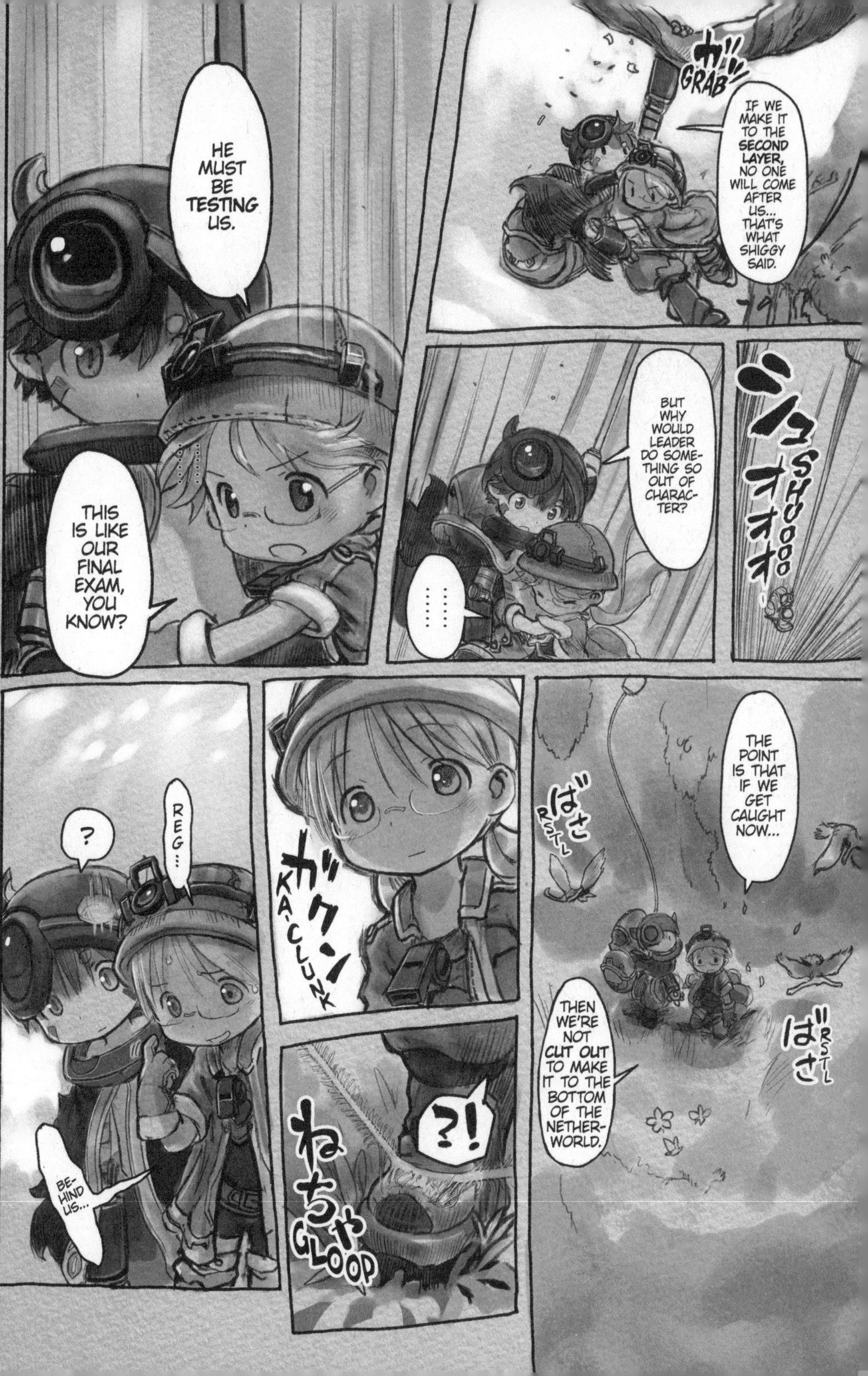
ガッ GRAB
IF WE MAKE IT TO THE SECOND LAYER, NO ONE WILL COME AFTER US... THAT'S WHAT SHIGGY SAID.
シュオオオ SHUOOO
BUT WHY WOULD LEADER DO SOMETHING SO OUT OF CHARACTER?
......
HE MUST BE TESTING US.
THIS IS LIKE OUR FINAL EXAM, YOU KNOW?
ばさ RSTL
THE POINT IS THAT IF WE GET CAUGHT NOW...
THEN WE'RE NOT CUT OUT TO MAKE IT TO THE BOTTOM OF THE NETHER-WORLD.
ばさ RSTL
ガクン KA-CLUNK
ねちゃ GLOOP
?!
REG...
?
BE-HIND US...

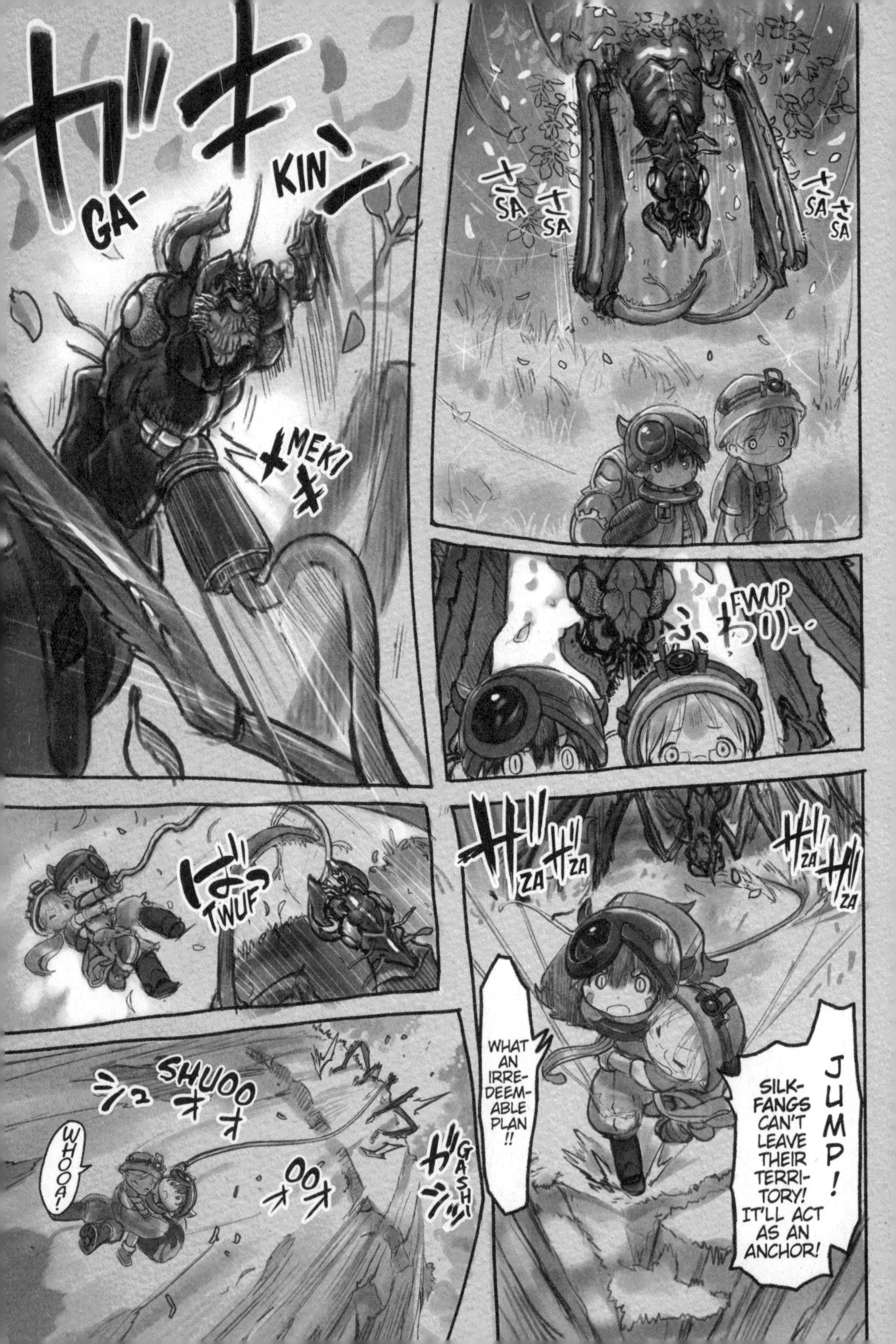

SA SA
SA SA
FWUP
GA-KIN
MEKI
ZA ZA
ZA ZA
JUMP!
SILK-FANGS CAN'T LEAVE THEIR TERRITORY! IT'LL ACT AS AN ANCHOR!
WHAT AN IRREDEEMABLE PLAN!!
TWUF
GASH
OOH
SHUOO
WHOOA!

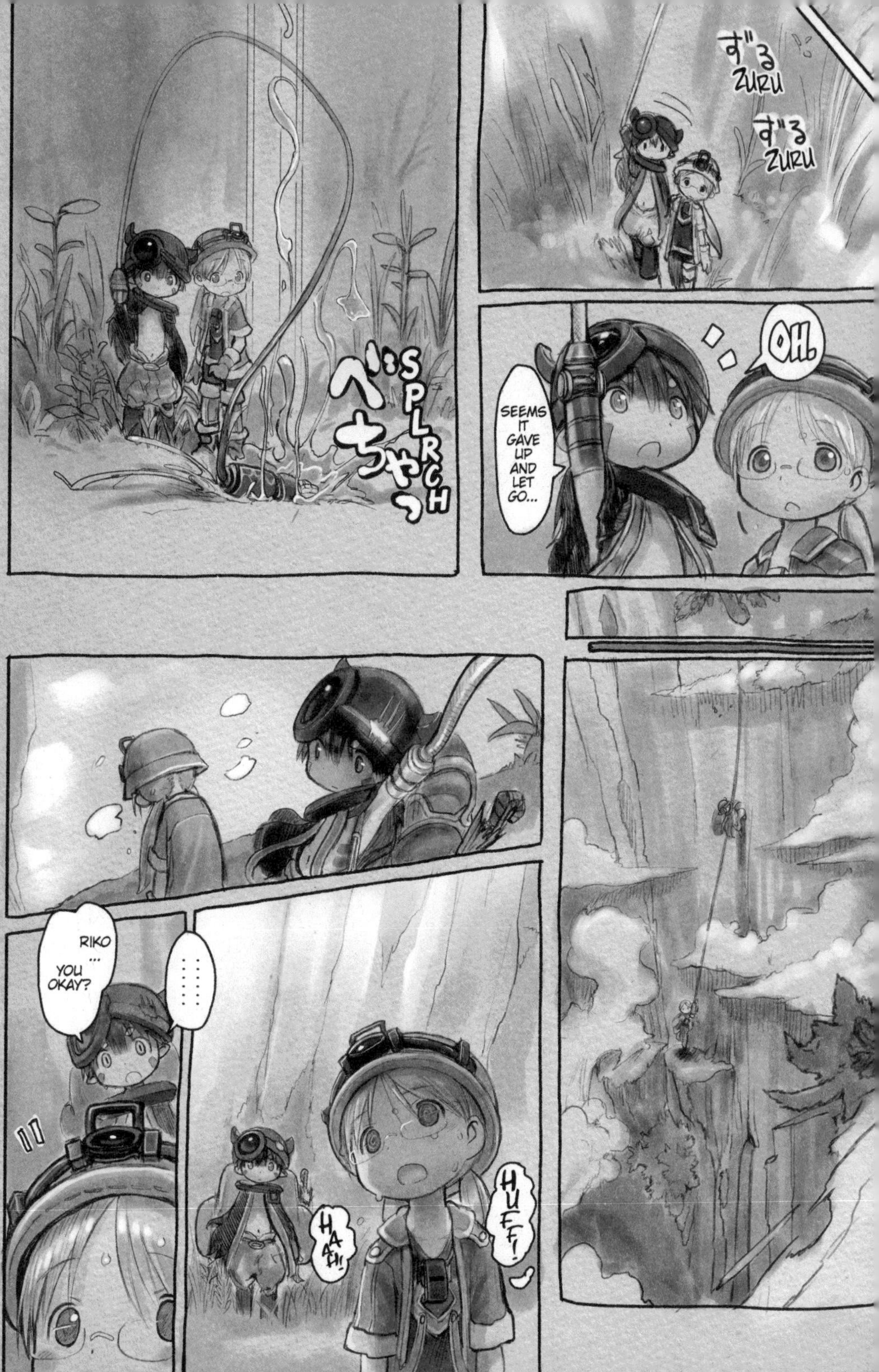
ず"る
ZURU
ず"る
ZURU
OH.
SEEMS IT GAVE UP AND LET GO...
べちゃっ
SPLRCH
HUFF!
HAAH!
......
RIKO ... YOU OKAY?
!!

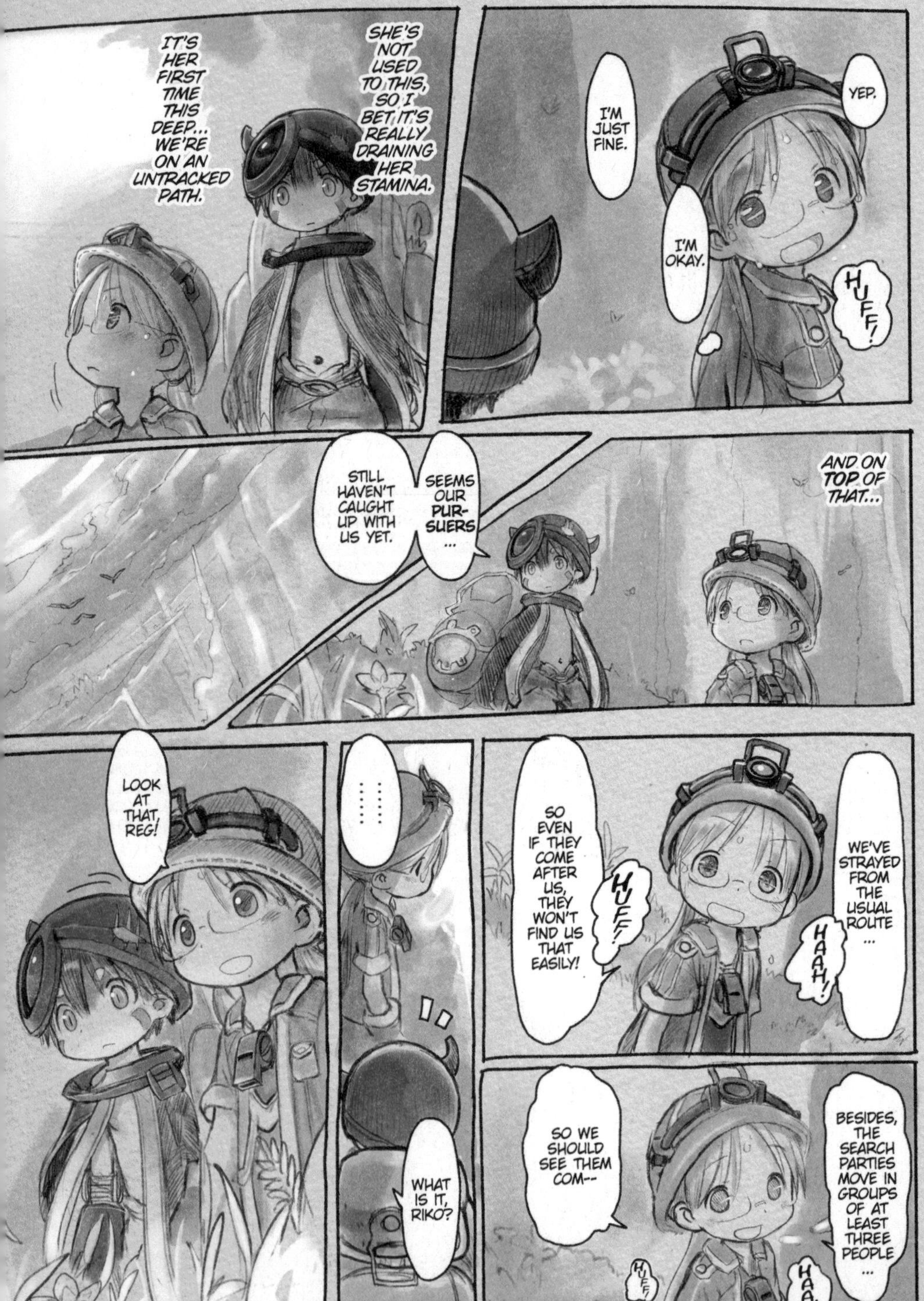
YEP.
I'M JUST FINE.
I'M OKAY.
HUFF!
SHE'S NOT USED TO THIS, SO I BET IT'S REALLY DRAINING HER STAMINA.
IT'S HER FIRST TIME THIS DEEP... WE'RE ON AN UNTRACKED PATH.
AND ON TOP OF THAT...
SEEMS OUR PURSUERS...
STILL HAVEN'T CAUGHT UP WITH US YET.
WE'VE STRAYED FROM THE USUAL ROUTE...
HAAH!
SO EVEN IF THEY COME AFTER US, THEY WON'T FIND US THAT EASILY!
HUFF!
BESIDES, THE SEARCH PARTIES MOVE IN GROUPS OF AT LEAST THREE PEOPLE...
HAAH!
SO WE SHOULD SEE THEM COM--
HUFF!
......
WHAT IS IT, RIKO?
LOOK AT THAT, REG!

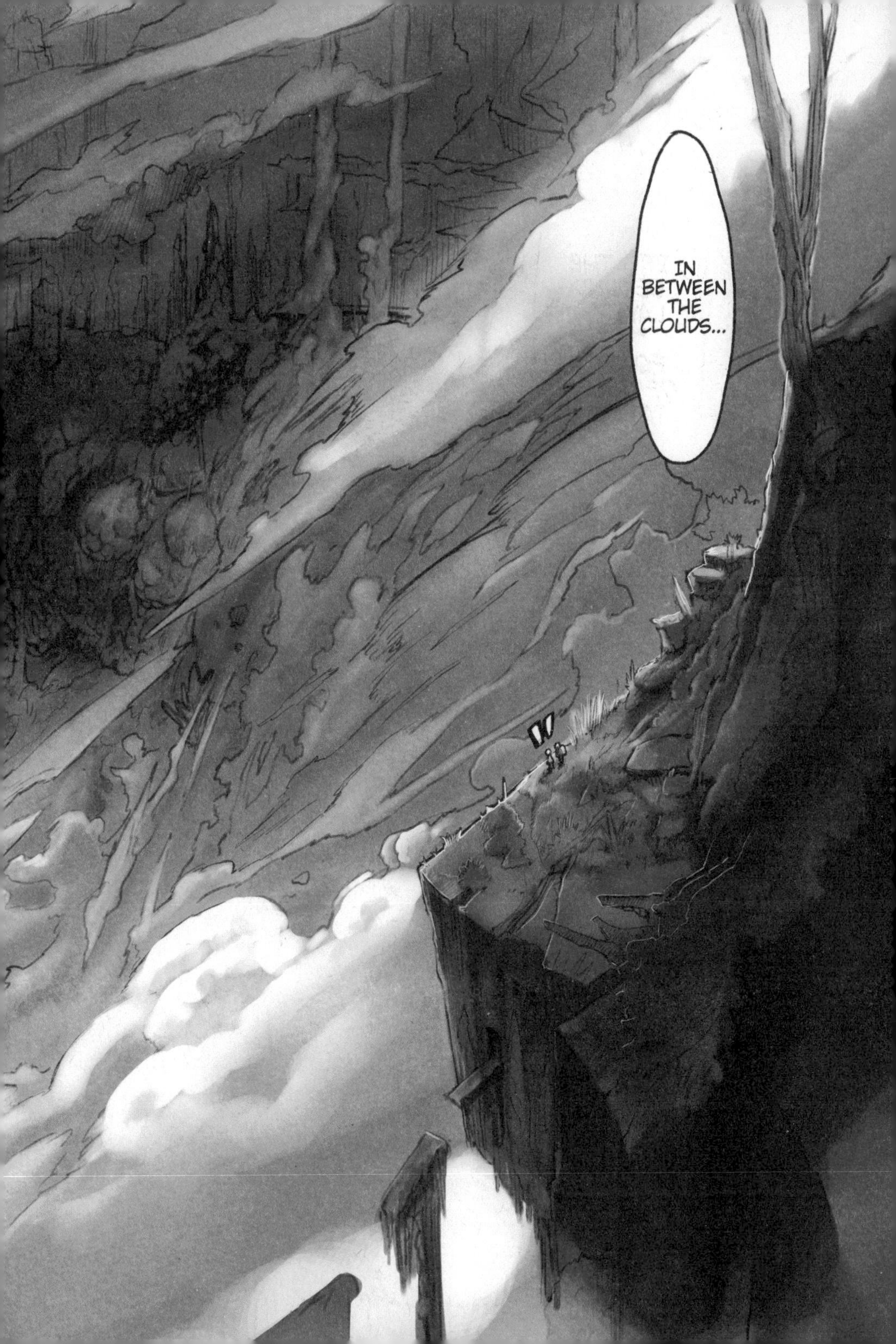
IN BETWEEN THE CLOUDS...

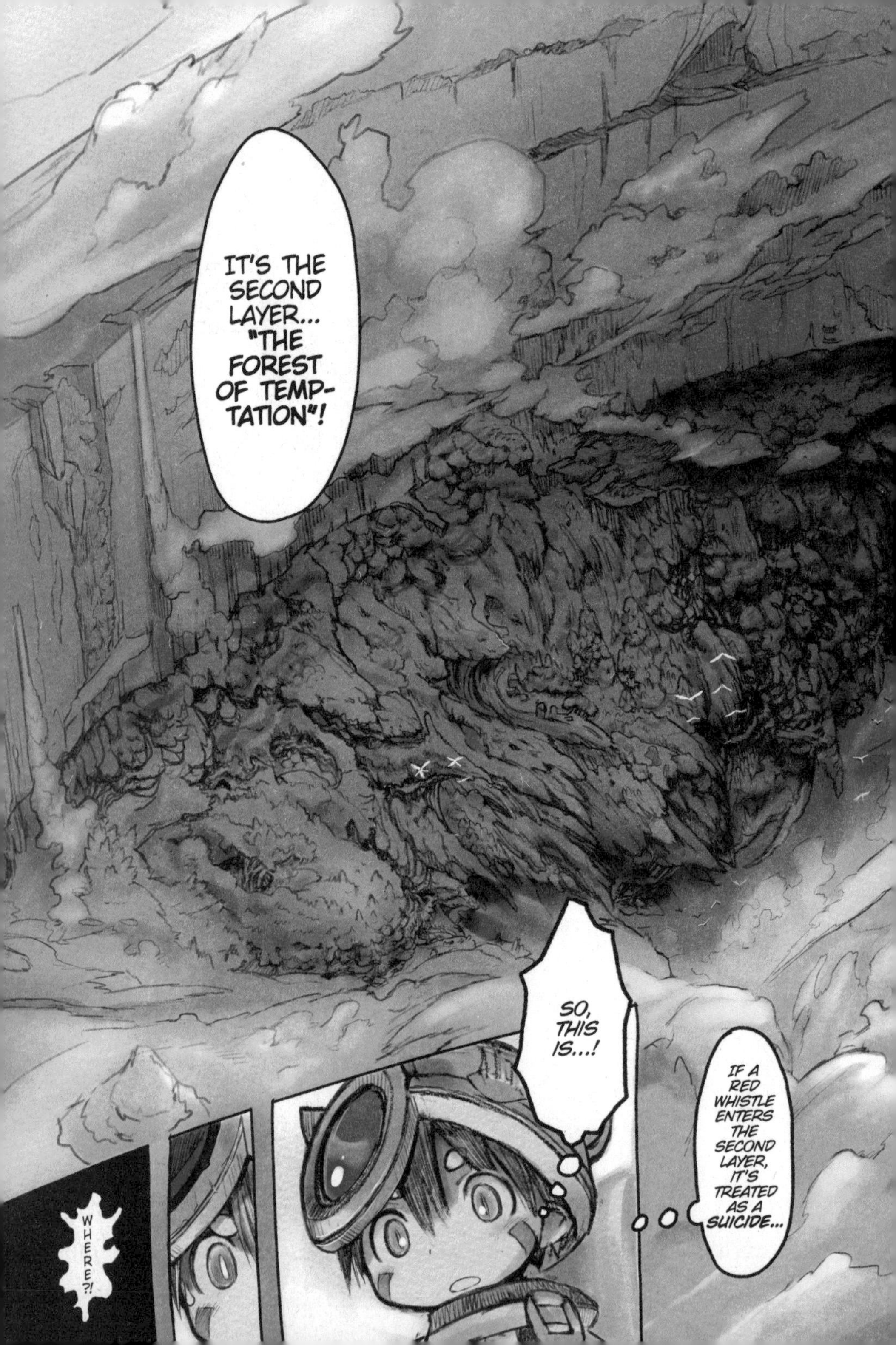
IT'S THE SECOND LAYER... "THE FOREST OF TEMP-TATION"!
SO, THIS IS...!
IF A RED WHISTLE ENTERS THE SECOND LAYER, IT'S TREATED AS A SUICIDE...
WHERE?!

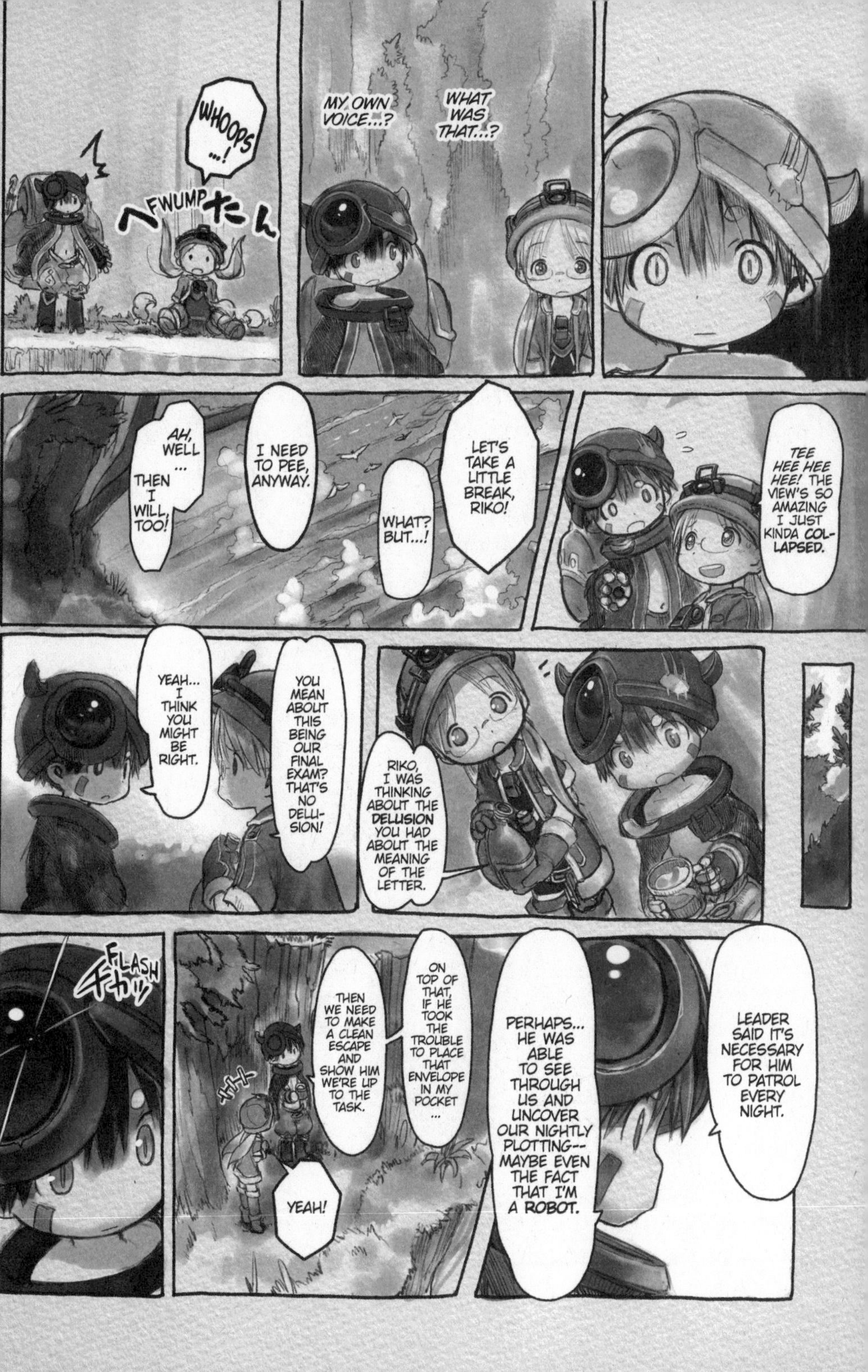
WHAT WAS THAT...?
MY OWN VOICE...?
WHOOPS ...!
FWUMP
TEE HEE HEE HEE! THE VIEW'S SO AMAZING I JUST KINDA COLLAPSED.
LET'S TAKE A LITTLE BREAK, RIKO!
WHAT? BUT...!
I NEED TO PEE, ANYWAY.
AH, WELL ... THEN I WILL, TOO!
RIKO, I WAS THINKING ABOUT THE DELUSION YOU HAD ABOUT THE MEANING OF THE LETTER.
YOU MEAN ABOUT THIS BEING OUR FINAL EXAM? THAT'S NO DELUSION!
YEAH... I THINK YOU MIGHT BE RIGHT.
LEADER SAID IT'S NECESSARY FOR HIM TO PATROL EVERY NIGHT.
PERHAPS... HE WAS ABLE TO SEE THROUGH US AND UNCOVER OUR NIGHTLY PLOTTING-- MAYBE EVEN THE FACT THAT I'M A ROBOT.
ON TOP OF THAT, IF HE TOOK THE TROUBLE TO PLACE THAT ENVELOPE IN MY POCKET ...
THEN WE NEED TO MAKE A CLEAN ESCAPE AND SHOW HIM WE'RE UP TO THE TASK.
YEAH!
FLASH

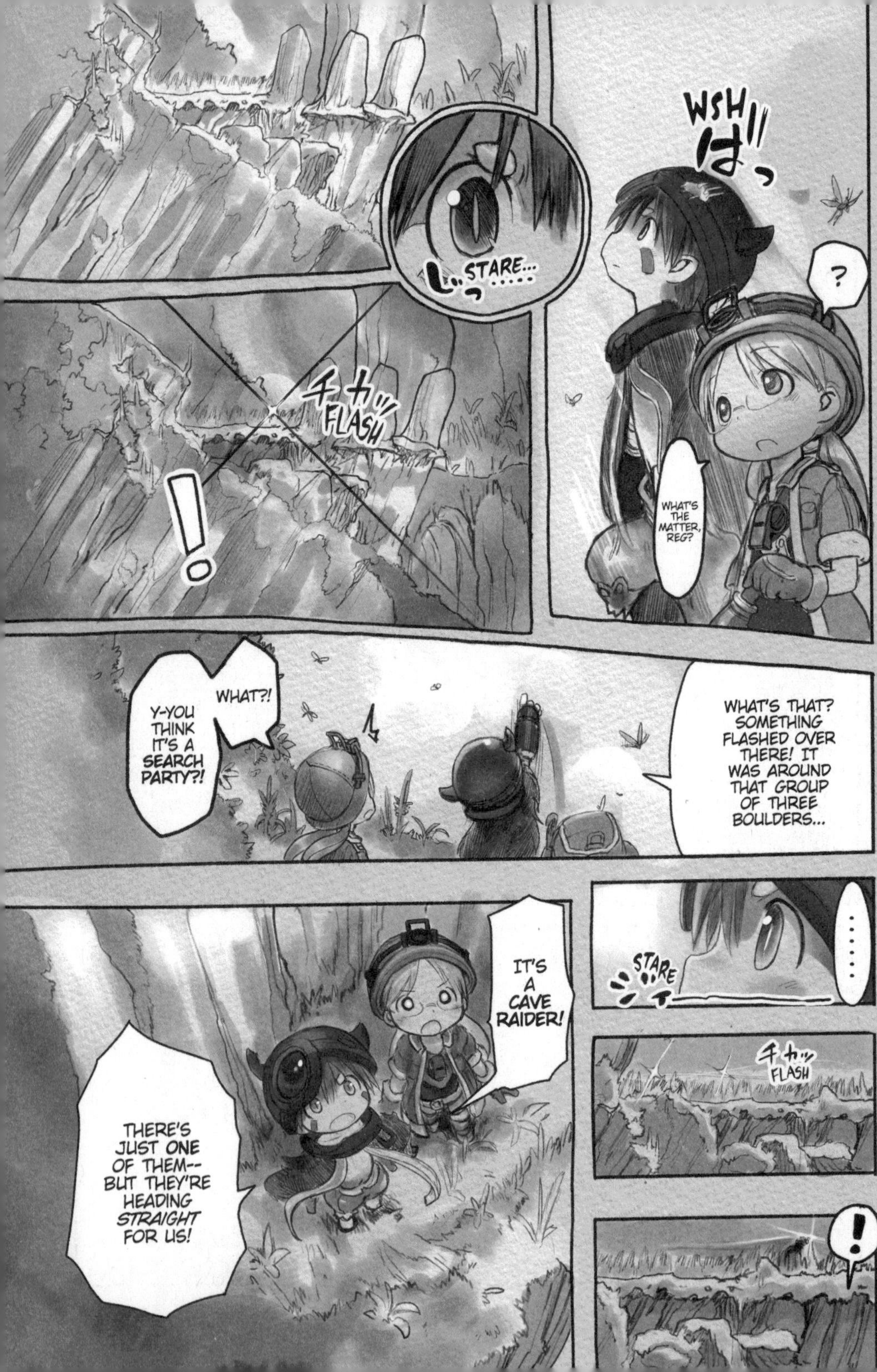
WSH ぱっ
?
WHAT'S THE MATTER, REG?
STARE...
チカッ FLASH
!
WHAT'S THAT? SOMETHING FLASHED OVER THERE! IT WAS AROUND THAT GROUP OF THREE BOULDERS...
WHAT?!
Y-YOU THINK IT'S A SEARCH PARTY?!
......
STARE
チカッ FLASH
!
IT'S A CAVE RAIDER!
THERE'S JUST ONE OF THEM--BUT THEY'RE HEADING *STRAIGHT* FOR US!

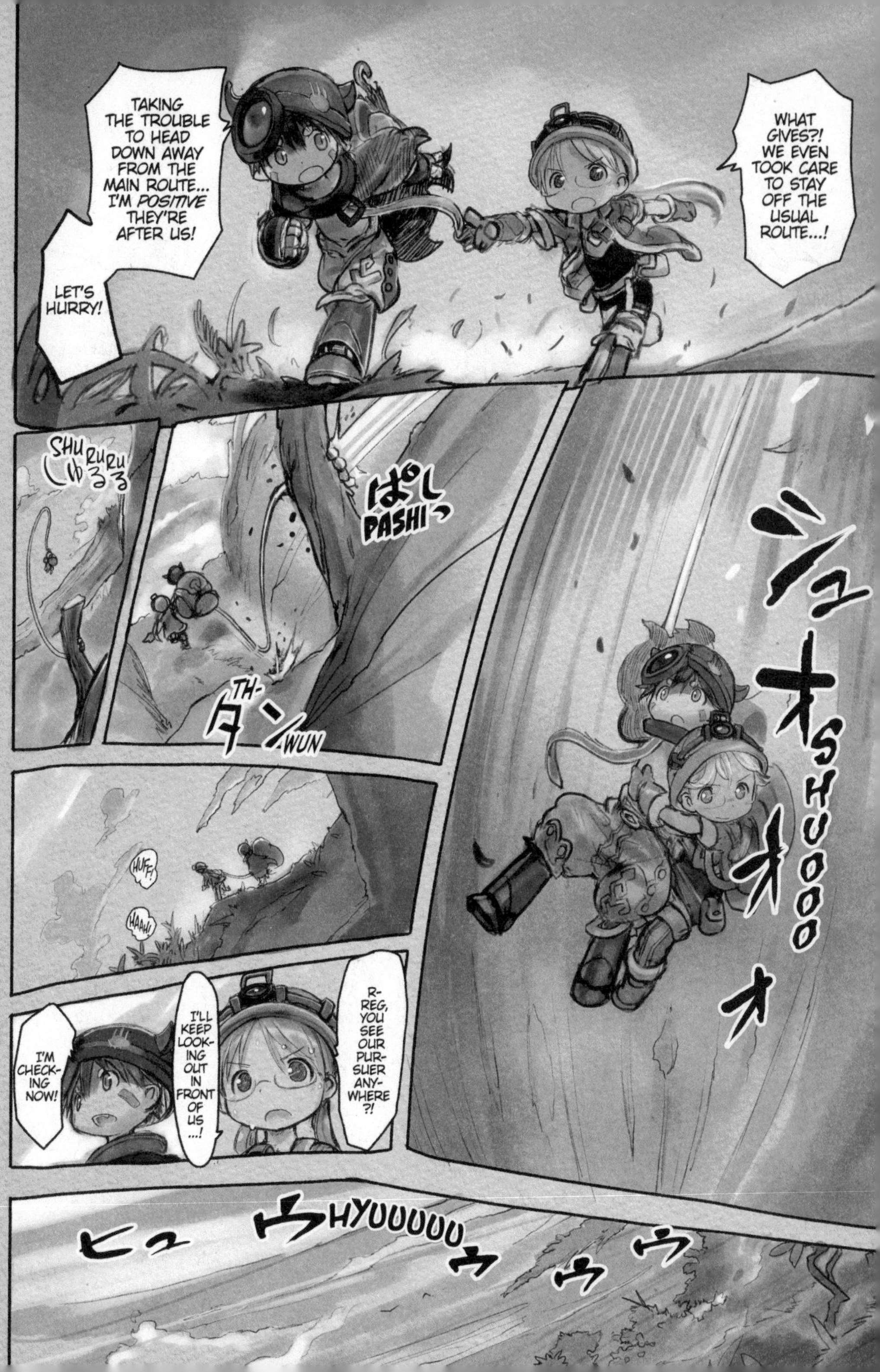
WHAT GIVES?! WE EVEN TOOK CARE TO STAY OFF THE USUAL ROUTE...!
TAKING THE TROUBLE TO HEAD DOWN AWAY FROM THE MAIN ROUTE... I'M *POSITIVE* THEY'RE AFTER US!
LET'S HURRY!
シュオオオ SHUOOOO
ぱしっ PASHI
TH- タン WUN
SHU RURU しゅるる
HUFF!
HAAH!
R-REG, YOU SEE OUR PURSUER ANYWHERE?!
I'LL KEEP LOOKING OUT IN FRONT OF US...!
I'M CHECKING NOW!
ヒュウ HYUUUUUU ウウウ

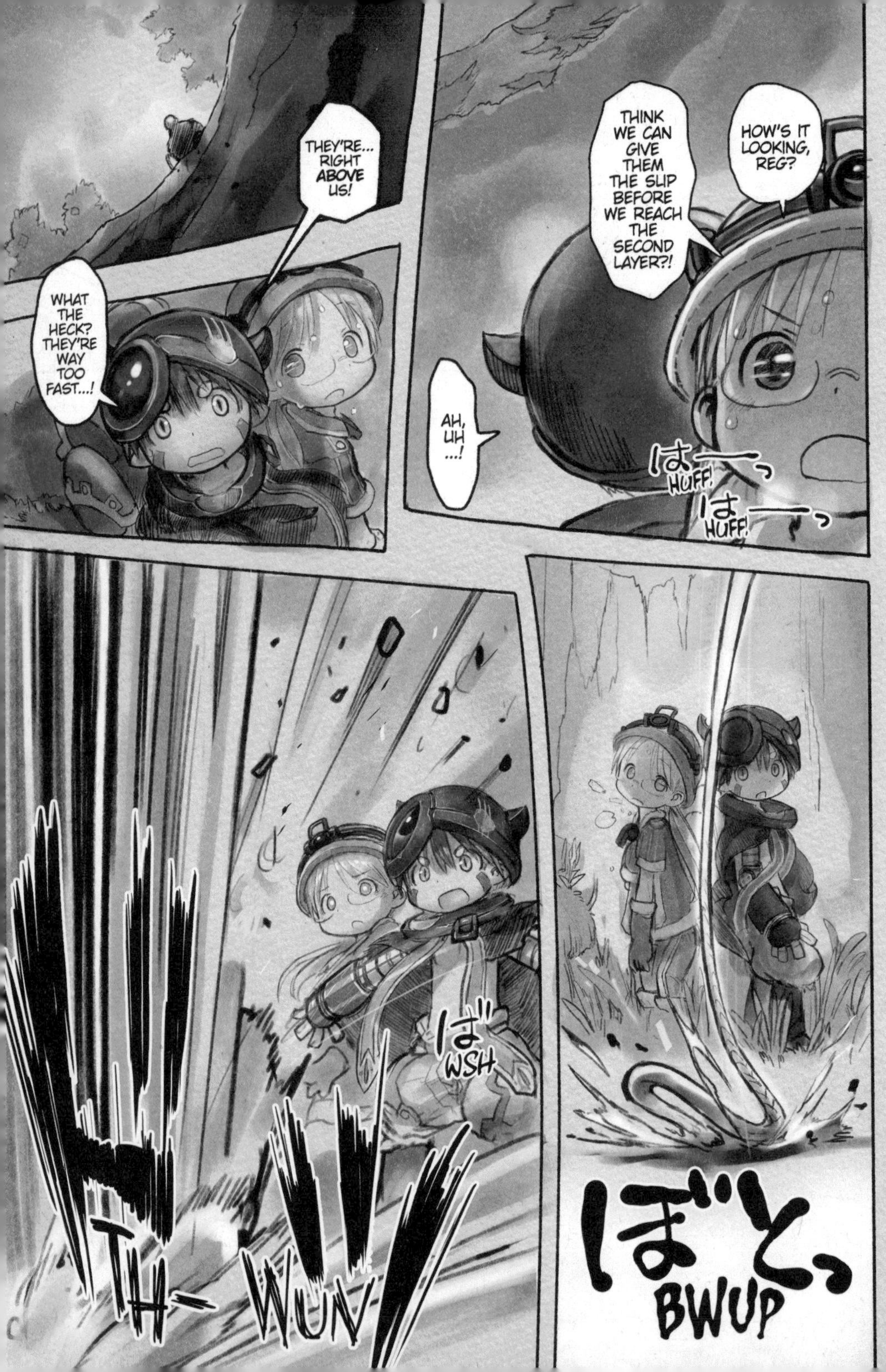
HOW'S IT LOOKING, REG?
THINK WE CAN GIVE THEM THE SLIP BEFORE WE REACH THE SECOND LAYER?!
AH, UH...!
はーっ
HUFF!
はーっ
HUFF!
THEY'RE... RIGHT ABOVE US!
WHAT THE HECK? THEY'RE WAY TOO FAST...!
ぼとっ
BWUP
ばっ
WSH
TH-WUN

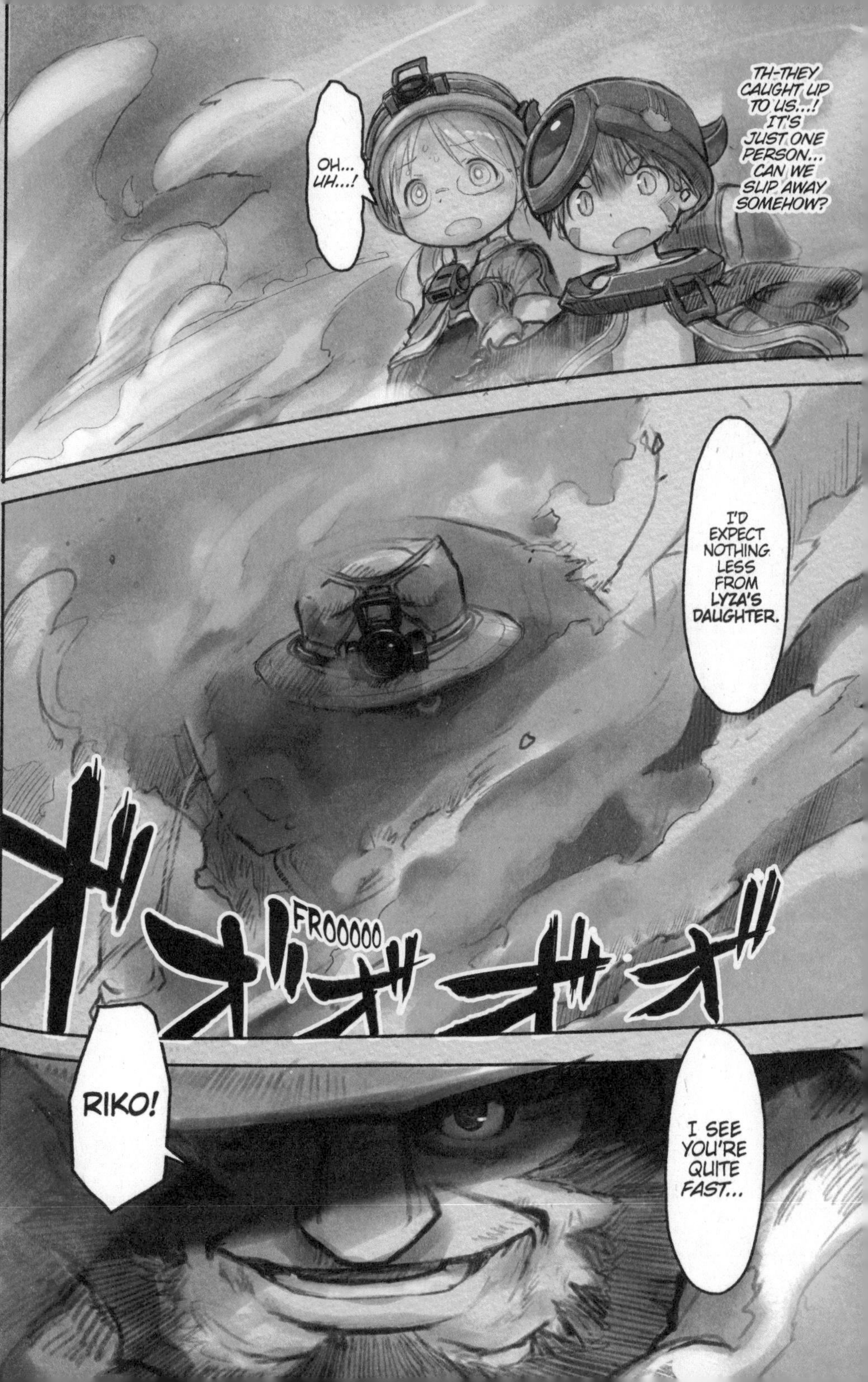
TH-THEY CAUGHT UP TO US...! IT'S JUST ONE PERSON... CAN WE SLIP AWAY SOMEHOW?
OH... UH...!
I'D EXPECT NOTHING LESS FROM LYZA'S DAUGHTER.
FROOOOO
I SEE YOU'RE QUITE FAST...
RIKO!

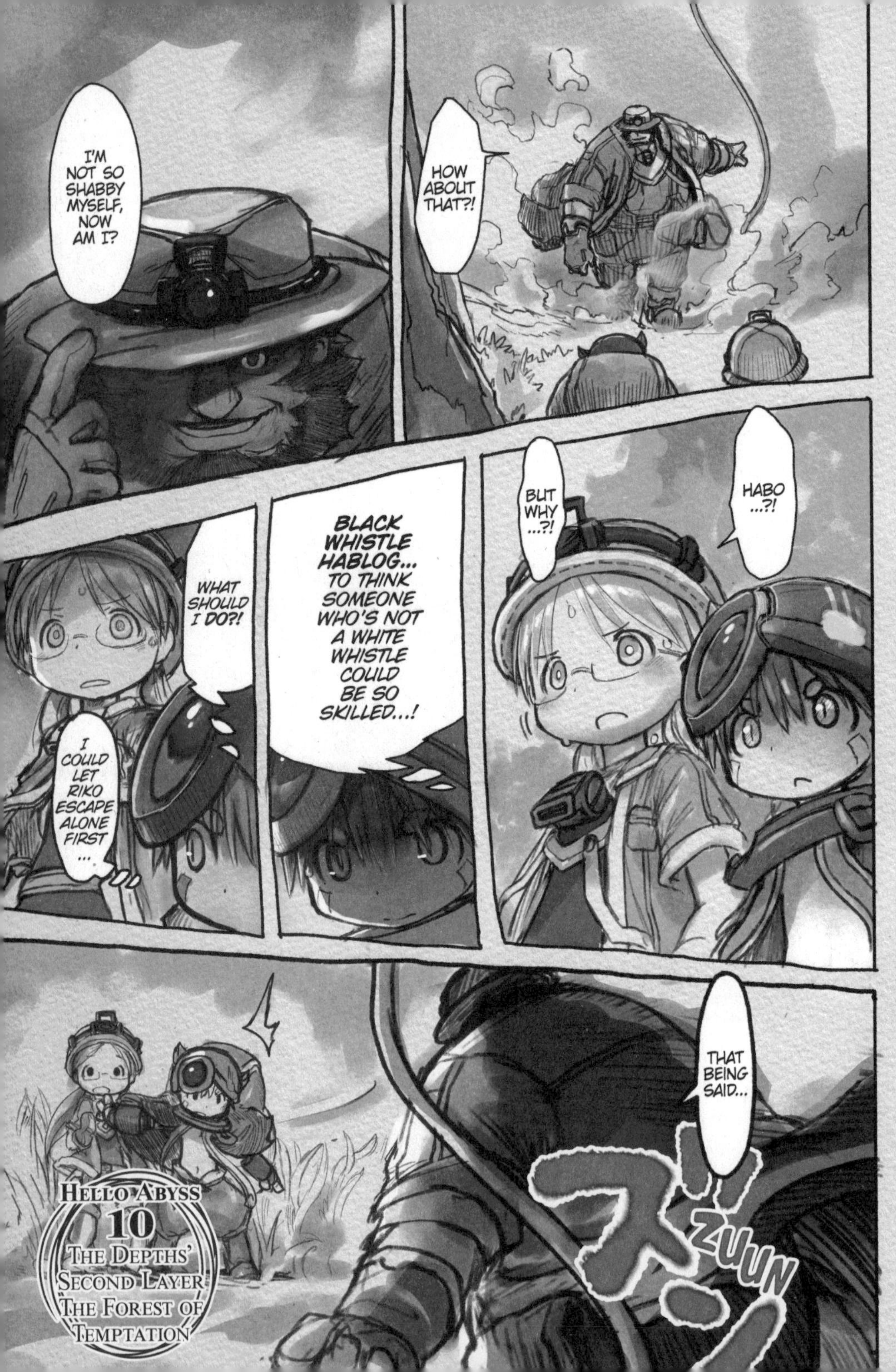

HOW ABOUT THAT?!
I'M NOT SO SHABBY MYSELF, NOW AM I?
HABO ...?!
BUT WHY ...?!
BLACK WHISTLE HABLOG... TO THINK SOMEONE WHO'S NOT A WHITE WHISTLE COULD BE SO SKILLED...!
WHAT SHOULD I DO?!
I COULD LET RIKO ESCAPE ALONE FIRST ...
THAT BEING SAID...
ZUUN
HELLO ABYSS
10
THE DEPTHS' SECOND LAYER THE FOREST OF TEMPTATION

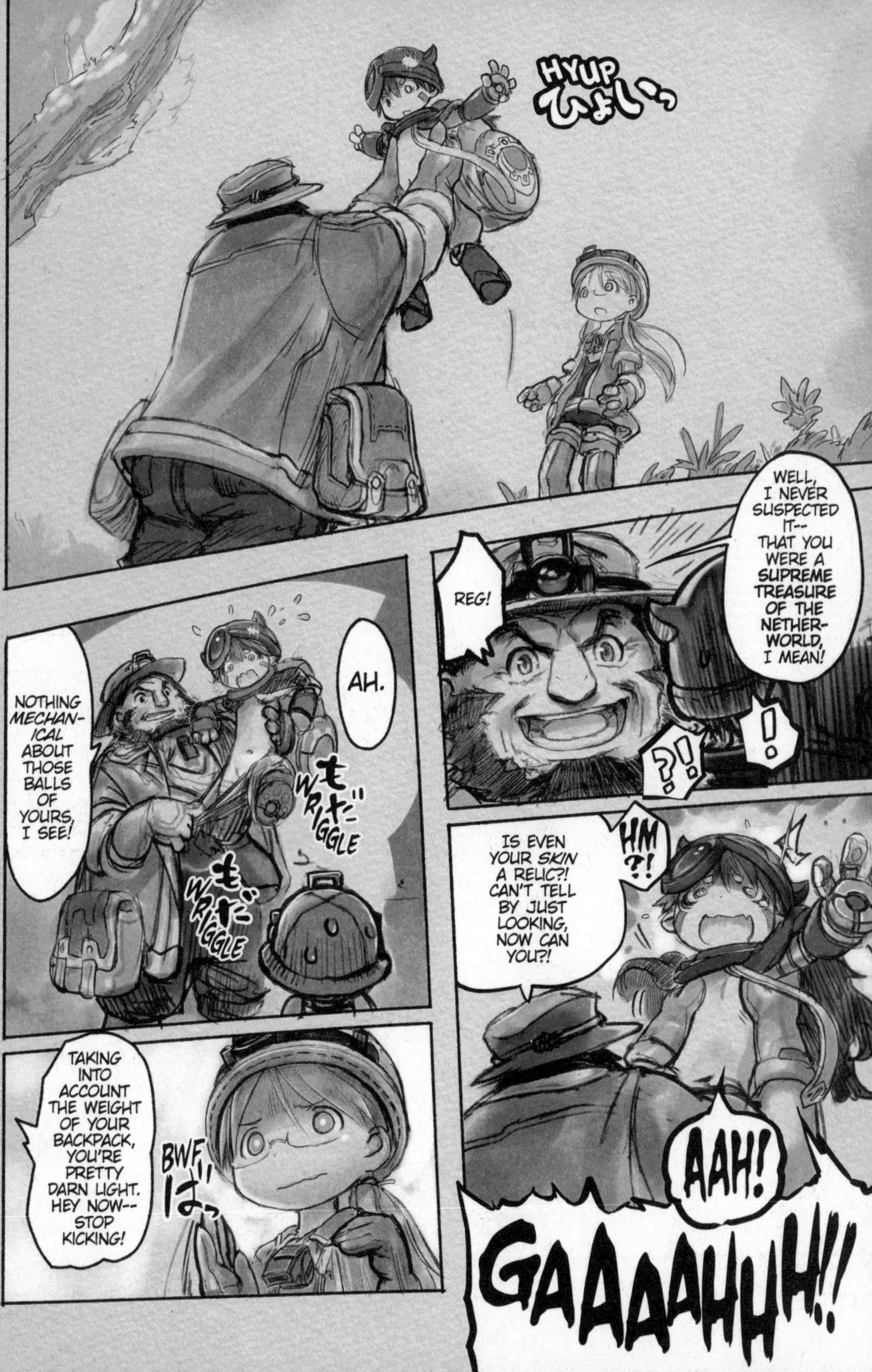
HYUP
ひょしっ
WELL, I NEVER SUSPECTED IT-- THAT YOU WERE A SUPREME TREASURE OF THE NETHER-WORLD, I MEAN!
REG!
!
?!
AH.
NOTHING MECHANICAL ABOUT THOSE BALLS OF YOURS, I SEE!
もぞ
WRIGGLE
もぞ
WRIGGLE
HM?!
IS EVEN YOUR SKIN A RELIC?! CAN'T TELL BY JUST LOOKING, NOW CAN YOU?!
AAH!
GAAAAHH!!
TAKING INTO ACCOUNT THE WEIGHT OF YOUR BACKPACK, YOU'RE PRETTY DARN LIGHT. HEY NOW-- STOP KICKING!
BWF
はっ

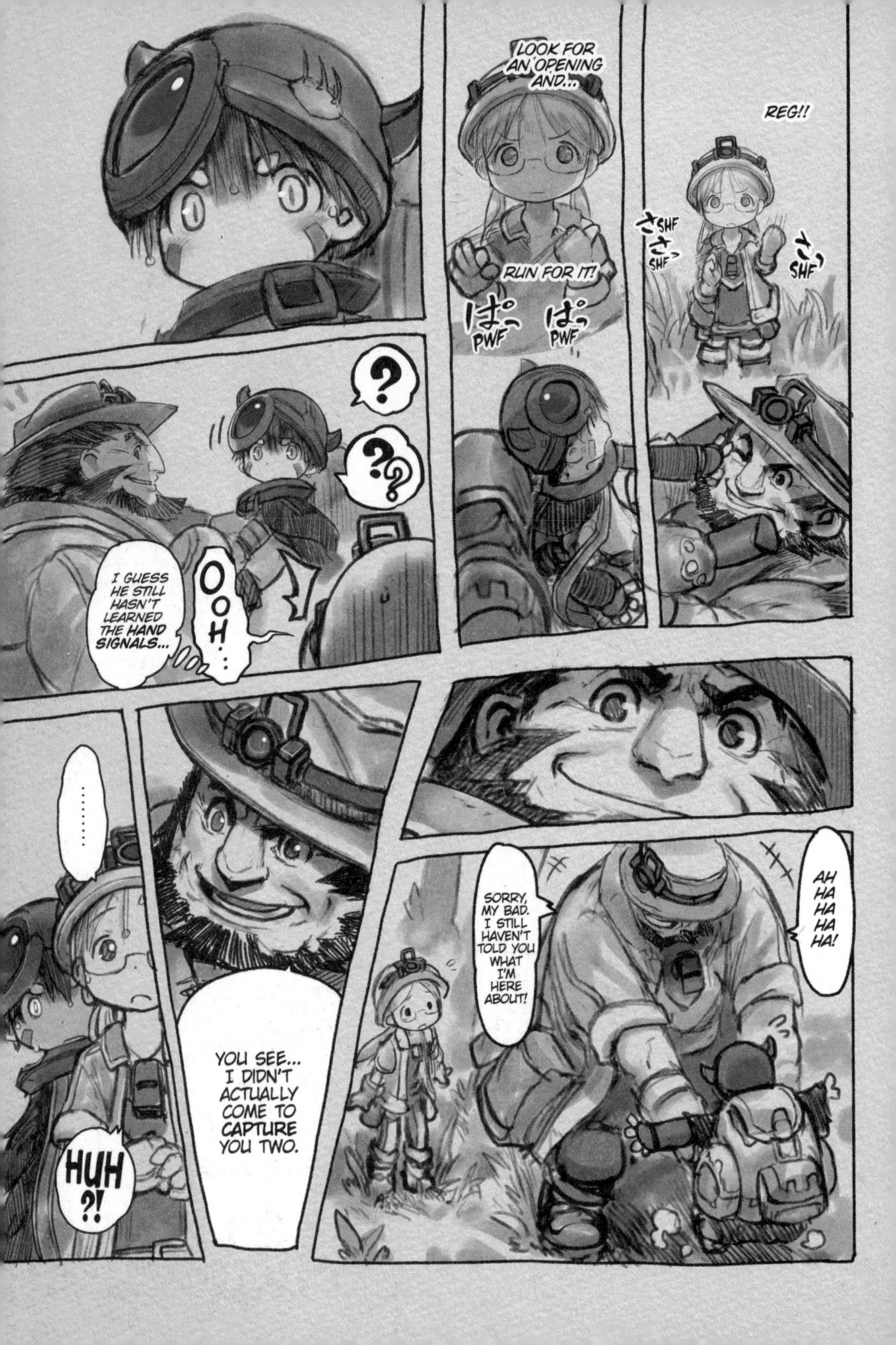
REG!!
さっ SHF
さっ SHF
さっ SHF
LOOK FOR AN OPENING AND...
RUN FOR IT!
ぱっ PWF
ぱっ PWF
?
??
OOH...
I GUESS HE STILL HASN'T LEARNED THE HAND SIGNALS...
AH HA HA HA HA HA!
SORRY, MY BAD. I STILL HAVEN'T TOLD YOU WHAT I'M HERE ABOUT!
YOU SEE... I DIDN'T ACTUALLY COME TO CAPTURE YOU TWO.
......
HUH?!

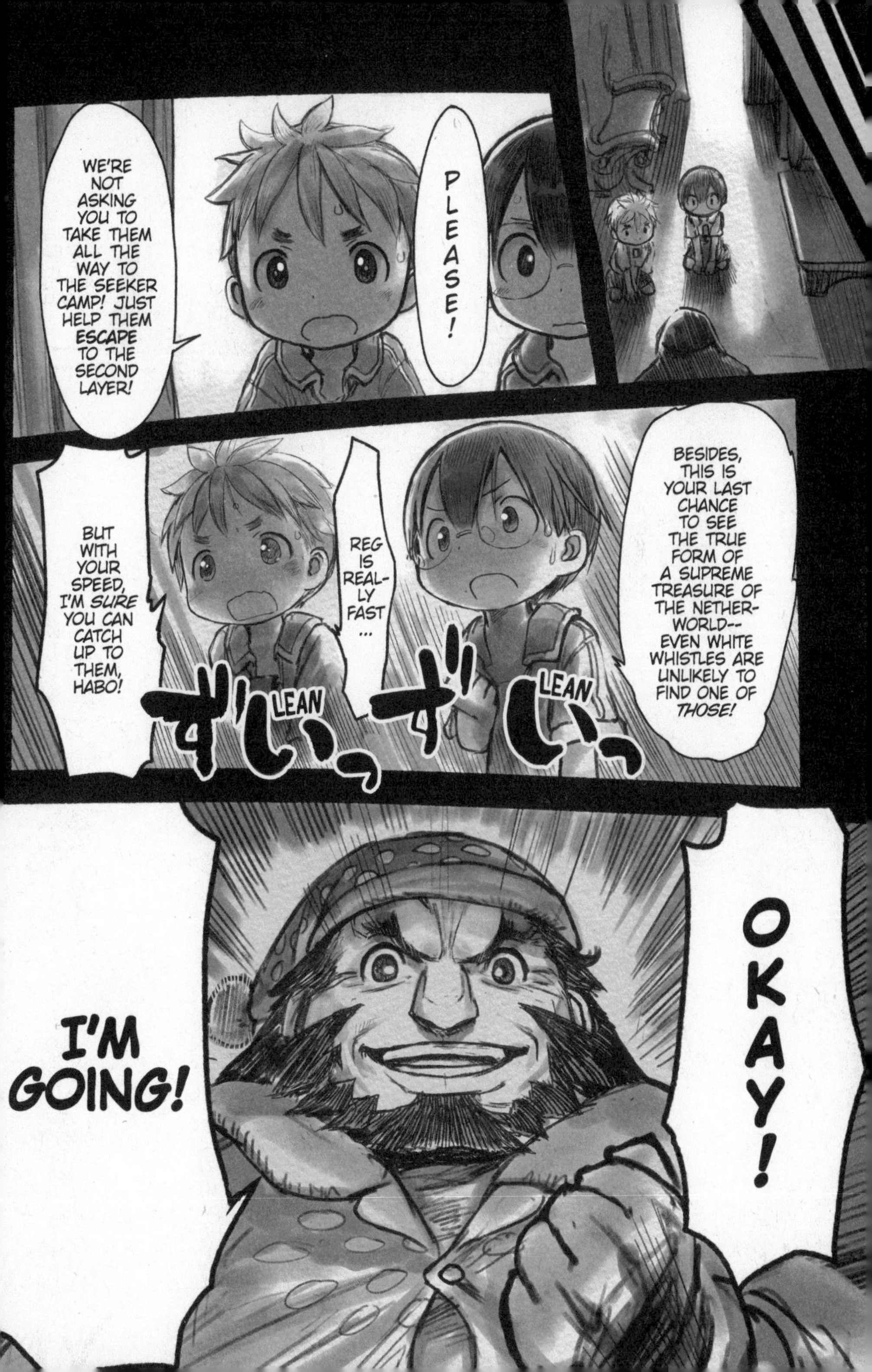
PLEASE!
WE'RE NOT ASKING YOU TO TAKE THEM ALL THE WAY TO THE SEEKER CAMP! JUST HELP THEM ESCAPE TO THE SECOND LAYER!
BESIDES, THIS IS YOUR LAST CHANCE TO SEE THE TRUE FORM OF A SUPREME TREASURE OF THE NETHER-WORLD-- EVEN WHITE WHISTLES ARE UNLIKELY TO FIND ONE OF THOSE!
LEAN
REG IS REAL-LY FAST...
BUT WITH YOUR SPEED, I'M SURE YOU CAN CATCH UP TO THEM, HABO!
LEAN
OKAY!
I'M GOING!

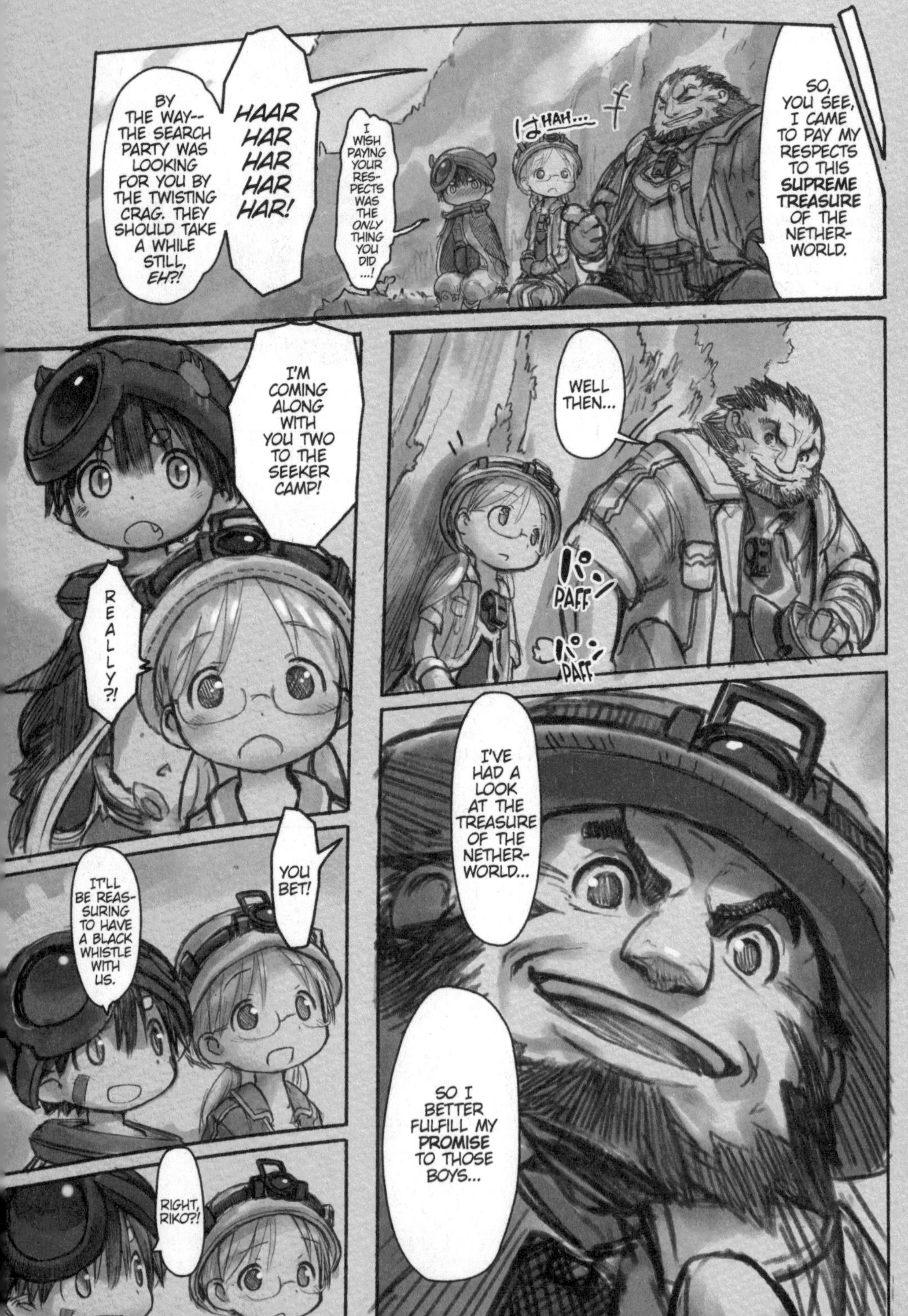
SO, YOU SEE, I CAME TO PAY MY RESPECTS TO THIS SUPREME TREASURE OF THE NETHER-WORLD.
は HAH...
I WISH PAYING YOUR RESPECTS WAS THE ONLY THING YOU DID ...!
HAAR HAR HAR HAR HAR!
BY THE WAY-- THE SEARCH PARTY WAS LOOKING FOR YOU BY THE TWISTING CRAG. THEY SHOULD TAKE A WHILE STILL, EH?!
WELL THEN...
パッ PAFF
パッ PAFF
I'M COMING ALONG WITH YOU TWO TO THE SEEKER CAMP!
REALLY?!
I'VE HAD A LOOK AT THE TREASURE OF THE NETHER-WORLD...
SO I BETTER FULFILL MY PROMISE TO THOSE BOYS...
YOU BET!
IT'LL BE REASSURING TO HAVE A BLACK WHISTLE WITH US.
RIGHT, RIKO?!

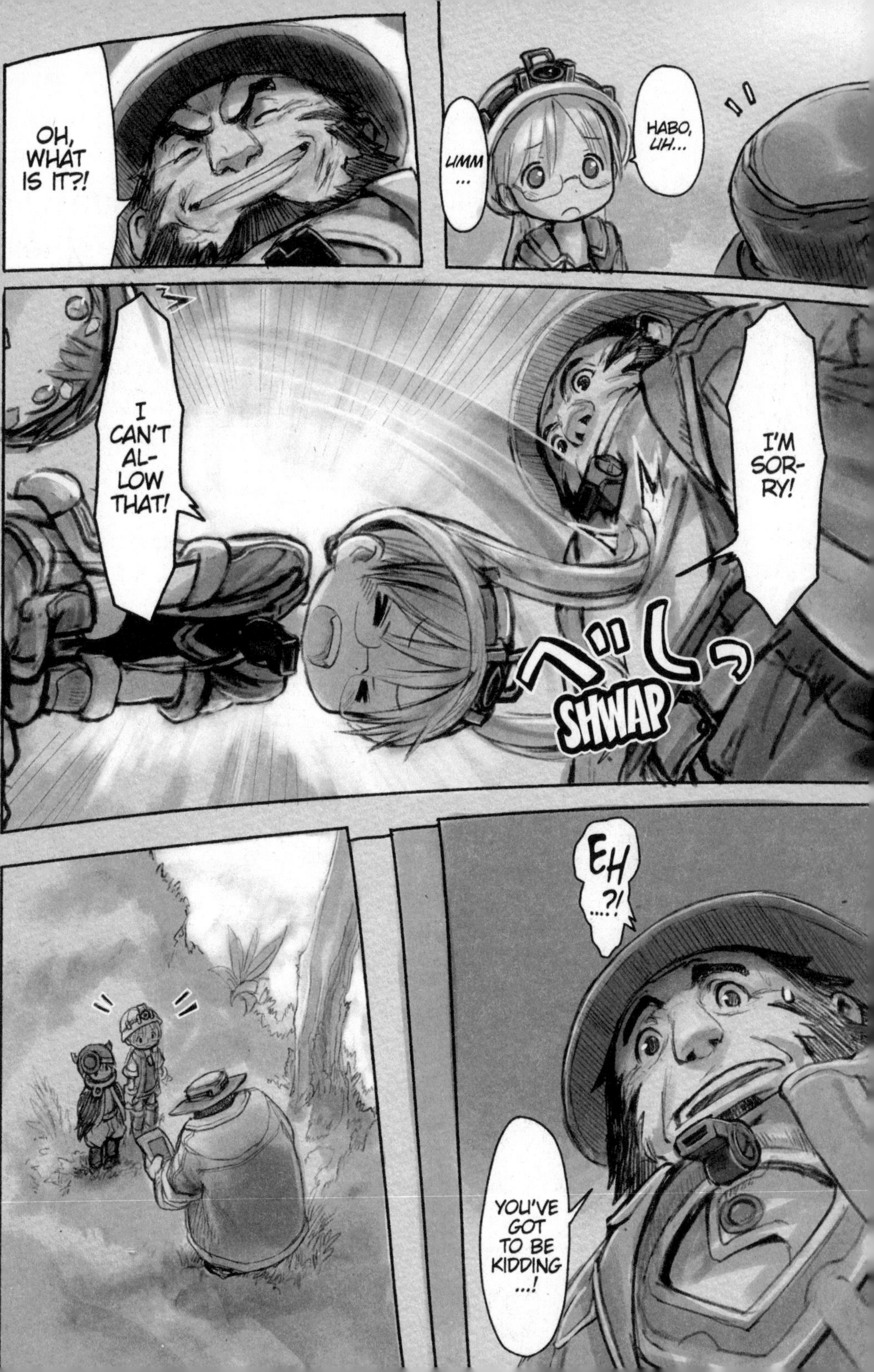
HABO, UH...
UMM ...
OH, WHAT IS IT?!
I'M SOR-RY!
I CAN'T AL-LOW THAT!
べしっ
SHWAP
EH ...?!
YOU'VE GOT TO BE KIDDING ...!

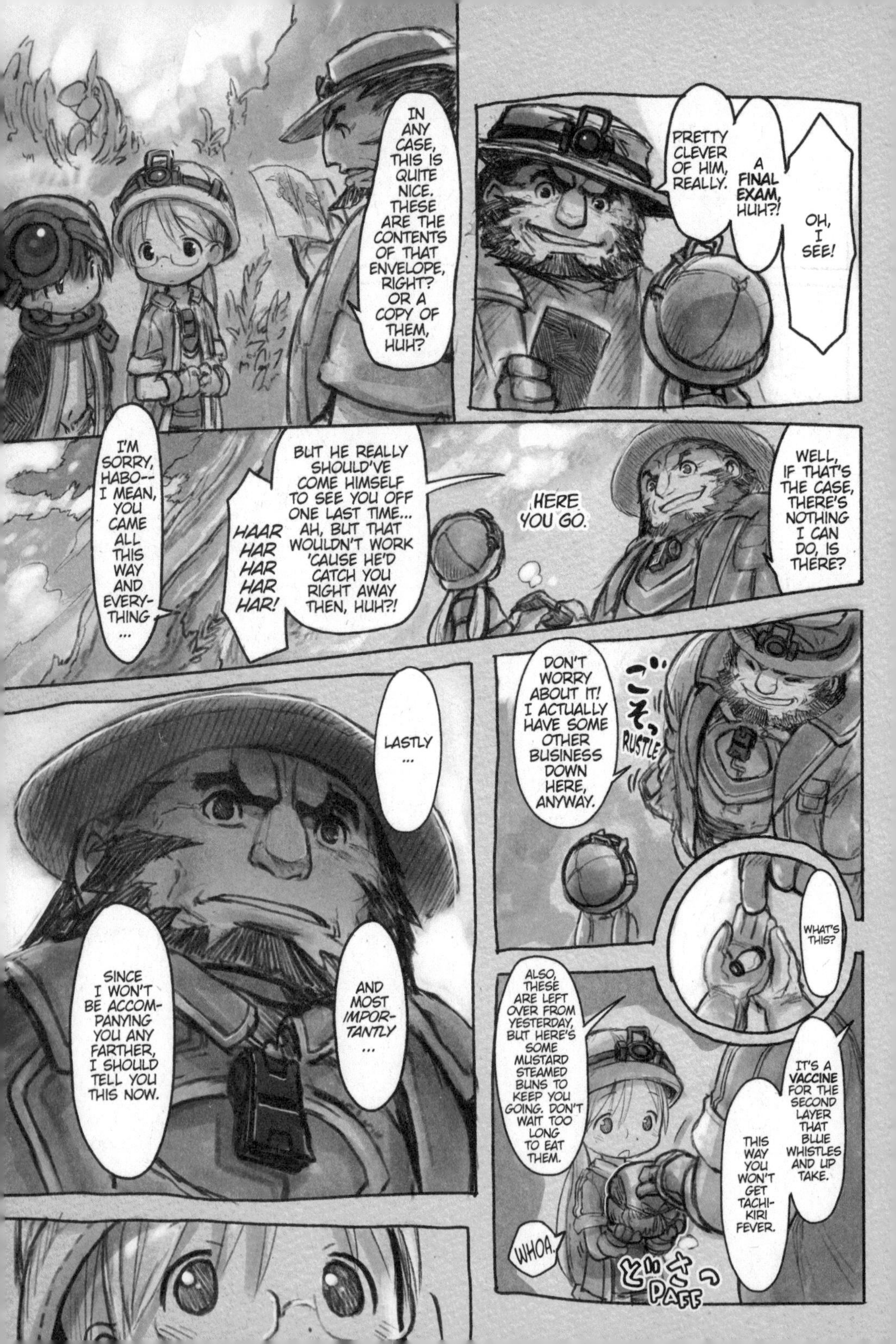

OH, I SEE!
A FINAL EXAM, HUH?!
PRETTY CLEVER OF HIM, REALLY.
IN ANY CASE, THIS IS QUITE NICE. THESE ARE THE CONTENTS OF THAT ENVELOPE, RIGHT? OR A COPY OF THEM, HUH?
WELL, IF THAT'S THE CASE, THERE'S NOTHING I CAN DO, IS THERE?
HERE YOU GO.
BUT HE REALLY SHOULD'VE COME HIMSELF TO SEE YOU OFF ONE LAST TIME... AH, BUT THAT WOULDN'T WORK 'CAUSE HE'D CATCH YOU RIGHT AWAY THEN, HUH?!
HAAR HAR HAR HAR HAR!
I'M SORRY, HABO-- I MEAN, YOU CAME ALL THIS WAY AND EVERYTHING...
DON'T WORRY ABOUT IT! I ACTUALLY HAVE SOME OTHER BUSINESS DOWN HERE, ANYWAY.
ごそ
RUSTLE
WHAT'S THIS?
IT'S A VACCINE FOR THE SECOND LAYER THAT BLUE WHISTLES AND UP TAKE.
THIS WAY YOU WON'T GET TACHI-KIRI FEVER.
ALSO, THESE ARE LEFT OVER FROM YESTERDAY, BUT HERE'S SOME MUSTARD STEAMED BUNS TO KEEP YOU GOING. DON'T WAIT TOO LONG TO EAT THEM.
WHOA.
とさっ
PAFF
LASTLY...
AND MOST IMPORTANTLY...
SINCE I WON'T BE ACCOMPANYING YOU ANY FARTHER, I SHOULD TELL YOU THIS NOW.

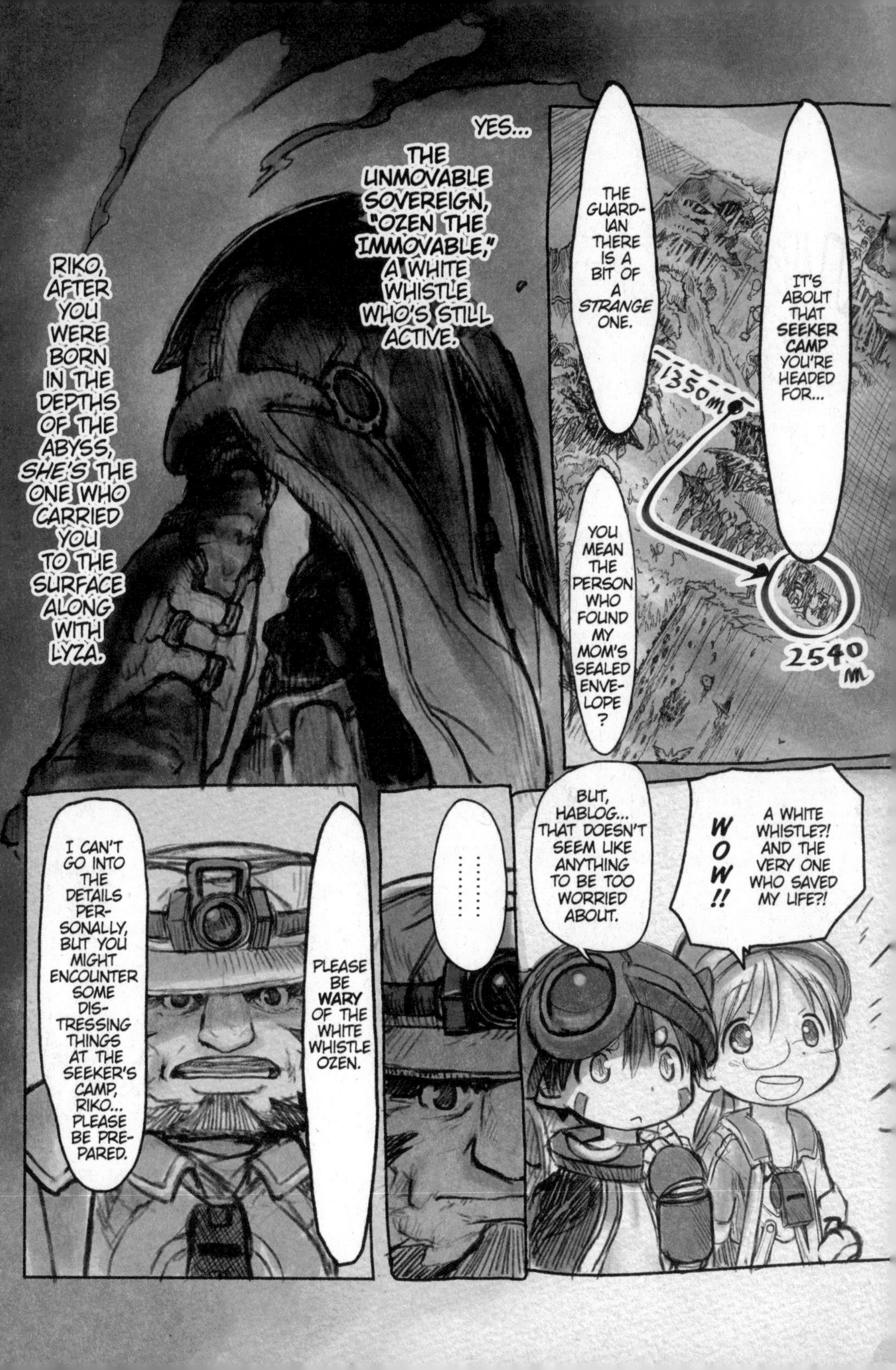
IT'S ABOUT THAT SEEKER CAMP YOU'RE HEADED FOR...
THE GUARDIAN THERE IS A BIT OF A STRANGE ONE.
1350m
2540m
YOU MEAN THE PERSON WHO FOUND MY MOM'S SEALED ENVELOPE?
YES...
THE UNMOVABLE SOVEREIGN, "OZEN THE IMMOVABLE," A WHITE WHISTLE WHO'S STILL ACTIVE.
RIKO, AFTER YOU WERE BORN IN THE DEPTHS OF THE ABYSS, SHE'S THE ONE WHO CARRIED YOU TO THE SURFACE ALONG WITH LYZA.
A WHITE WHISTLE?! AND THE VERY ONE WHO SAVED MY LIFE?!
WOW!!
BUT, HABLOG... THAT DOESN'T SEEM LIKE ANYTHING TO BE TOO WORRIED ABOUT.
......
PLEASE BE WARY OF THE WHITE WHISTLE OZEN.
I CAN'T GO INTO THE DETAILS PERSONALLY, BUT YOU MIGHT ENCOUNTER SOME DISTRESSING THINGS AT THE SEEKER'S CAMP, RIKO... PLEASE BE PREPARED.

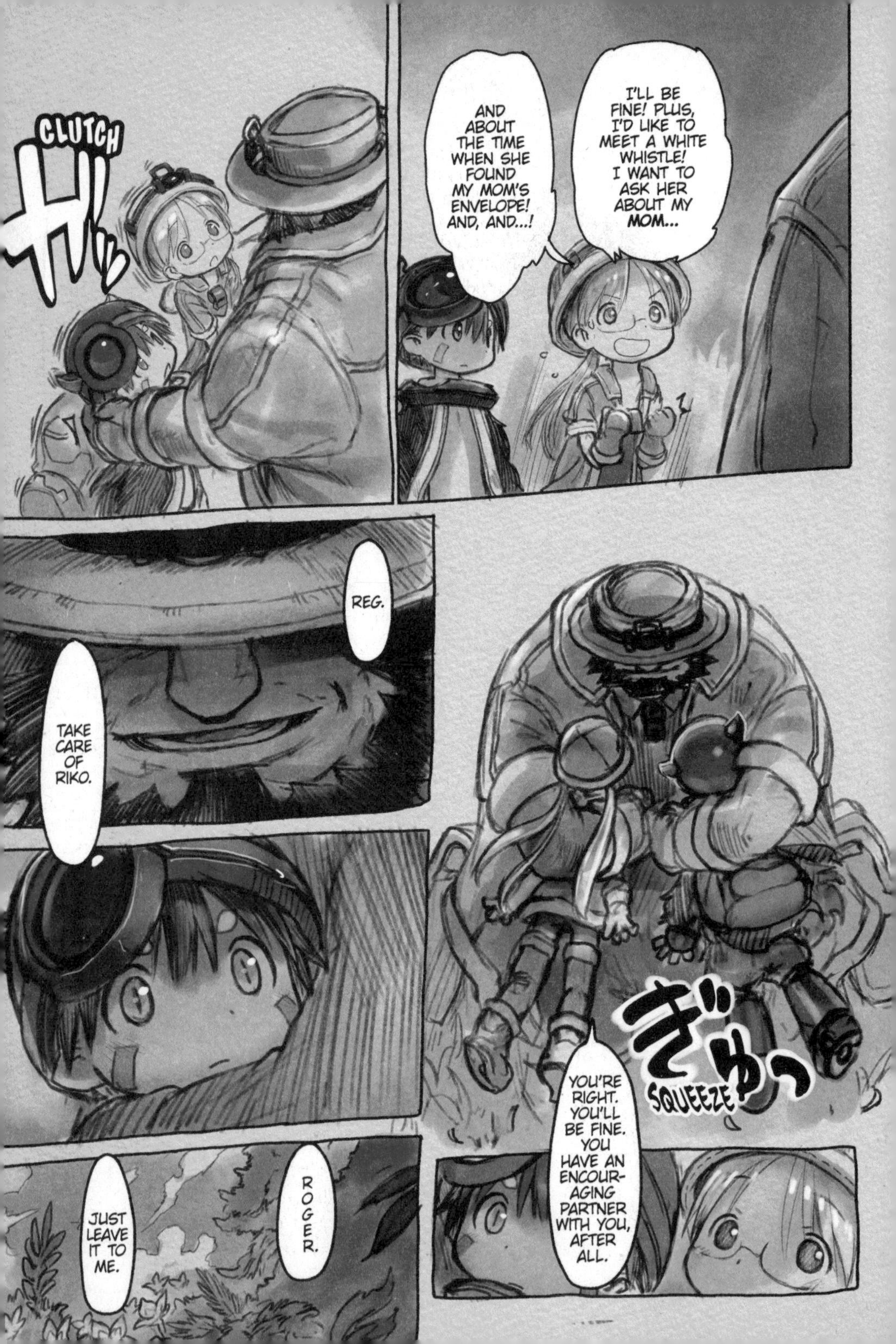
I'LL BE FINE! PLUS, I'D LIKE TO MEET A WHITE WHISTLE! I WANT TO ASK HER ABOUT MY MOM...
AND ABOUT THE TIME WHEN SHE FOUND MY MOM'S ENVELOPE! AND, AND...!
CLUTCH
ぎゅっ
SQUEEZE
YOU'RE RIGHT. YOU'LL BE FINE. YOU HAVE AN ENCOURAGING PARTNER WITH YOU, AFTER ALL.
REG.
TAKE CARE OF RIKO.
ROGER.
JUST LEAVE IT TO ME.

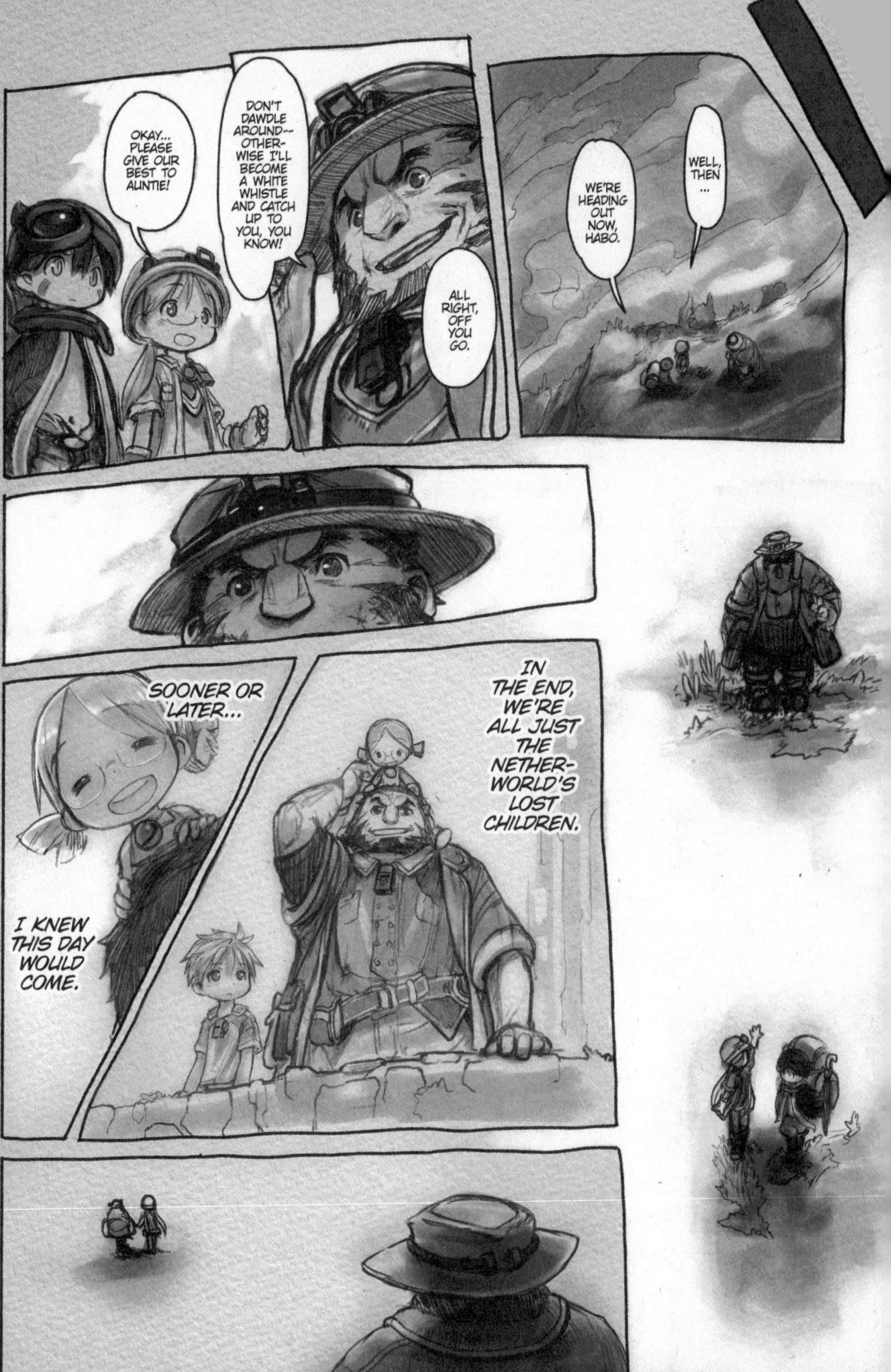
WELL, THEN ...
WE'RE HEADING OUT NOW, HABO.
ALL RIGHT, OFF YOU GO.
OKAY... PLEASE GIVE OUR BEST TO AUNTIE!
DON'T DAWDLE AROUND-- OTHER-WISE I'LL BECOME A WHITE WHISTLE AND CATCH UP TO YOU, YOU KNOW!
IN THE END, WE'RE ALL JUST THE NETHER-WORLD'S LOST CHILDREN.
SOONER OR LATER...
I KNEW THIS DAY WOULD COME.

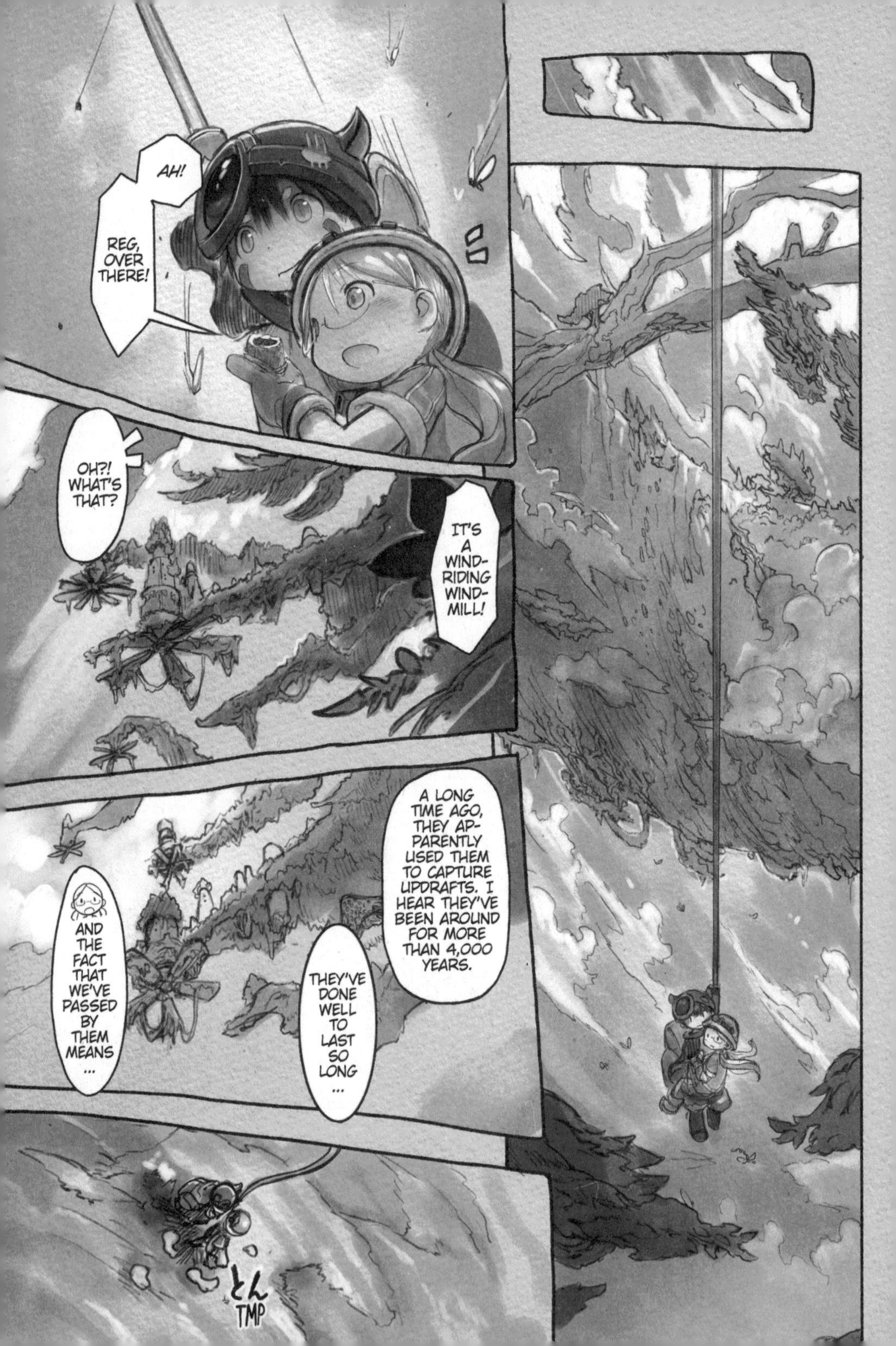
AH!
REG, OVER THERE!
IT'S A WIND-RIDING WINDMILL!
OH?! WHAT'S THAT?
A LONG TIME AGO, THEY APPARENTLY USED THEM TO CAPTURE UPDRAFTS. I HEAR THEY'VE BEEN AROUND FOR MORE THAN 4,000 YEARS.
THEY'VE DONE WELL TO LAST SO LONG...
AND THE FACT THAT WE'VE PASSED BY THEM MEANS...
とん
TMP

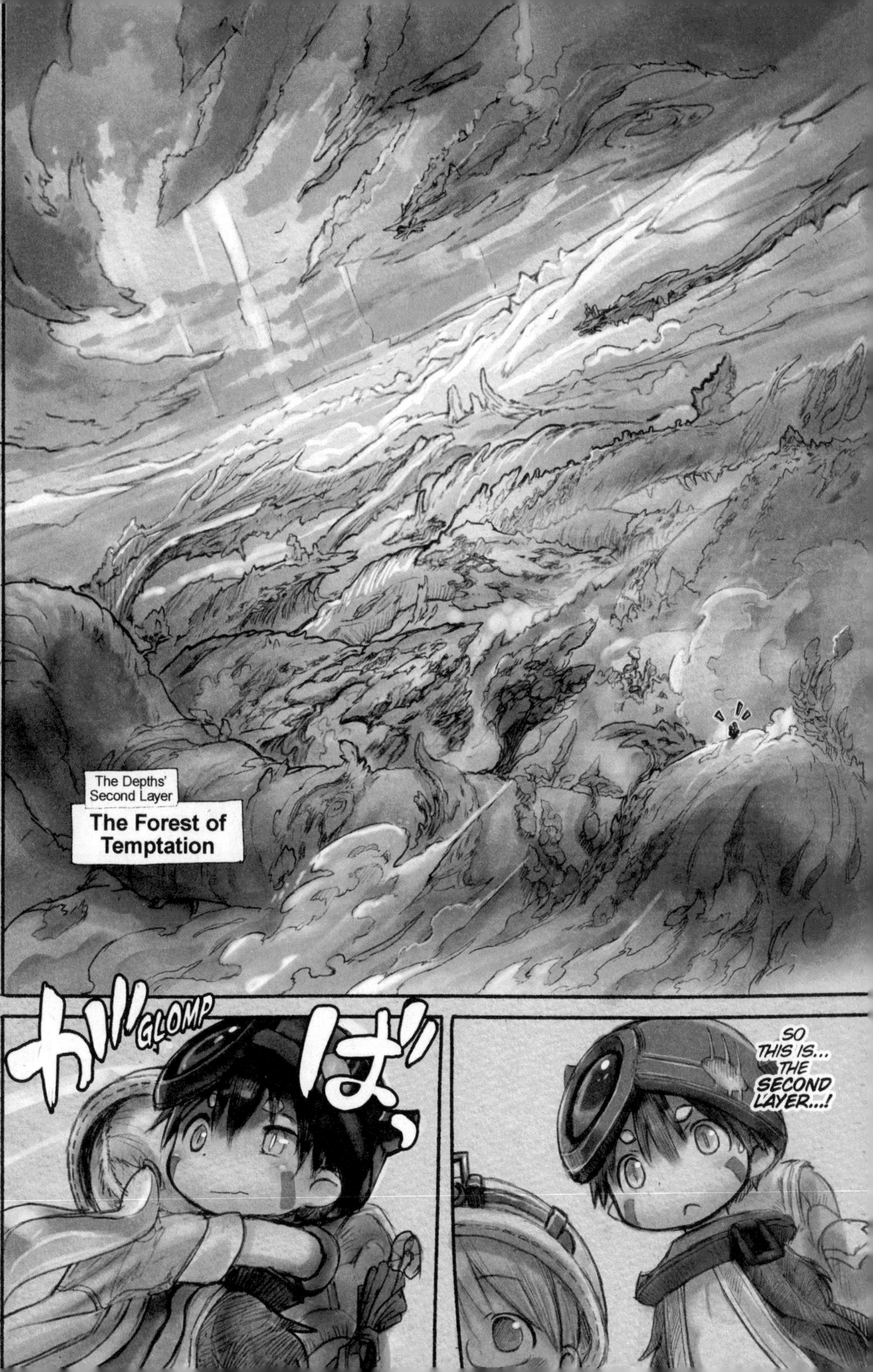
The Depths' Second Layer
The Forest of Temptation
SO THIS IS... THE SECOND LAYER...!
GLOMP

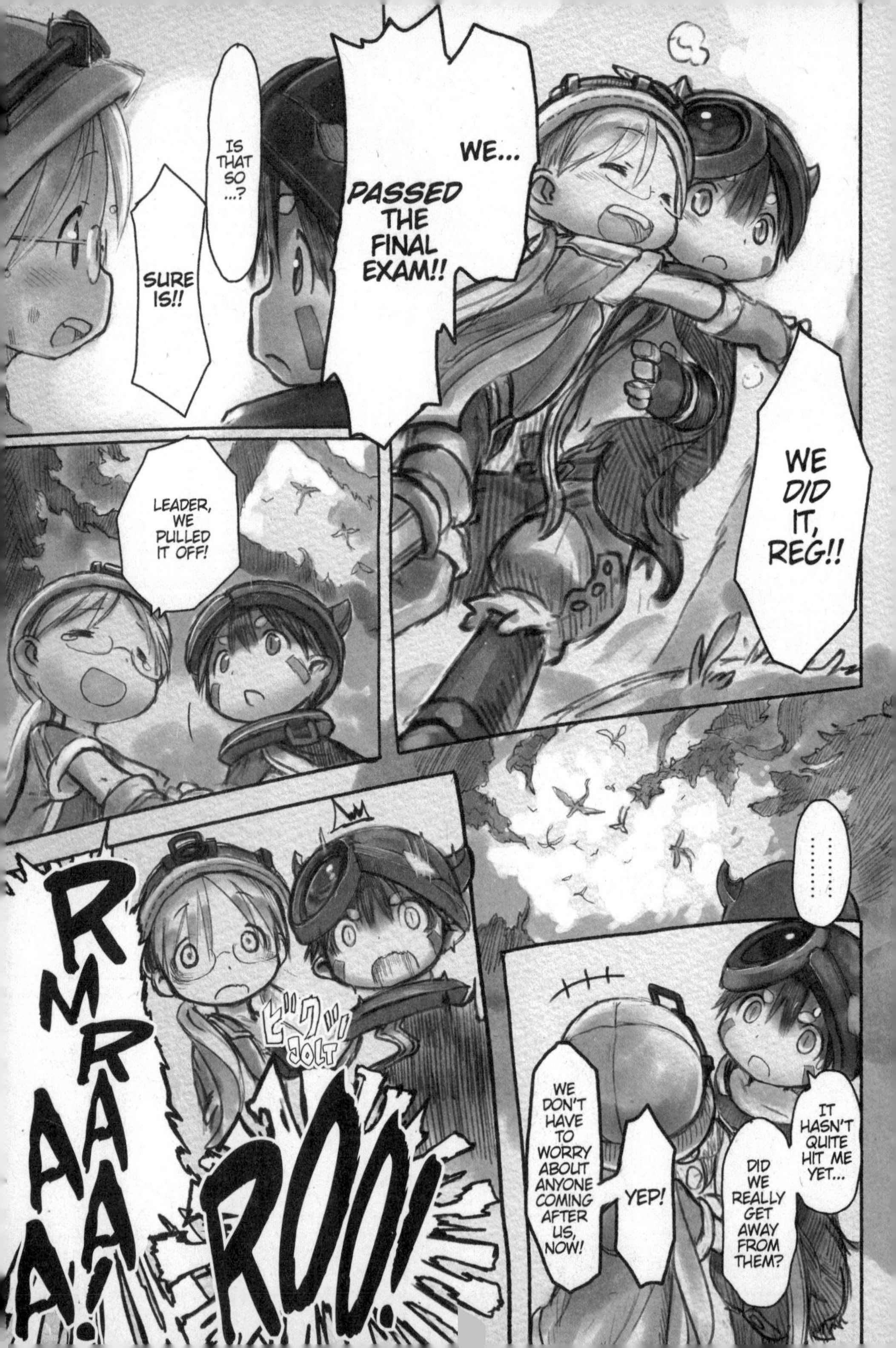
WE... PASSED THE FINAL EXAM!!
WE DID IT, REG!!
IS THAT SO ...?
SURE IS!!
LEADER, WE PULLED IT OFF!
......
IT HASN'T QUITE HIT ME YET...
DID WE REALLY GET AWAY FROM THEM?
YEP!
WE DON'T HAVE TO WORRY ABOUT ANYONE COMING AFTER US, NOW!
JOLT
RMRAAAAA!
ROOO!

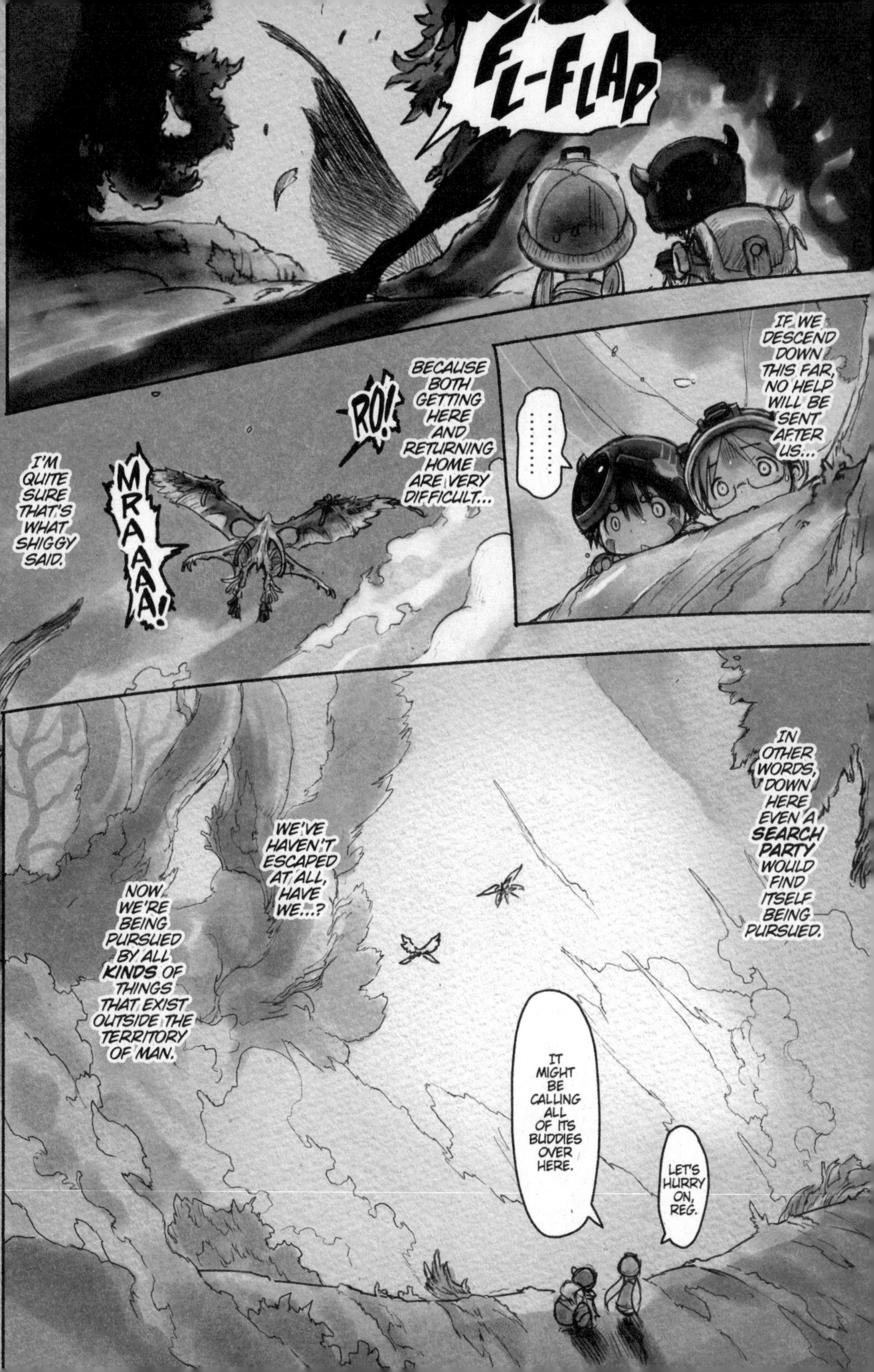
FL-FLAP
IF WE DESCEND DOWN THIS FAR, NO HELP WILL BE SENT AFTER US...
......
BECAUSE BOTH GETTING HERE AND RETURNING HOME ARE VERY DIFFICULT...
RO!
MRAAAAA!
I'M QUITE SURE THAT'S WHAT SHIGGY SAID.
IN OTHER WORDS, DOWN HERE EVEN A SEARCH PARTY WOULD FIND ITSELF BEING PURSUED.
WE'VE HAVEN'T ESCAPED AT ALL, HAVE WE...?
NOW WE'RE BEING PURSUED BY ALL KINDS OF THINGS THAT EXIST OUTSIDE THE TERRITORY OF MAN.
IT MIGHT BE CALLING ALL OF ITS BUDDIES OVER HERE.
LET'S HURRY ON, REG.

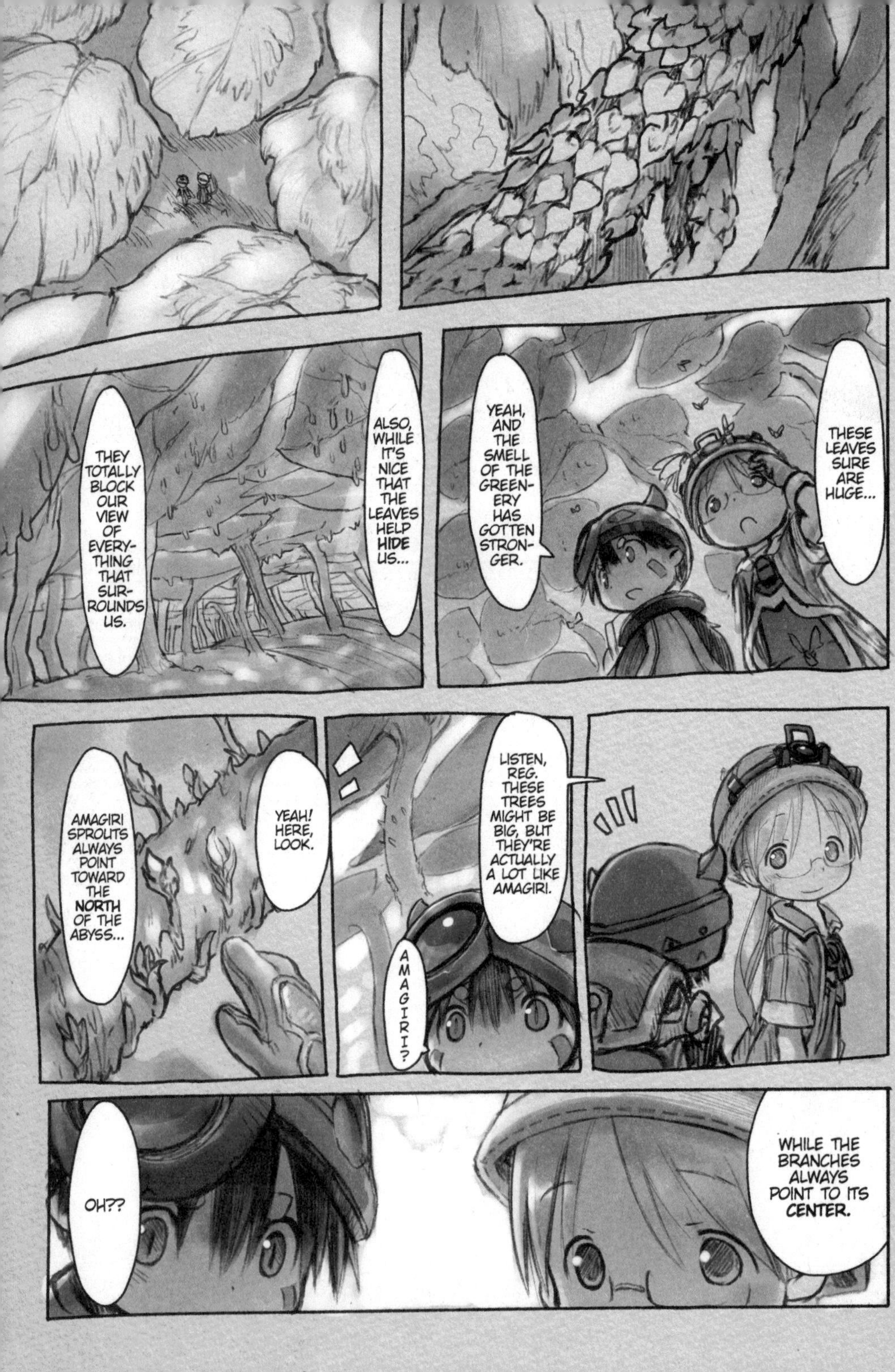
THESE LEAVES SURE ARE HUGE...
YEAH, AND THE SMELL OF THE GREENERY HAS GOTTEN STRONGER.
ALSO, WHILE IT'S NICE THAT THE LEAVES HELP **HIDE** US...
THEY TOTALLY BLOCK OUR VIEW OF EVERYTHING THAT SURROUNDS US.
LISTEN, REG. THESE TREES MIGHT BE BIG, BUT THEY'RE ACTUALLY A LOT LIKE AMAGIRI.
AMAGIRI?
YEAH! HERE, LOOK.
AMAGIRI SPROUTS ALWAYS POINT TOWARD THE **NORTH** OF THE ABYSS...
WHILE THE BRANCHES ALWAYS POINT TO ITS **CENTER.**
OH??

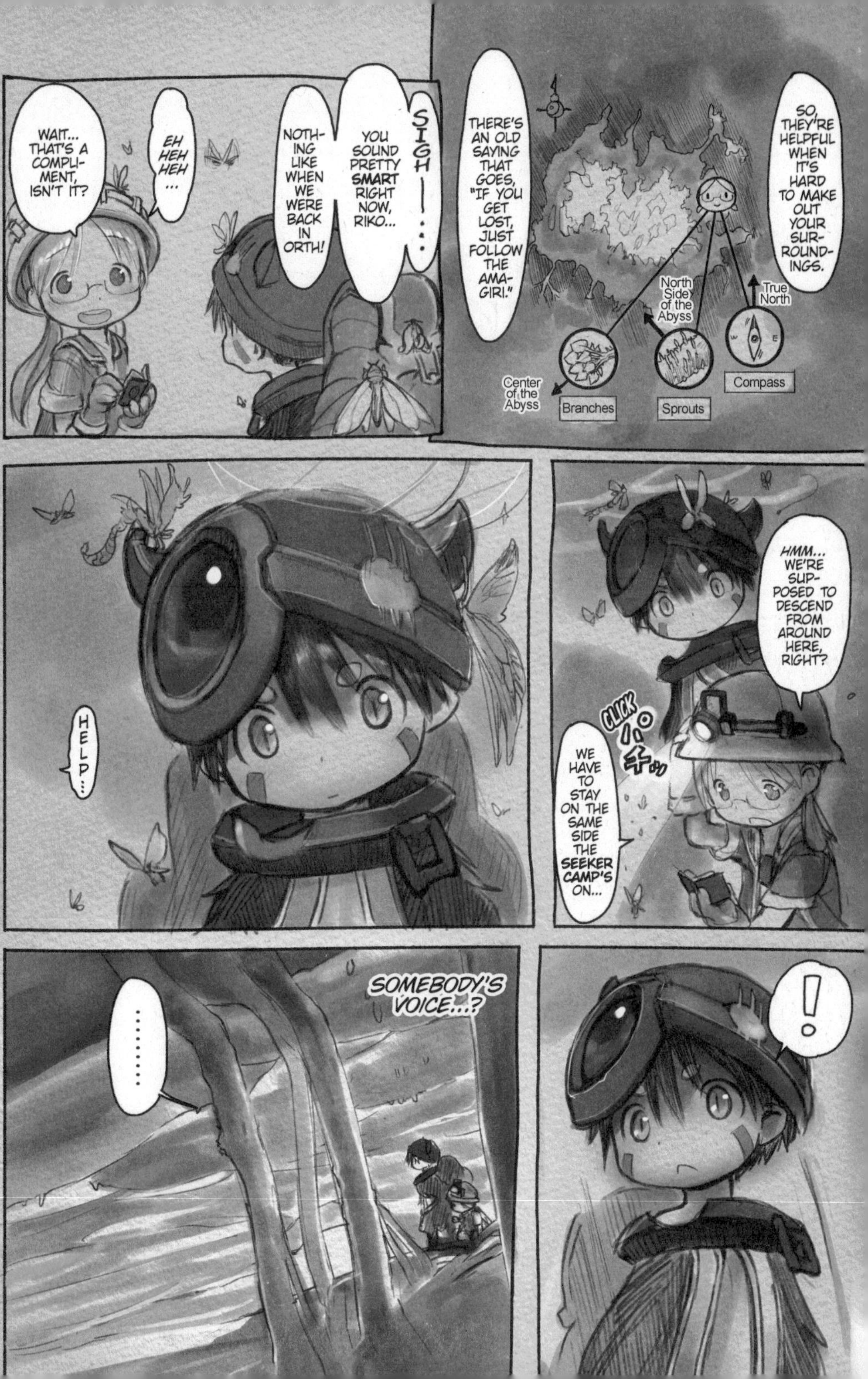
SO, THEY'RE HELPFUL WHEN IT'S HARD TO MAKE OUT YOUR SURROUNDINGS.
THERE'S AN OLD SAYING THAT GOES, "IF YOU GET LOST, JUST FOLLOW THE AMAGIRI."
True North
Compass
North Side of the Abyss
Sprouts
Branches
Center of the Abyss
SIGH...
YOU SOUND PRETTY **SMART** RIGHT NOW, RIKO...
NOTHING LIKE WHEN WE WERE BACK IN ORTH!
EH HEH HEH...
WAIT... THAT'S A COMPLIMENT, ISN'T IT?
HMM... WE'RE SUPPOSED TO DESCEND FROM AROUND HERE, RIGHT?
CLICK
WE HAVE TO STAY ON THE SAME SIDE THE **SEEKER CAMP'S** ON...
HELP...
!
SOMEBODY'S VOICE...?
......

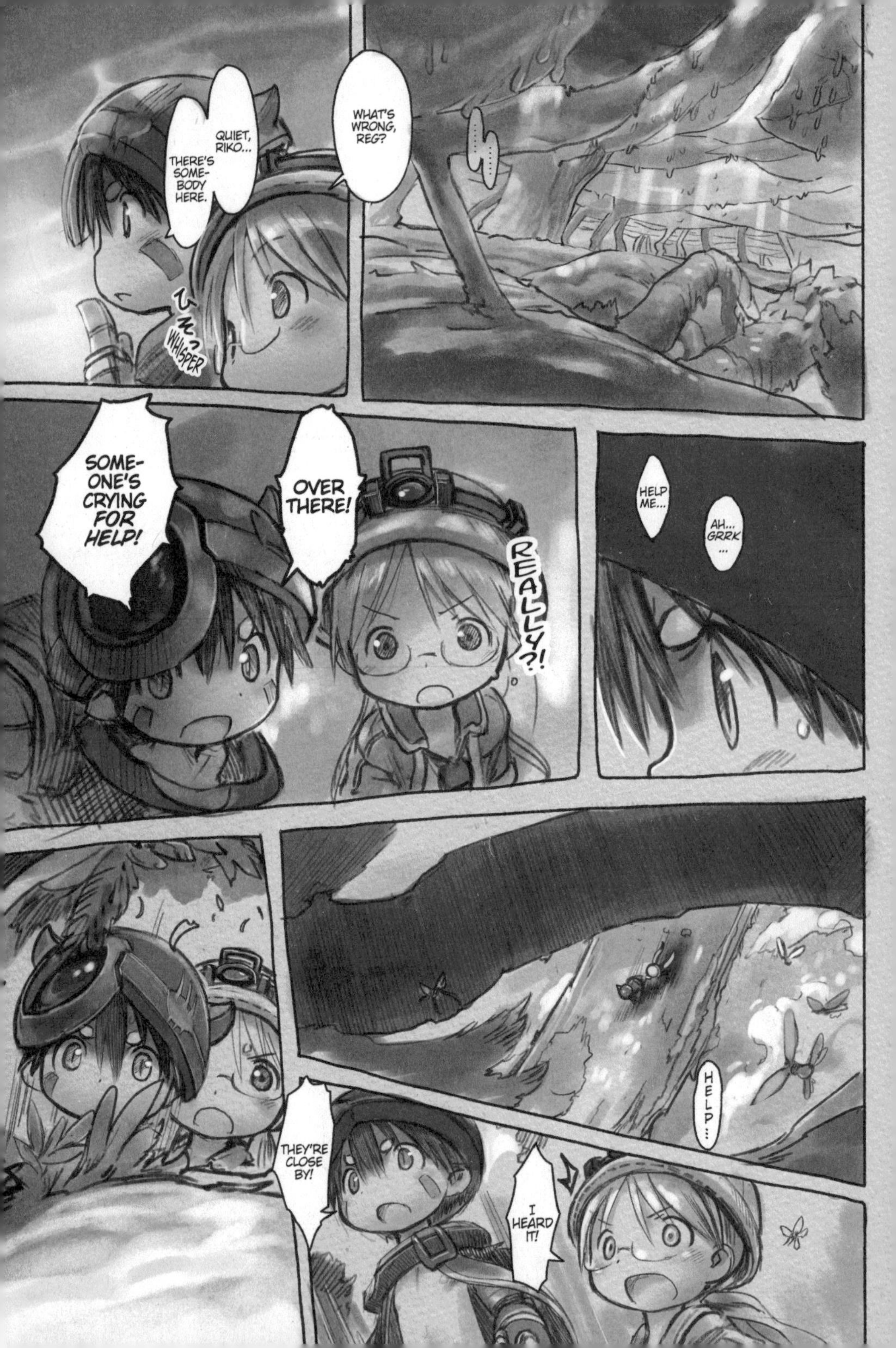
......
WHAT'S WRONG, REG?
QUIET, RIKO... THERE'S SOME-BODY HERE.
ひそっ WHISPER
HELP ME...
AH... GRRK ...
OVER THERE!
SOME-ONE'S CRYING FOR HELP!
REALLY?!
HELP...
I HEARD IT!
THEY'RE CLOSE BY!

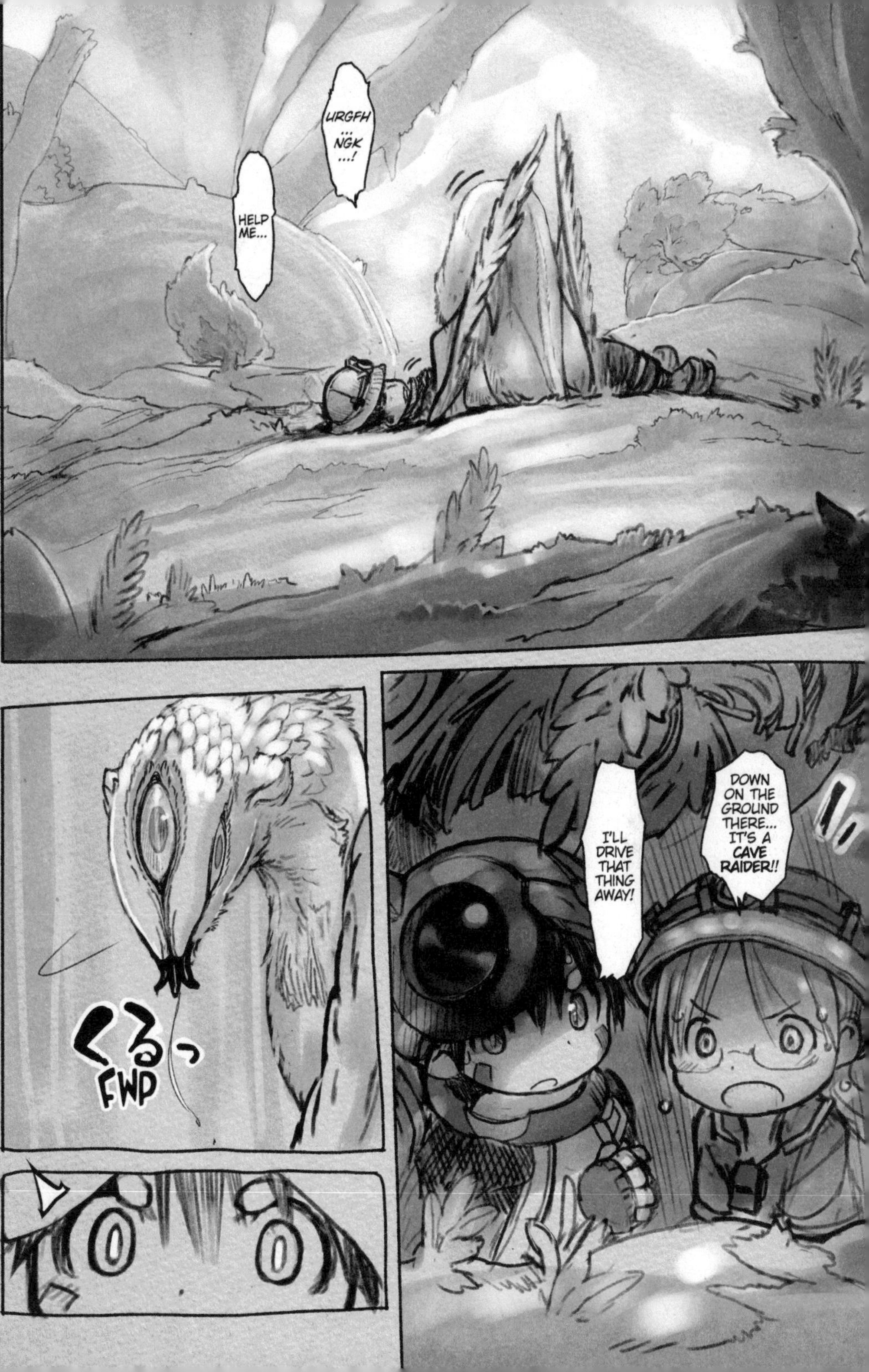
URGFH... NGK...!
HELP ME...
DOWN ON THE GROUND THERE... IT'S A CAVE RAIDER!!
I'LL DRIVE THAT THING AWAY!
くるっ
FWP

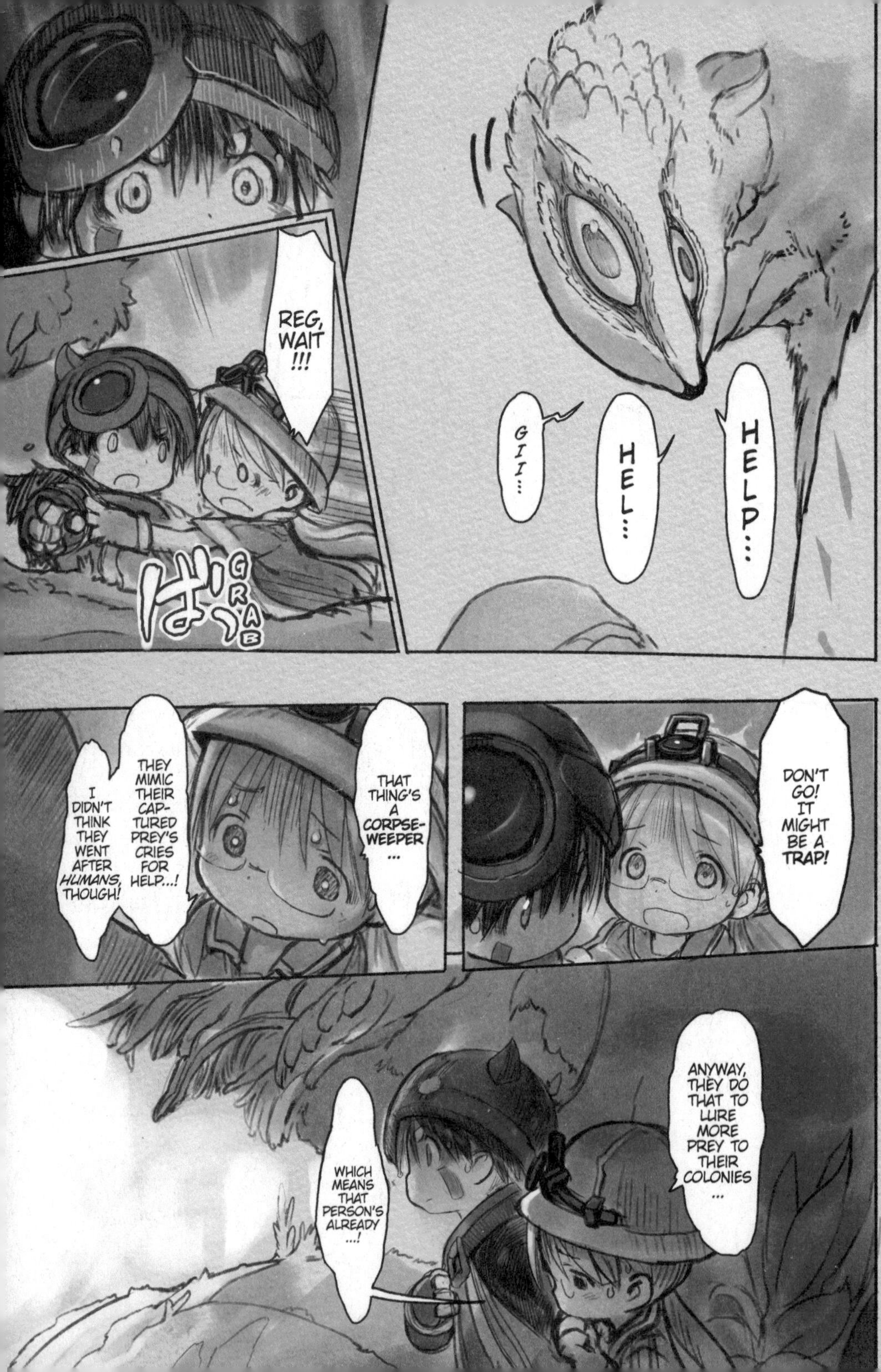
HELP...
HEL...
GII...
REG, WAIT!!!
ばっ GRAB
DON'T GO! IT MIGHT BE A TRAP!
THAT THING'S A CORPSE-WEEPER...
THEY MIMIC THEIR CAP-TURED PREY'S CRIES FOR HELP...!
I DIDN'T THINK THEY WENT AFTER HUMANS, THOUGH!
ANYWAY, THEY DO THAT TO LURE MORE PREY TO THEIR COLONIES...
WHICH MEANS THAT PERSON'S ALREADY...!

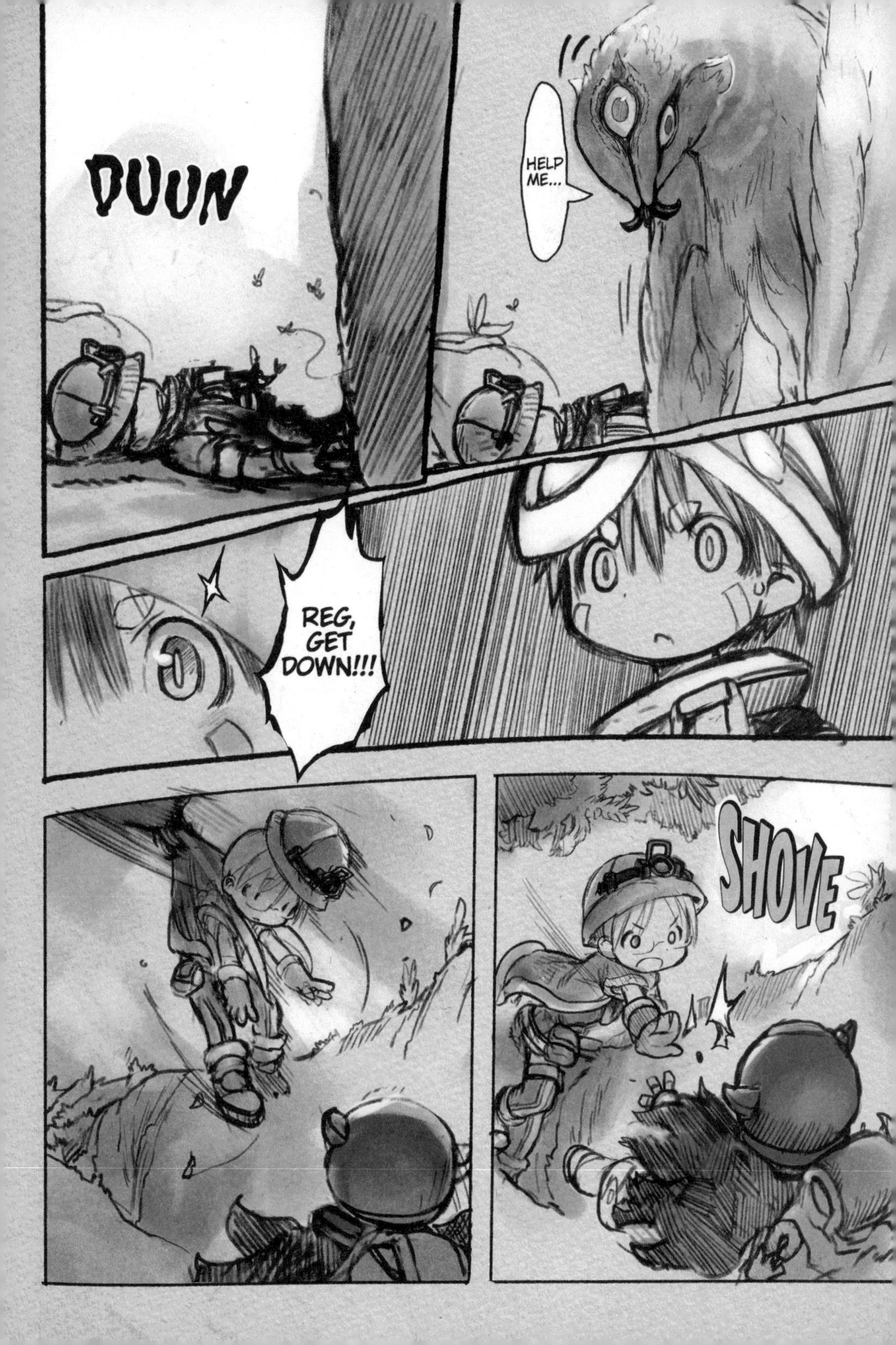
HELP ME...
DUUN
REG, GET DOWN!!!
SHOVE

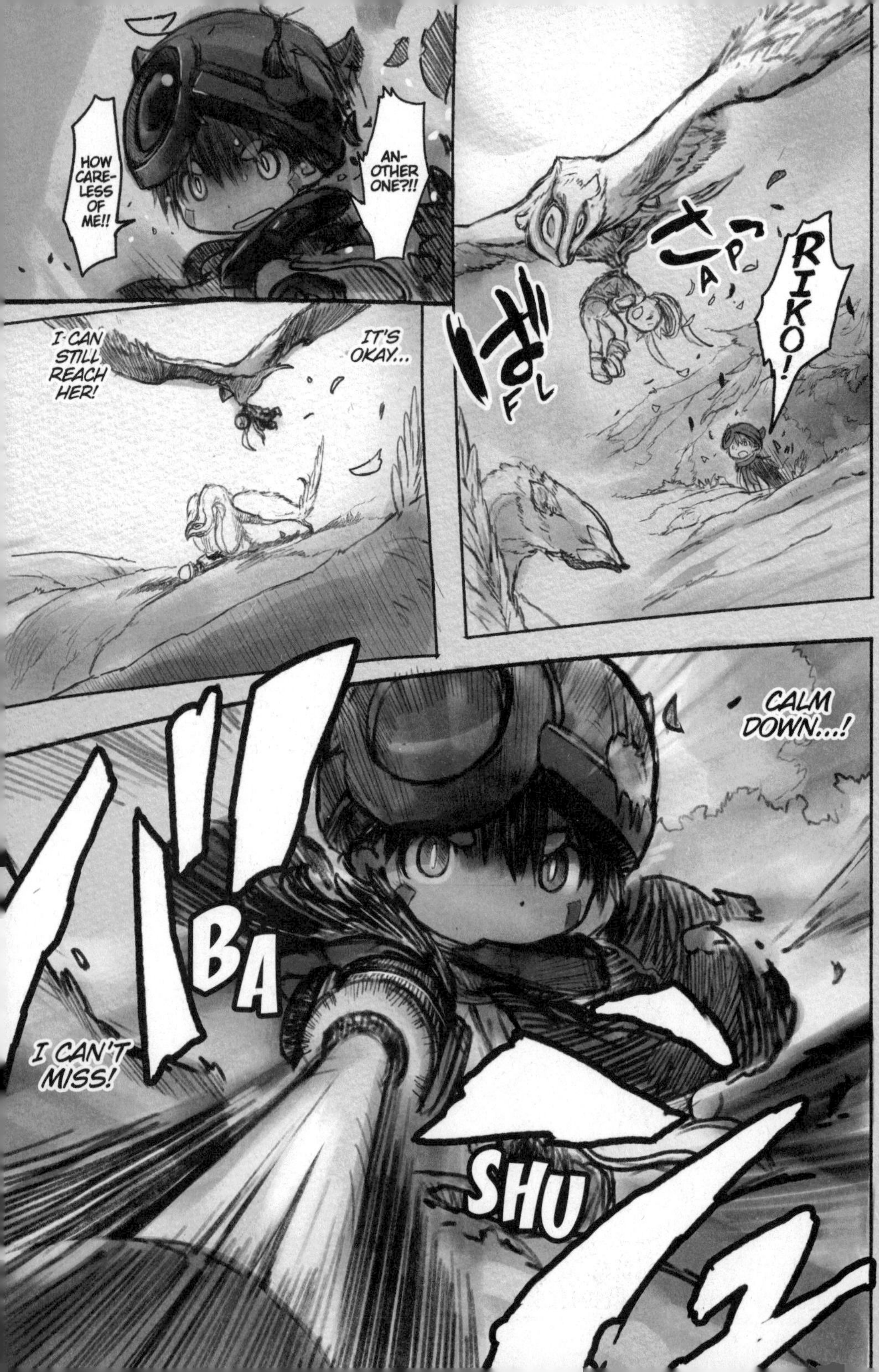
RIKO!
CAP
FL
AN-OTHER ONE?!!
HOW CARE-LESS OF ME!!
IT'S OKAY...
I CAN STILL REACH HER!
CALM DOWN...!
BA
SHU
I CAN'T MISS!

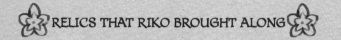

RELICS THAT RIKO BROUGHT ALONG

STAR COMPASS
GRADE-4 RELIC (ESTIMATED)

RIKO NAMED THIS RELIC, WHICH SHE UNEARTHED IN THE FIRST LAYER. THE INNER COMPASS-LIKE PART DOESN'T BUDGE A BIT WHEN THE OUTER SPHERE IS SPUN. RIKO INSISTS THAT IT IS POINTING TO THE BOTTOM OF THE NETHERWORLD...

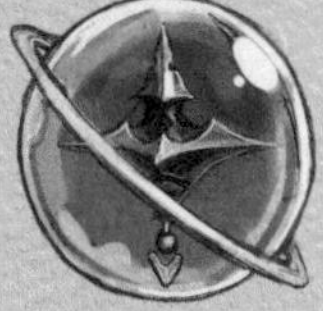

THE LATERAL PROTRUSIONS DO NOT SEEM TO POINT IN THE CARDINAL DIRECTIONS OF NORTH, SOUTH, EAST, AND WEST.

SCALED UMBRELLA
GRADE-4 RELIC

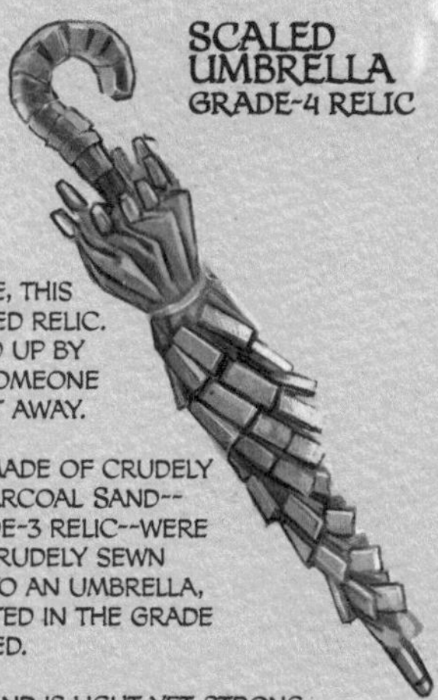

TO BE PRECISE, THIS IS A PROCESSED RELIC. IT WAS PICKED UP BY RIKO AFTER SOMEONE ELSE THREW IT AWAY.

THE PLATES, MADE OF CRUDELY SINTERED CHARCOAL SAND--ITSELF A GRADE-3 RELIC--WERE EVEN MORE CRUDELY SEWN TOGETHER INTO AN UMBRELLA, WHICH RESULTED IN THE GRADE BEING LOWERED.

CHARCOAL SAND IS LIGHT YET STRONG. THIS UMBRELLA MAKES GOOD USE OF THOSE CHARACTERISTICS, AND RIKO THINKS IT WILL MAKE FOR AN EFFECTIVE SHIELD.

SILKFANG

THEIR MOUTHS CONTAIN POISONOUS SPINES WITH PARALYTIC PROPERTIES.

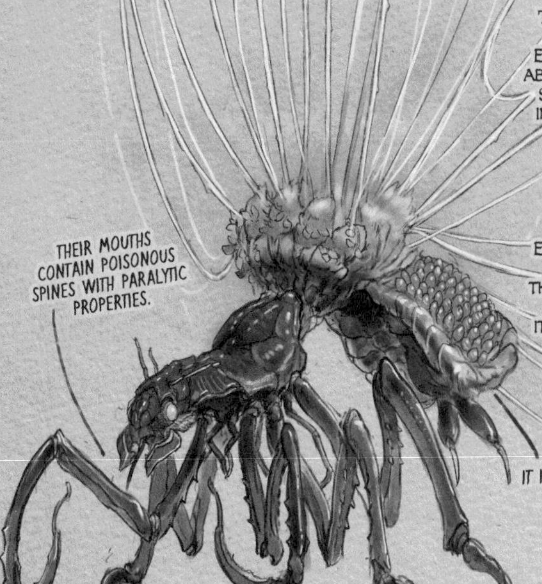

THESE LARGE BUGS LIVE IN THE FIRST LAYER.

EACH HAS ITS OWN DOME-SHAPED TERRITORY ABOUT TEN METERS IN SIZE, WITHIN WHICH THEY STRETCH OUT THEIR STICKY FEELERS AND LIE IN WAIT. IN THIS WAY, THEIR TERRITORY ITSELF BECOMES A TRAP FOR CATCHING PREY.

WHILE THEY MOVE WITH ASTONISHING SPEED IN THEIR OWN TERRITORY, THEY KINDLY NEVER VENTURE OUTSIDE OF IT.

EACH HAS ITS OWN DOME-SHAPED TERRITORY ABOUT TEN METERS IN SIZE, WITHIN WHICH THEY STRETCH OUT THEIR STICKY FEELERS AND LIE IN WAIT. IN THIS WAY, THEIR TERRITORY ITSELF BECOMES A TRAP FOR CATCHING PREY.

THEY REST IN THEIR WEBS AT THE TOP OF THEIR DOMES UNTIL PREY WANDERS INTO THEIR TERRITORY.

IT IS NOT KNOWN IF THEY ARE EDIBLE.

DANGER LEVEL:
★★
(REQUIRES CAUTION)

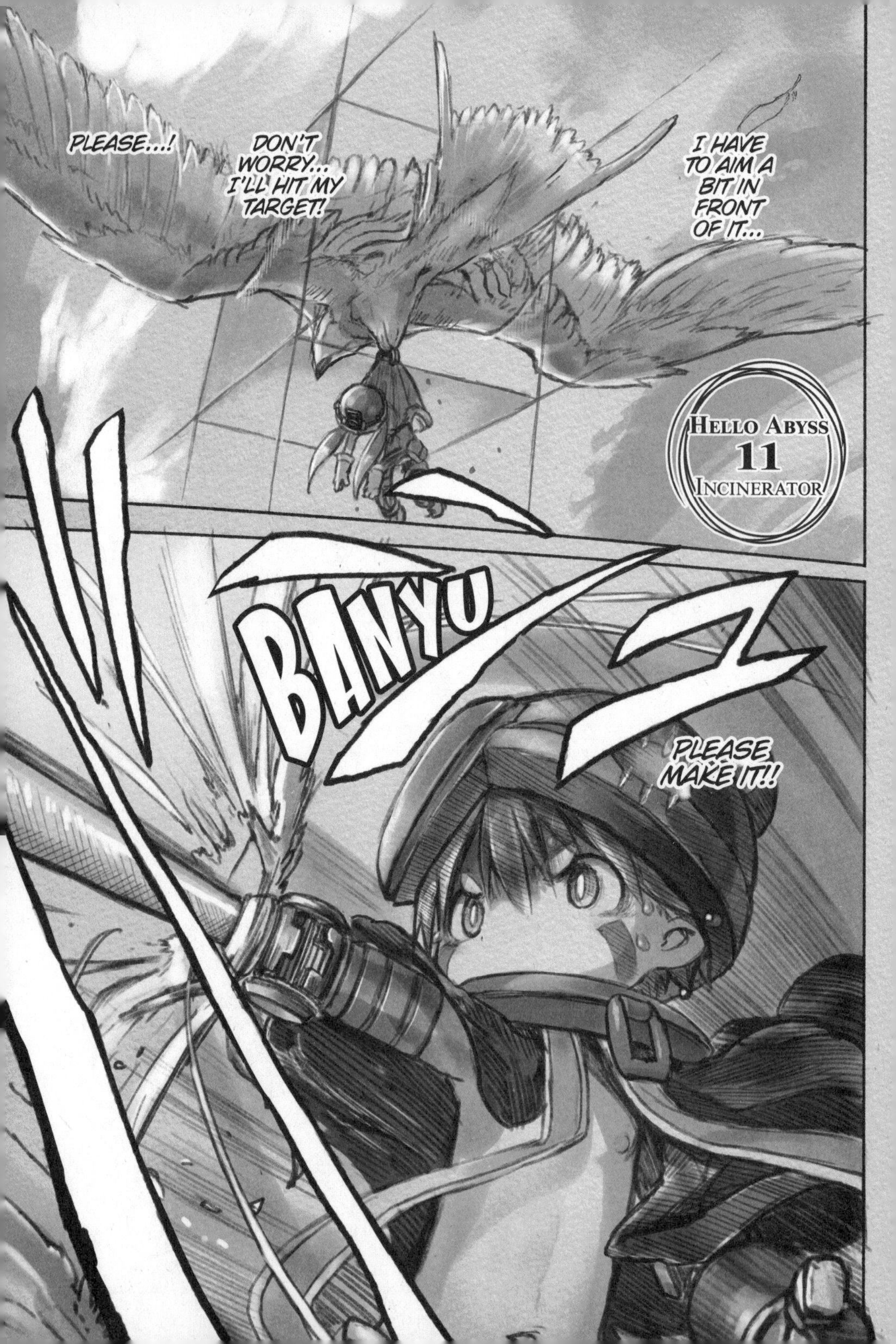
I HAVE TO AIM A BIT IN FRONT OF IT...
DON'T WORRY... I'LL HIT MY TARGET!
PLEASE...!
HELLO ABYSS 11 INCINERATOR
BANYU
PLEASE MAKE IT!!

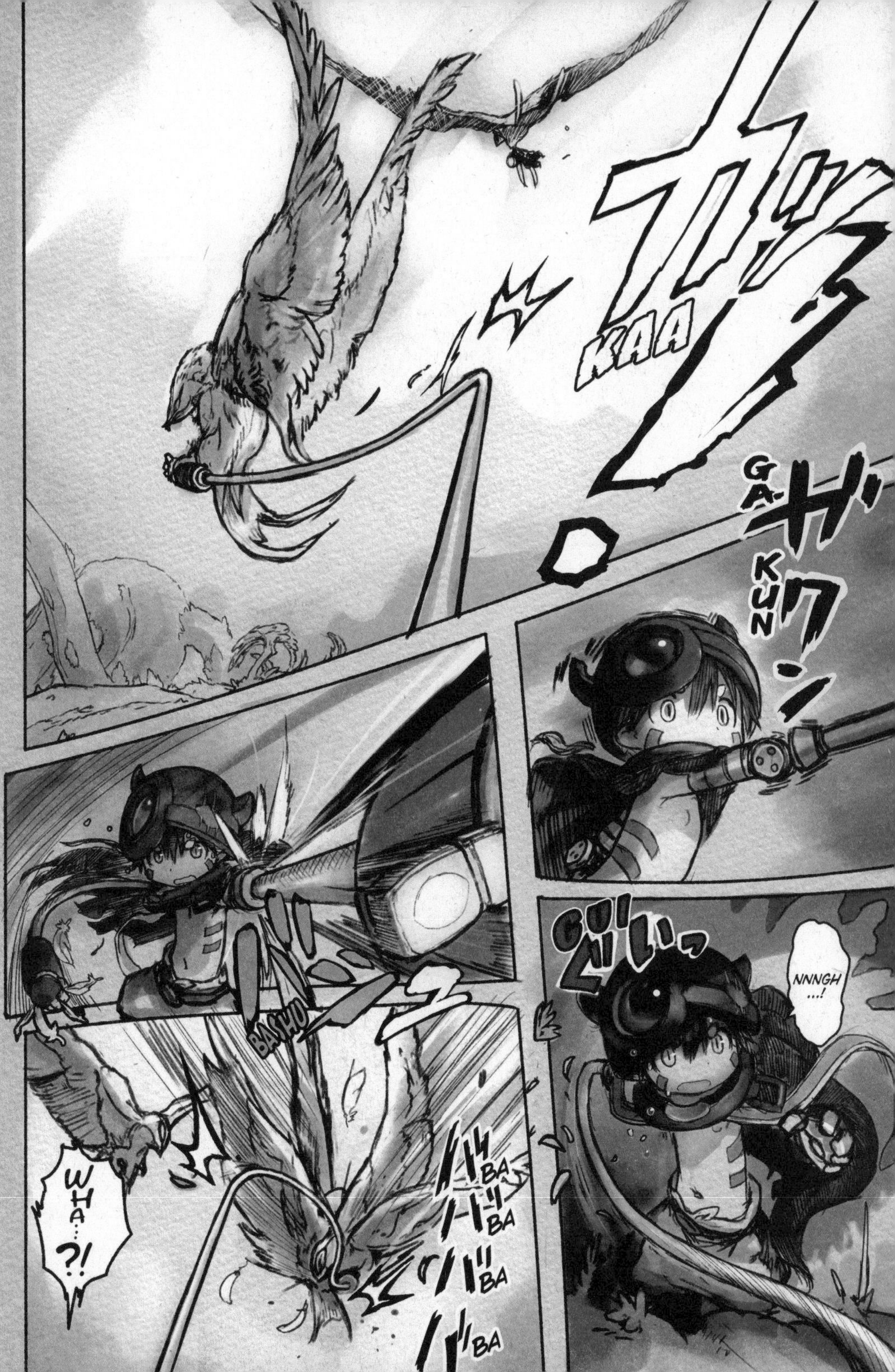

KAA
GA KUN
NNNGH ...!
BASHU
BA BA BA BA
WHA...?!

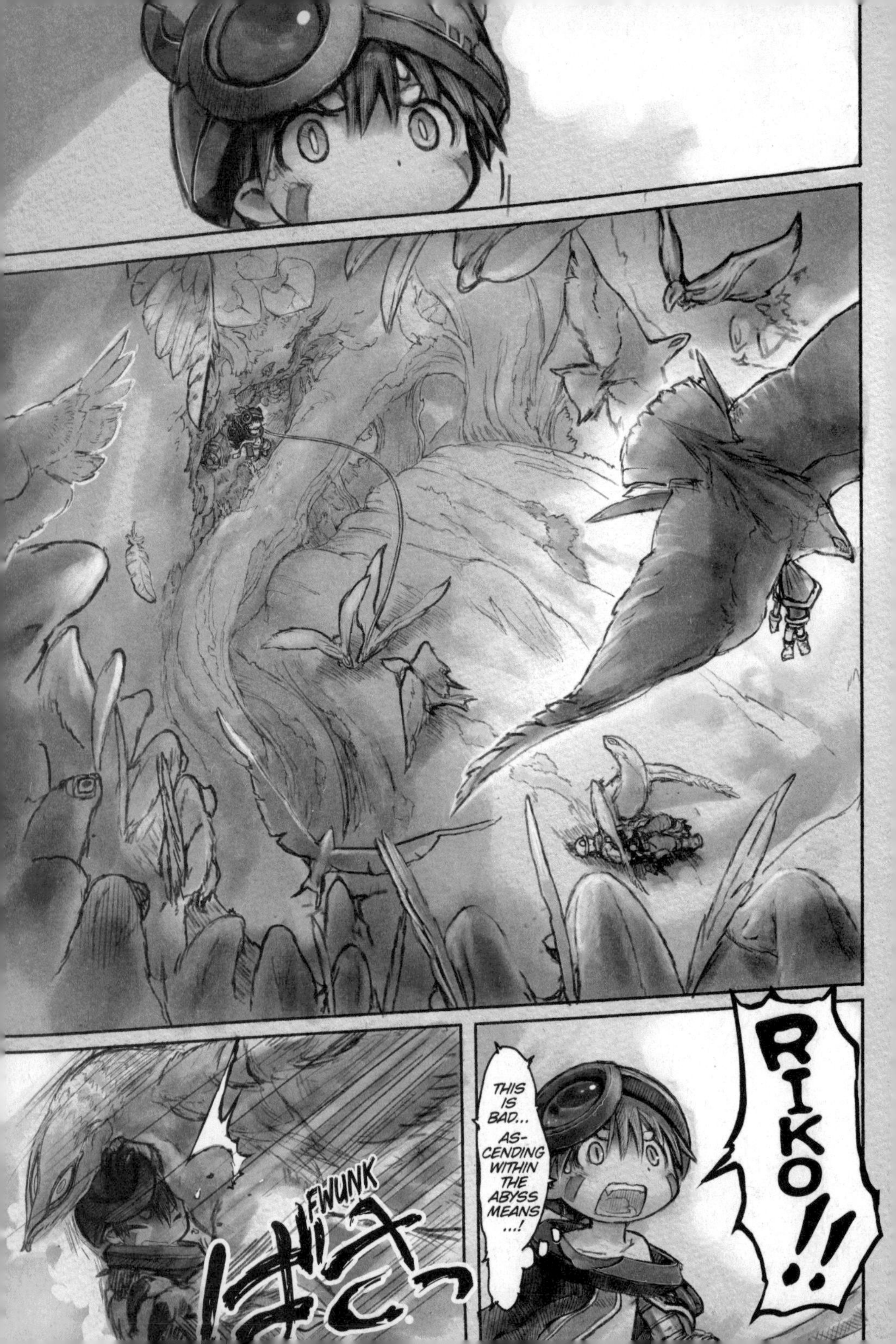
RIKO!!
THIS IS BAD... ASCENDING WITHIN THE ABYSS MEANS ...!
FWUNK
ばさっ

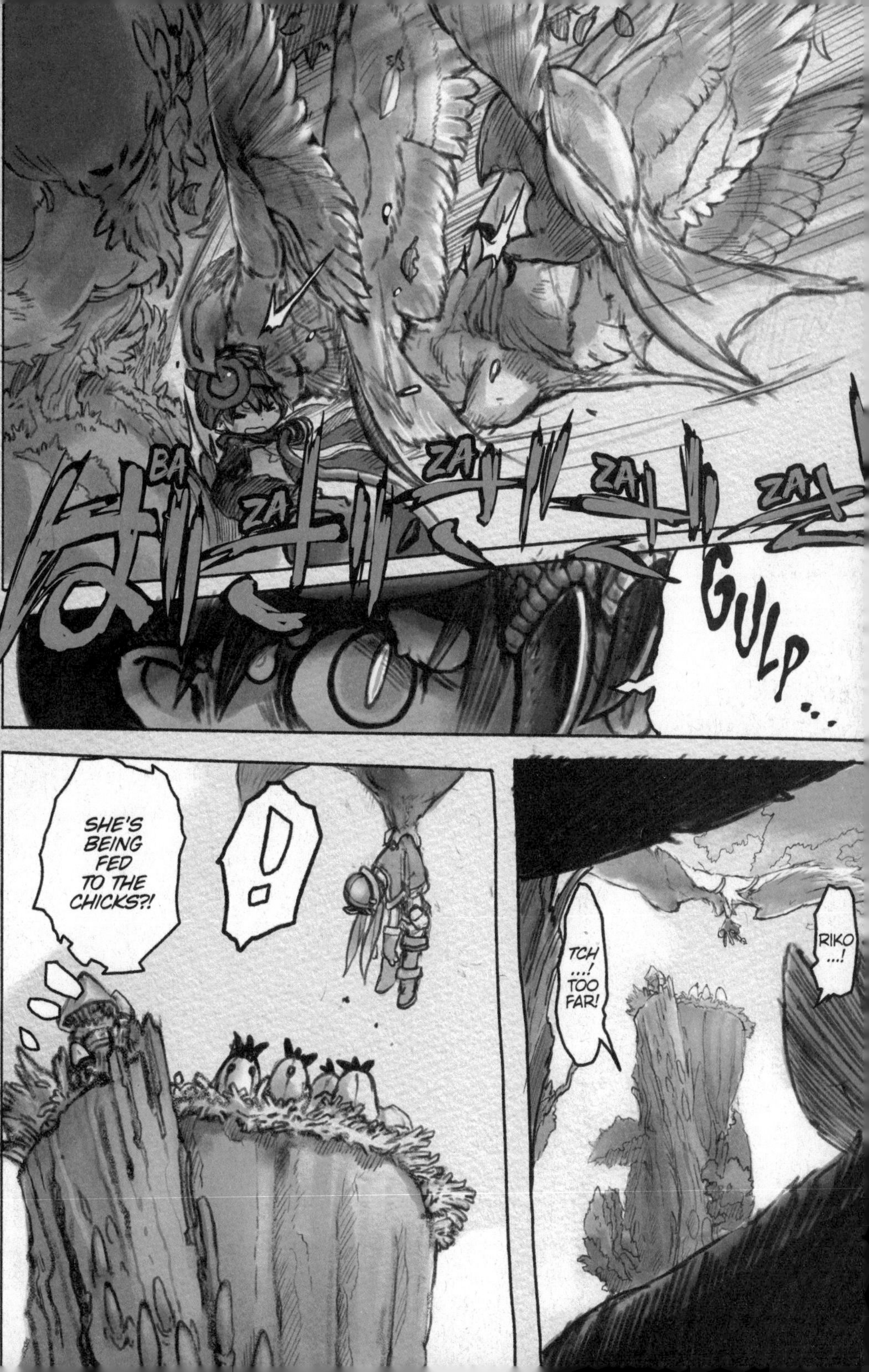
BA ZA ZA ZA ZA
GULP...
RIKO...!
TCH...! TOO FAR!
!
SHE'S BEING FED TO THE CHICKS?!

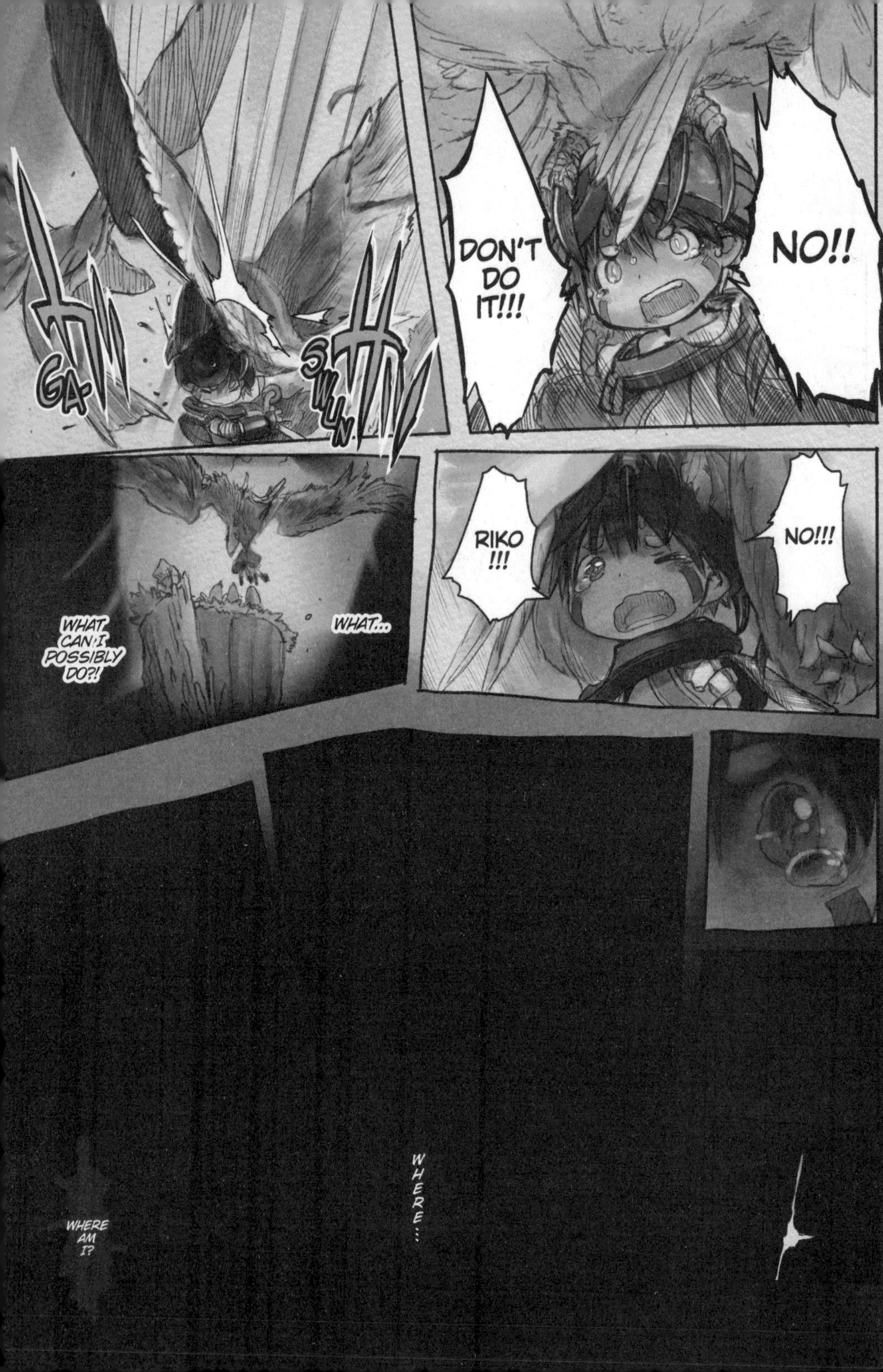
NO!!
DON'T DO IT!!!
SWUN
GA
NO!!!
RIKO!!!
WHAT...
WHAT CAN I POSSIBLY DO?!
WHERE...
WHERE AM I?

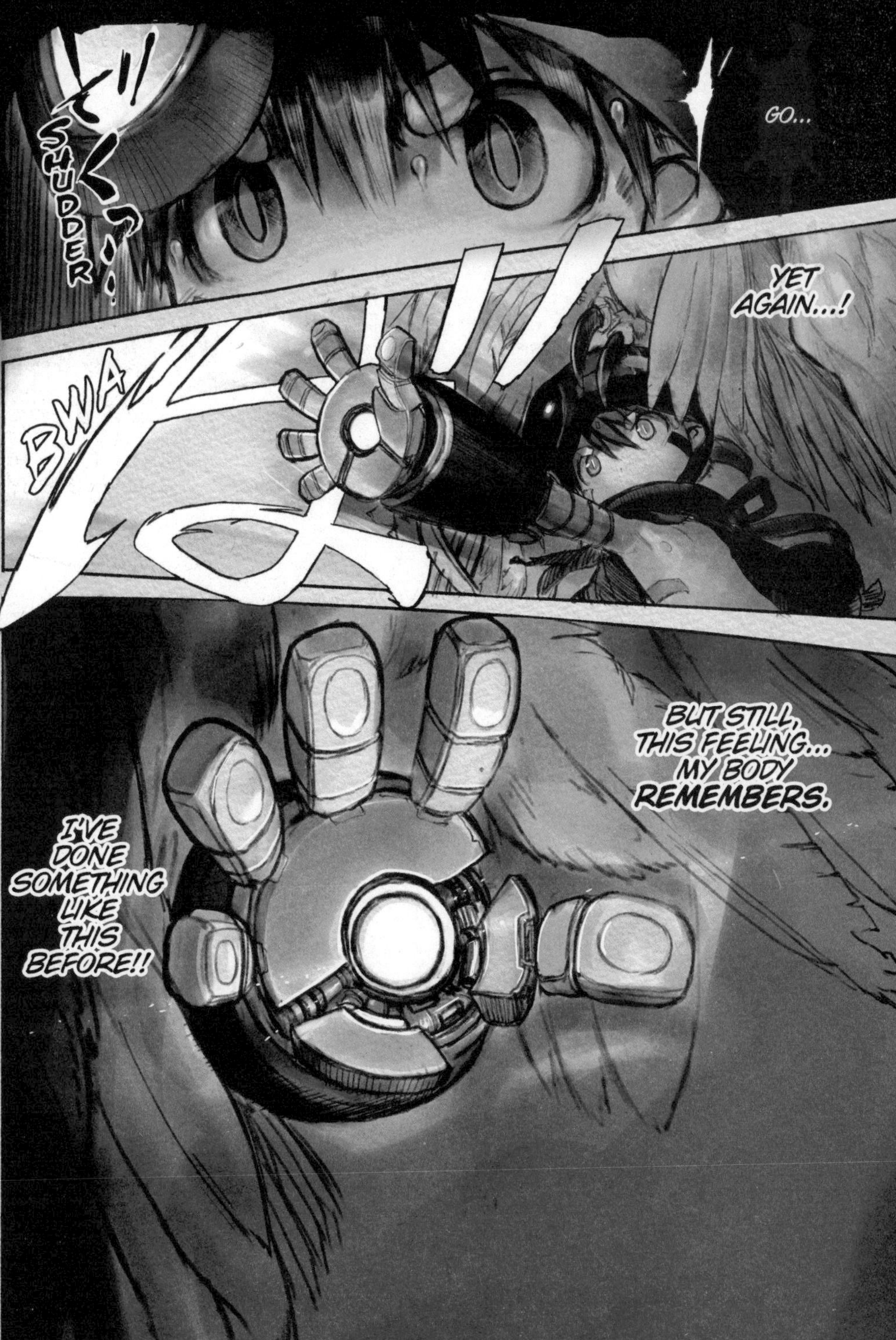
GO...
SHUDDER
YET AGAIN...!
BWA
BUT STILL, THIS FEELING... MY BODY REMEMBERS.
I'VE DONE SOMETHING LIKE THIS BEFORE!!

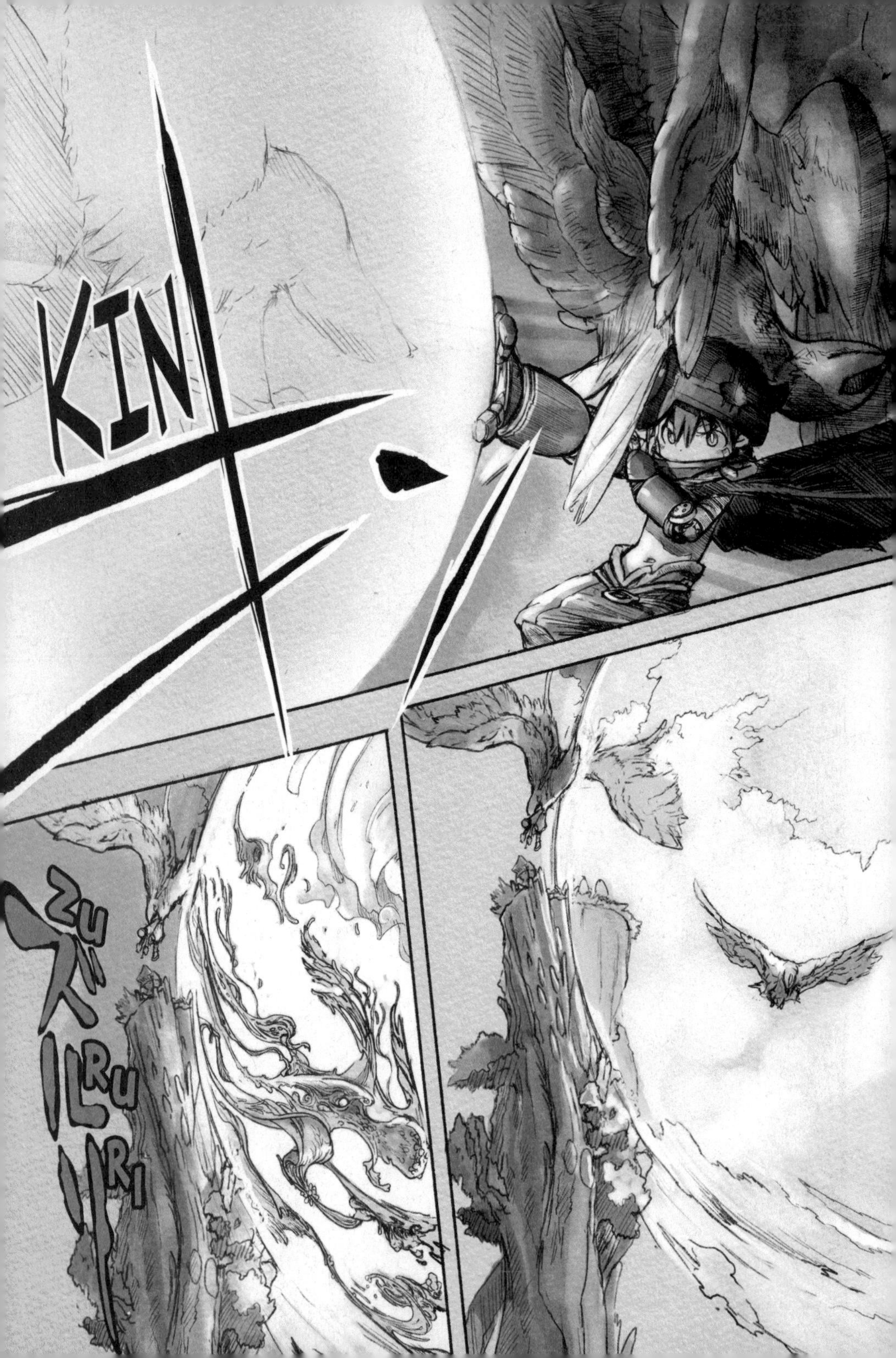
KIN
ズルリ
ZURURI

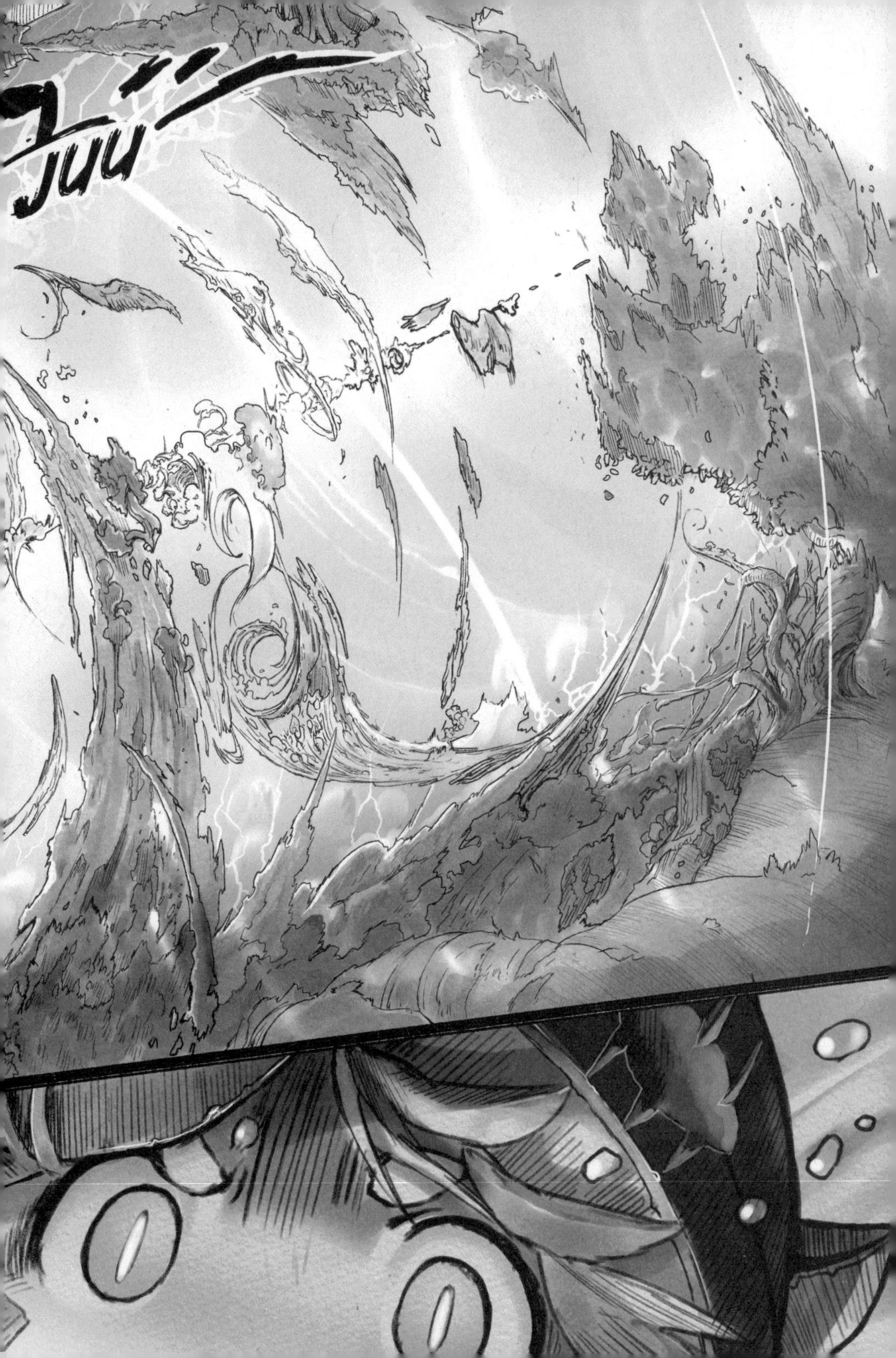
JUU

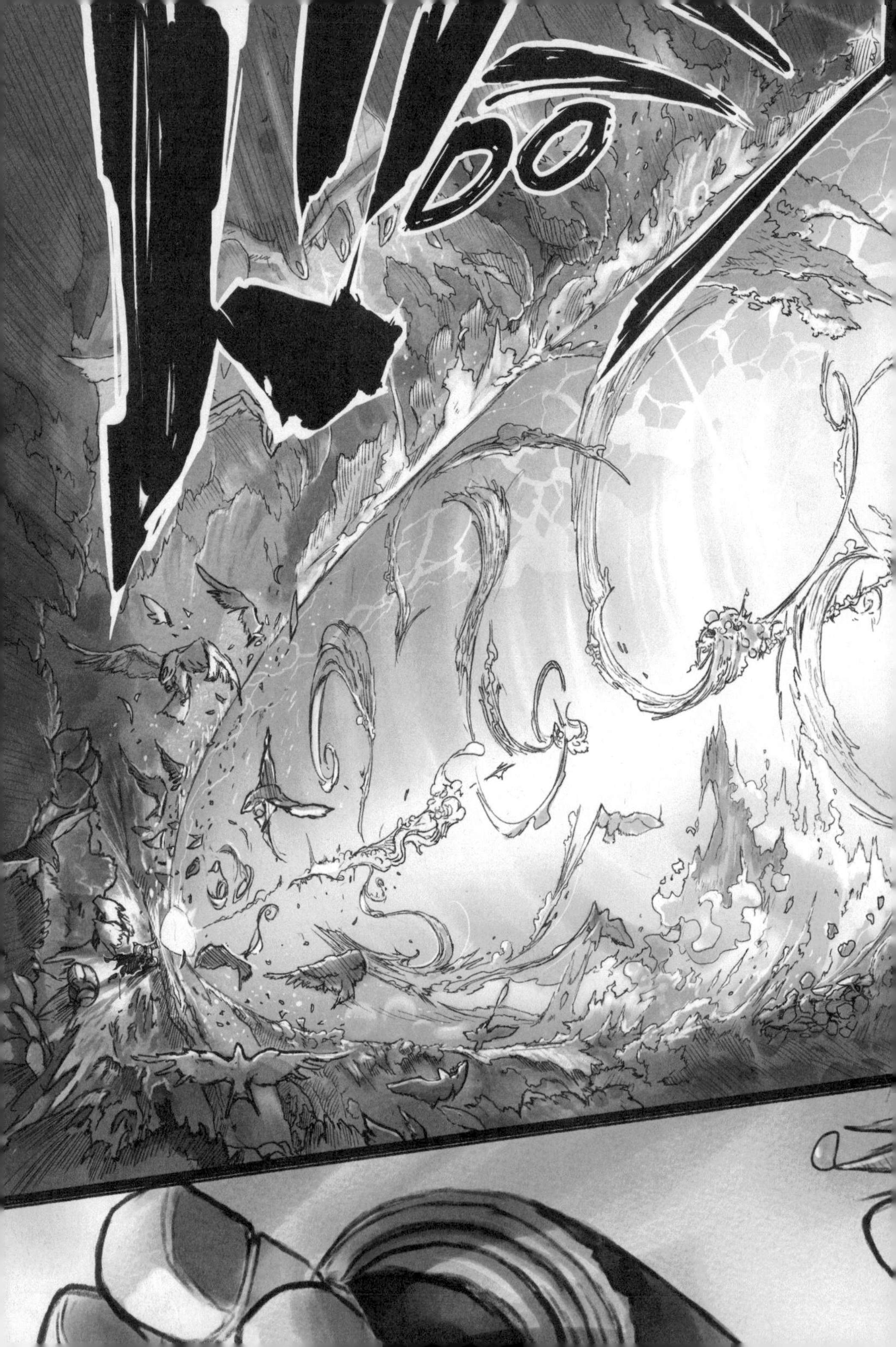
DO

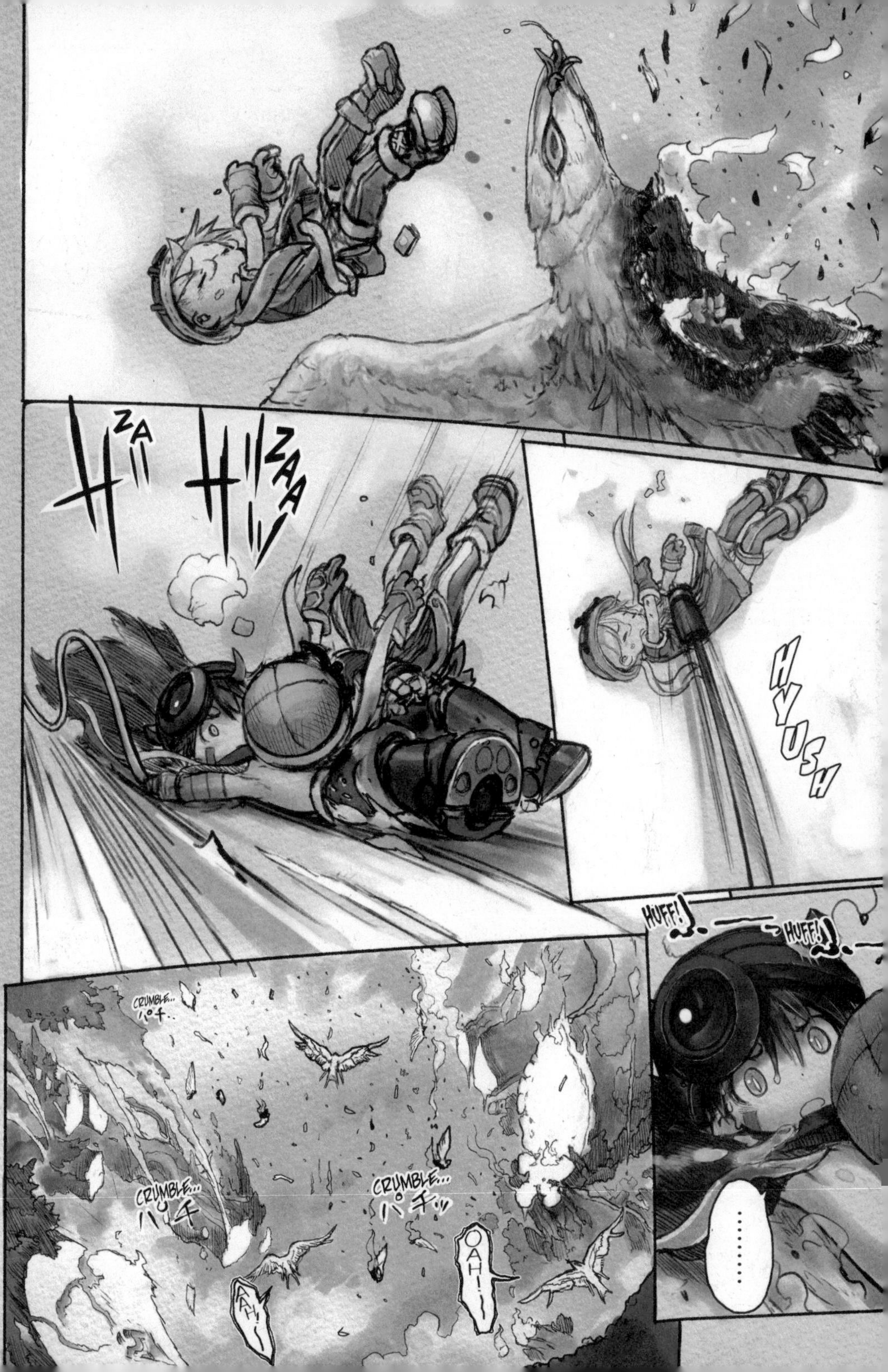
HYUSH
HZAA
HZAA
HUFF!
HUFF!
......
CRUMBLE...
パチ..
CRUMBLE...
パチッ
CRUMBLE...
パチ
OAH!
AAH!

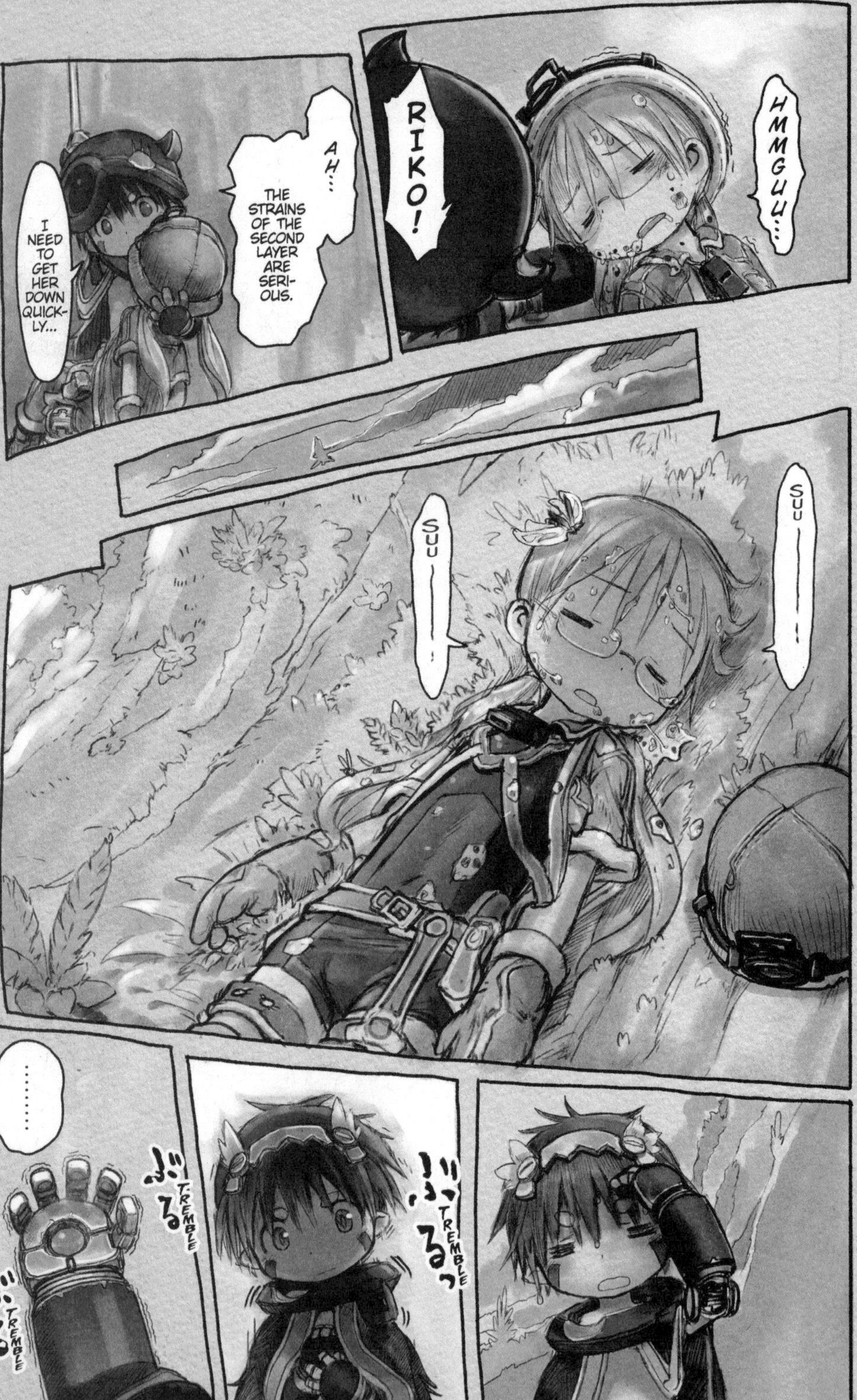
HMMGUU...
RIKO!
AH...
THE STRAINS OF THE SECOND LAYER ARE SERIOUS.
I NEED TO GET HER DOWN QUICKLY...
SUU—!
SUU—!
ぶるっ TREMBLE
ぶる TREMBLE
......
ぶる TREMBLE

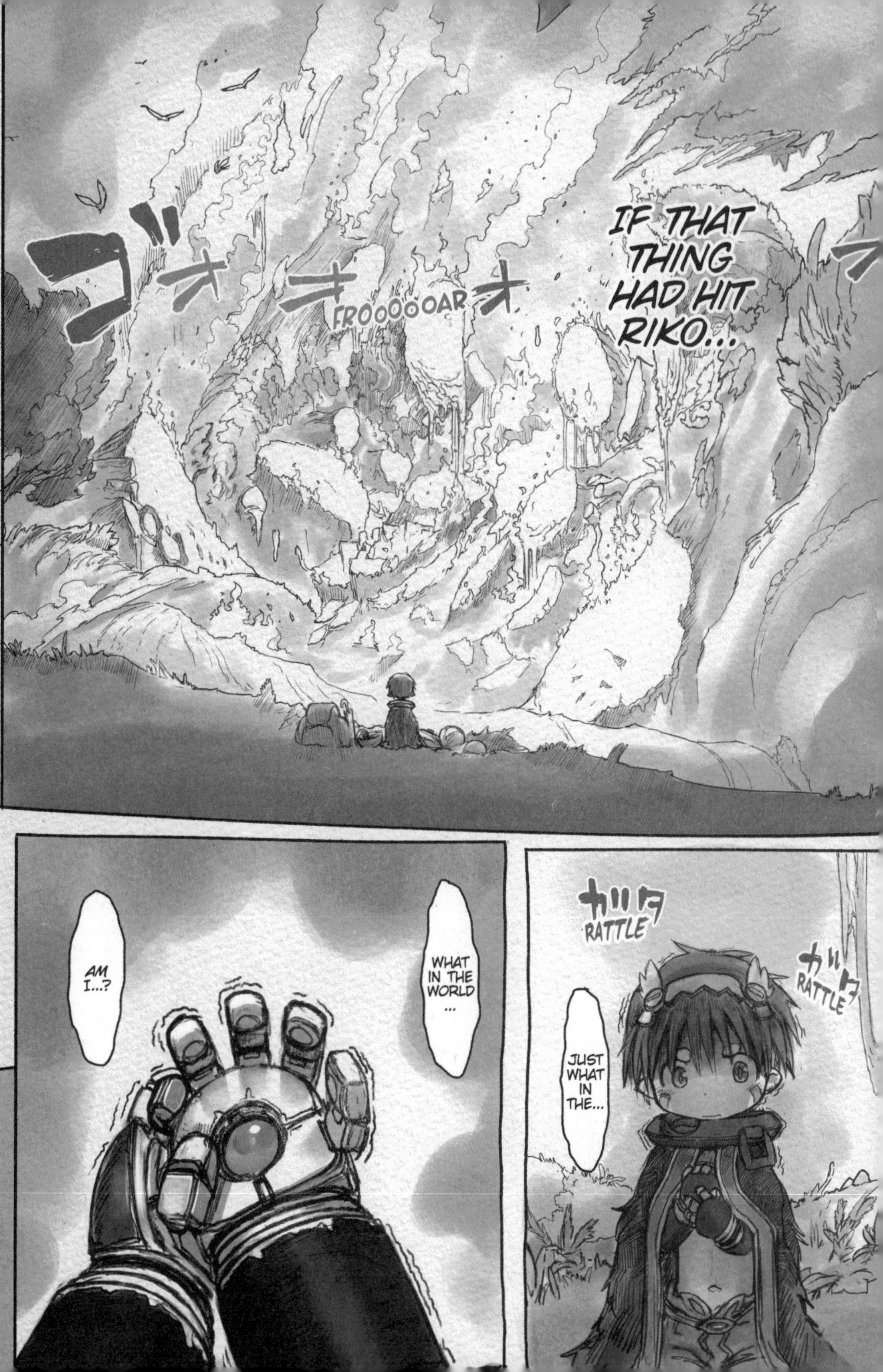
FROOOOOAR
IF THAT THING HAD HIT RIKO...
RATTLE
RATTLE
JUST WHAT IN THE...
WHAT IN THE WORLD ...
AM I...?

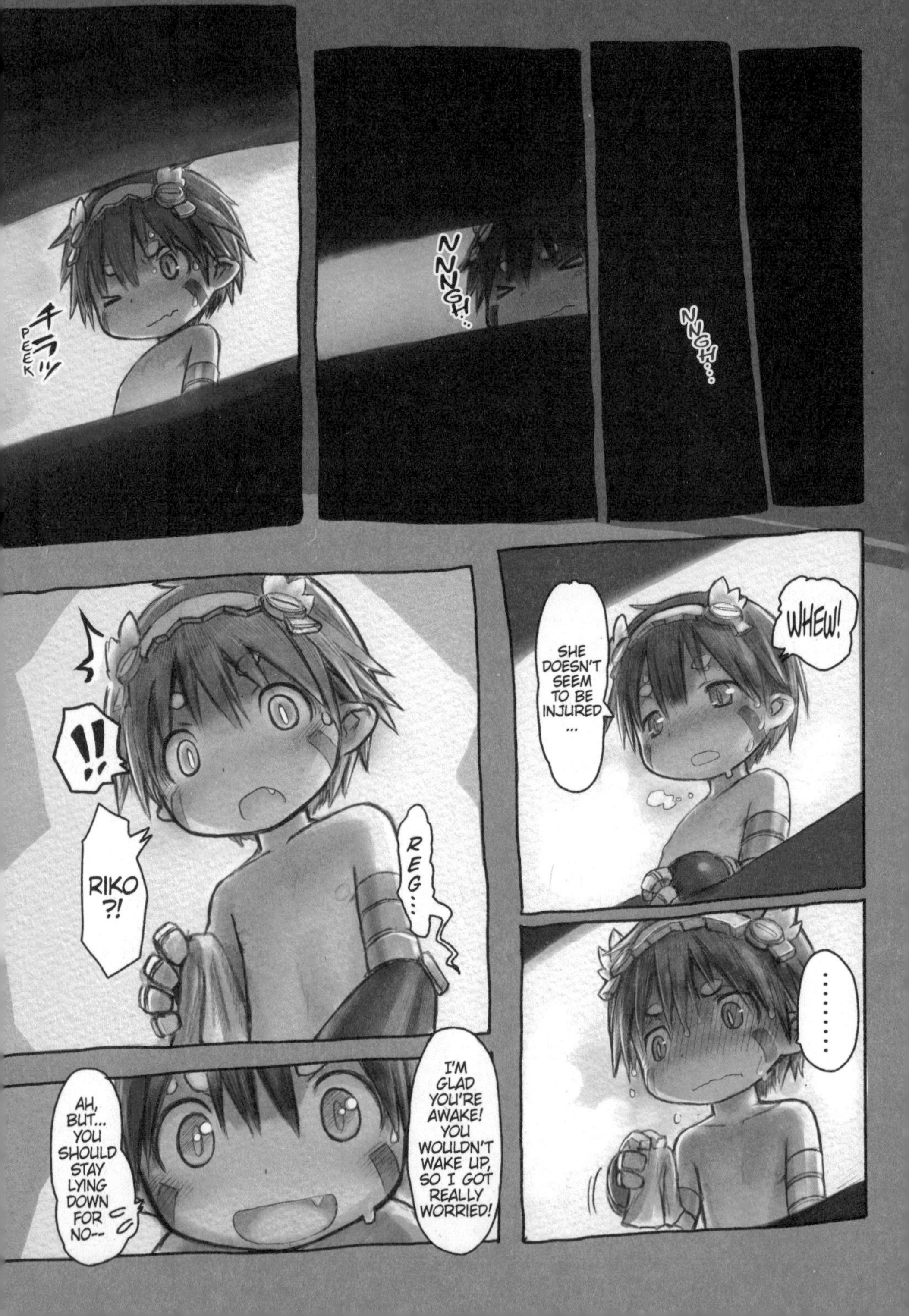
NNGH...
NNNGH..
チラッ
PEEK
WHEW!
SHE DOESN'T SEEM TO BE INJURED...
REG...
!!
RIKO?!
......
I'M GLAD YOU'RE AWAKE! YOU WOULDN'T WAKE UP, SO I GOT REALLY WORRIED!
AH, BUT... YOU SHOULD STAY LYING DOWN FOR NO--

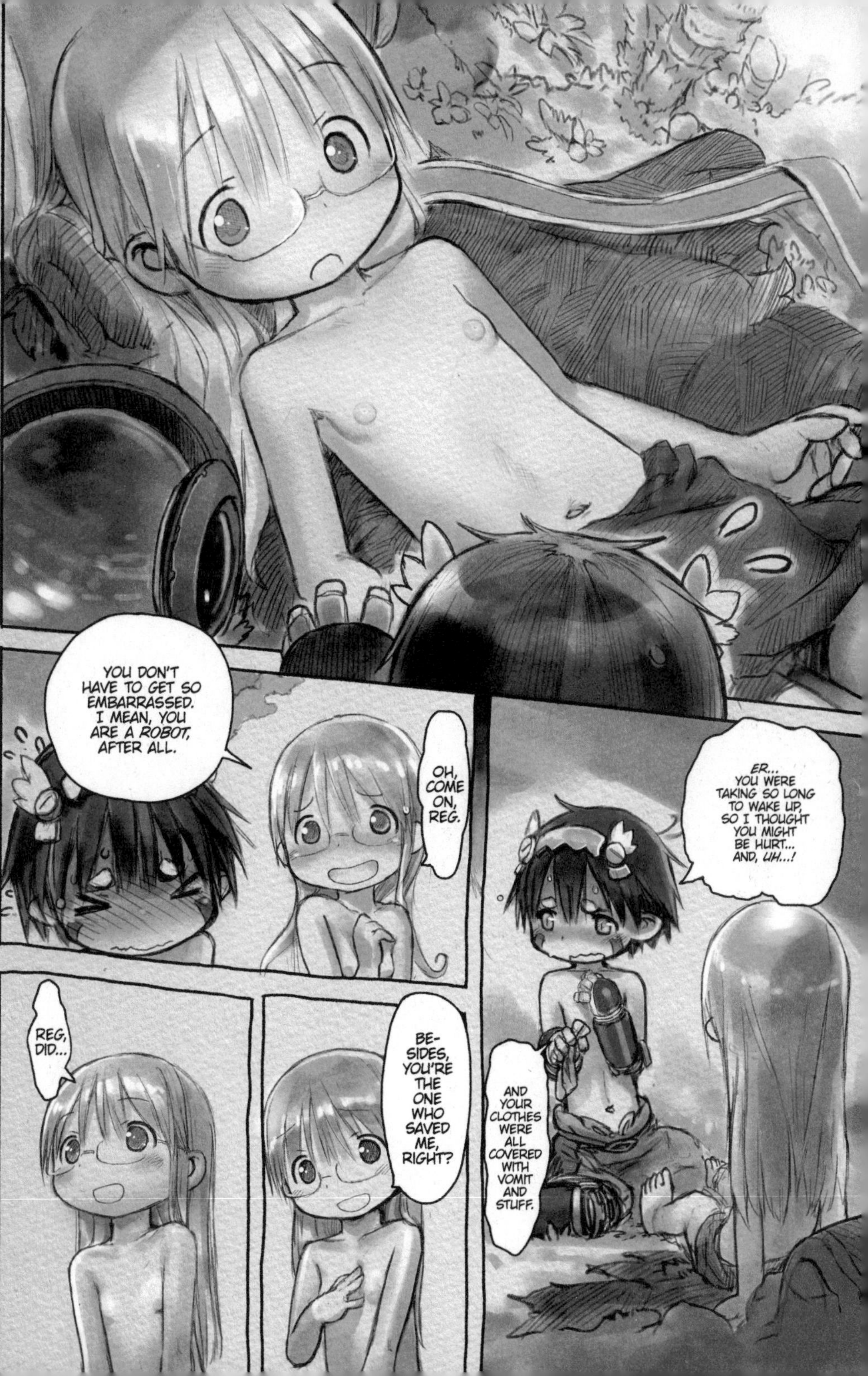
ER... YOU WERE TAKING SO LONG TO WAKE UP, SO I THOUGHT YOU MIGHT BE HURT... AND, UH...!
AND YOUR CLOTHES WERE ALL COVERED WITH VOMIT AND STUFF.
OH, COME ON, REG.
YOU DON'T HAVE TO GET SO EMBARRASSED. I MEAN, YOU ARE A ROBOT, AFTER ALL.
BE-SIDES, YOU'RE THE ONE WHO SAVED ME, RIGHT?
REG, DID...

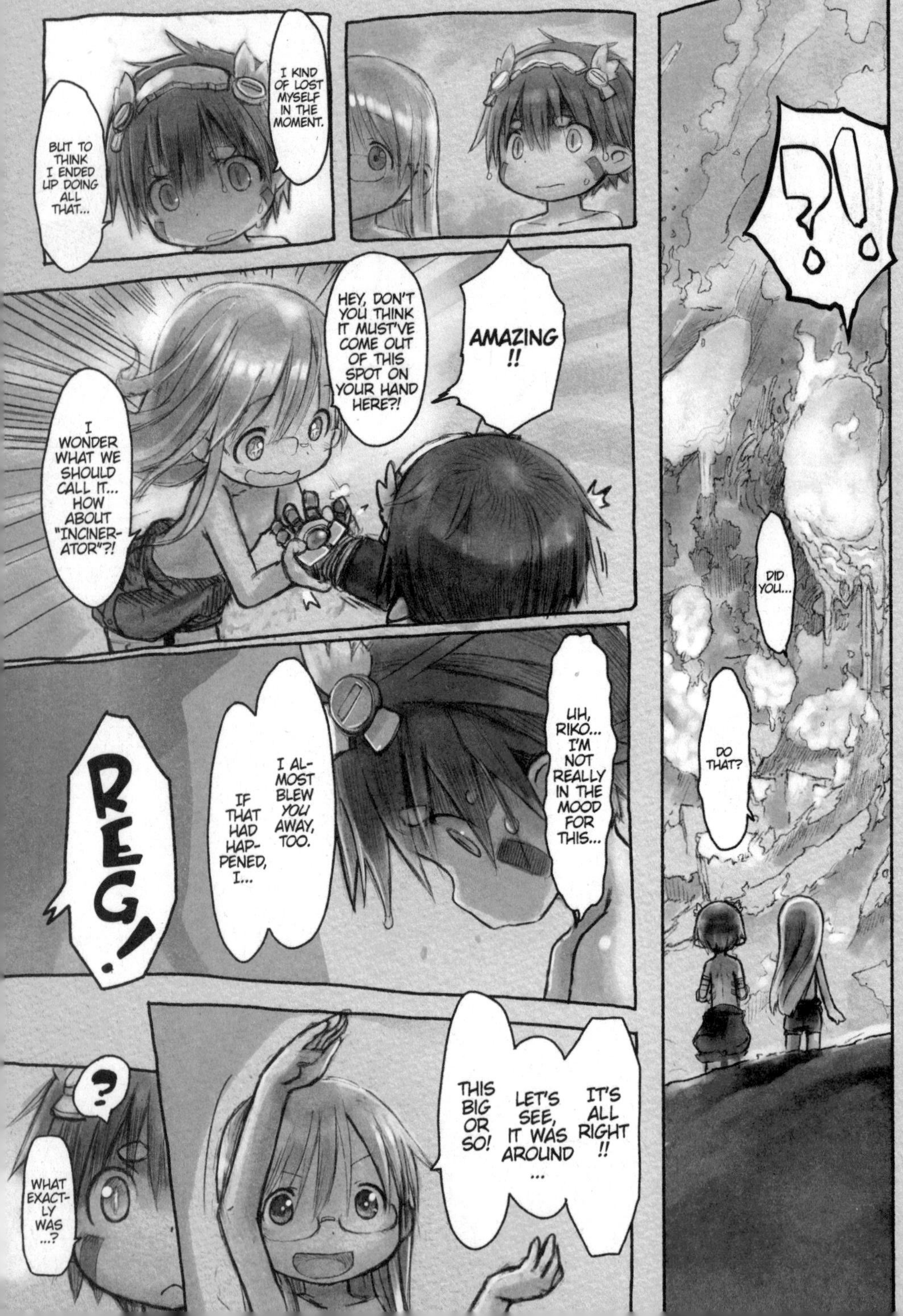
?!
DID YOU...
DO THAT?
I KIND OF LOST MYSELF IN THE MOMENT.
BUT TO THINK I ENDED UP DOING ALL THAT...
AMAZING!!
HEY, DON'T YOU THINK IT MUST'VE COME OUT OF THIS SPOT ON YOUR HAND HERE?!
I WONDER WHAT WE SHOULD CALL IT... HOW ABOUT "INCINERATOR"?!
UH, RIKO... I'M NOT REALLY IN THE MOOD FOR THIS...
I ALMOST BLEW *YOU* AWAY, TOO.
IF THAT HAD HAPPENED, I...
REG!
IT'S ALL RIGHT!!
LET'S SEE, IT WAS AROUND...
THIS BIG OR SO!
?
WHAT EXACTLY WAS...?

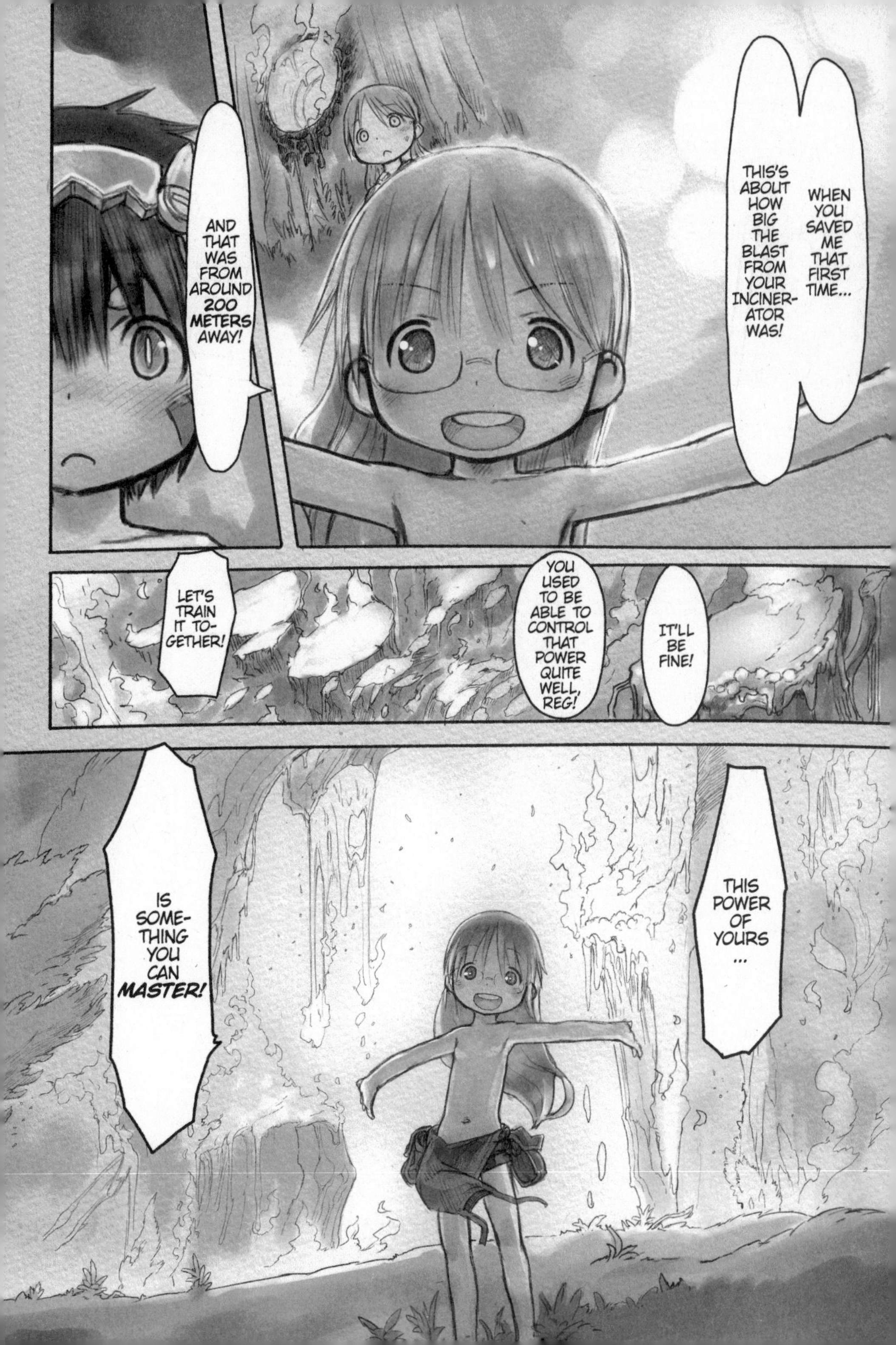
WHEN YOU SAVED ME THAT FIRST TIME...
THIS'S ABOUT HOW BIG THE BLAST FROM YOUR INCINERATOR WAS!
AND THAT WAS FROM AROUND 200 METERS AWAY!
IT'LL BE FINE!
YOU USED TO BE ABLE TO CONTROL THAT POWER QUITE WELL, REG!
LET'S TRAIN IT TOGETHER!
THIS POWER OF YOURS ...
IS SOMETHING YOU CAN *MASTER!*

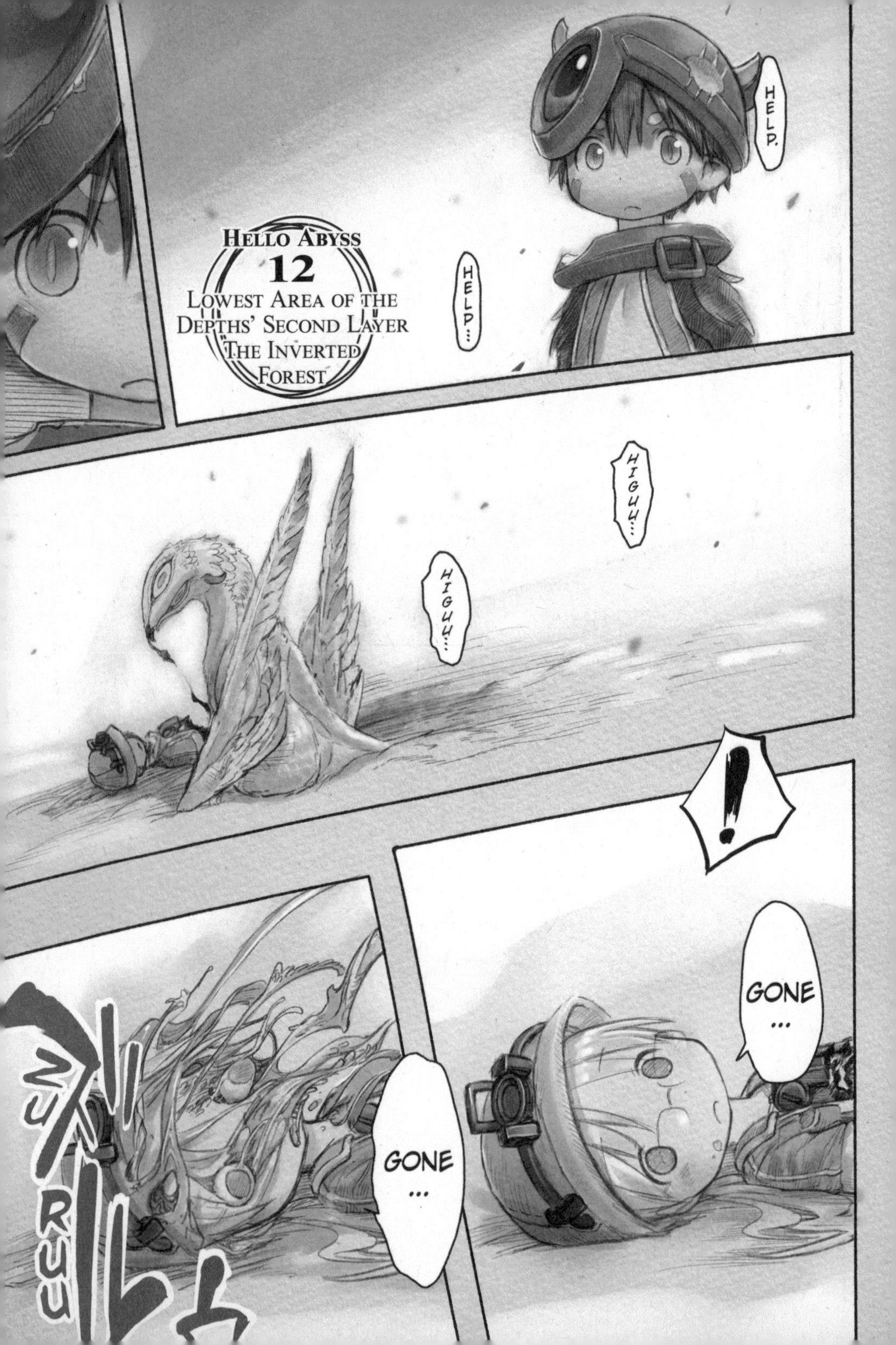
HELP.
HELP...
HELLO ABYSS 12
LOWEST AREA OF THE DEPTHS' SECOND LAYER
THE INVERTED FOREST
HIGUH...
HIGUH...
!
GONE ...
GONE ...
ZURU

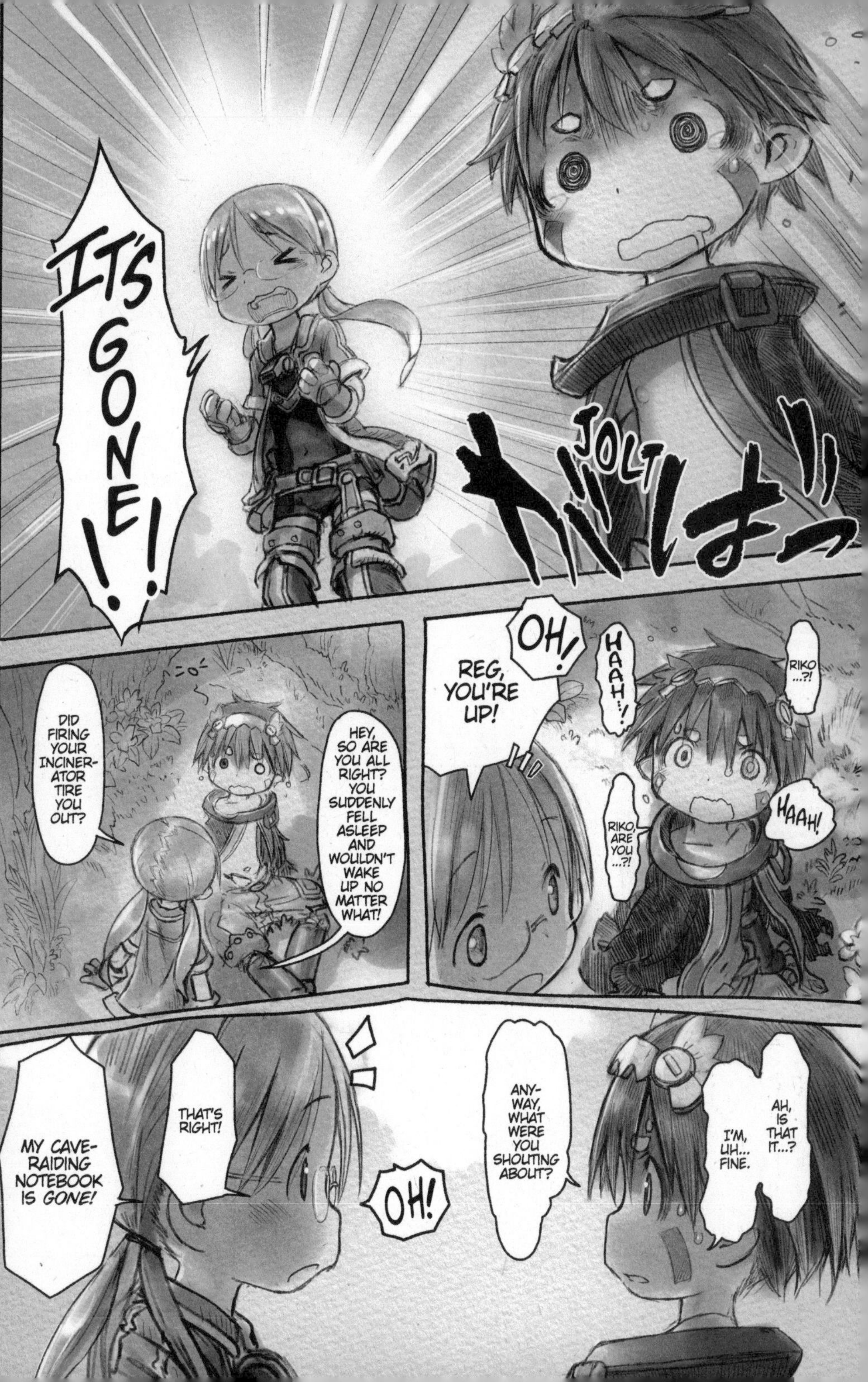
JOLT
ガバはっ
IT'S GONE!!
RIKO...?!
HAAAH...!
OH!
REG, YOU'RE UP!
HAAAH!
RIKO, ARE YOU...?!
HEY, SO ARE YOU ALL RIGHT? YOU SUDDENLY FELL ASLEEP AND WOULDN'T WAKE UP NO MATTER WHAT!
DID FIRING YOUR INCINERATOR TIRE YOU OUT?
AH, IS THAT IT...?
I'M, UH... FINE.
ANYWAY, WHAT WERE YOU SHOUTING ABOUT?
OH!
THAT'S RIGHT!
MY CAVE-RAIDING NOTEBOOK IS GONE!

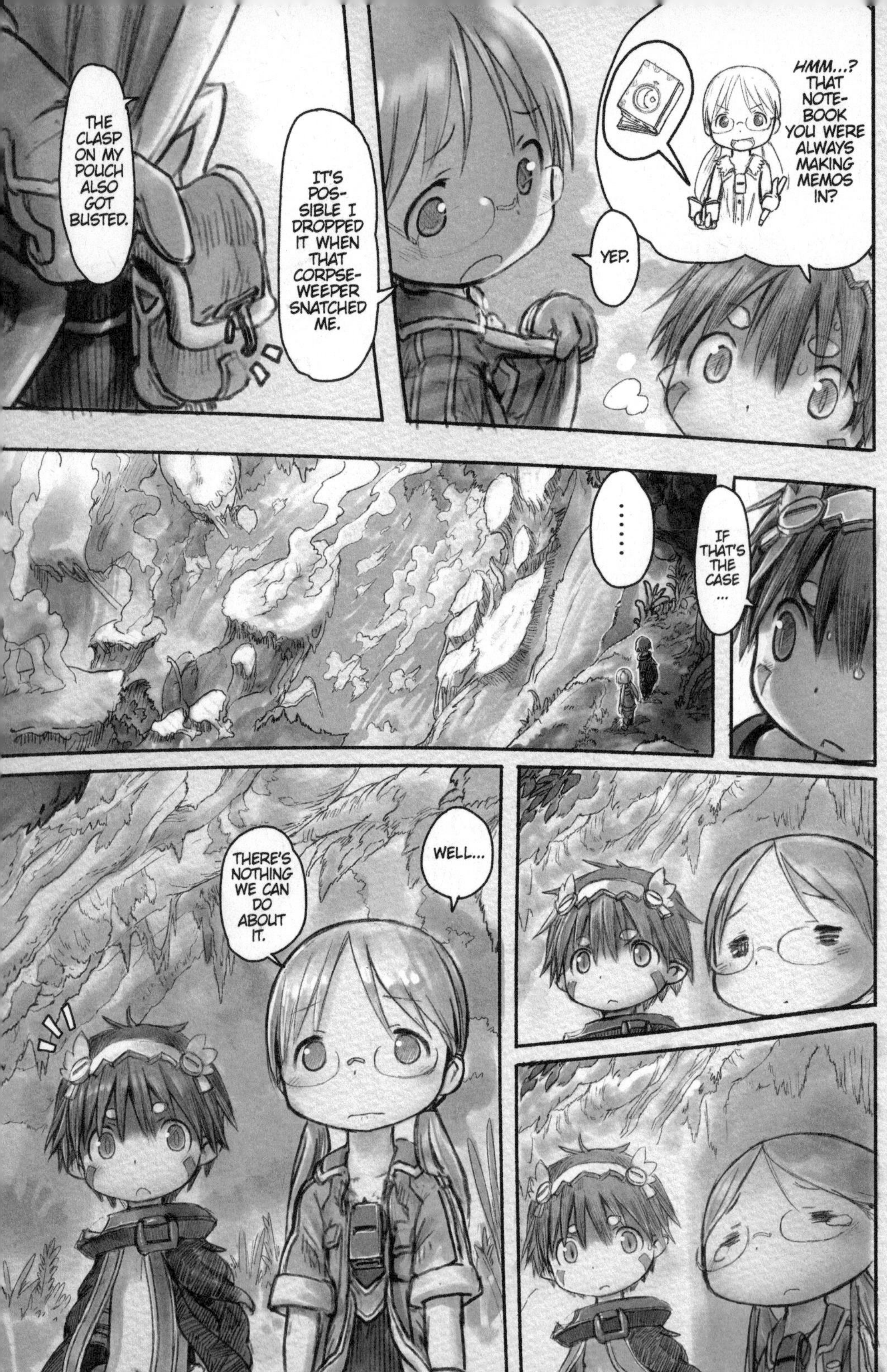
HMM...? THAT NOTEBOOK YOU WERE ALWAYS MAKING MEMOS IN?
YEP.
IT'S POSSIBLE I DROPPED IT WHEN THAT CORPSE-WEEPER SNATCHED ME.
THE CLASP ON MY POUCH ALSO GOT BUSTED.
IF THAT'S THE CASE ...
......
WELL...
THERE'S NOTHING WE CAN DO ABOUT IT.

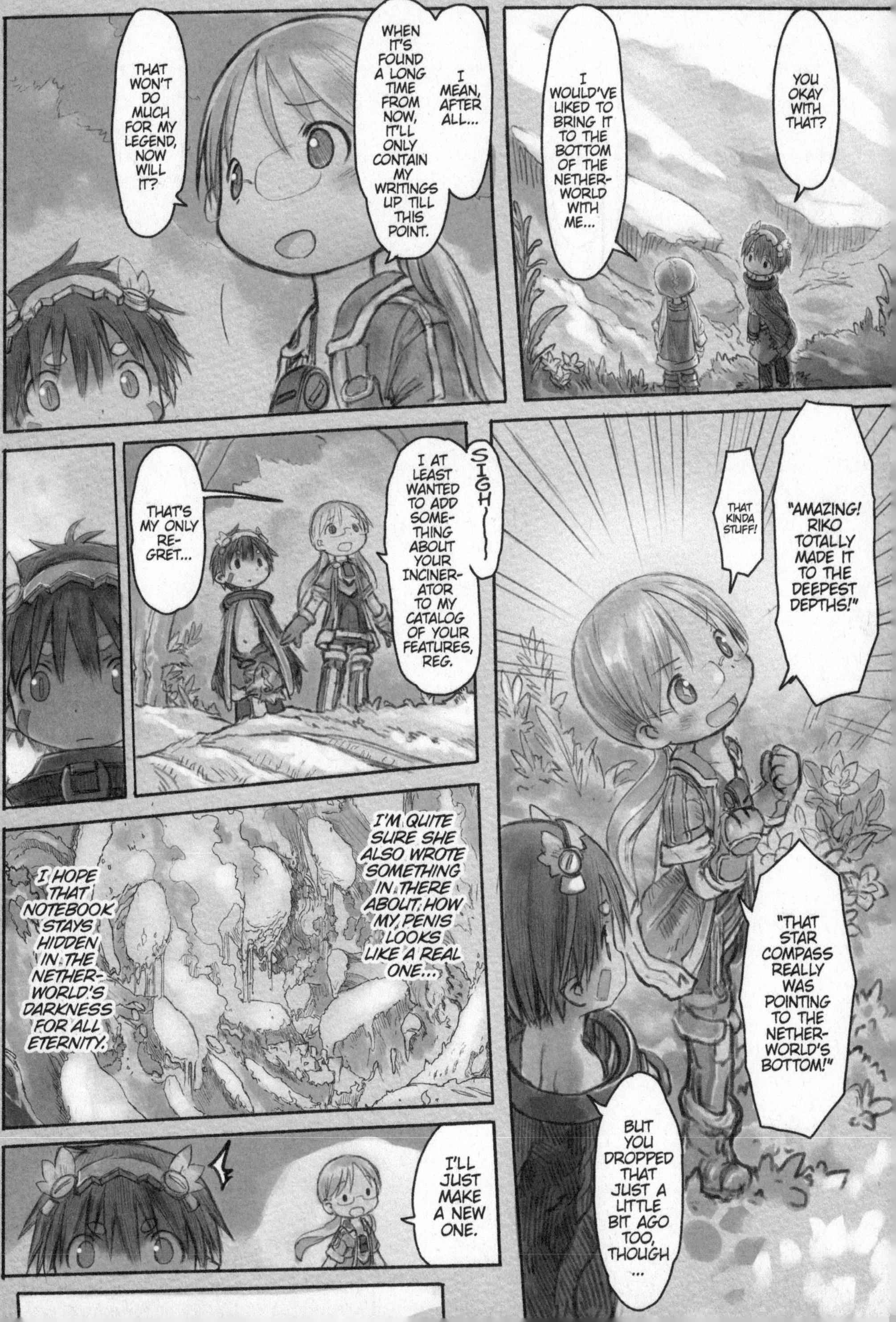
YOU OKAY WITH THAT?
I WOULD'VE LIKED TO BRING IT TO THE BOTTOM OF THE NETHER-WORLD WITH ME...
I MEAN, AFTER ALL...
WHEN IT'S FOUND A LONG TIME FROM NOW, IT'LL ONLY CONTAIN MY WRITINGS UP TILL THIS POINT.
THAT WON'T DO MUCH FOR MY LEGEND, NOW WILL IT?
"AMAZING! RIKO TOTALLY MADE IT TO THE DEEPEST DEPTHS!"
THAT KINDA STUFF!
"THAT STAR COMPASS REALLY WAS POINTING TO THE NETHER-WORLD'S BOTTOM!"
BUT YOU DROPPED THAT JUST A LITTLE BIT AGO TOO, THOUGH...
SIGH
I AT LEAST WANTED TO ADD SOME-THING ABOUT YOUR INCINER-ATOR TO MY CATALOG OF YOUR FEATURES, REG.
THAT'S MY ONLY RE-GRET...
I'M QUITE SURE SHE ALSO WROTE SOMETHING IN THERE ABOUT HOW MY PENIS LOOKS LIKE A REAL ONE...
I HOPE THAT NOTEBOOK STAYS HIDDEN IN THE NETHER-WORLD'S DARKNESS FOR ALL ETERNITY.
I'LL JUST MAKE A NEW ONE.

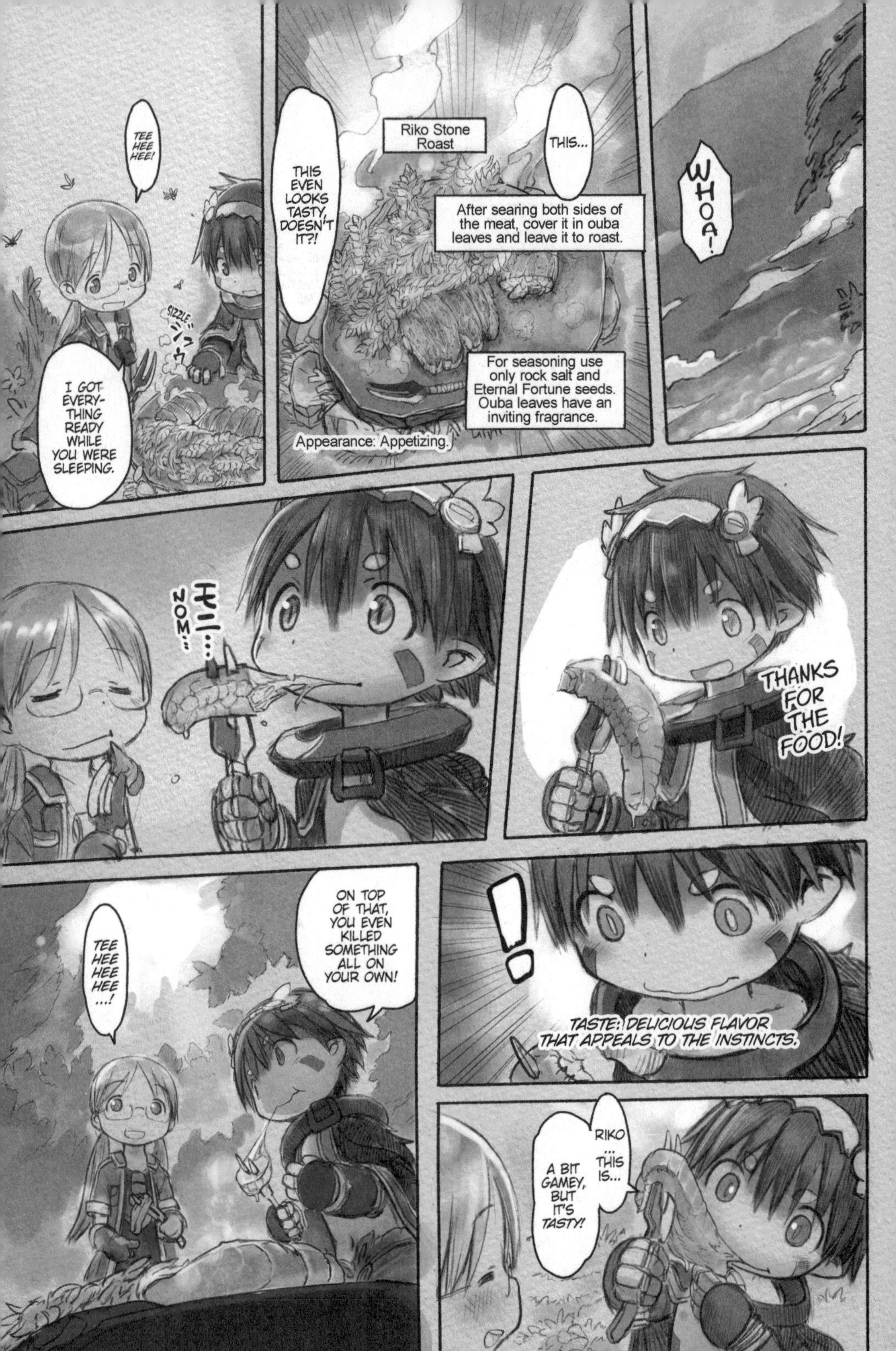
WHOA!
THIS...
Riko Stone Roast
After searing both sides of the meat, cover it in ouba leaves and leave it to roast.
THIS EVEN LOOKS TASTY, DOESN'T IT?!
For seasoning use only rock salt and Eternal Fortune seeds. Ouba leaves have an inviting fragrance.
Appearance: Appetizing.
TEE HEE HEE!
SIZZLE
I GOT EVERY-THING READY WHILE YOU WERE SLEEPING.
THANKS FOR THE FOOD!
NOM...
!
TASTE: DELICIOUS FLAVOR THAT APPEALS TO THE INSTINCTS.
RIKO ... THIS IS...
A BIT GAMEY, BUT IT'S TASTY!
ON TOP OF THAT, YOU EVEN KILLED SOMETHING ALL ON YOUR OWN!
TEE HEE HEE HEE ...!

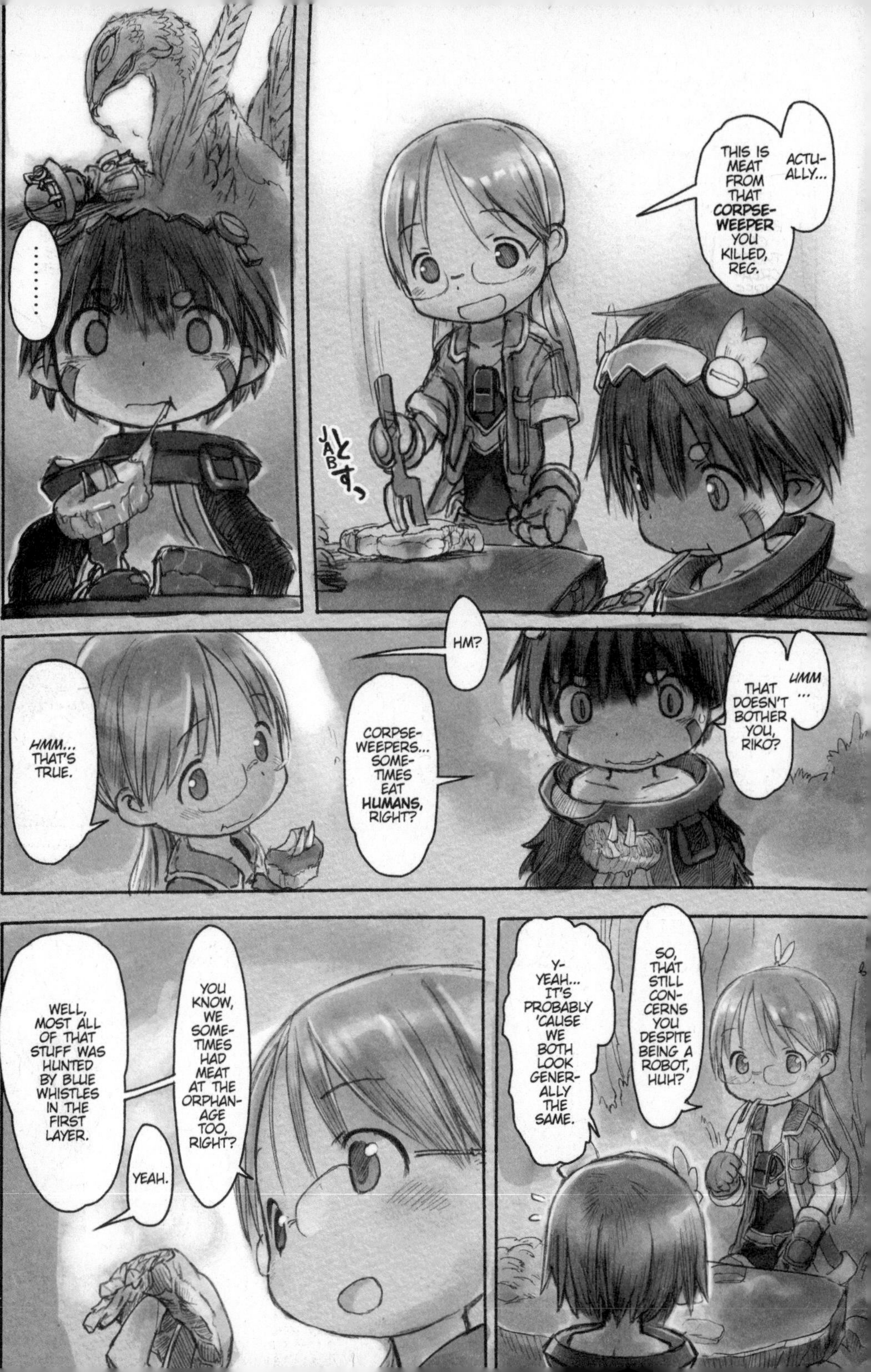
ACTUALLY...
THIS IS MEAT FROM THAT CORPSE-WEEPER YOU KILLED, REG.
JAB
......
UMM ... THAT DOESN'T BOTHER YOU, RIKO?
HM?
CORPSE-WEEPERS... SOMETIMES EAT HUMANS, RIGHT?
HMM... THAT'S TRUE.
SO, THAT STILL CONCERNS YOU DESPITE BEING A ROBOT, HUH?
Y-YEAH... IT'S PROBABLY 'CAUSE WE BOTH LOOK GENERALLY THE SAME.
YOU KNOW, WE SOMETIMES HAD MEAT AT THE ORPHANAGE TOO, RIGHT?
YEAH.
WELL, MOST ALL OF THAT STUFF WAS HUNTED BY BLUE WHISTLES IN THE FIRST LAYER.

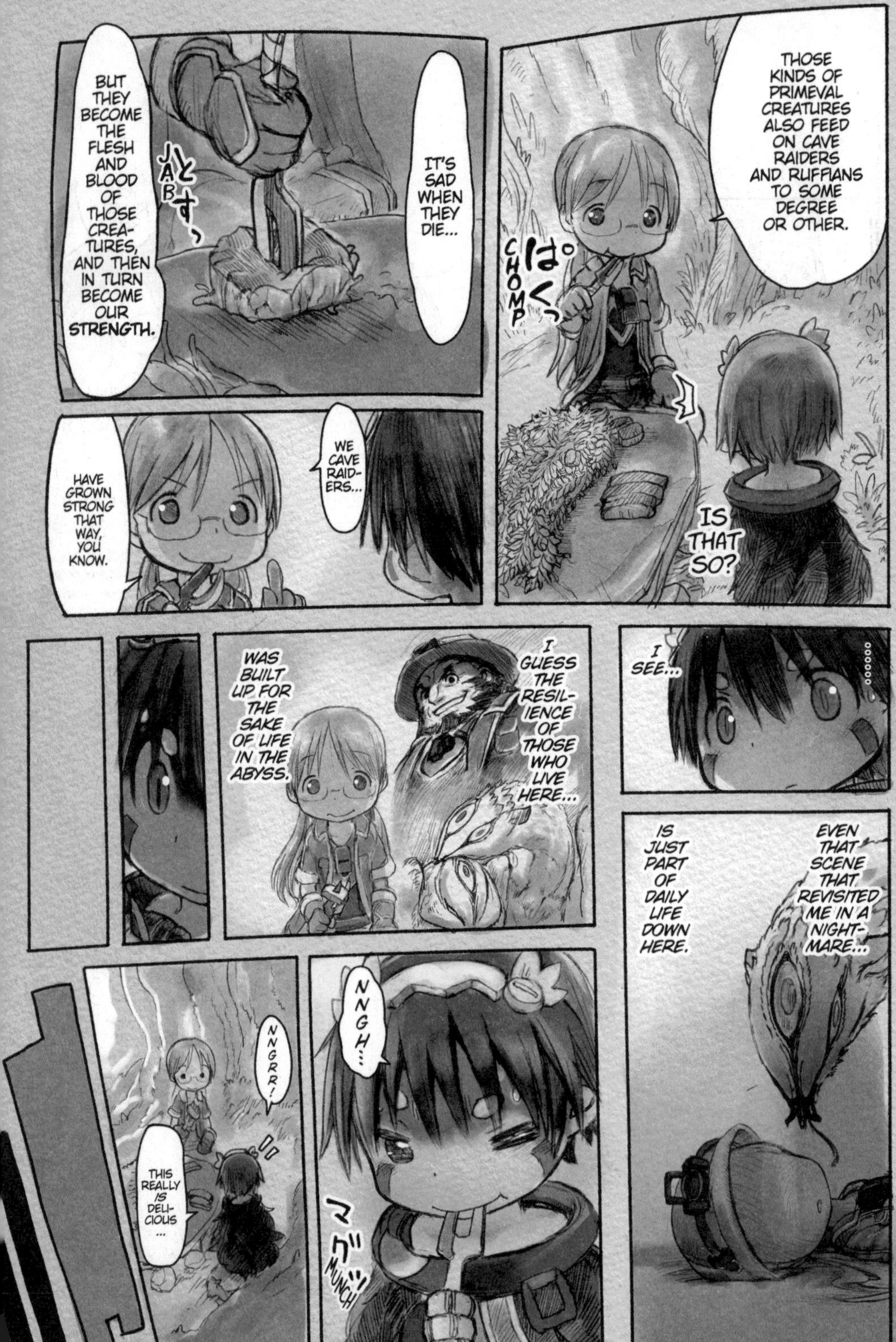
THOSE KINDS OF PRIMEVAL CREATURES ALSO FEED ON CAVE RAIDERS AND RUFFIANS TO SOME DEGREE OR OTHER.
CHOMP
IS THAT SO?
IT'S SAD WHEN THEY DIE...
JAB
BUT THEY BECOME THE FLESH AND BLOOD OF THOSE CREATURES, AND THEN IN TURN BECOME OUR STRENGTH.
WE CAVE RAIDERS...
HAVE GROWN STRONG THAT WAY, YOU KNOW.
I SEE...
I GUESS THE RESILIENCE OF THOSE WHO LIVE HERE...
WAS BUILT UP FOR THE SAKE OF LIFE IN THE ABYSS.
EVEN THAT SCENE THAT REVISITED ME IN A NIGHTMARE...
IS JUST PART OF DAILY LIFE DOWN HERE.
NNGH...
MUNCH
NNGRR!
THIS REALLY IS DELICIOUS...

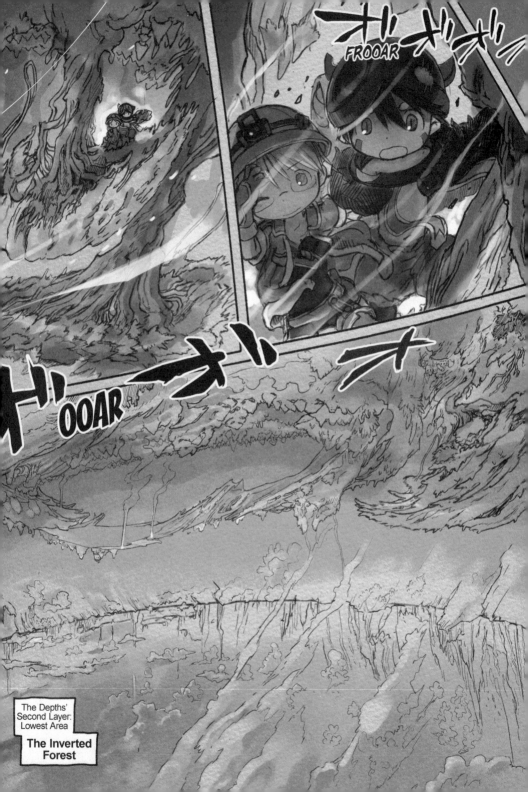

The Depths'
Second Layer:
Lowest Area

**The Inverted
Forest**

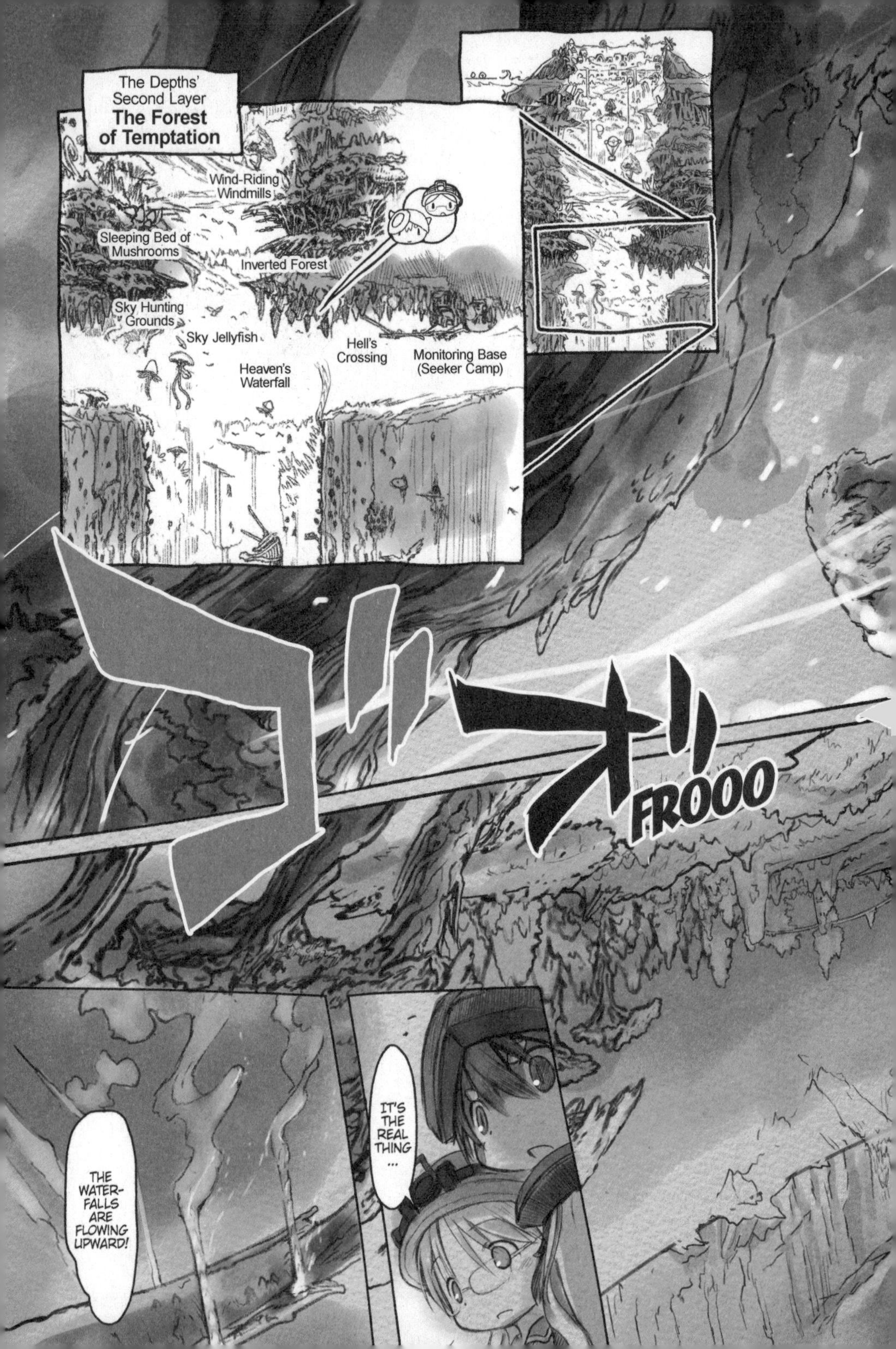
The Depths' Second Layer
The Forest of Temptation
Wind-Riding Windmills
Sleeping Bed of Mushrooms
Inverted Forest
Sky Hunting Grounds
Sky Jellyfish
Hell's Crossing
Monitoring Base (Seeker Camp)
Heaven's Waterfall
FROOO
IT'S THE REAL THING...
THE WATER-FALLS ARE FLOWING UPWARD!

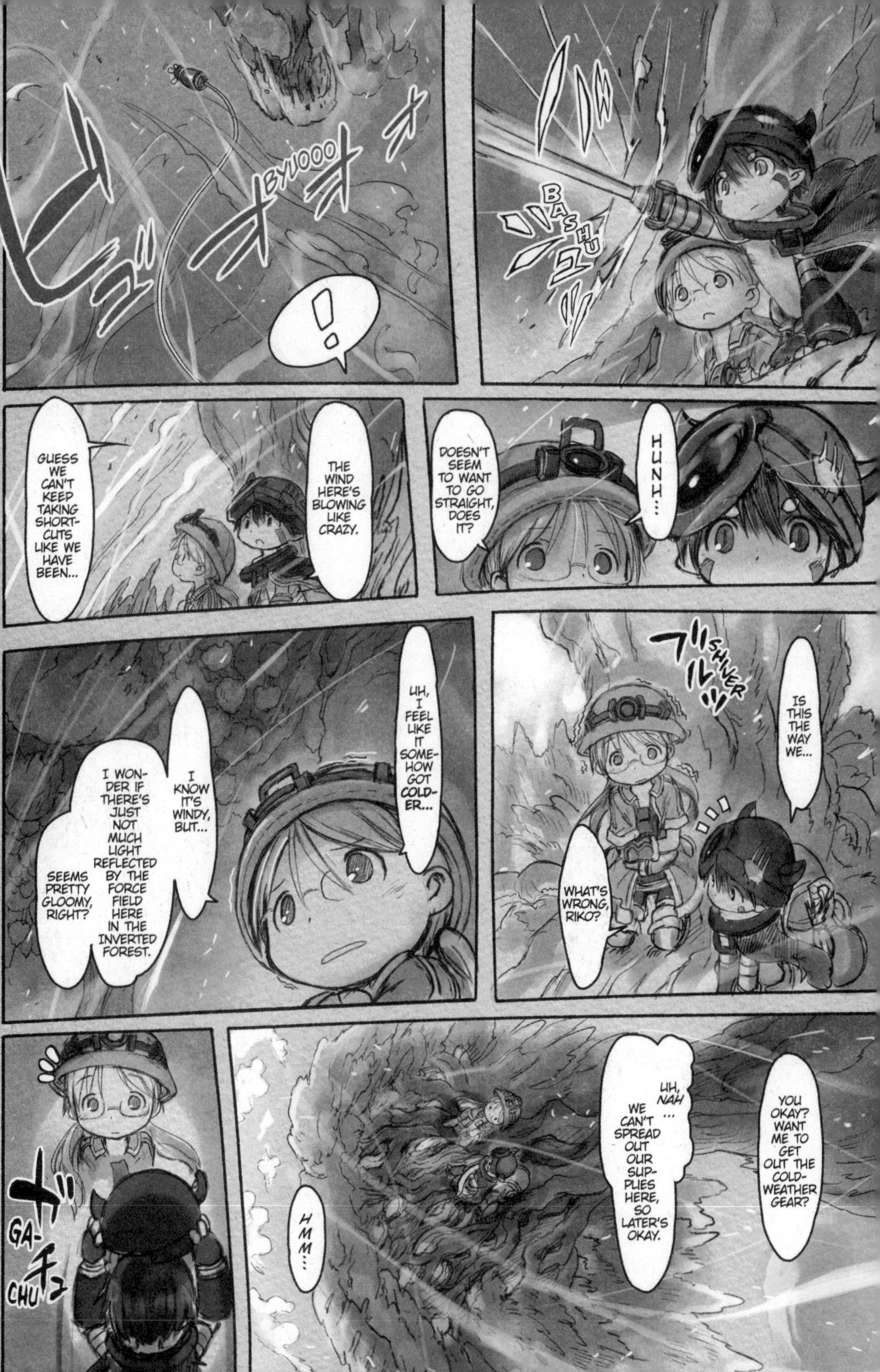
BASHU
BYUOOO
!
HUNH...
DOESN'T SEEM TO WANT TO GO STRAIGHT, DOES IT?
THE WIND HERE'S BLOWING LIKE CRAZY.
GUESS WE CAN'T KEEP TAKING SHORT-CUTS LIKE WE HAVE BEEN...
SHIVER
IS THIS THE WAY WE...
WHAT'S WRONG, RIKO?
UH, I FEEL LIKE IT SOMEHOW GOT **COLDER**...
I KNOW IT'S WINDY, BUT...
I WONDER IF THERE'S JUST NOT MUCH LIGHT REFLECTED BY THE FORCE FIELD HERE IN THE INVERTED FOREST.
SEEMS PRETTY GLOOMY, RIGHT?
YOU OKAY? WANT ME TO GET OUT THE COLD-WEATHER GEAR?
UH, *NAH*... WE CAN'T SPREAD OUT OUR SUP-PLIES HERE, SO LATER'S OKAY.
HMM...
GA-CHU

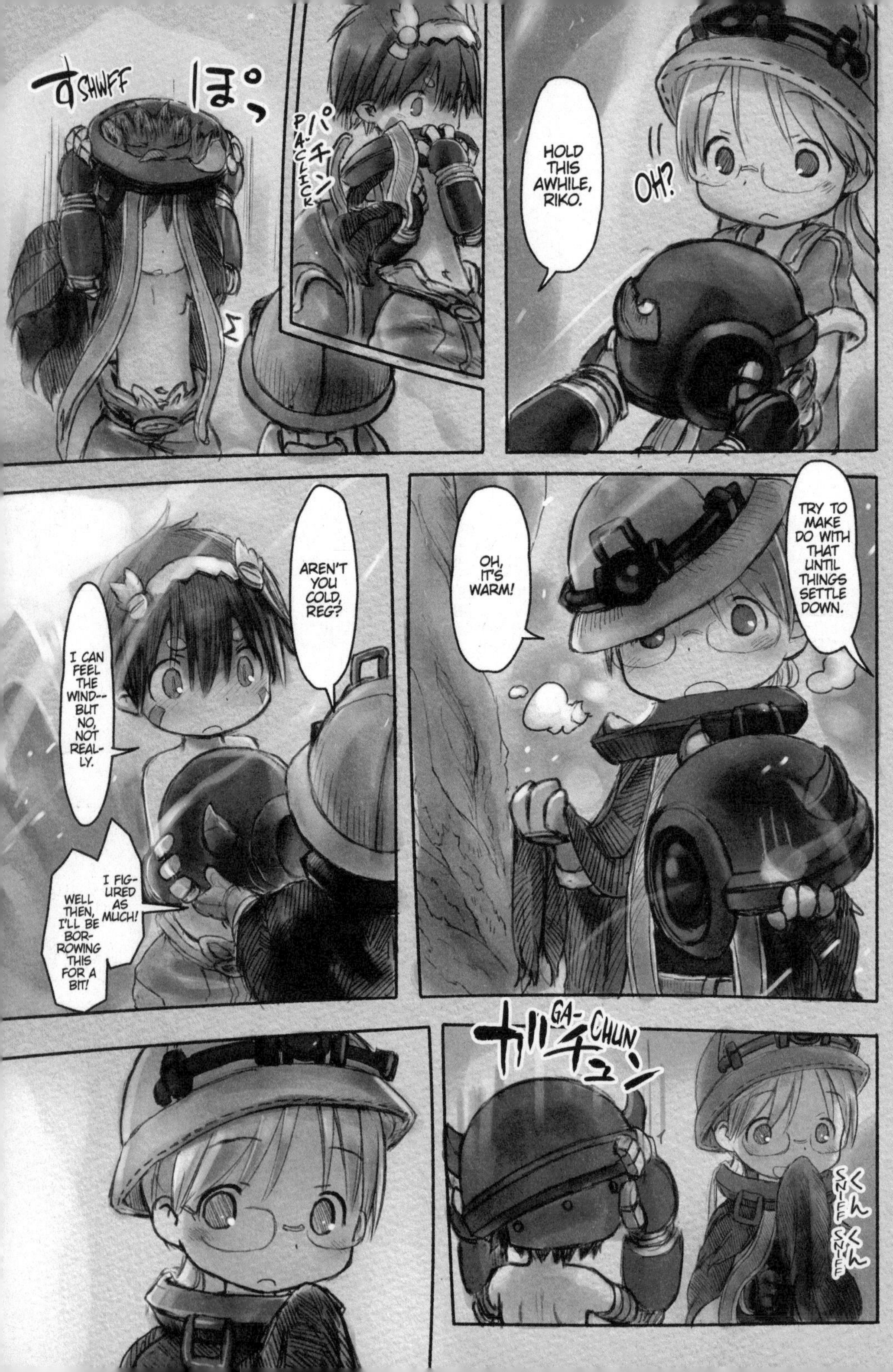
HOLD THIS AWHILE, RIKO.
OH?
パチン PA-CLICK
すSHWFF
ぽっ
TRY TO MAKE DO WITH THAT UNTIL THINGS SETTLE DOWN.
OH, IT'S WARM!
AREN'T YOU COLD, REG?
I CAN FEEL THE WIND-- BUT NO, NOT REALLY.
I FIGURED AS MUCH!
WELL THEN, I'LL BE BORROWING THIS FOR A BIT!
カチュン GA-CHUN
くんくん SNIFF SNIFF

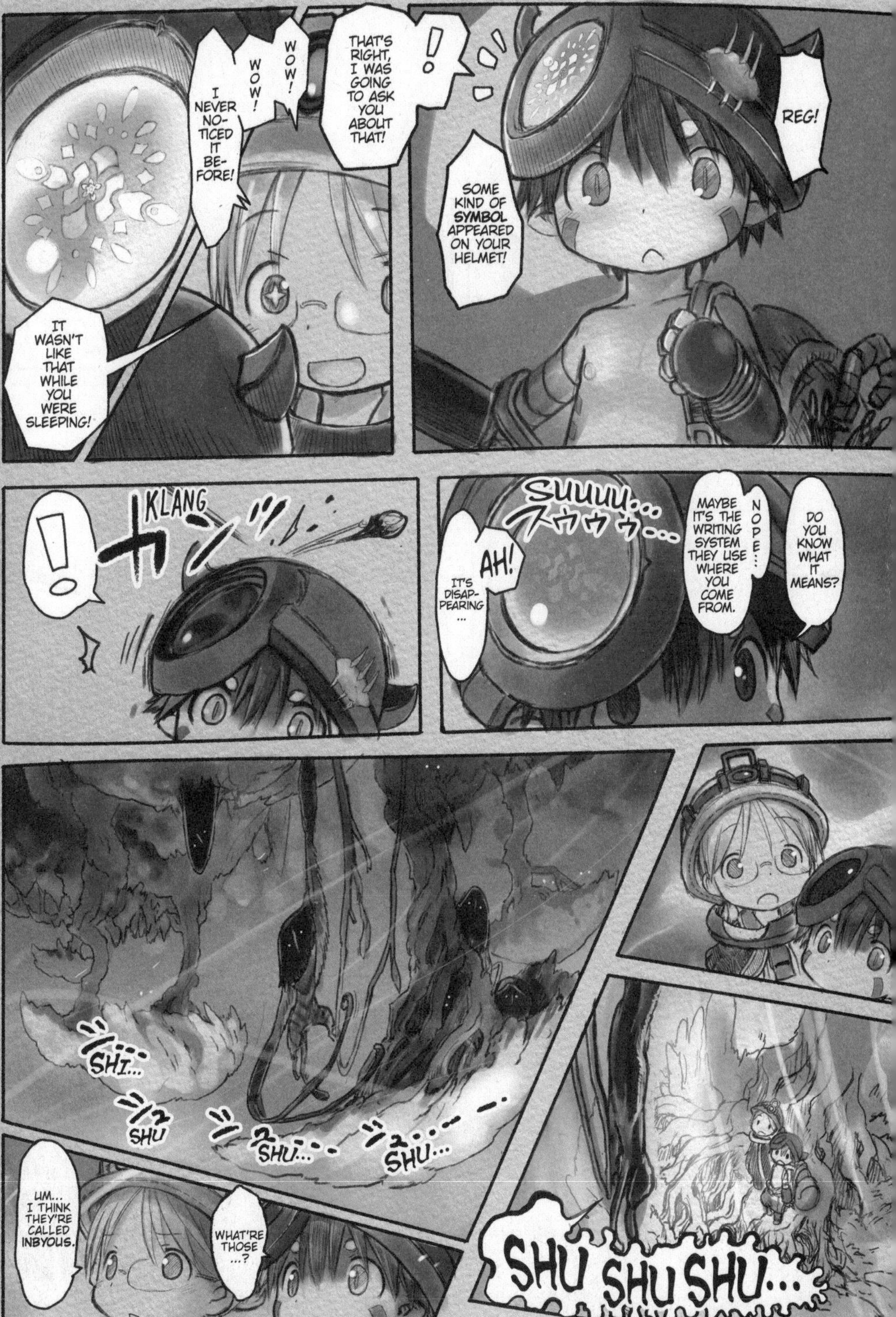
REG!
!
SOME KIND OF SYMBOL APPEARED ON YOUR HELMET!
THAT'S RIGHT, I WAS GOING TO ASK YOU ABOUT THAT!
WOW! WOW!
I NEVER NOTICED IT BEFORE!
IT WASN'T LIKE THAT WHILE YOU WERE SLEEPING!
DO YOU KNOW WHAT IT MEANS?
NOPE...
MAYBE IT'S THE WRITING SYSTEM THEY USE WHERE YOU COME FROM.
SUUUU...
AH!
IT'S DISAPPEARING...
KLANG
!
SHU SHU SHU...
SHI...
SHU
SHU...
SHU...
WHAT'RE THOSE...?
UM... I THINK THEY'RE CALLED INBYOUS.

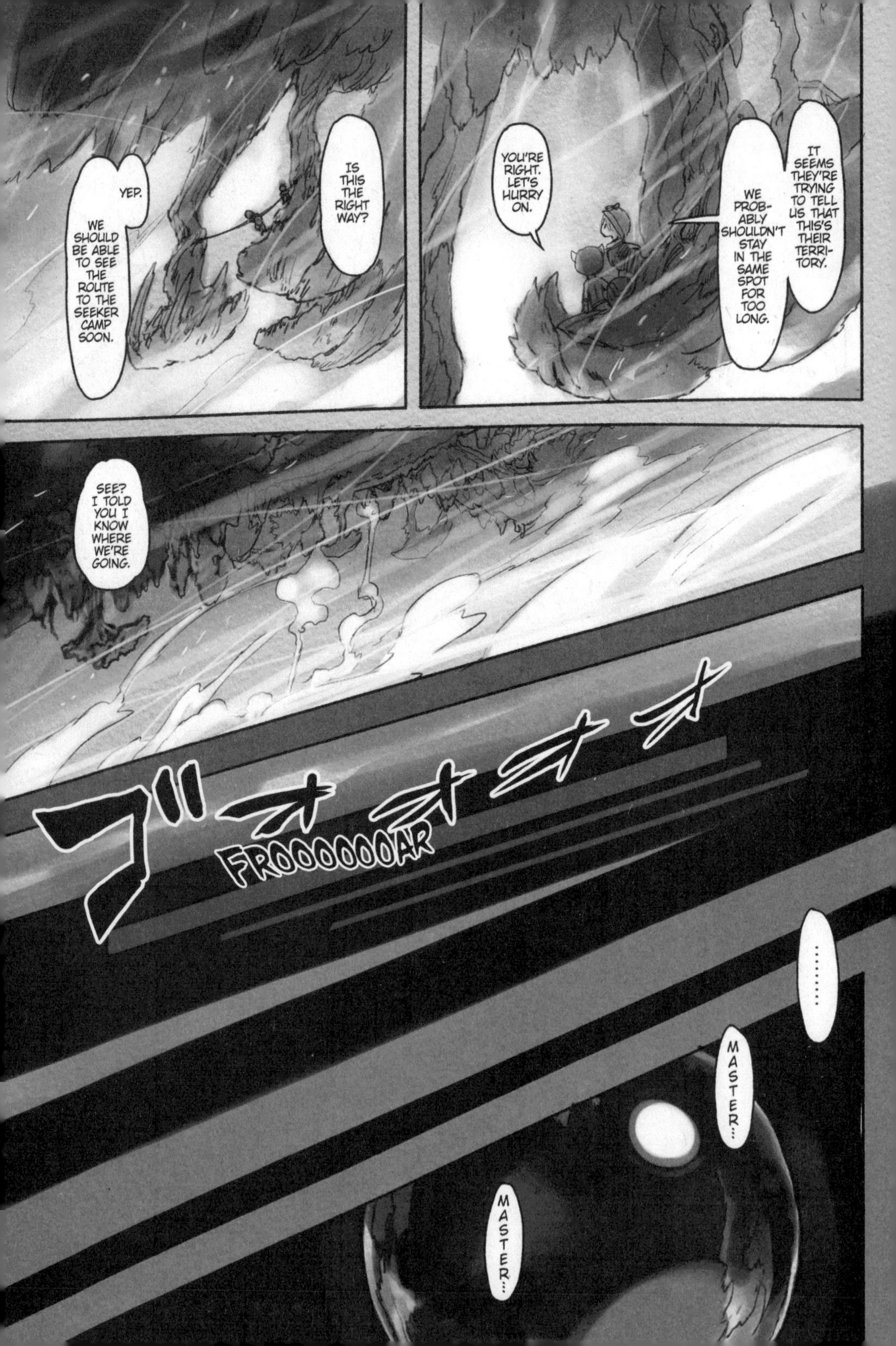
IT SEEMS THEY'RE TRYING TO TELL US THAT THIS'S THEIR TERRITORY.
WE PROBABLY SHOULDN'T STAY IN THE SAME SPOT FOR TOO LONG.
YOU'RE RIGHT. LET'S HURRY ON.
IS THIS THE RIGHT WAY?
YEP.
WE SHOULD BE ABLE TO SEE THE ROUTE TO THE SEEKER CAMP SOON.
SEE? I TOLD YOU I KNOW WHERE WE'RE GOING.
ブオオオオ
FROOOOOOAR
....
MASTER...
MASTER...

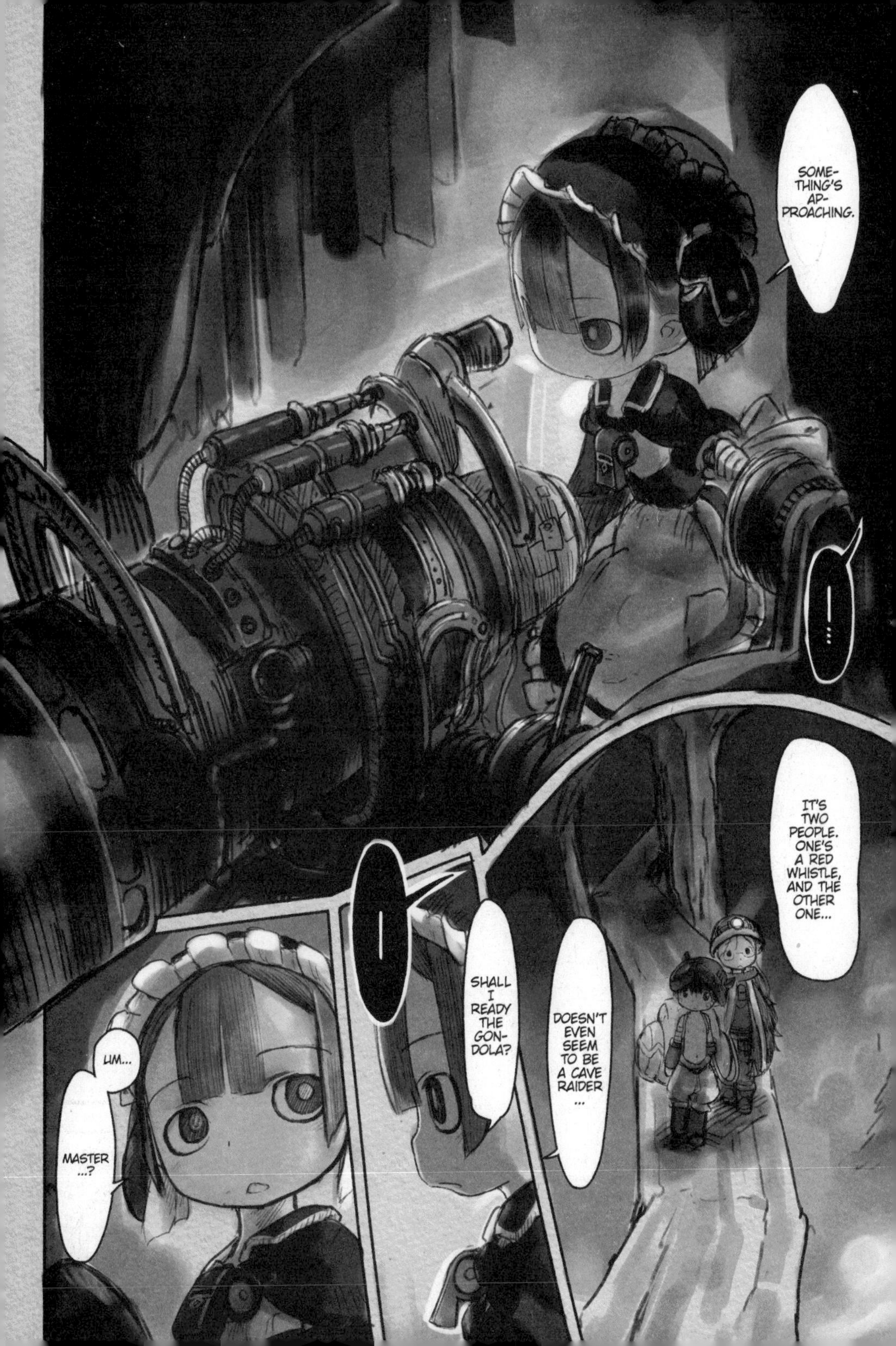

SOMETHING'S APPROACHING.
!...
IT'S TWO PEOPLE. ONE'S A RED WHISTLE, AND THE OTHER ONE...
DOESN'T EVEN SEEM TO BE A CAVE RAIDER ...
!
SHALL I READY THE GONDOLA?
UM...
MASTER ...?

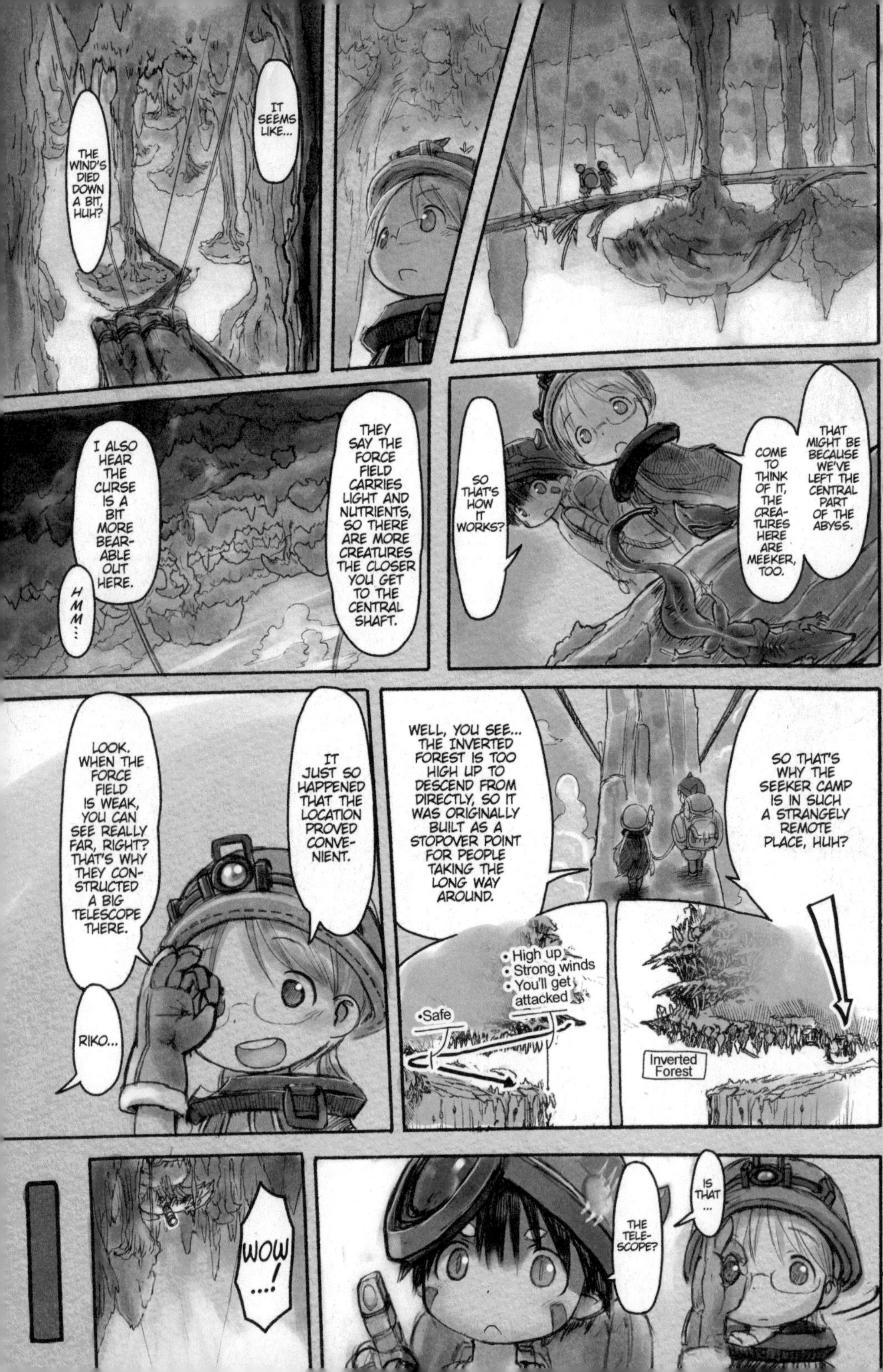
IT SEEMS LIKE...
THE WIND'S DIED DOWN A BIT, HUH?
THAT MIGHT BE BECAUSE WE'VE LEFT THE CENTRAL PART OF THE ABYSS.
COME TO THINK OF IT, THE CREATURES HERE ARE MEEKER, TOO.
SO THAT'S HOW IT WORKS?
THEY SAY THE FORCE FIELD CARRIES LIGHT AND NUTRIENTS, SO THERE ARE MORE CREATURES THE CLOSER YOU GET TO THE CENTRAL SHAFT.
I ALSO HEAR THE CURSE IS A BIT MORE BEARABLE OUT HERE.
HMM...
SO THAT'S WHY THE SEEKER CAMP IS IN SUCH A STRANGELY REMOTE PLACE, HUH?
Inverted Forest
WELL, YOU SEE... THE INVERTED FOREST IS TOO HIGH UP TO DESCEND FROM DIRECTLY, SO IT WAS ORIGINALLY BUILT AS A STOPOVER POINT FOR PEOPLE TAKING THE LONG WAY AROUND.
• High up
• Strong winds
• You'll get attacked
•Safe
IT JUST SO HAPPENED THAT THE LOCATION PROVED CONVENIENT.
LOOK. WHEN THE FORCE FIELD IS WEAK, YOU CAN SEE REALLY FAR, RIGHT? THAT'S WHY THEY CONSTRUCTED A BIG TELESCOPE THERE.
RIKO...
IS THAT ...
THE TELESCOPE?
WOW ...!

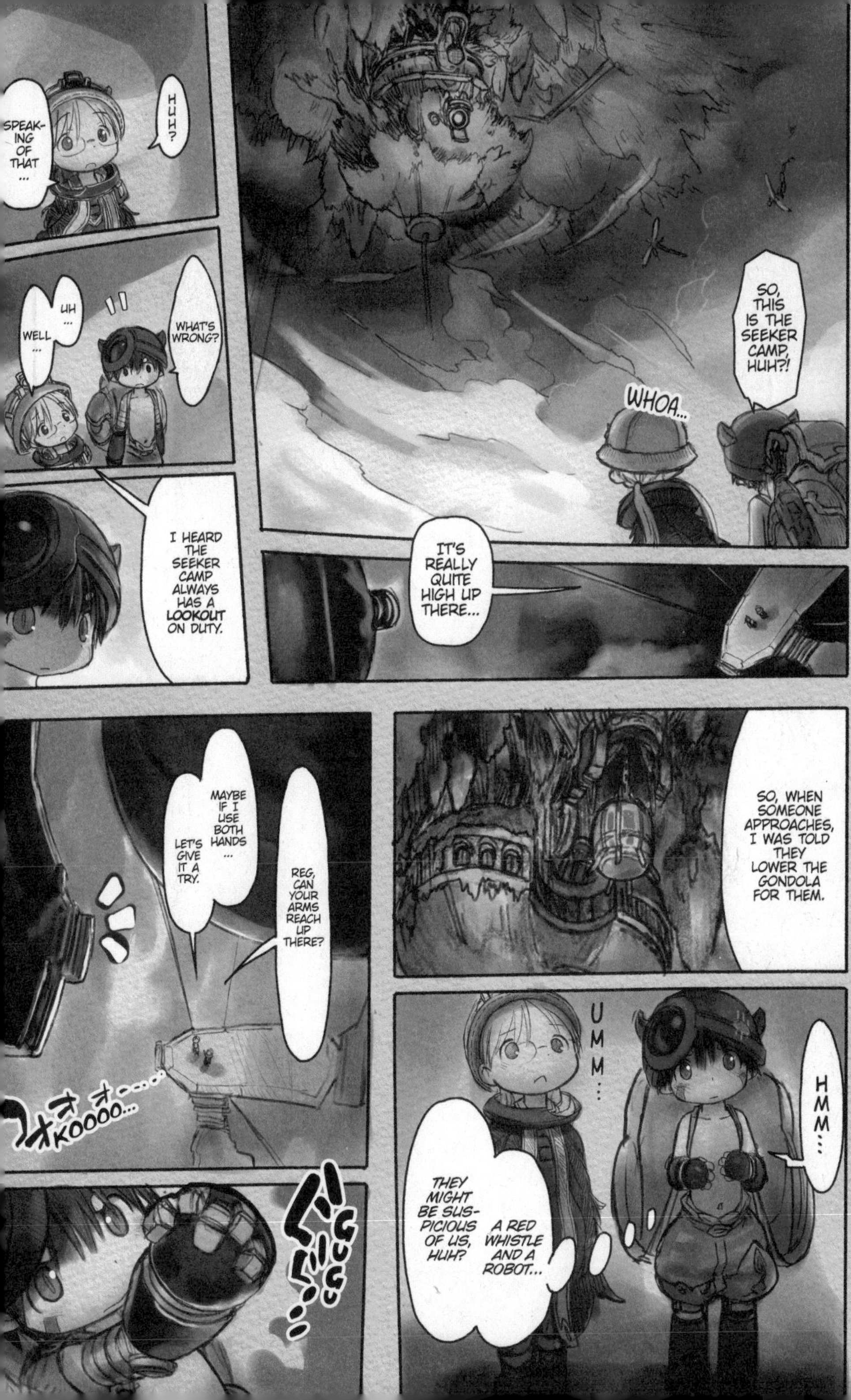

SO, THIS IS THE SEEKER CAMP, HUH?!
WHOA...
IT'S REALLY QUITE HIGH UP THERE...
HUH?
SPEAKING OF THAT...
WHAT'S WRONG?
UH... WELL...
I HEARD THE SEEKER CAMP ALWAYS HAS A LOOKOUT ON DUTY.
SO, WHEN SOMEONE APPROACHES, I WAS TOLD THEY LOWER THE GONDOLA FOR THEM.
HMM...
UMM...
A RED WHISTLE AND A ROBOT...
THEY MIGHT BE SUSPICIOUS OF US, HUH?
REG, CAN YOUR ARMS REACH UP THERE?
MAYBE IF I USE BOTH HANDS...
LET'S GIVE IT A TRY.
KOOOO...

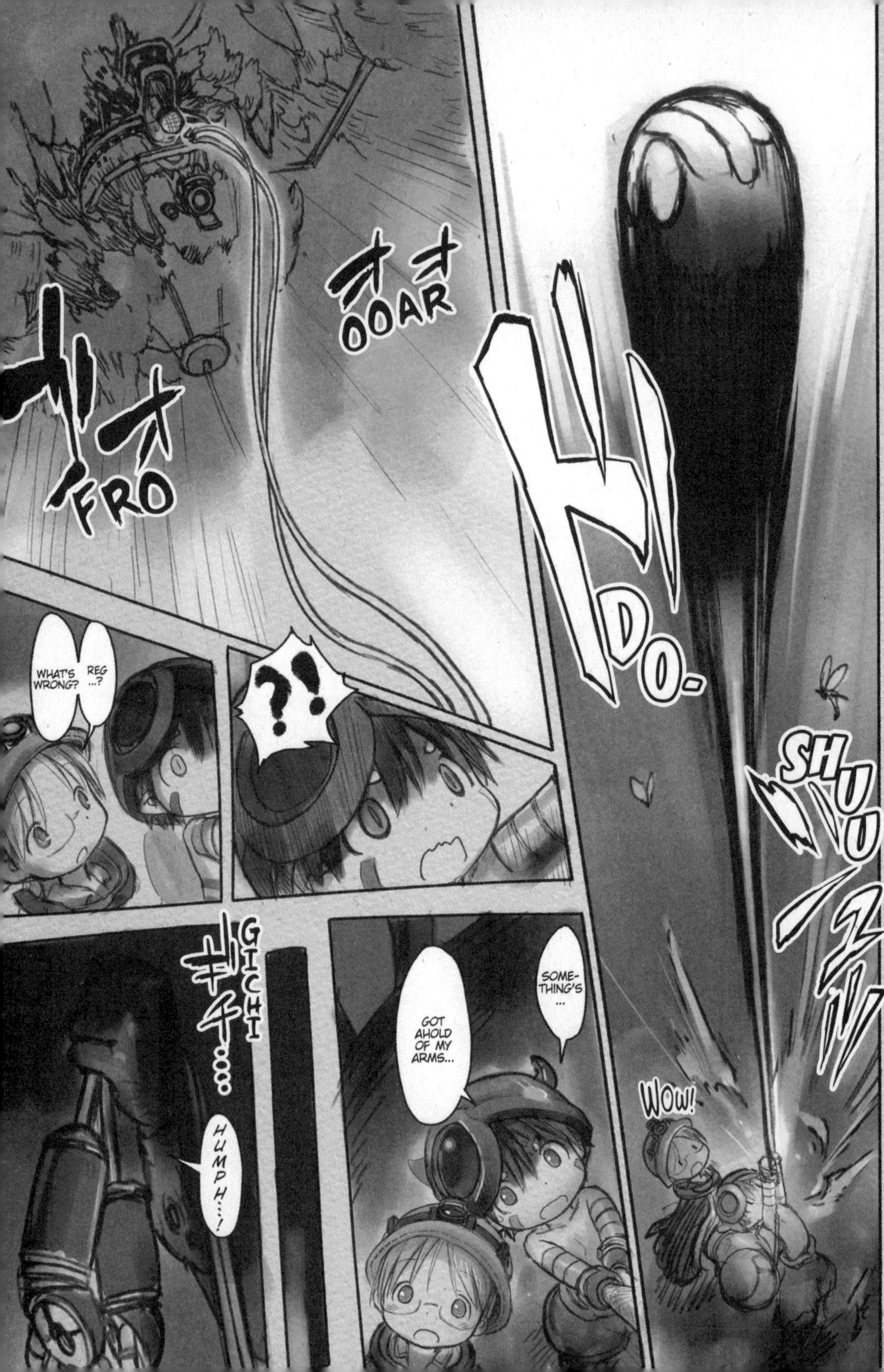
DO-
SHUUN
WOW!
OOAR
FRO
?!
REG ...?
WHAT'S WRONG?
SOME-THING'S...
GOT AHOLD OF MY ARMS...
GICHI...
HUMPH...!

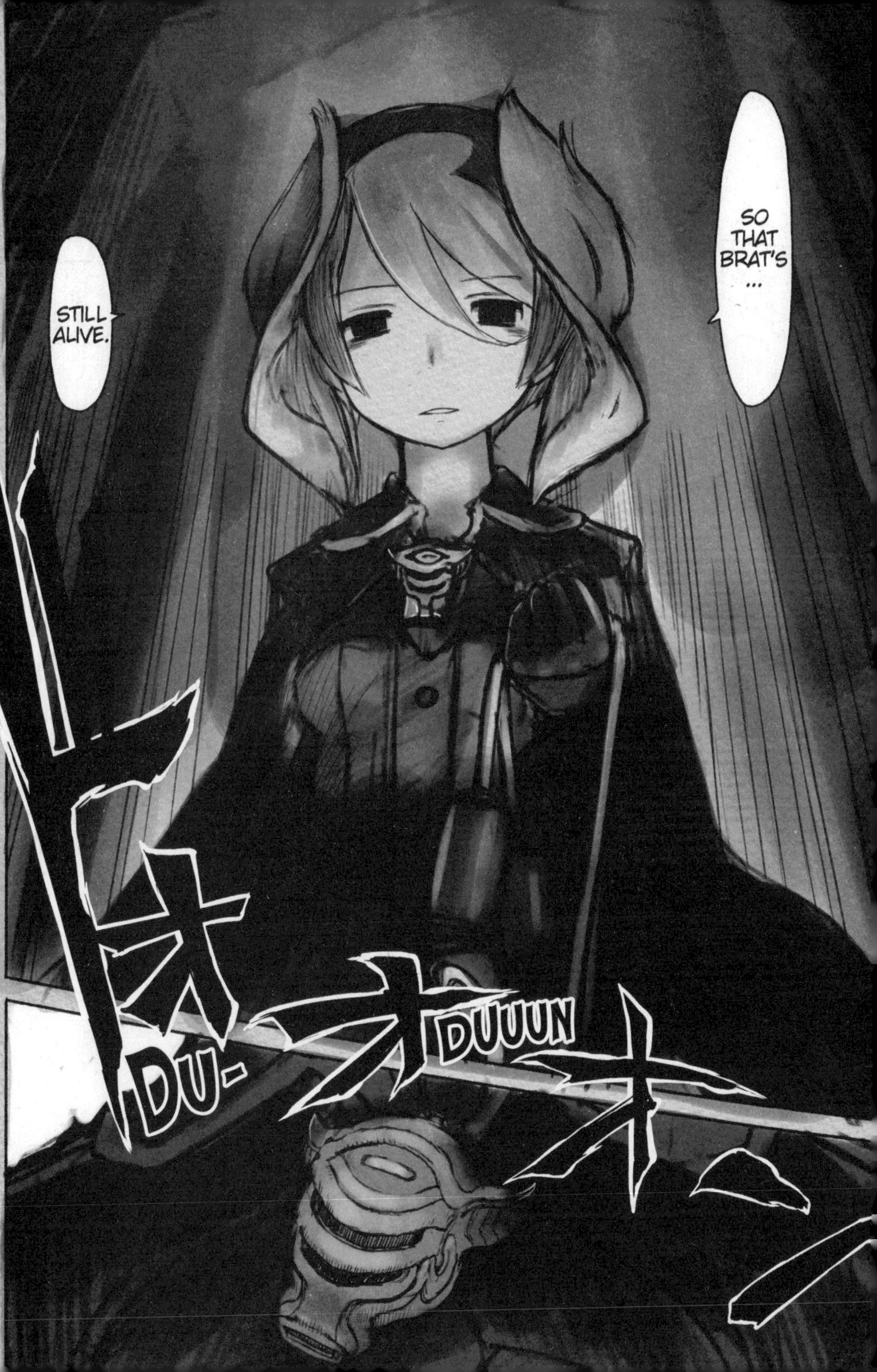

...
SO THAT BRAT'S ...
...
STILL ALIVE.
ドオ
DU-
オ
DUUUN
オン

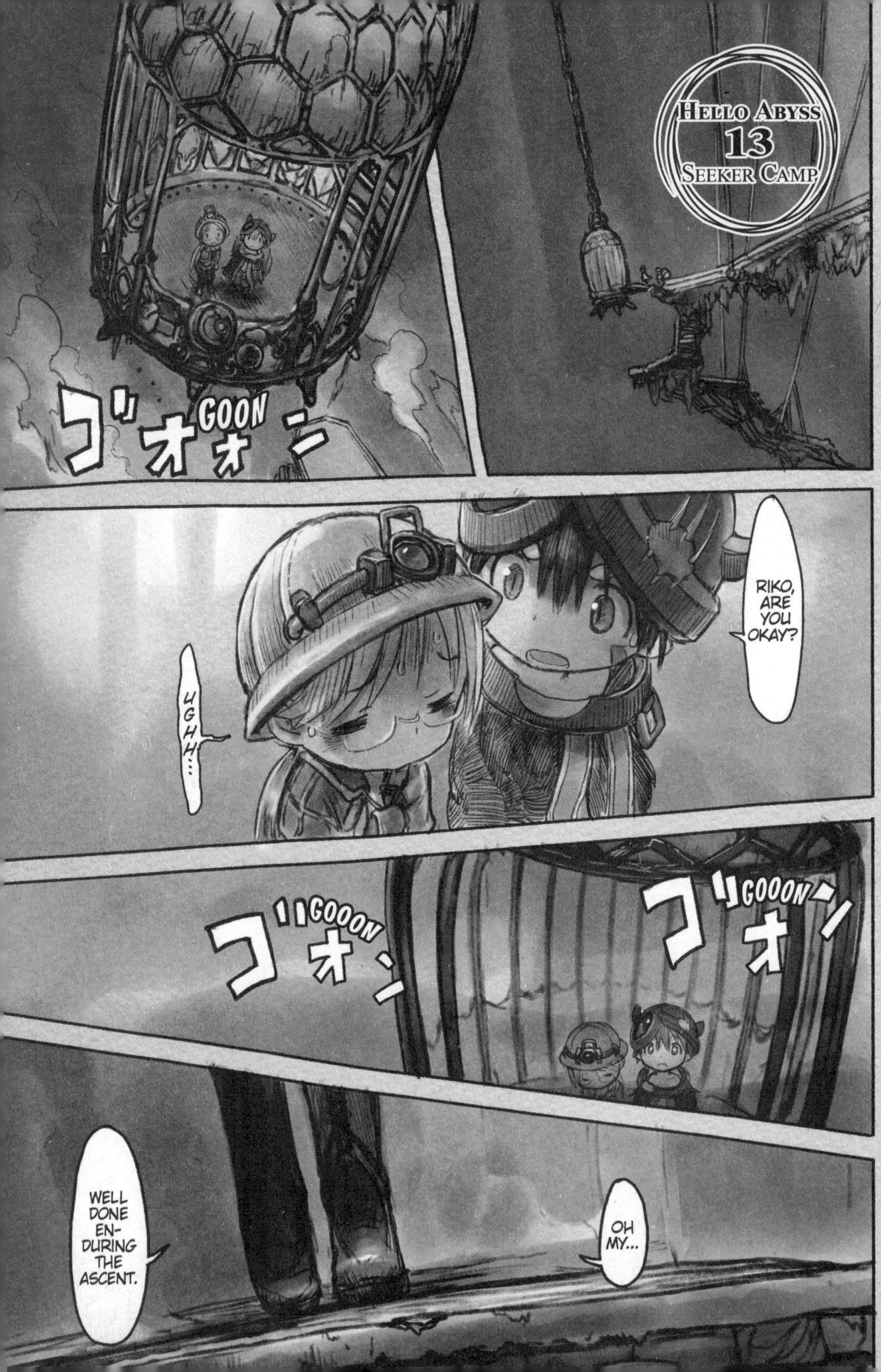
HELLO ABYSS
13
SEEKER CAMP
GOON
RIKO, ARE YOU OKAY?
UGHH...
GOOOON
GOOOON
OH MY...
WELL DONE EN-DURING THE ASCENT.

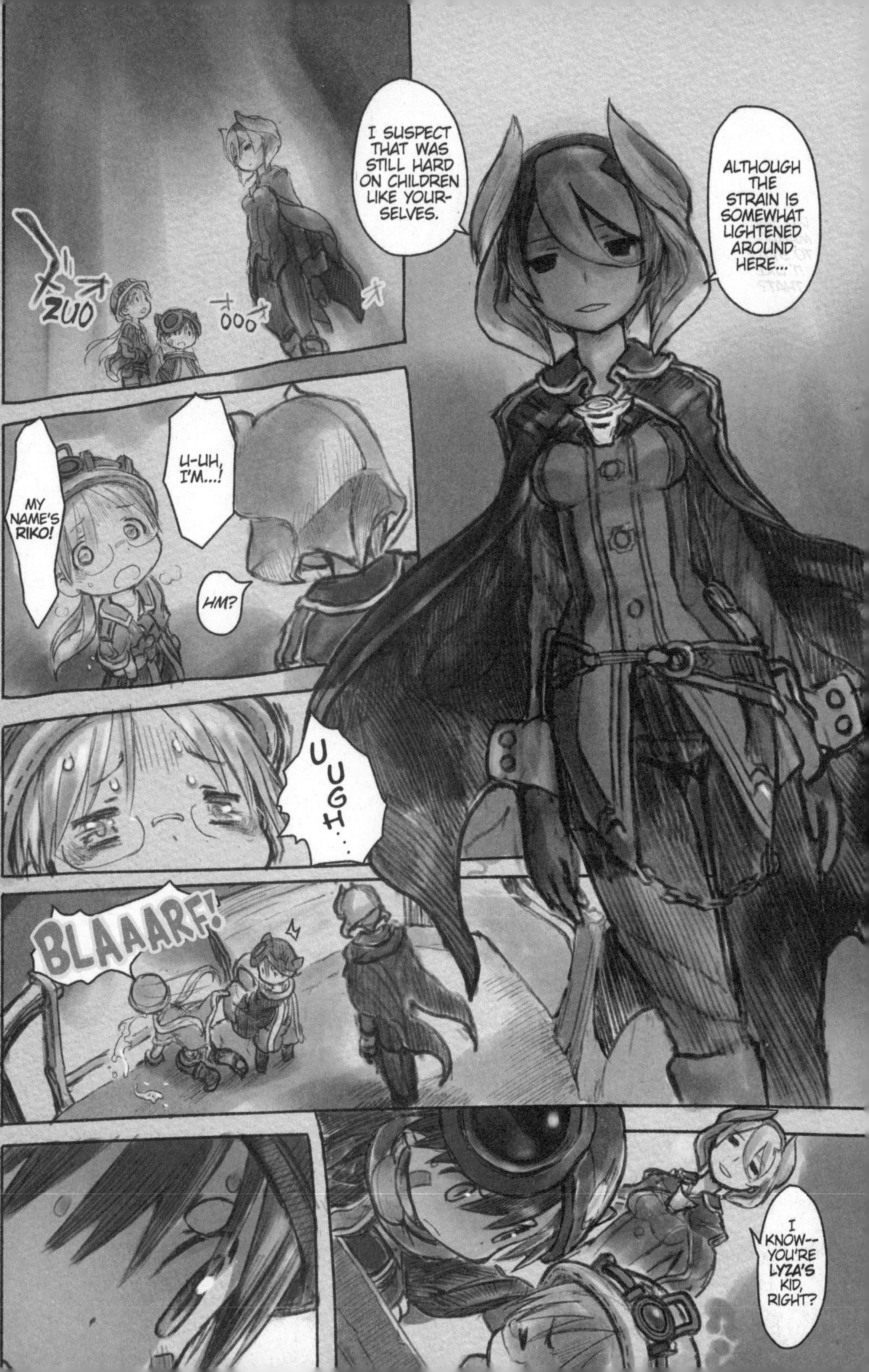
ALTHOUGH THE STRAIN IS SOMEWHAT LIGHTENED AROUND HERE...
I SUSPECT THAT WAS STILL HARD ON CHILDREN LIKE YOUR-SELVES.
ZUO
OOO
U-UH, I'M...!
MY NAME'S RIKO!
HM?
UUGH...
BLAAARF!
I KNOW--YOU'RE LYZA'S KID, RIGHT?

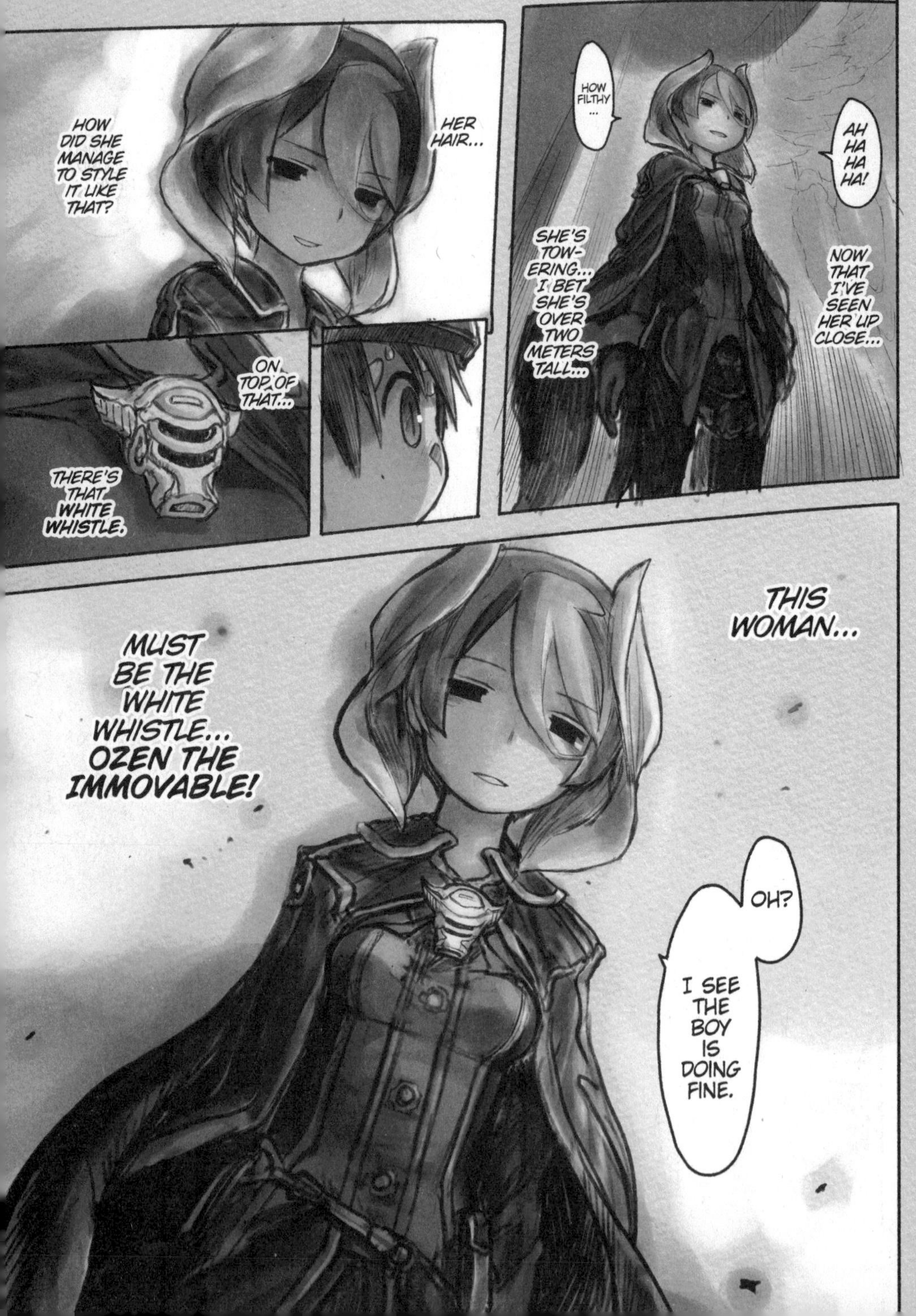
HOW FILTHY...
AH HA HA HA!
NOW THAT I'VE SEEN HER UP CLOSE...
SHE'S TOW-ERING... I BET SHE'S OVER TWO METERS TALL...
HER HAIR...
HOW DID SHE MANAGE TO STYLE IT LIKE THAT?
ON TOP OF THAT...
THERE'S THAT WHITE WHISTLE.
THIS WOMAN...
MUST BE THE WHITE WHISTLE... OZEN THE IMMOVABLE!
OH?
I SEE THE BOY IS DOING FINE.

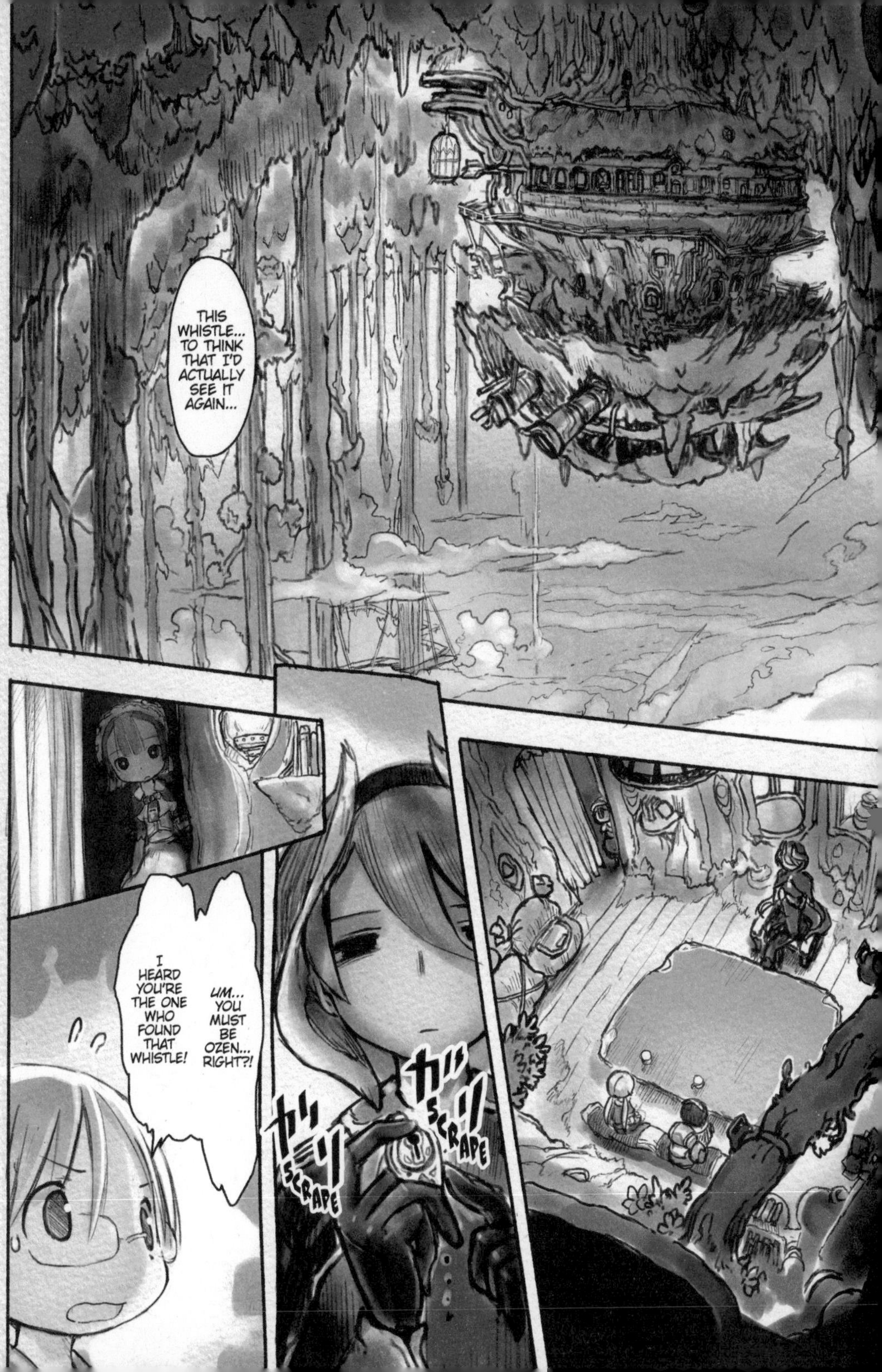
THIS WHISTLE... TO THINK THAT I'D ACTUALLY SEE IT AGAIN...
カリ SCRAPE
カリ SCRAPE
UM... YOU MUST BE OZEN... RIGHT?!
I HEARD YOU'RE THE ONE WHO FOUND THAT WHISTLE!

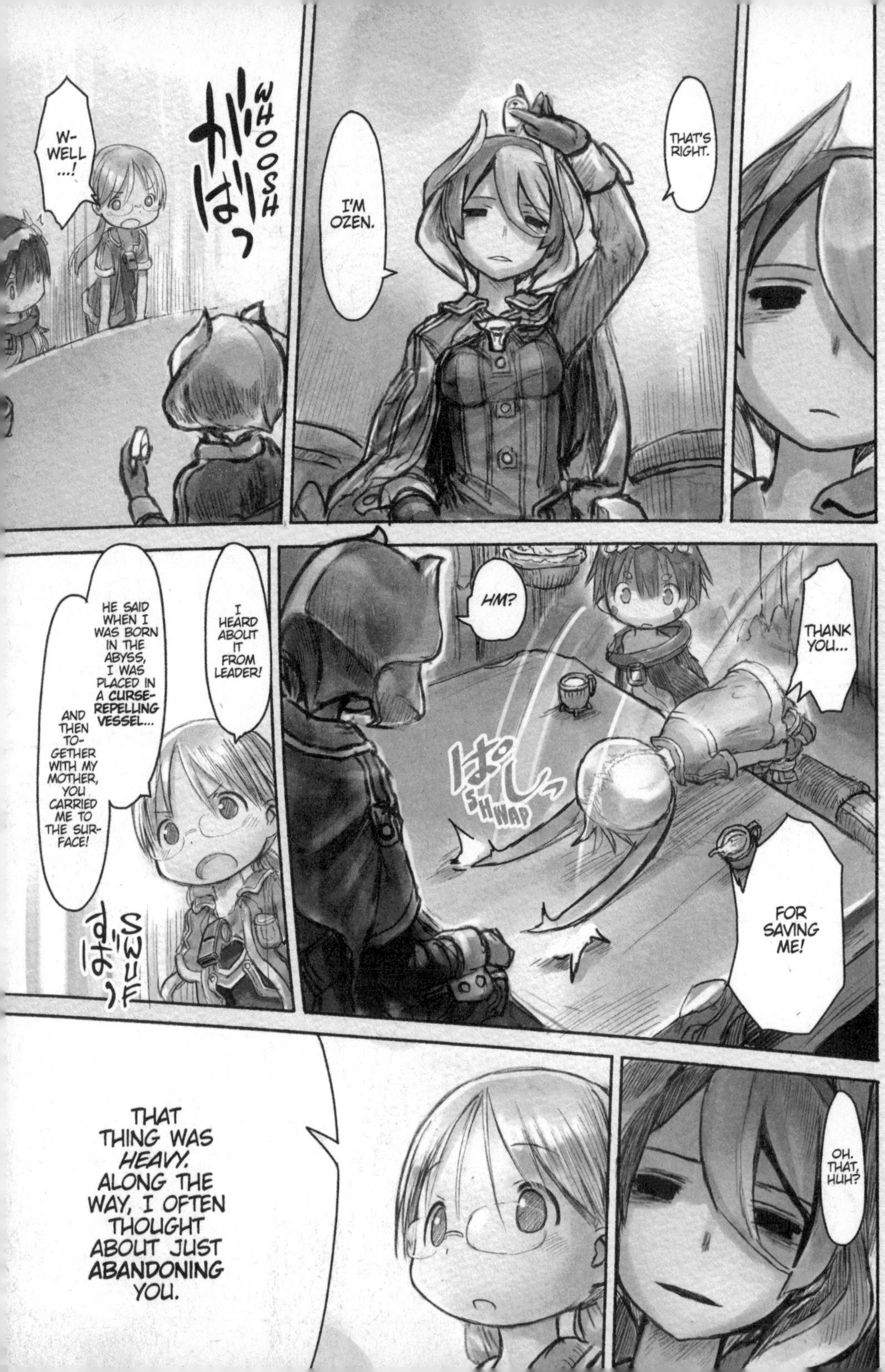
THAT'S RIGHT.
I'M OZEN.
がばっ
WHOOSH
W-WELL ...!
THANK YOU...
HM?
FOR SAVING ME!
ぱしっ
SHWAP
I HEARD ABOUT IT FROM LEADER!
HE SAID WHEN I WAS BORN IN THE ABYSS, I WAS PLACED IN A CURSE-REPELLING VESSEL...
AND THEN TOGETHER WITH MY MOTHER, YOU CARRIED ME TO THE SURFACE!
すばっ
SWUF
OH. THAT, HUH?
THAT THING WAS HEAVY. ALONG THE WAY, I OFTEN THOUGHT ABOUT JUST ABANDONING YOU.

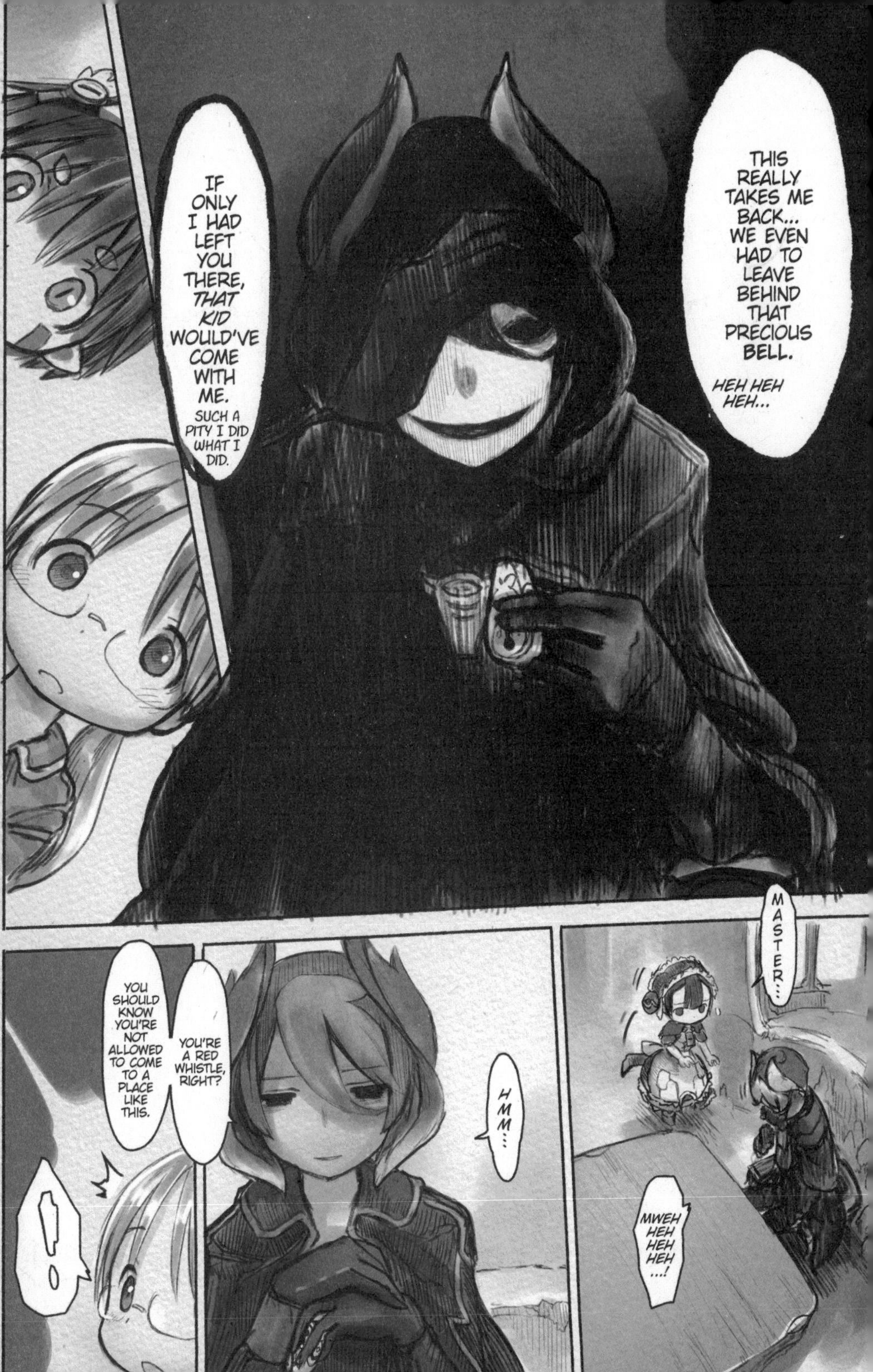
THIS REALLY TAKES ME BACK... WE EVEN HAD TO LEAVE BEHIND THAT PRECIOUS BELL.
HEH HEH HEH...
IF ONLY I HAD LEFT YOU THERE, *THAT KID* WOULD'VE COME WITH ME.
SUCH A PITY I DID WHAT I DID.
MASTER...
MWEH HEH HEH HEH...!
HMM...
YOU'RE A RED WHISTLE, RIGHT?
YOU SHOULD KNOW YOU'RE NOT ALLOWED TO COME TO A PLACE LIKE THIS.
!

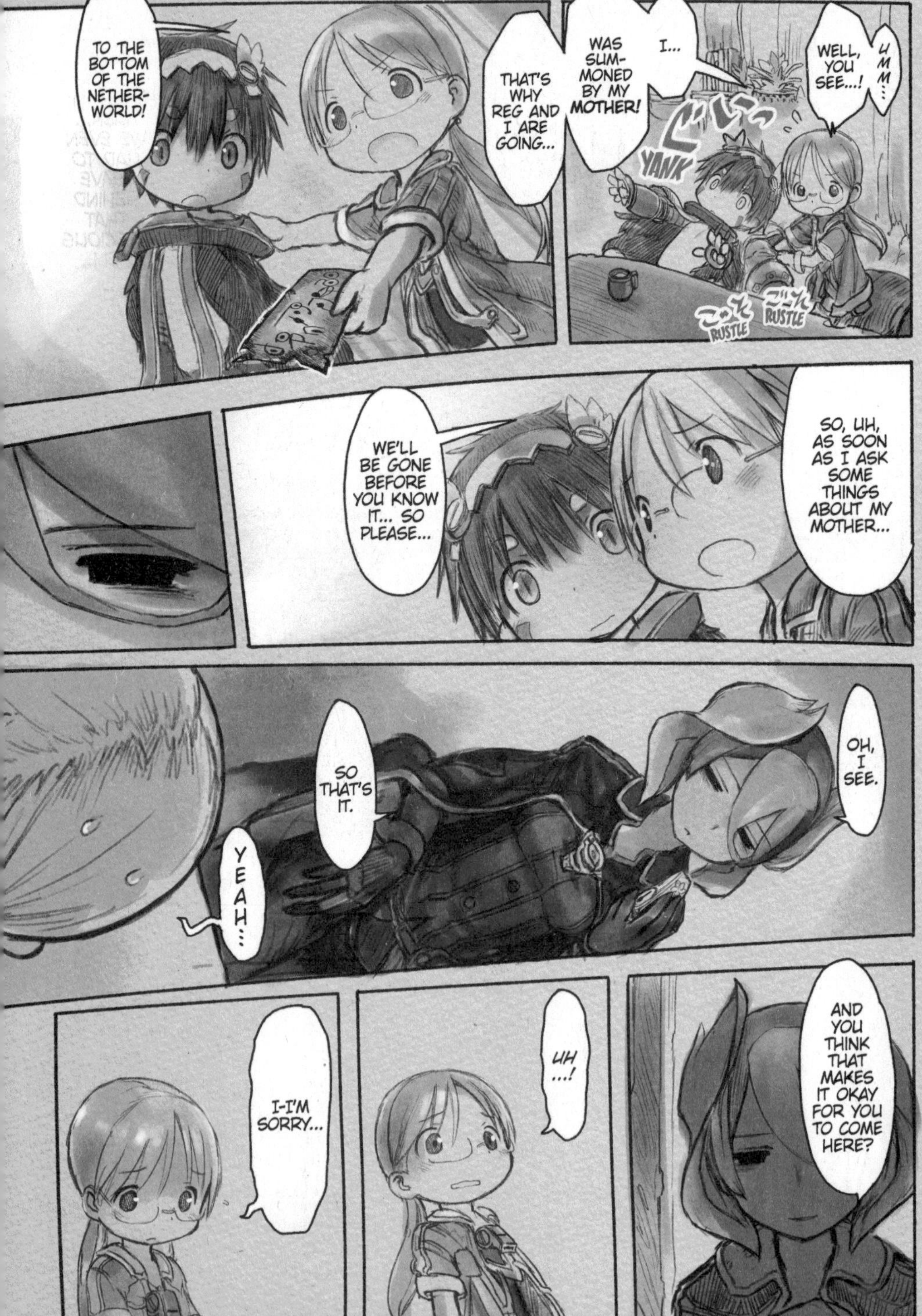
UMM...
WELL, YOU SEE...!
I...
WAS SUMMONED BY MY MOTHER!
YANK
RUSTLE
RUSTLE
THAT'S WHY REG AND I ARE GOING...
TO THE BOTTOM OF THE NETHERWORLD!
SO, UH, AS SOON AS I ASK SOME THINGS ABOUT MY MOTHER...
WE'LL BE GONE BEFORE YOU KNOW IT... SO PLEASE...
OH, I SEE.
SO THAT'S IT.
YEAH...
AND YOU THINK THAT MAKES IT OKAY FOR YOU TO COME HERE?
UH...!
I-I'M SORRY...

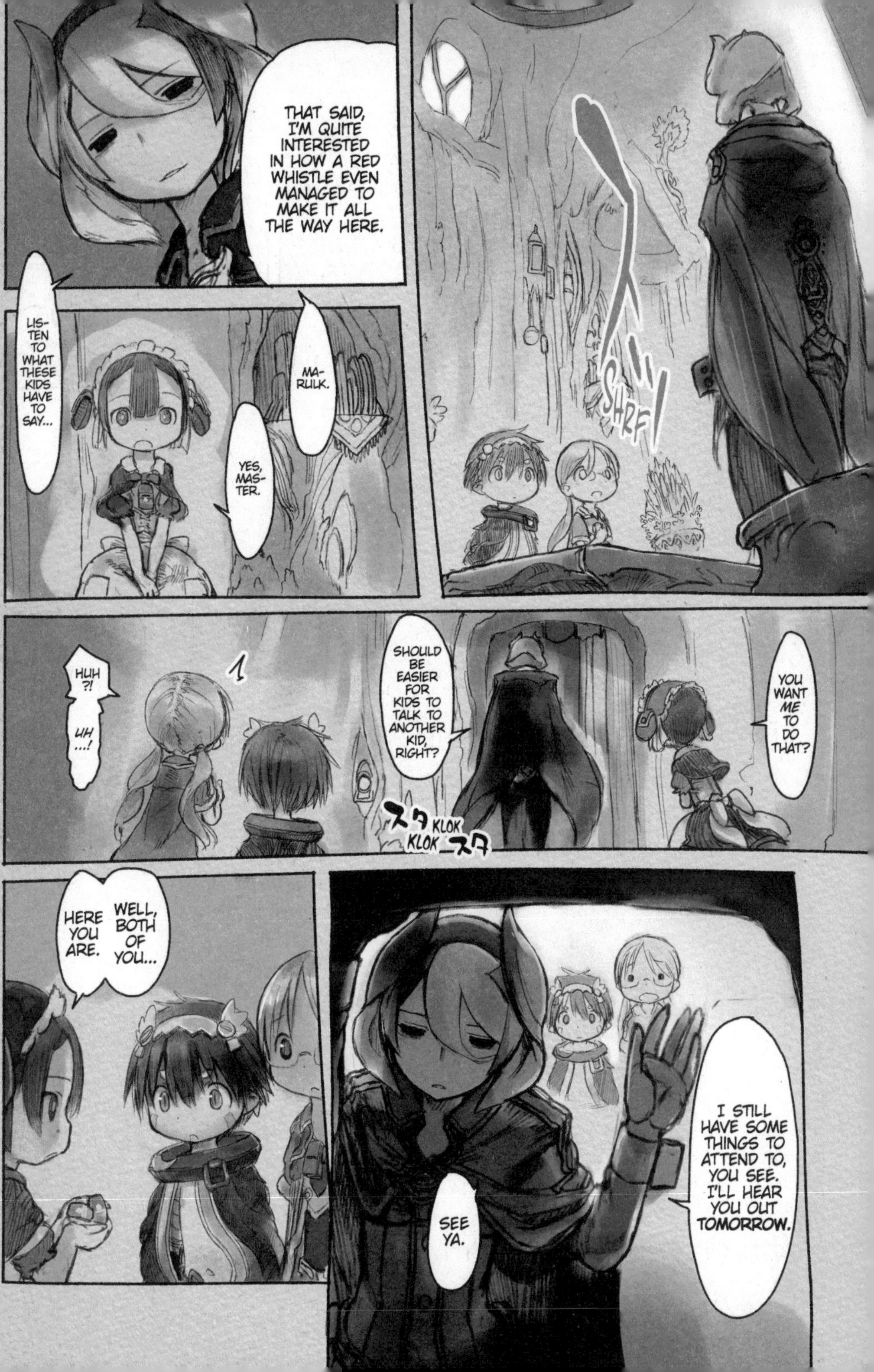
SHRF
THAT SAID, I'M QUITE INTERESTED IN HOW A RED WHISTLE EVEN MANAGED TO MAKE IT ALL THE WAY HERE.
MA-RULK.
LIS-TEN TO WHAT THESE KIDS HAVE TO SAY...
YES, MAS-TER.
YOU WANT ME TO DO THAT?
SHOULD BE EASIER FOR KIDS TO TALK TO ANOTHER KID, RIGHT?
HUH ?!
UH ...!
KLOK KLOK
I STILL HAVE SOME THINGS TO ATTEND TO, YOU SEE. I'LL HEAR YOU OUT TOMORROW.
SEE YA.
WELL, BOTH OF YOU...
HERE YOU ARE.

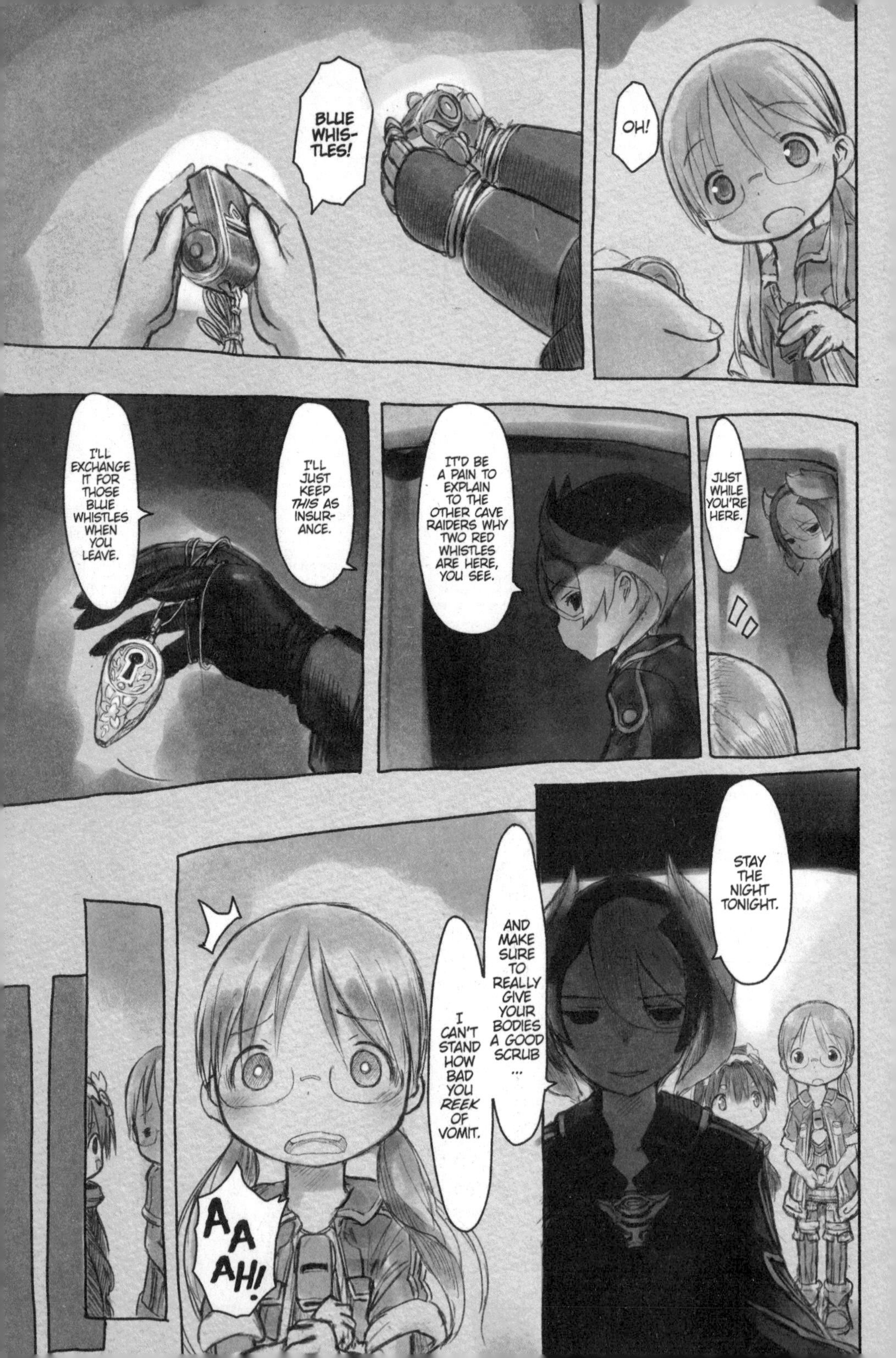
OH!
BLUE WHISTLES!
JUST WHILE YOU'RE HERE.
IT'D BE A PAIN TO EXPLAIN TO THE OTHER CAVE RAIDERS WHY TWO RED WHISTLES ARE HERE, YOU SEE.
I'LL JUST KEEP *THIS* AS INSURANCE.
I'LL EXCHANGE IT FOR THOSE BLUE WHISTLES WHEN YOU LEAVE.
STAY THE NIGHT TONIGHT.
AND MAKE SURE TO REALLY GIVE YOUR BODIES A GOOD SCRUB...
I CAN'T STAND HOW BAD YOU *REEK* OF VOMIT.
AAAH!

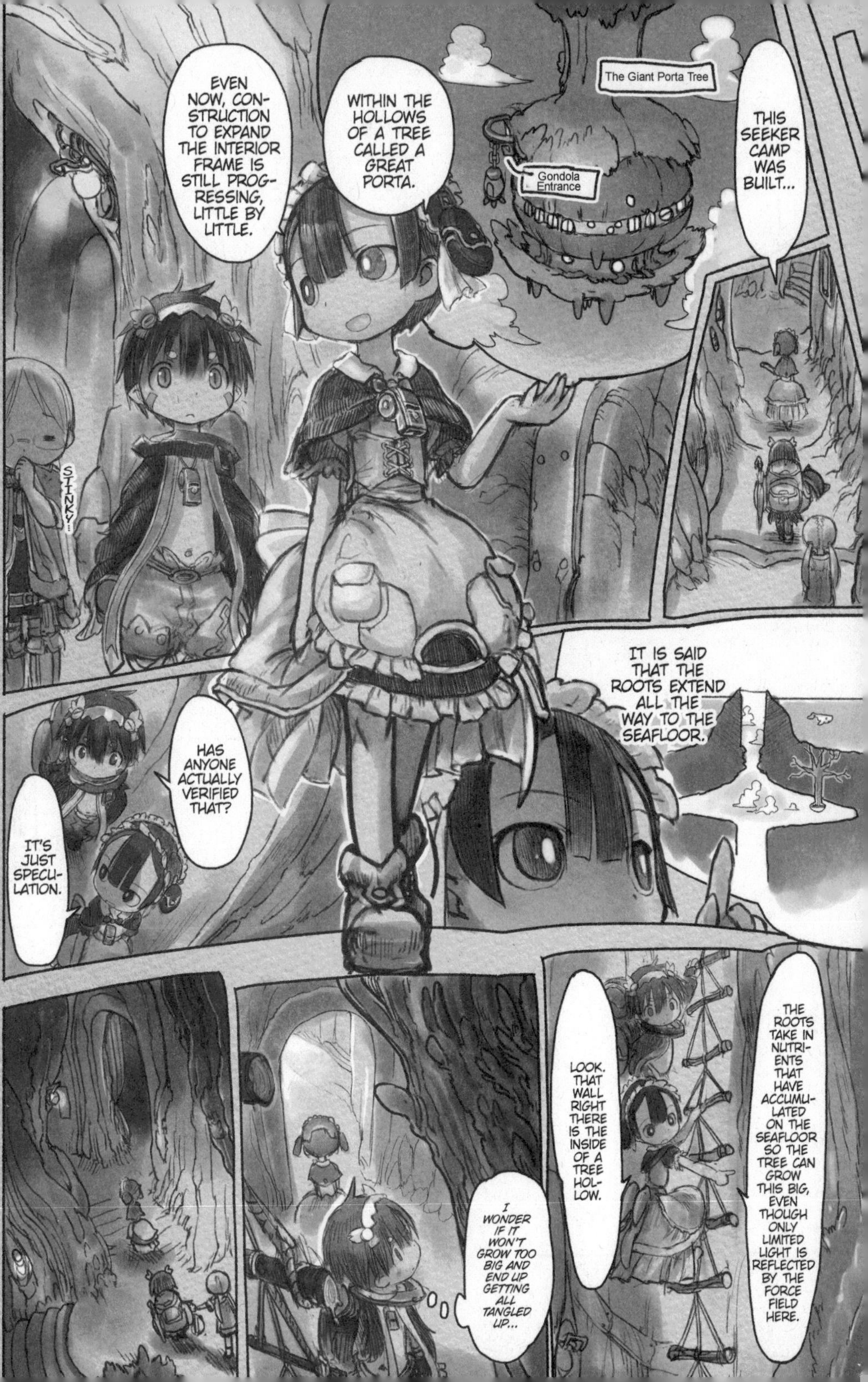
THIS SEEKER CAMP WAS BUILT...
The Giant Porta Tree
Gondola Entrance
WITHIN THE HOLLOWS OF A TREE CALLED A GREAT PORTA.
EVEN NOW, CONSTRUCTION TO EXPAND THE INTERIOR FRAME IS STILL PROGRESSING, LITTLE BY LITTLE.
STINKY...
IT IS SAID THAT THE ROOTS EXTEND ALL THE WAY TO THE SEAFLOOR.
HAS ANYONE ACTUALLY VERIFIED THAT?
IT'S JUST SPECULATION.
THE ROOTS TAKE IN NUTRIENTS THAT HAVE ACCUMULATED ON THE SEAFLOOR SO THE TREE CAN GROW THIS BIG, EVEN THOUGH ONLY LIMITED LIGHT IS REFLECTED BY THE FORCE FIELD HERE.
LOOK. THAT WALL RIGHT THERE IS THE INSIDE OF A TREE HOLLOW.
I WONDER IF IT WON'T GROW TOO BIG AND END UP GETTING ALL TANGLED UP...

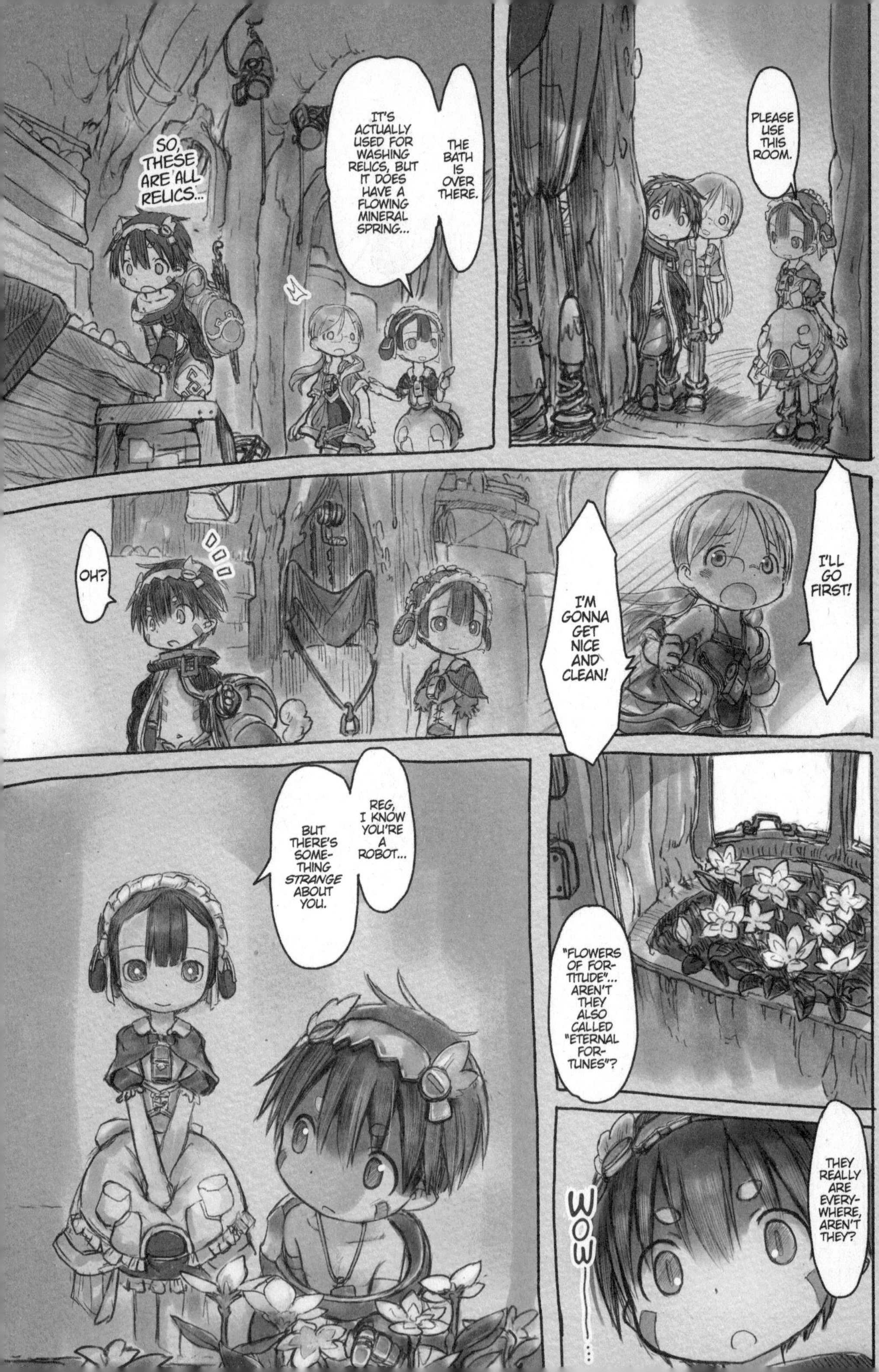
PLEASE USE THIS ROOM.
THE BATH IS OVER THERE.
IT'S ACTUALLY USED FOR WASHING RELICS, BUT IT DOES HAVE A FLOWING MINERAL SPRING...
SO, THESE ARE ALL RELICS...
I'LL GO FIRST!
I'M GONNA GET NICE AND CLEAN!
OH?
"FLOWERS OF FOR-TITUDE"... AREN'T THEY ALSO CALLED "ETERNAL FOR-TUNES"?
THEY REALLY ARE EVERY-WHERE, AREN'T THEY?
WOW......
REG, I KNOW YOU'RE A ROBOT...
BUT THERE'S SOME-THING *STRANGE* ABOUT YOU.

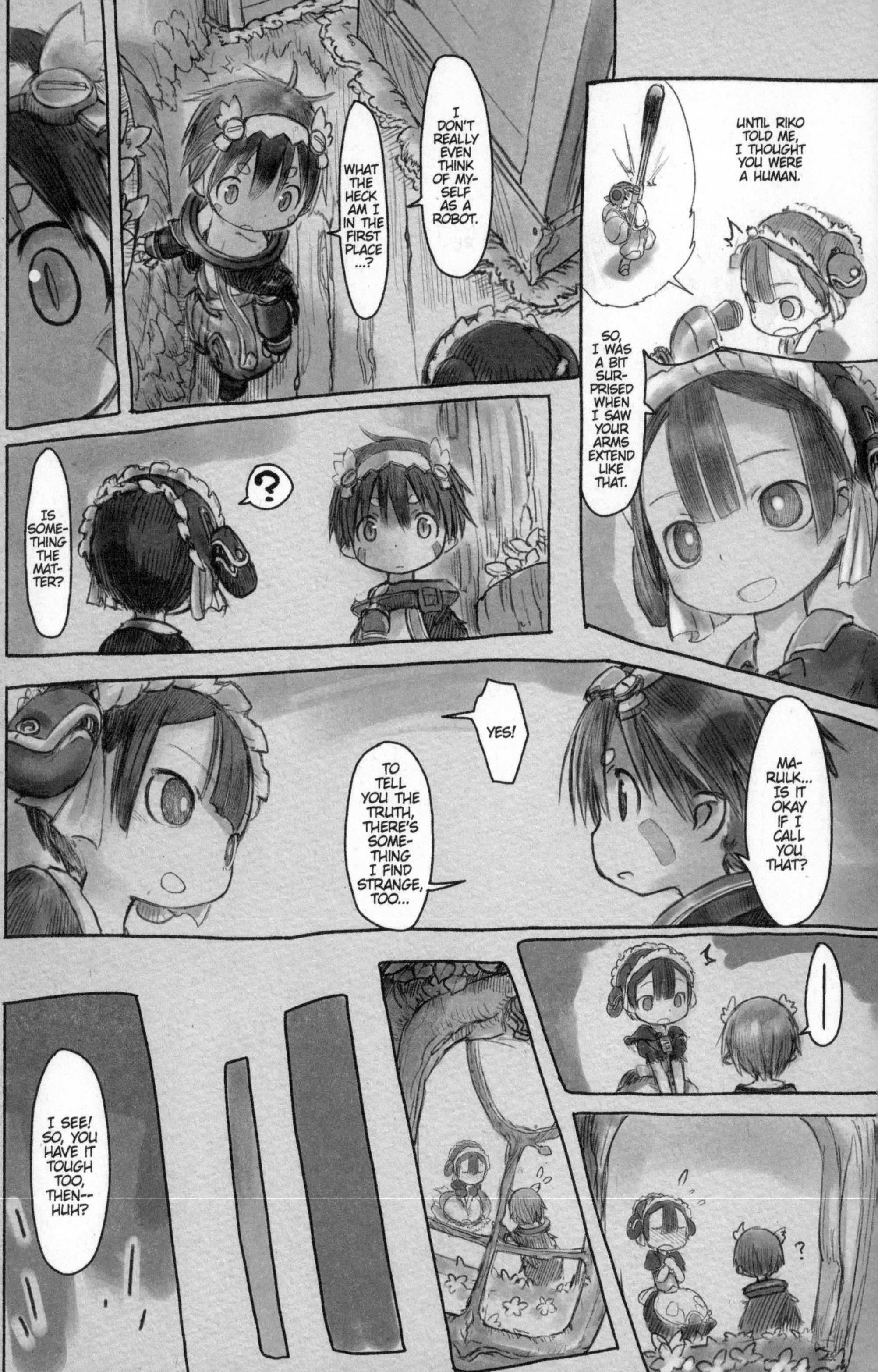
UNTIL RIKO TOLD ME, I THOUGHT YOU WERE A HUMAN.
SO, I WAS A BIT SUR-PRISED WHEN I SAW YOUR ARMS EXTEND LIKE THAT.
I DON'T REALLY EVEN THINK OF MY-SELF AS A ROBOT.
WHAT THE HECK AM I IN THE FIRST PLACE ...?
?
IS SOME-THING THE MAT-TER?
MA-RULK... IS IT OKAY IF I CALL YOU THAT?
YES!
TO TELL YOU THE TRUTH, THERE'S SOME-THING I FIND STRANGE, TOO...
!
?
I SEE! SO, YOU HAVE IT TOUGH TOO, THEN-- HUH?

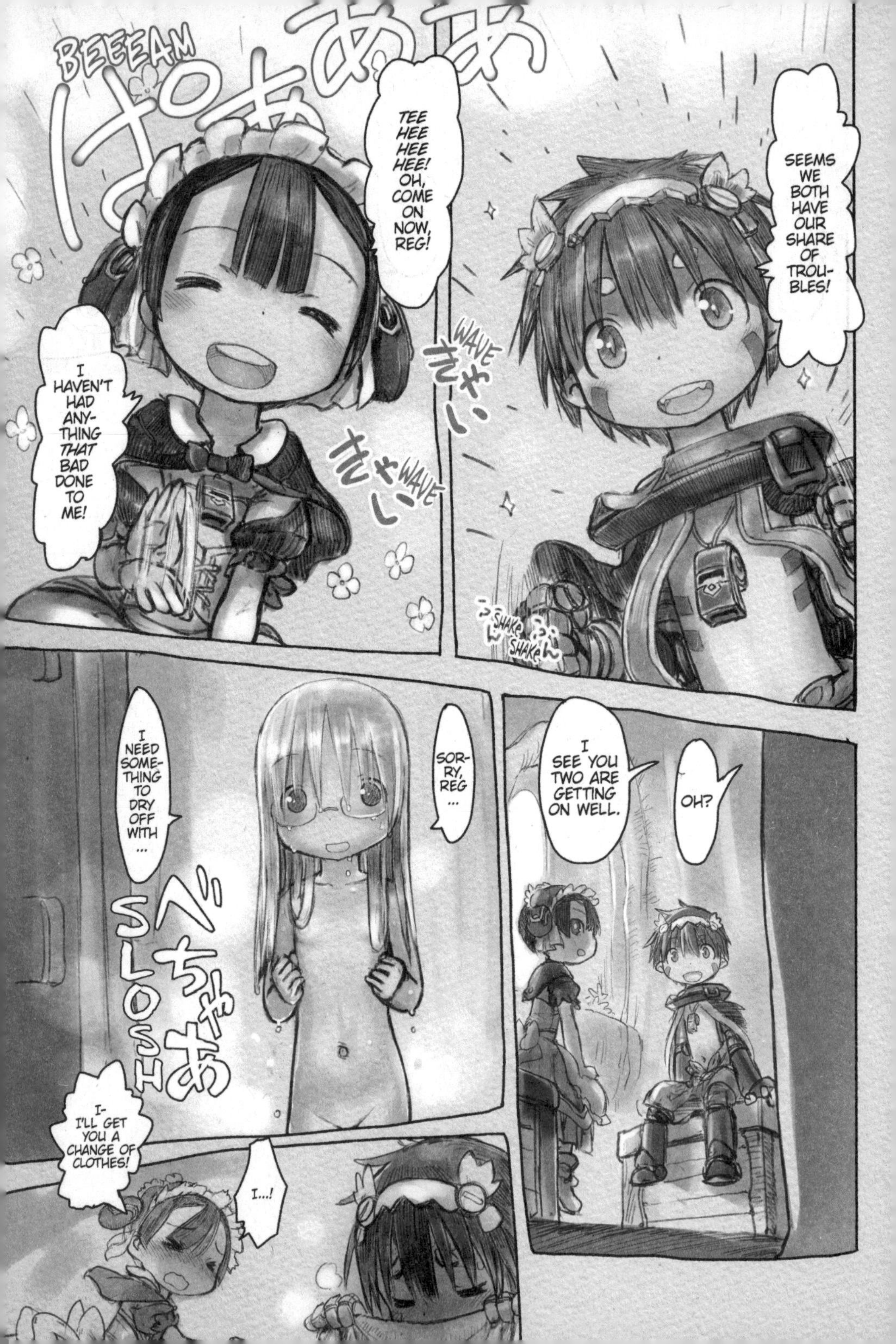
SEEMS WE BOTH HAVE OUR SHARE OF TROUBLES!
SHAKE SHAKE
BEEEAM
TEE HEE HEE HEE! OH, COME ON NOW, REG!
WAVE WAVE
I HAVEN'T HAD ANYTHING *THAT* BAD DONE TO ME!
OH?
I SEE YOU TWO ARE GETTING ON WELL.
SORRY, REG...
I NEED SOMETHING TO DRY OFF WITH...
SLOSH
I...!
I- I'LL GET YOU A CHANGE OF CLOTHES!

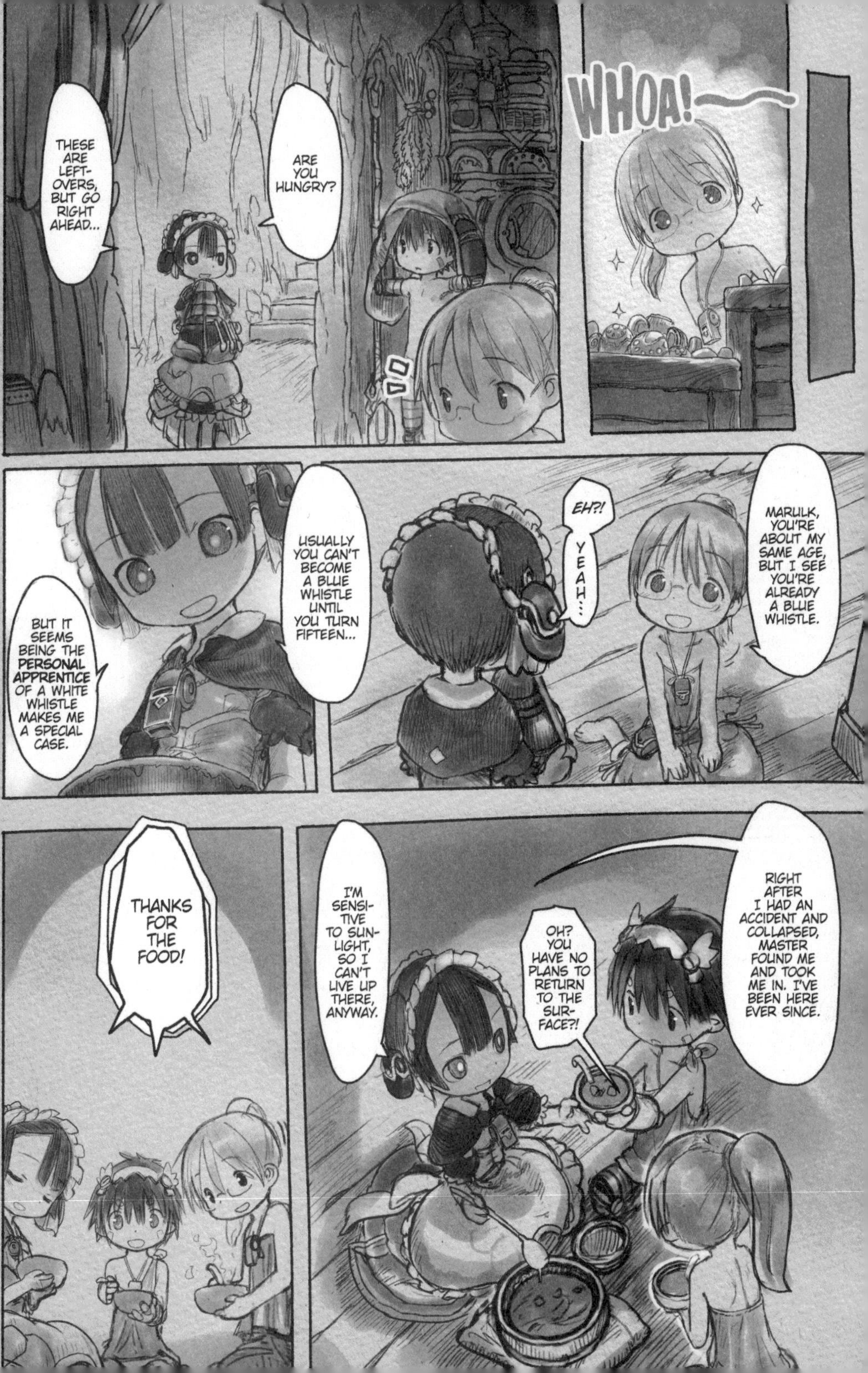
WHOA!~~
ARE YOU HUNGRY?
THESE ARE LEFT-OVERS, BUT GO RIGHT AHEAD...
MARULK, YOU'RE ABOUT MY SAME AGE, BUT I SEE YOU'RE ALREADY A BLUE WHISTLE.
EH?!
YEAH...
USUALLY YOU CAN'T BECOME A BLUE WHISTLE UNTIL YOU TURN FIFTEEN...
BUT IT SEEMS BEING THE **PERSONAL APPRENTICE** OF A WHITE WHISTLE MAKES ME A SPECIAL CASE.
RIGHT AFTER I HAD AN ACCIDENT AND COLLAPSED, MASTER FOUND ME AND TOOK ME IN. I'VE BEEN HERE EVER SINCE.
OH? YOU HAVE NO PLANS TO RETURN TO THE SUR-FACE?!
I'M SENSI-TIVE TO SUN-LIGHT, SO I CAN'T LIVE UP THERE, ANYWAY.
THANKS FOR THE FOOD!

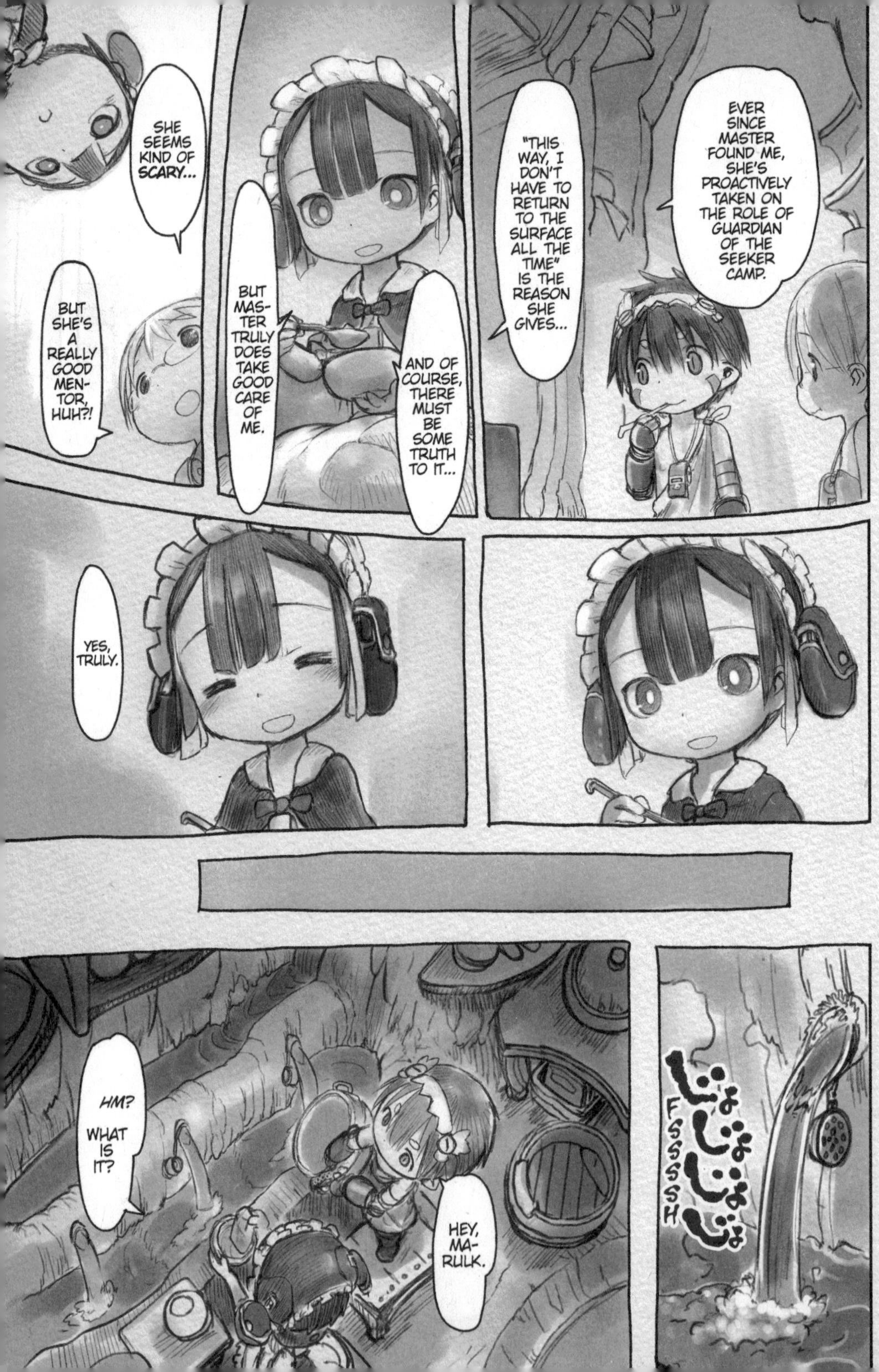
EVER SINCE MASTER FOUND ME, SHE'S PROACTIVELY TAKEN ON THE ROLE OF GUARDIAN OF THE SEEKER CAMP.
"THIS WAY, I DON'T HAVE TO RETURN TO THE SURFACE ALL THE TIME" IS THE REASON SHE GIVES...
AND OF COURSE, THERE MUST BE SOME TRUTH TO IT...
BUT MASTER TRULY DOES TAKE GOOD CARE OF ME.
SHE SEEMS KIND OF SCARY...
BUT SHE'S A REALLY GOOD MENTOR, HUH?!
YES, TRULY.
じょじょじょじょじょ
FSSSSH
HEY, MARULK.
HM? WHAT IS IT?

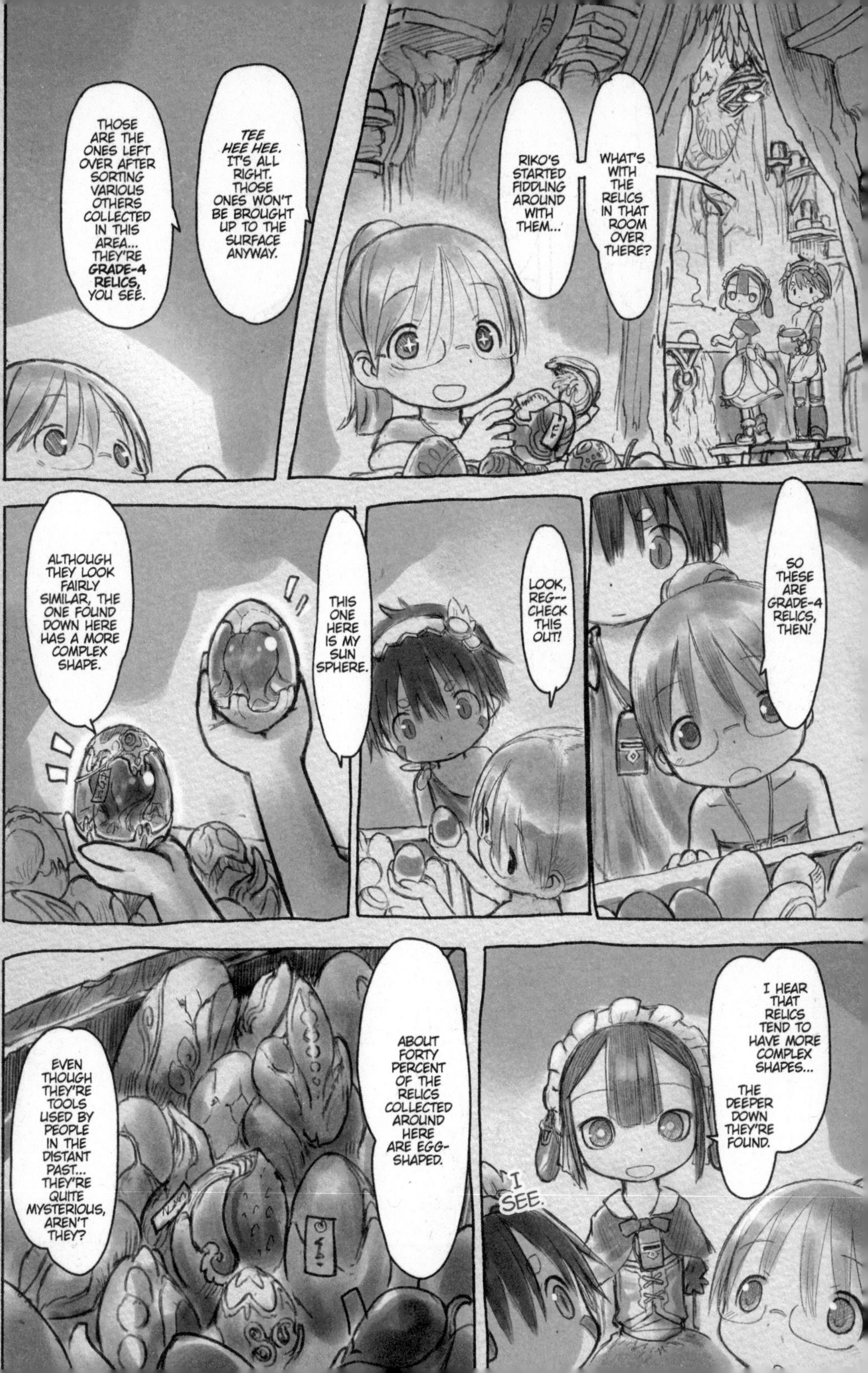
WHAT'S WITH THE RELICS IN THAT ROOM OVER THERE?
RIKO'S STARTED FIDDLING AROUND WITH THEM...
TEE HEE HEE. IT'S ALL RIGHT. THOSE ONES WON'T BE BROUGHT UP TO THE SURFACE ANYWAY.
THOSE ARE THE ONES LEFT OVER AFTER SORTING VARIOUS OTHERS COLLECTED IN THIS AREA... THEY'RE **GRADE-4 RELICS,** YOU SEE.
SO THESE ARE GRADE-4 RELICS, THEN!
LOOK, REG-- CHECK THIS OUT!
THIS ONE HERE IS MY SUN SPHERE.
ALTHOUGH THEY LOOK FAIRLY SIMILAR, THE ONE FOUND DOWN HERE HAS A MORE COMPLEX SHAPE.
I HEAR THAT RELICS TEND TO HAVE MORE COMPLEX SHAPES...
THE DEEPER DOWN THEY'RE FOUND.
I SEE.
ABOUT FORTY PERCENT OF THE RELICS COLLECTED AROUND HERE ARE EGG-SHAPED.
EVEN THOUGH THEY'RE TOOLS USED BY PEOPLE IN THE DISTANT PAST... THEY'RE QUITE MYSTERIOUS, AREN'T THEY?

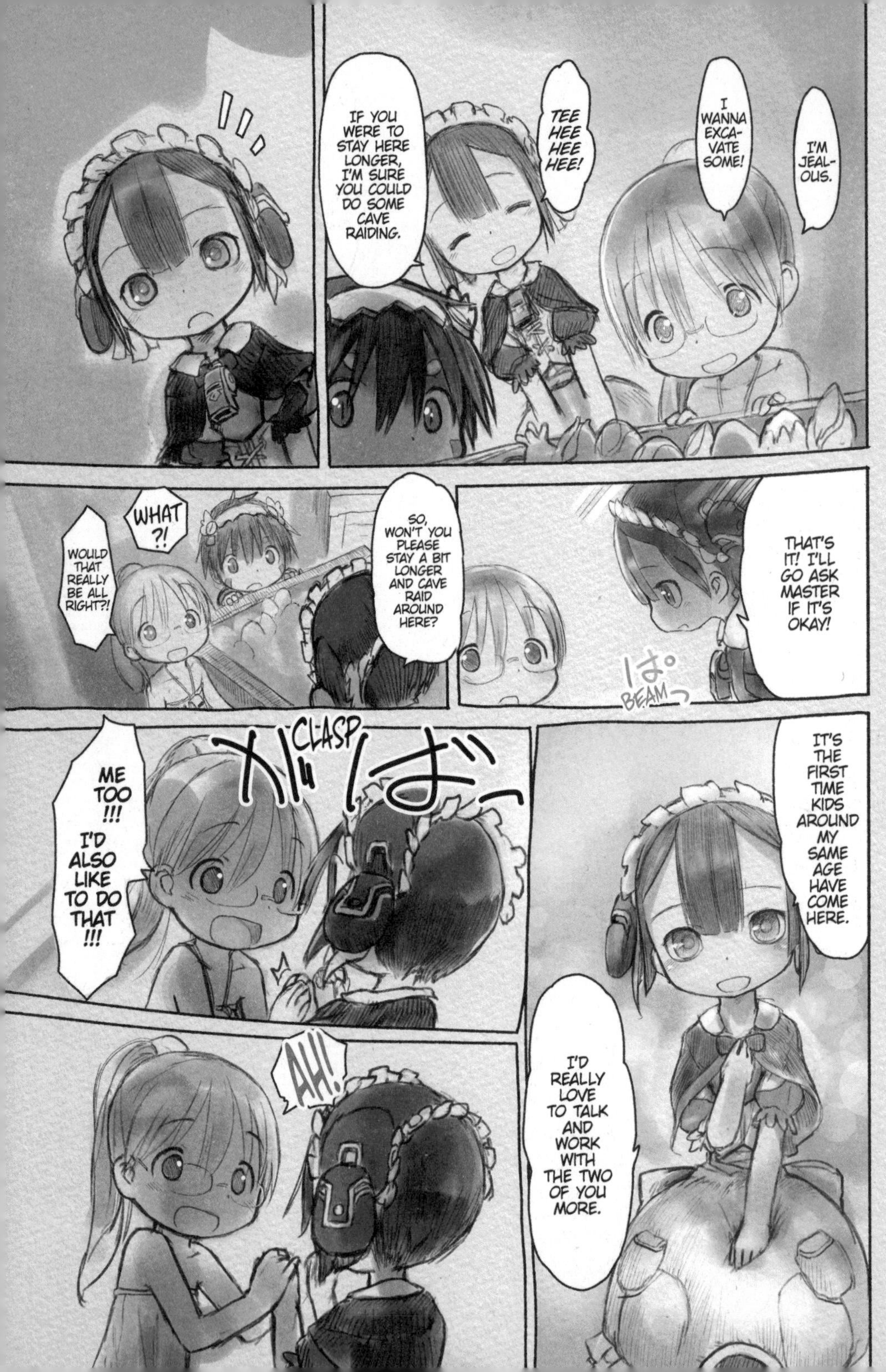
I'M JEALOUS.
I WANNA EXCAVATE SOME!
TEE HEE HEE HEE!
IF YOU WERE TO STAY HERE LONGER, I'M SURE YOU COULD DO SOME CAVE RAIDING.
THAT'S IT! I'LL GO ASK MASTER IF IT'S OKAY!
ぱっ
BEAM
SO, WON'T YOU PLEASE STAY A BIT LONGER AND CAVE RAID AROUND HERE?
WHAT?!
WOULD THAT REALLY BE ALL RIGHT?!
IT'S THE FIRST TIME KIDS AROUND MY SAME AGE HAVE COME HERE.
I'D REALLY LOVE TO TALK AND WORK WITH THE TWO OF YOU MORE.
CLASP
ME TOO!!! I'D ALSO LIKE TO DO THAT!!!
AH!

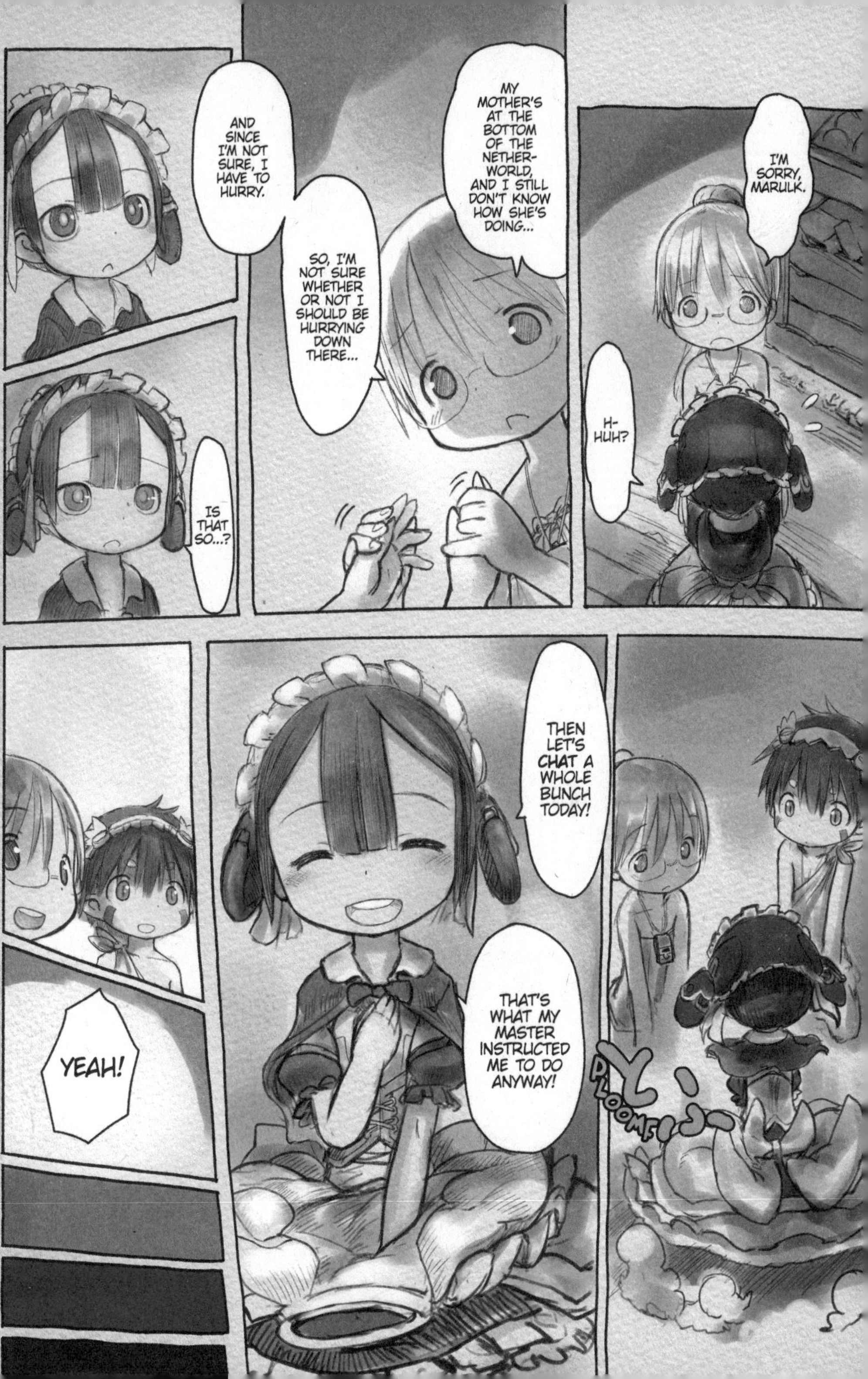

I'M SORRY, MARULK.
H-HUH?
MY MOTHER'S AT THE BOTTOM OF THE NETHER-WORLD, AND I STILL DON'T KNOW HOW SHE'S DOING...
SO, I'M NOT SURE WHETHER OR NOT I SHOULD BE HURRYING DOWN THERE...
AND SINCE I'M NOT SURE, I HAVE TO HURRY.
IS THAT SO...?
PLOOMF
THEN LET'S CHAT A WHOLE BUNCH TODAY!
THAT'S WHAT MY MASTER INSTRUCTED ME TO DO ANYWAY!
YEAH!

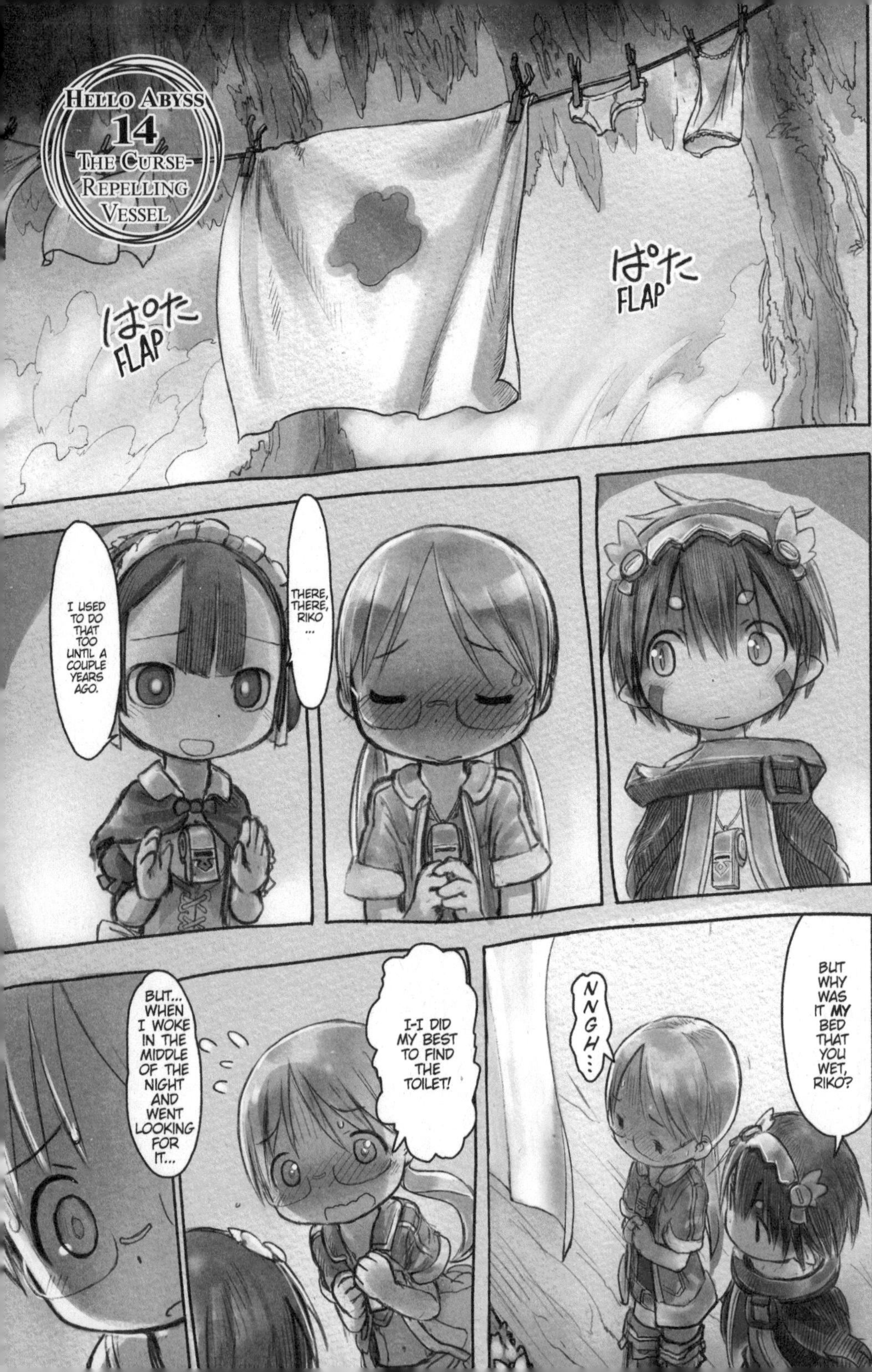
HELLO ABYSS 14 THE CURSE-REPELLING VESSEL
ぱた FLAP
ぱた FLAP
THERE, THERE, RIKO...
I USED TO DO THAT TOO UNTIL A COUPLE YEARS AGO.
BUT WHY WAS IT MY BED THAT YOU WET, RIKO?
NNGH...
I-I DID MY BEST TO FIND THE TOILET!
BUT... WHEN I WOKE IN THE MIDDLE OF THE NIGHT AND WENT LOOKING FOR IT...

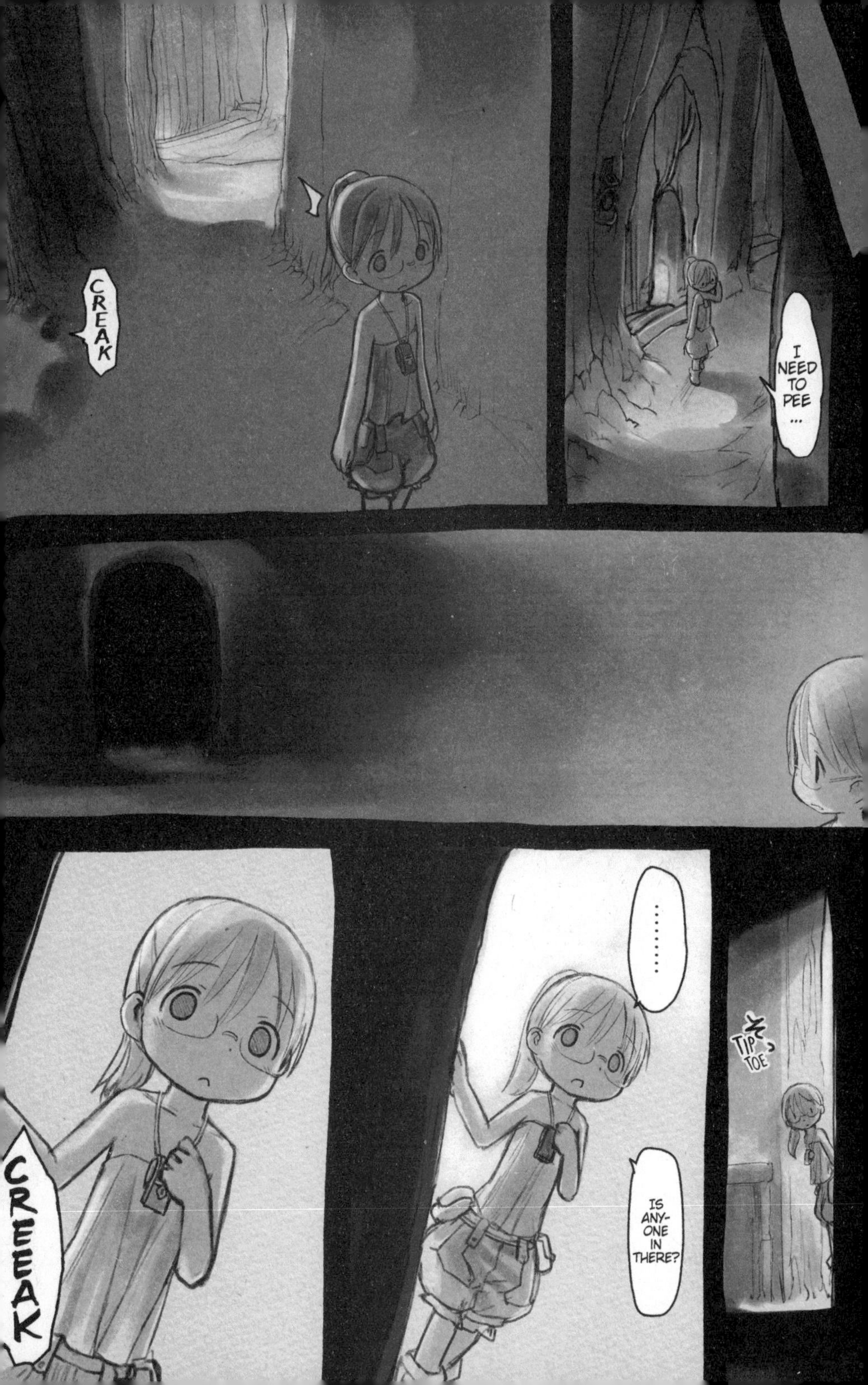
I NEED TO PEE ...
CREAK
TIP TOE
....
IS ANY-ONE IN THERE?
CREEEAK

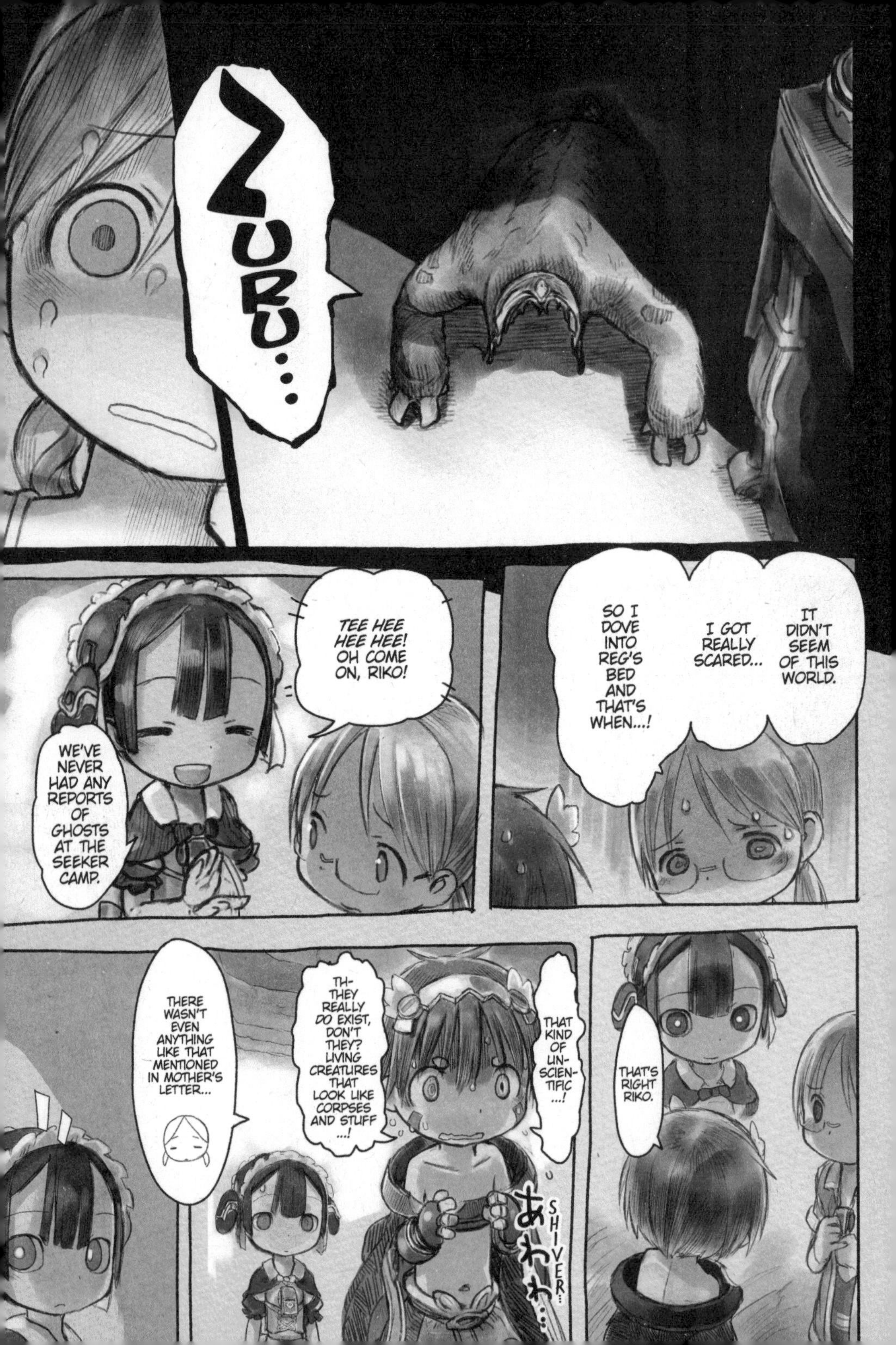
ZURU...
IT DIDN'T SEEM OF THIS WORLD.
I GOT REALLY SCARED...
SO I DOVE INTO REG'S BED AND THAT'S WHEN...!
TEE HEE HEE HEE! OH COME ON, RIKO!
WE'VE NEVER HAD ANY REPORTS OF GHOSTS AT THE SEEKER CAMP.
THAT'S RIGHT RIKO.
THAT KIND OF UN-SCIENTIFIC ...!
TH-THEY REALLY DO EXIST, DON'T THEY? LIVING CREATURES THAT LOOK LIKE CORPSES AND STUFF ...!
THERE WASN'T EVEN ANYTHING LIKE THAT MENTIONED IN MOTHER'S LETTER...
あわわ
SHIVER...

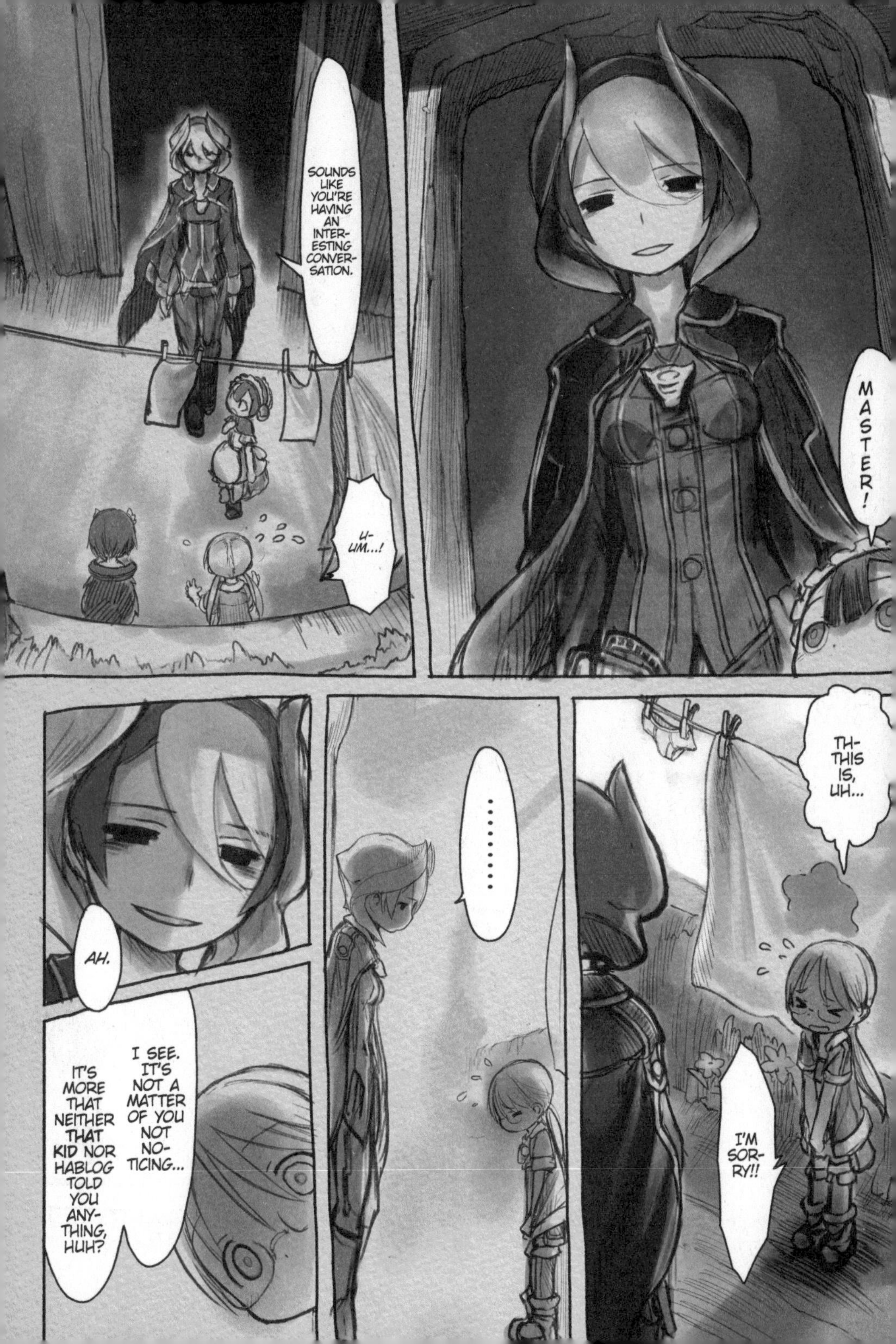
MASTER!
SOUNDS LIKE YOU'RE HAVING AN INTERESTING CONVERSATION.
U-UM...!
TH-THIS IS, UH...
I'M SORRY!!
......
AH.
I SEE. IT'S NOT A MATTER OF YOU NOT NOTICING...
IT'S MORE THAT NEITHER THAT KID NOR HABLOG TOLD YOU ANYTHING, HUH?

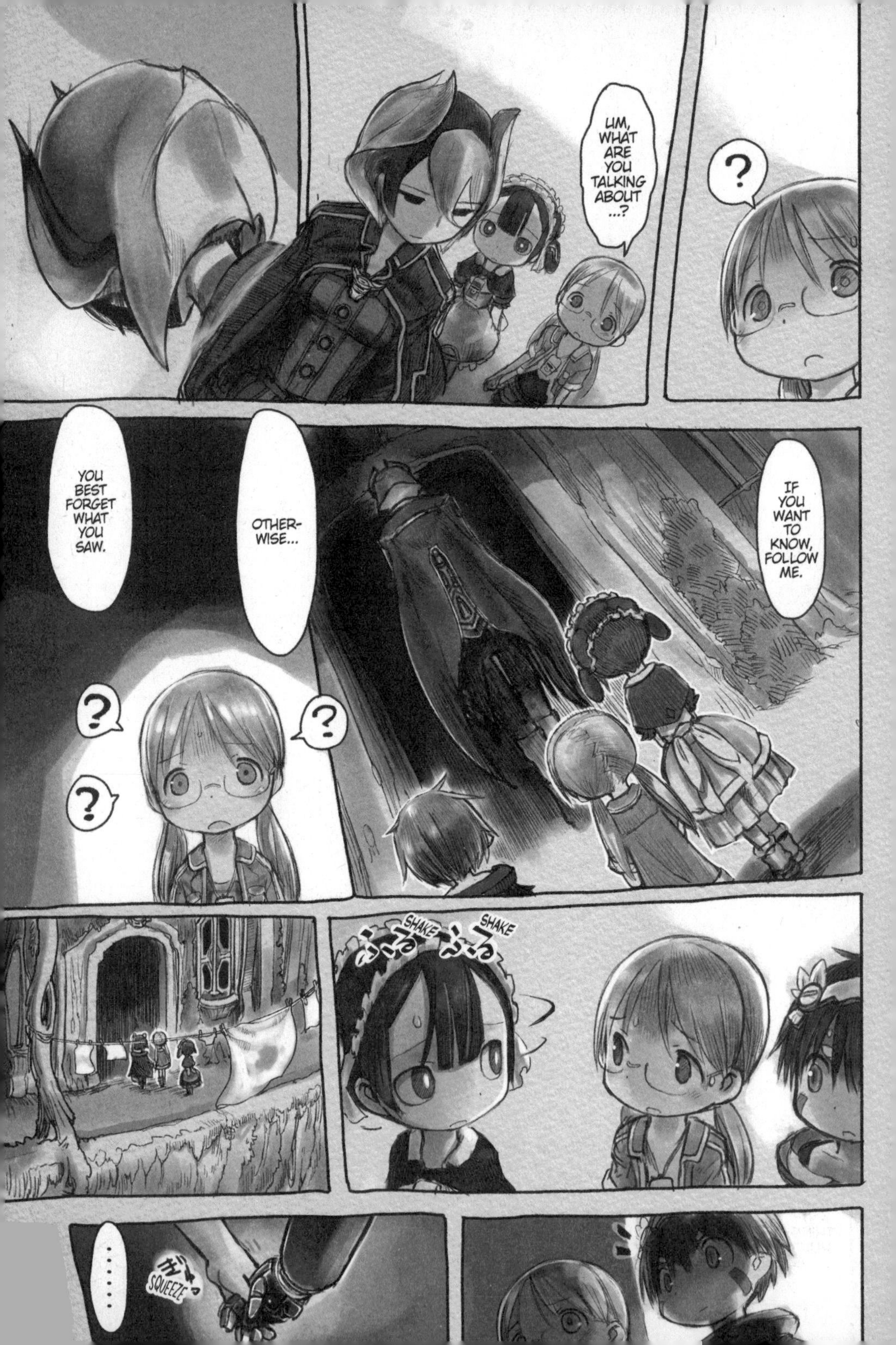
?
UM, WHAT ARE YOU TALKING ABOUT ...?
IF YOU WANT TO KNOW, FOLLOW ME.
OTHER-WISE...
YOU BEST FORGET WHAT YOU SAW.
?
?
?
SHAKE SHAKE
......
SQUEEZE

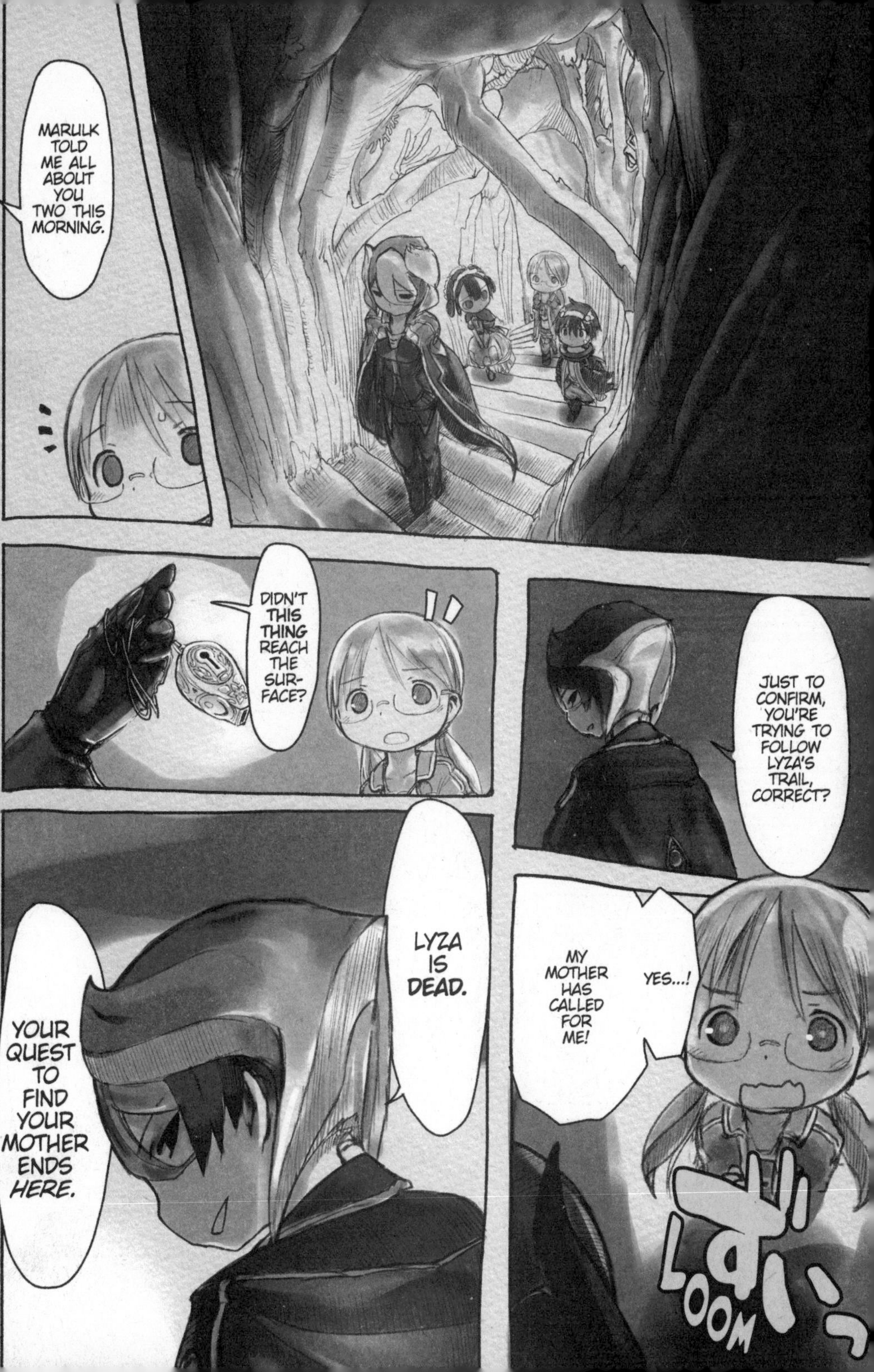
MARULK TOLD ME ALL ABOUT YOU TWO THIS MORNING.
JUST TO CONFIRM, YOU'RE TRYING TO FOLLOW LYZA'S TRAIL, CORRECT?
DIDN'T THIS THING REACH THE SUR-FACE?
YES...!
MY MOTHER HAS CALLED FOR ME!
LOOM
LYZA IS DEAD.
YOUR QUEST TO FIND YOUR MOTHER ENDS HERE.

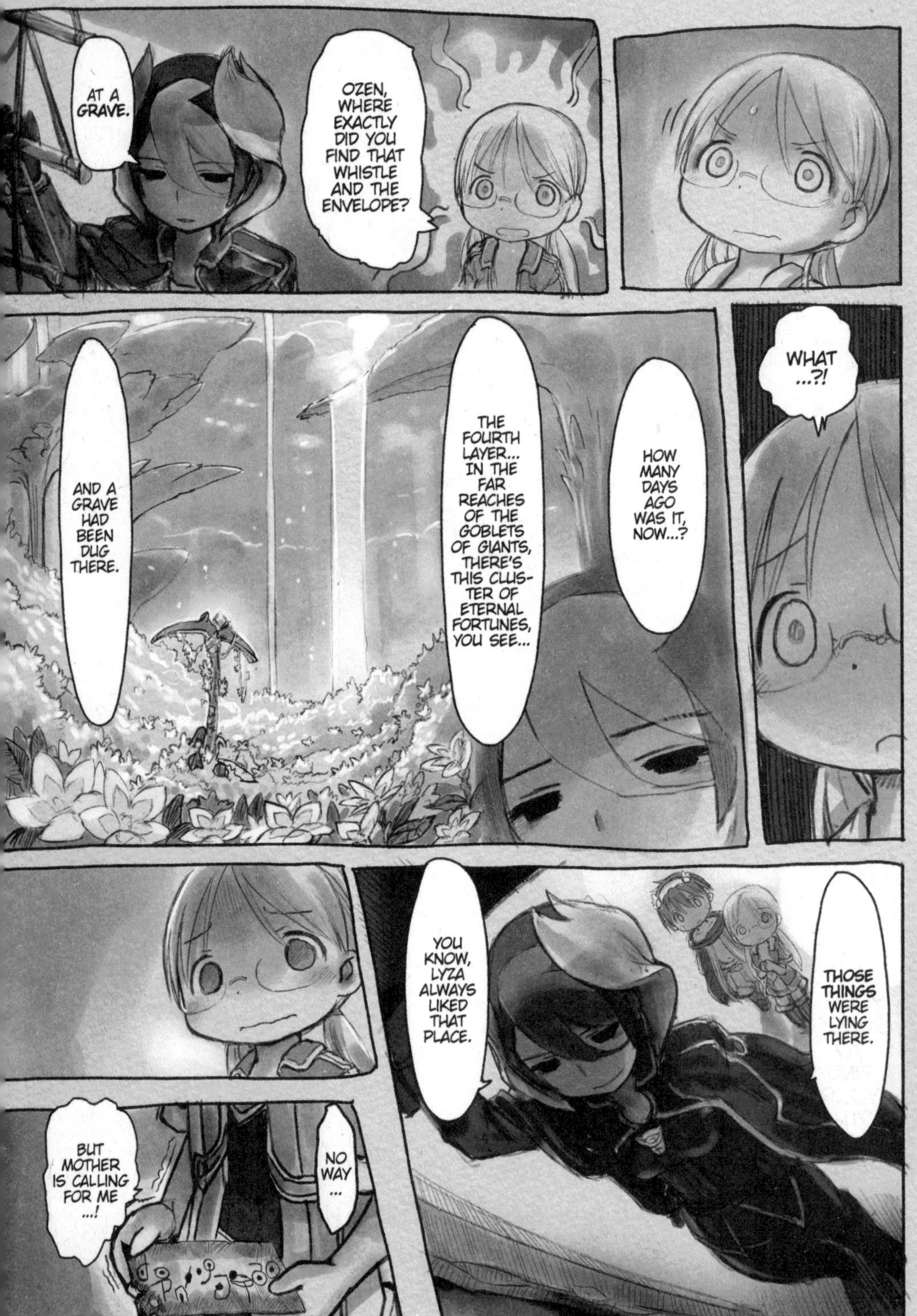
OZEN, WHERE EXACTLY DID YOU FIND THAT WHISTLE AND THE ENVELOPE?
AT A GRAVE.
WHAT ...?!
HOW MANY DAYS AGO WAS IT, NOW...?
THE FOURTH LAYER... IN THE FAR REACHES OF THE GOBLETS OF GIANTS, THERE'S THIS CLUSTER OF ETERNAL FORTUNES, YOU SEE...
AND A GRAVE HAD BEEN DUG THERE.
THOSE THINGS WERE LYING THERE.
YOU KNOW, LYZA ALWAYS LIKED THAT PLACE.
NO WAY ...
BUT MOTHER IS CALLING FOR ME ...!

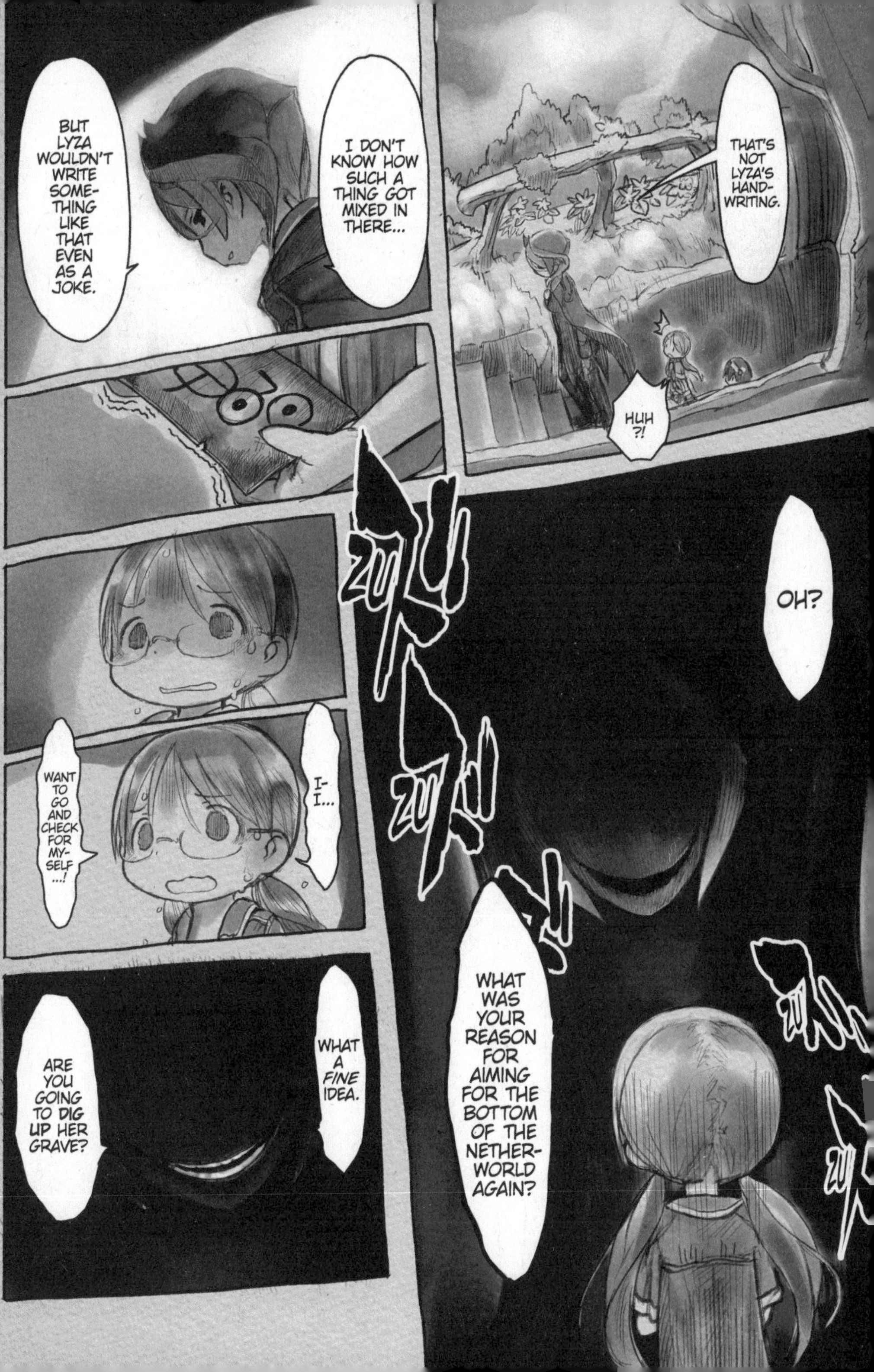
THAT'S NOT LYZA'S HAND-WRITING.
HUH ?!
I DON'T KNOW HOW SUCH A THING GOT MIXED IN THERE...
BUT LYZA WOULDN'T WRITE SOME-THING LIKE THAT EVEN AS A JOKE.
ZU
ZU
OH?
WHAT WAS YOUR REASON FOR AIMING FOR THE BOTTOM OF THE NETHER-WORLD AGAIN?
ZU
ZU
I-I...
WANT TO GO AND CHECK FOR MY-SELF...!
WHAT A *FINE* IDEA.
ARE YOU GOING TO DIG UP HER GRAVE?

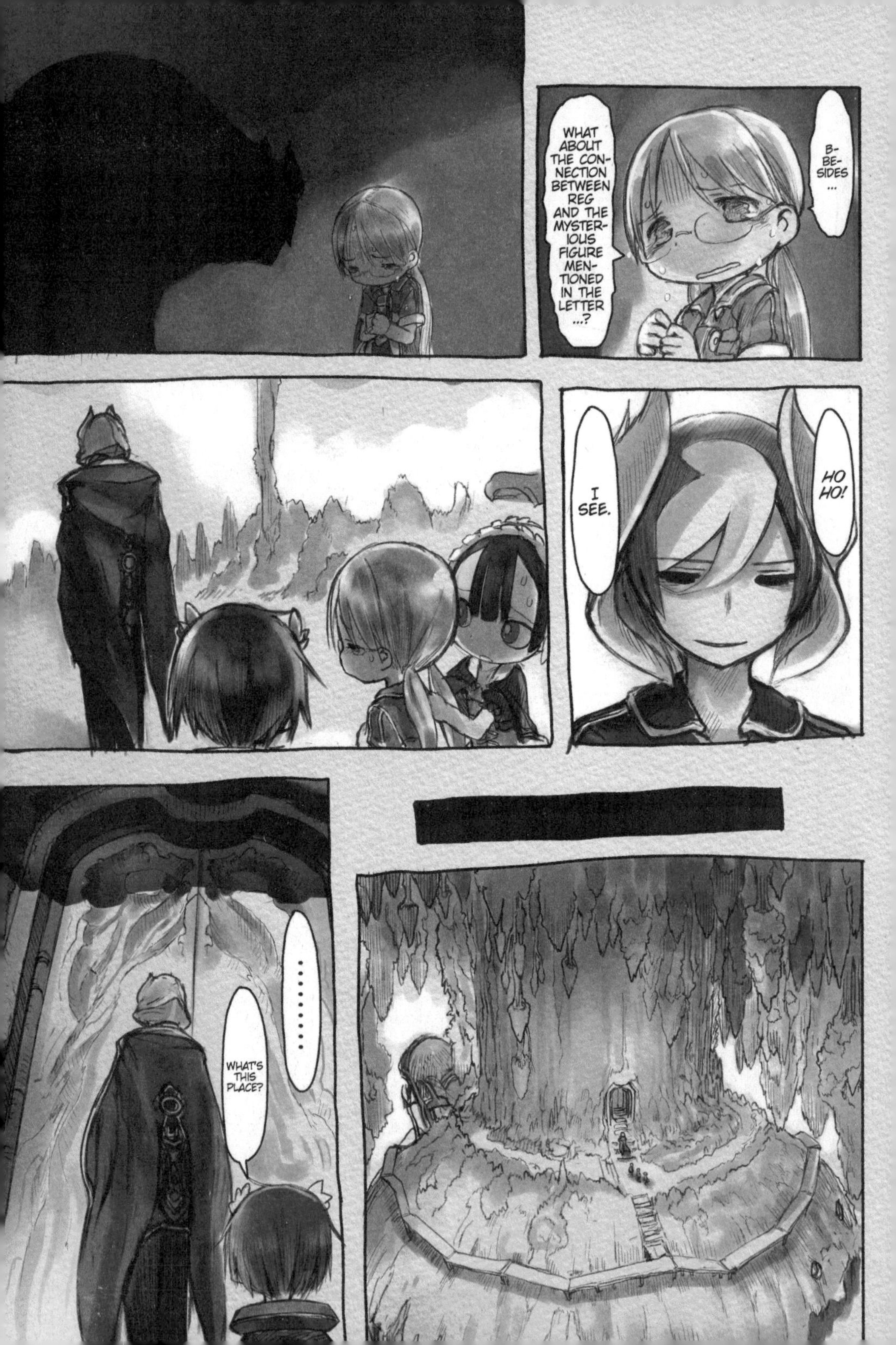
B-BE-SIDES...
WHAT ABOUT THE CONNECTION BETWEEN REG AND THE MYSTERIOUS FIGURE MENTIONED IN THE LETTER...?
HO HO!
I SEE.
......
WHAT'S THIS PLACE?

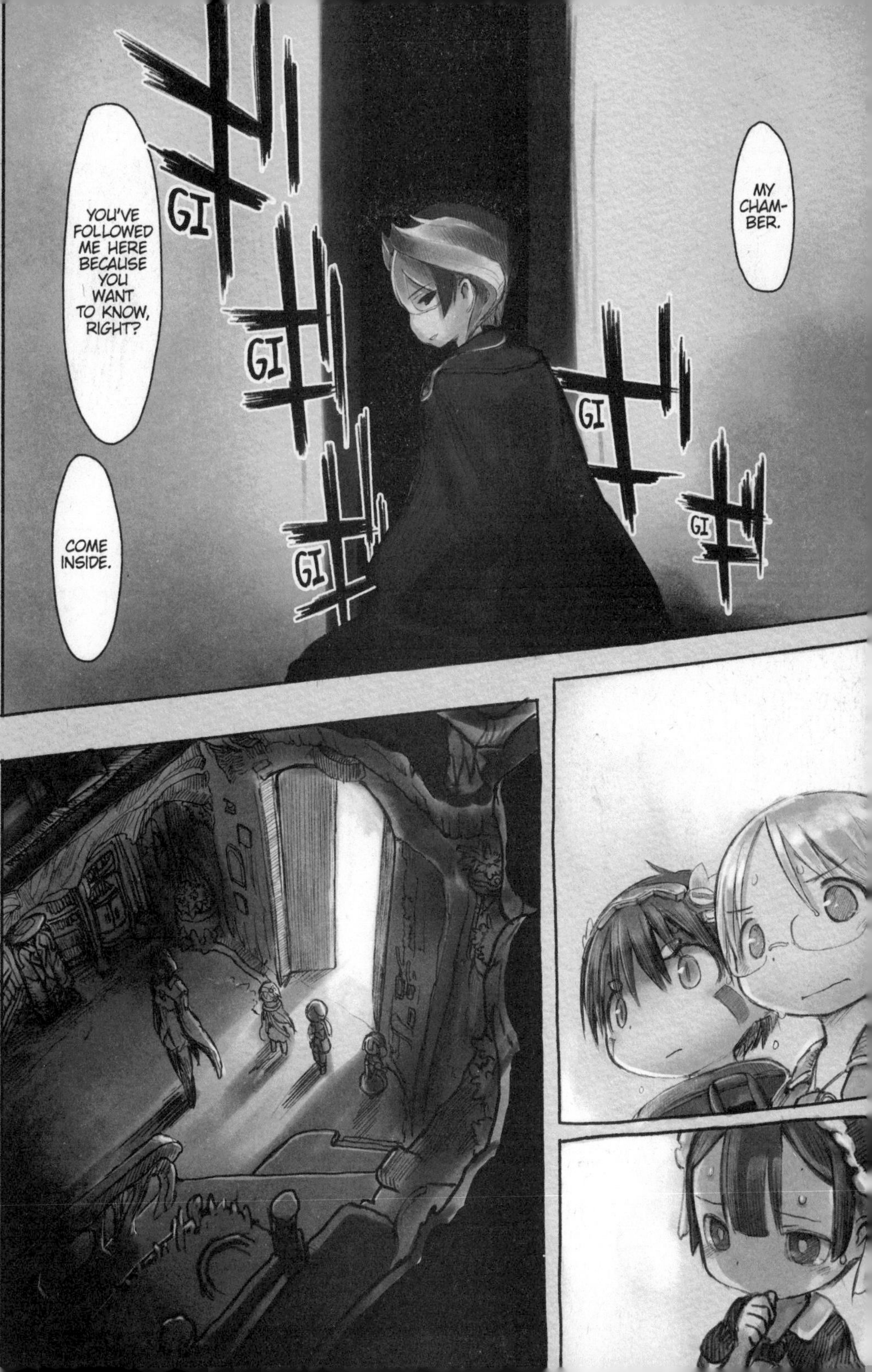
MY CHAMBER.
GI
GI
GI
GI
GI
YOU'VE FOLLOWED ME HERE BECAUSE YOU WANT TO KNOW, RIGHT?
COME INSIDE.

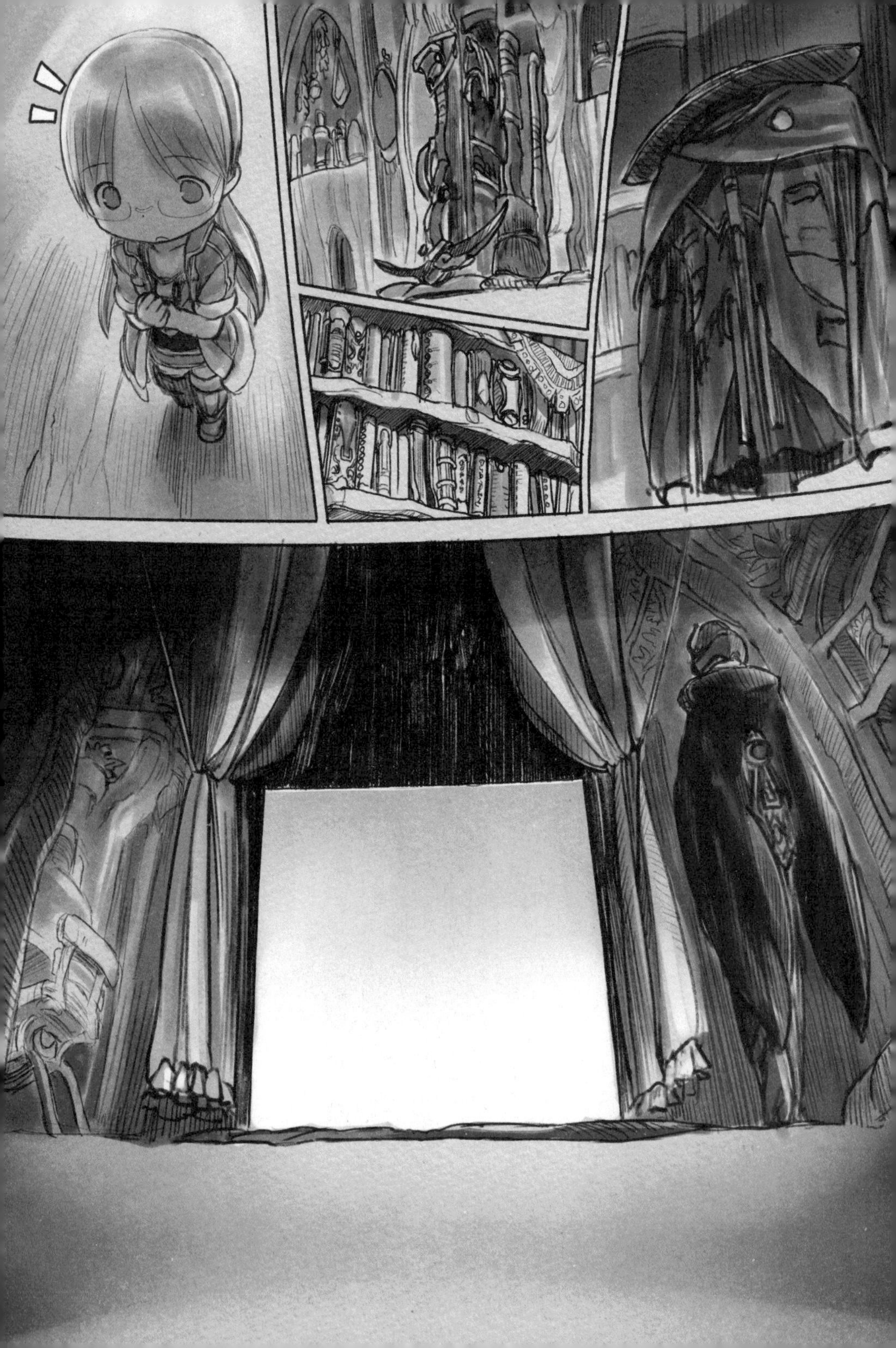

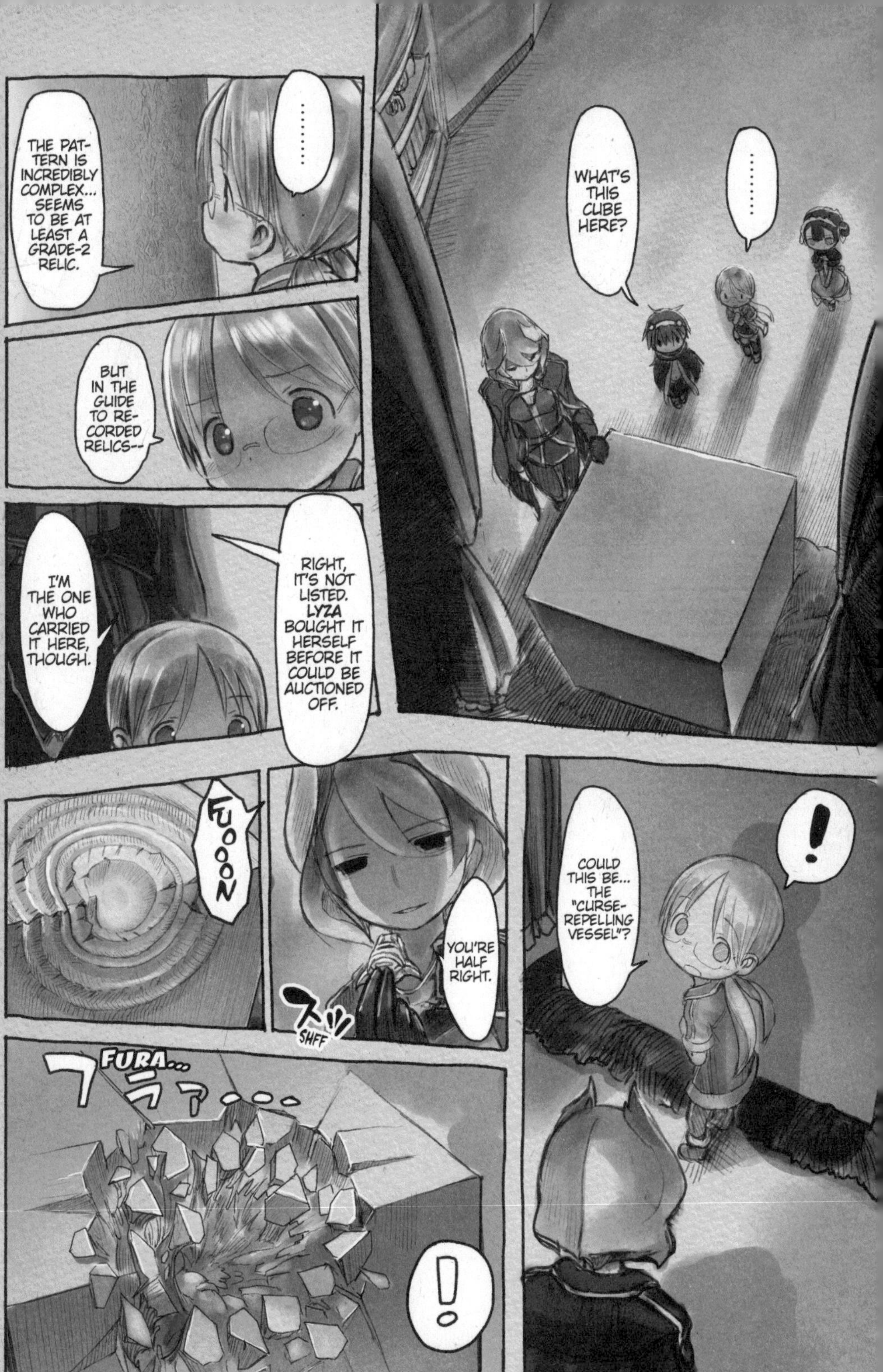

......
WHAT'S THIS CUBE HERE?
......
THE PATTERN IS INCREDIBLY COMPLEX... SEEMS TO BE AT LEAST A GRADE-2 RELIC.
BUT IN THE GUIDE TO RECORDED RELICS--
RIGHT, IT'S NOT LISTED. LYZA BOUGHT IT HERSELF BEFORE IT COULD BE AUCTIONED OFF.
I'M THE ONE WHO CARRIED IT HERE, THOUGH.
!
COULD THIS BE... THE "CURSE-REPELLING VESSEL"?
YOU'RE HALF RIGHT.
SHFF
FUOOON
FURA...
!

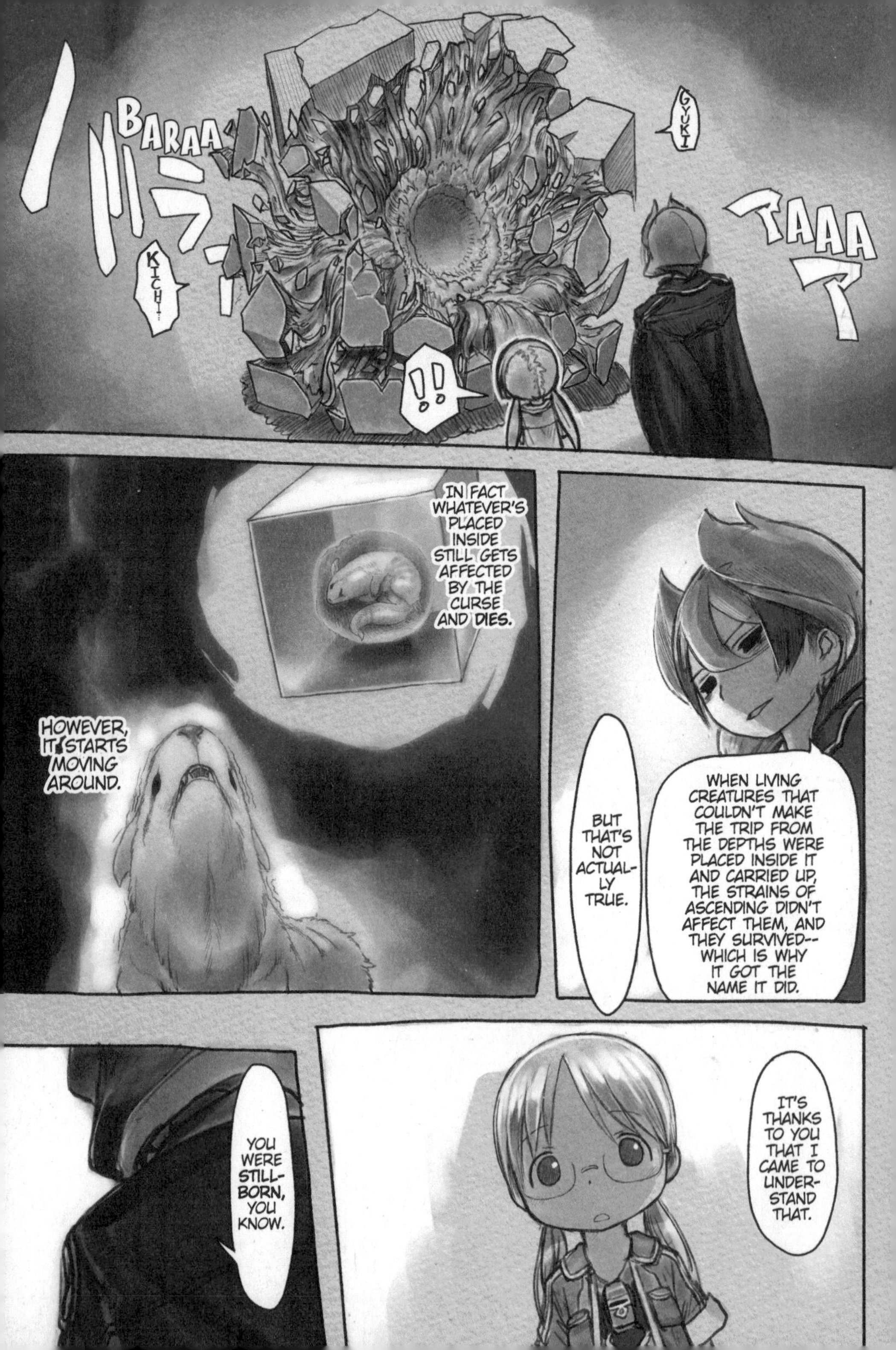
GYUKI
TAAA
BARAA
KICHI...
!!
WHEN LIVING CREATURES THAT COULDN'T MAKE THE TRIP FROM THE DEPTHS WERE PLACED INSIDE IT AND CARRIED UP, THE STRAINS OF ASCENDING DIDN'T AFFECT THEM, AND THEY SURVIVED--WHICH IS WHY IT GOT THE NAME IT DID.
BUT THAT'S NOT ACTUALLY TRUE.
IN FACT WHATEVER'S PLACED INSIDE STILL GETS AFFECTED BY THE CURSE AND DIES.
HOWEVER, IT STARTS MOVING AROUND.
IT'S THANKS TO YOU THAT I CAME TO UNDERSTAND THAT.
YOU WERE STILLBORN, YOU KNOW.

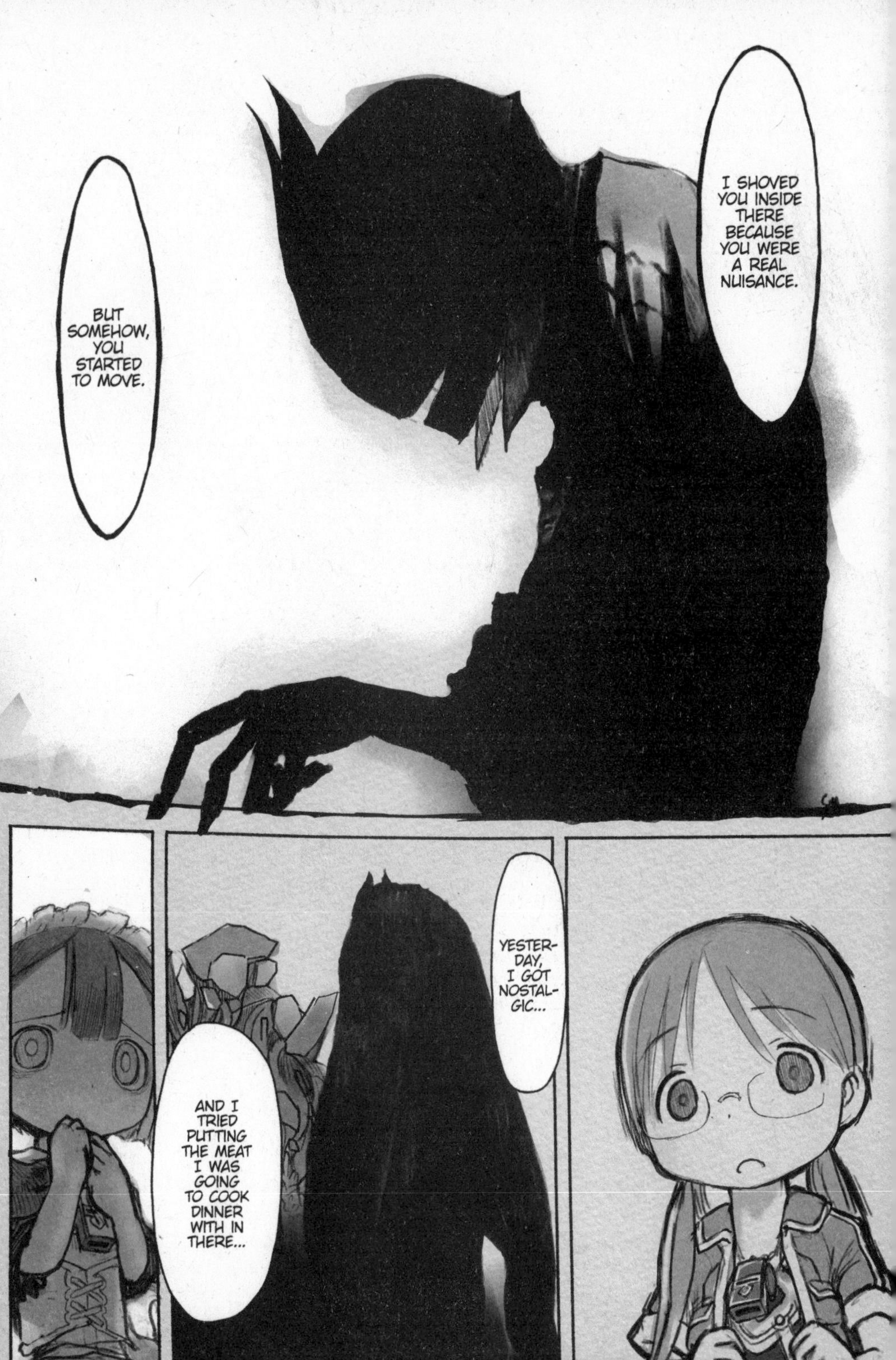
I SHOVED YOU INSIDE THERE BECAUSE YOU WERE A REAL NUISANCE.
BUT SOMEHOW, YOU STARTED TO MOVE.
YESTER-DAY, I GOT NOSTAL-GIC...
AND I TRIED PUTTING THE MEAT I WAS GOING TO COOK DINNER WITH IN THERE...

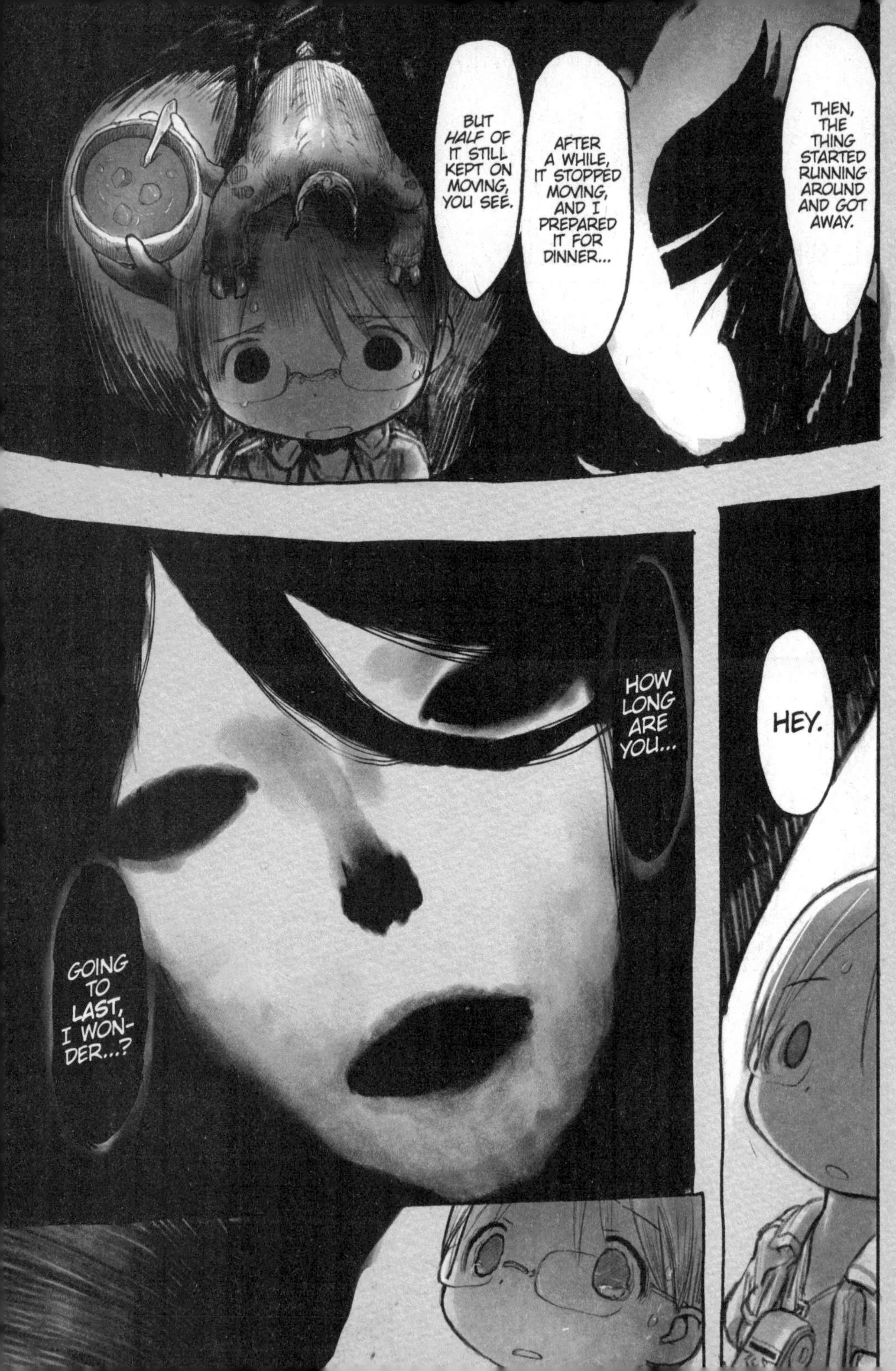
THEN, THE THING STARTED RUNNING AROUND AND GOT AWAY.
AFTER A WHILE, IT STOPPED MOVING, AND I PREPARED IT FOR DINNER...
BUT *HALF* OF IT STILL KEPT ON MOVING, YOU SEE.
HEY.
HOW LONG ARE YOU...
GOING TO LAST, I WONDER...?

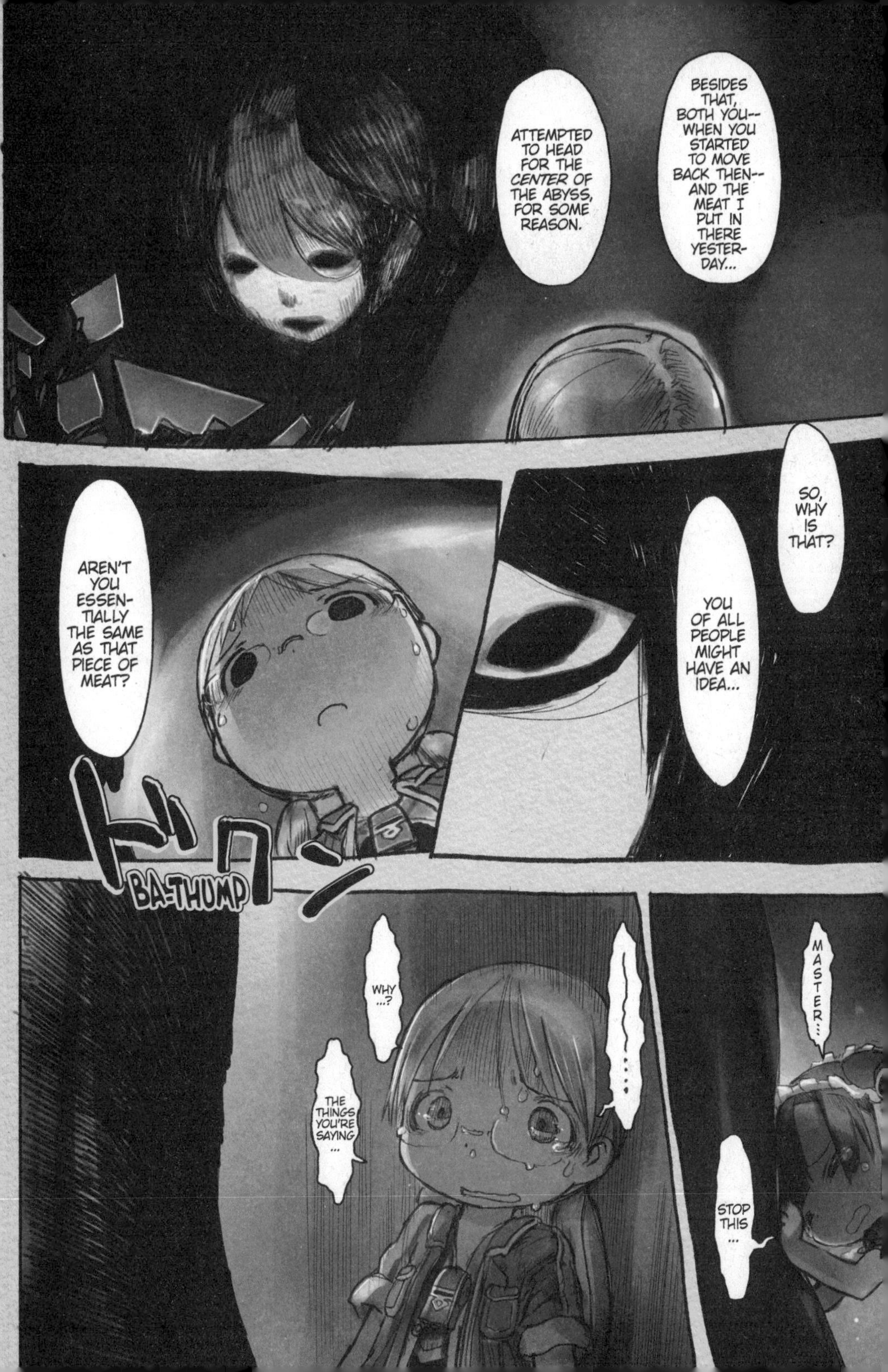
BESIDES THAT, BOTH YOU-- WHEN YOU STARTED TO MOVE BACK THEN-- AND THE MEAT I PUT IN THERE YESTER-DAY...
ATTEMPTED TO HEAD FOR THE CENTER OF THE ABYSS, FOR SOME REASON.
SO, WHY IS THAT?
YOU OF ALL PEOPLE MIGHT HAVE AN IDEA...
AREN'T YOU ESSEN-TIALLY THE SAME AS THAT PIECE OF MEAT?
BA-THUMP
MASTER...
STOP THIS...
......
WHY...?
THE THINGS YOU'RE SAYING...

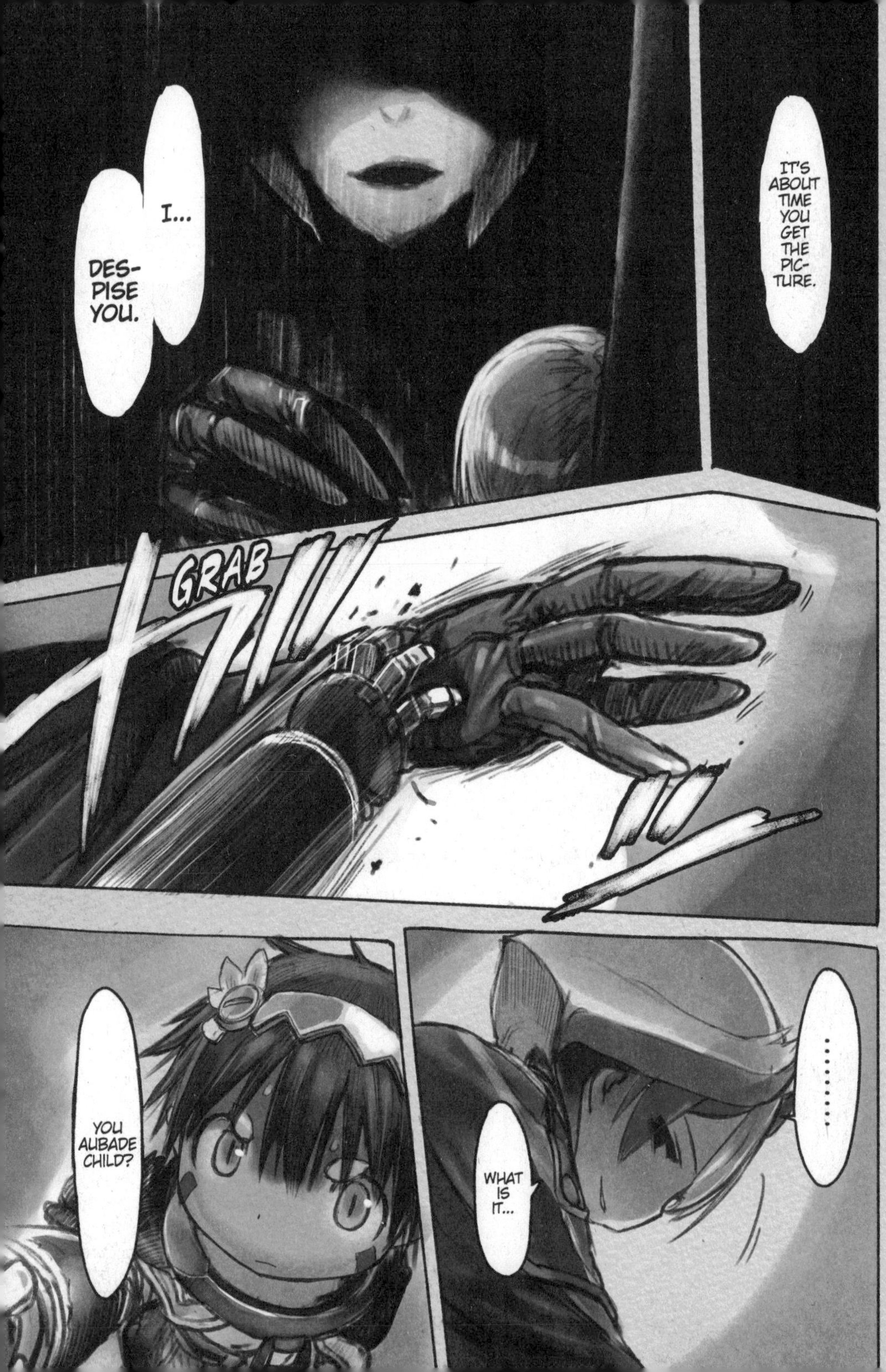

IT'S ABOUT TIME YOU GET THE PICTURE.
I...
DESPISE YOU.
GRAB
......
WHAT IS IT...
YOU AUBADE CHILD?

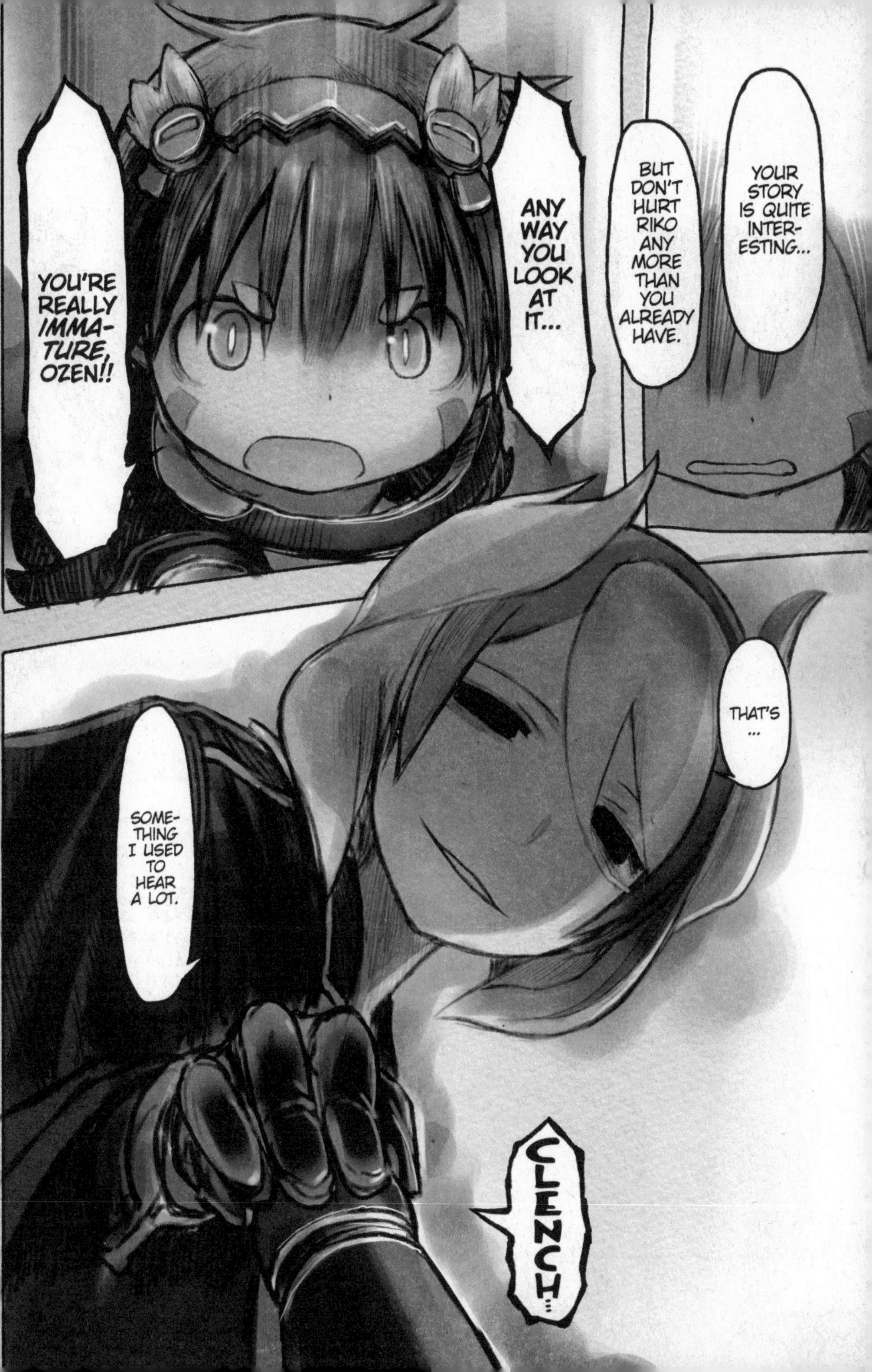
YOUR STORY IS QUITE INTERESTING...
BUT DON'T HURT RIKO ANY MORE THAN YOU ALREADY HAVE.
ANY WAY YOU LOOK AT IT...
YOU'RE REALLY *IMMATURE*, OZEN!!
THAT'S ...
SOMETHING I USED TO HEAR A LOT.
CLENCH...

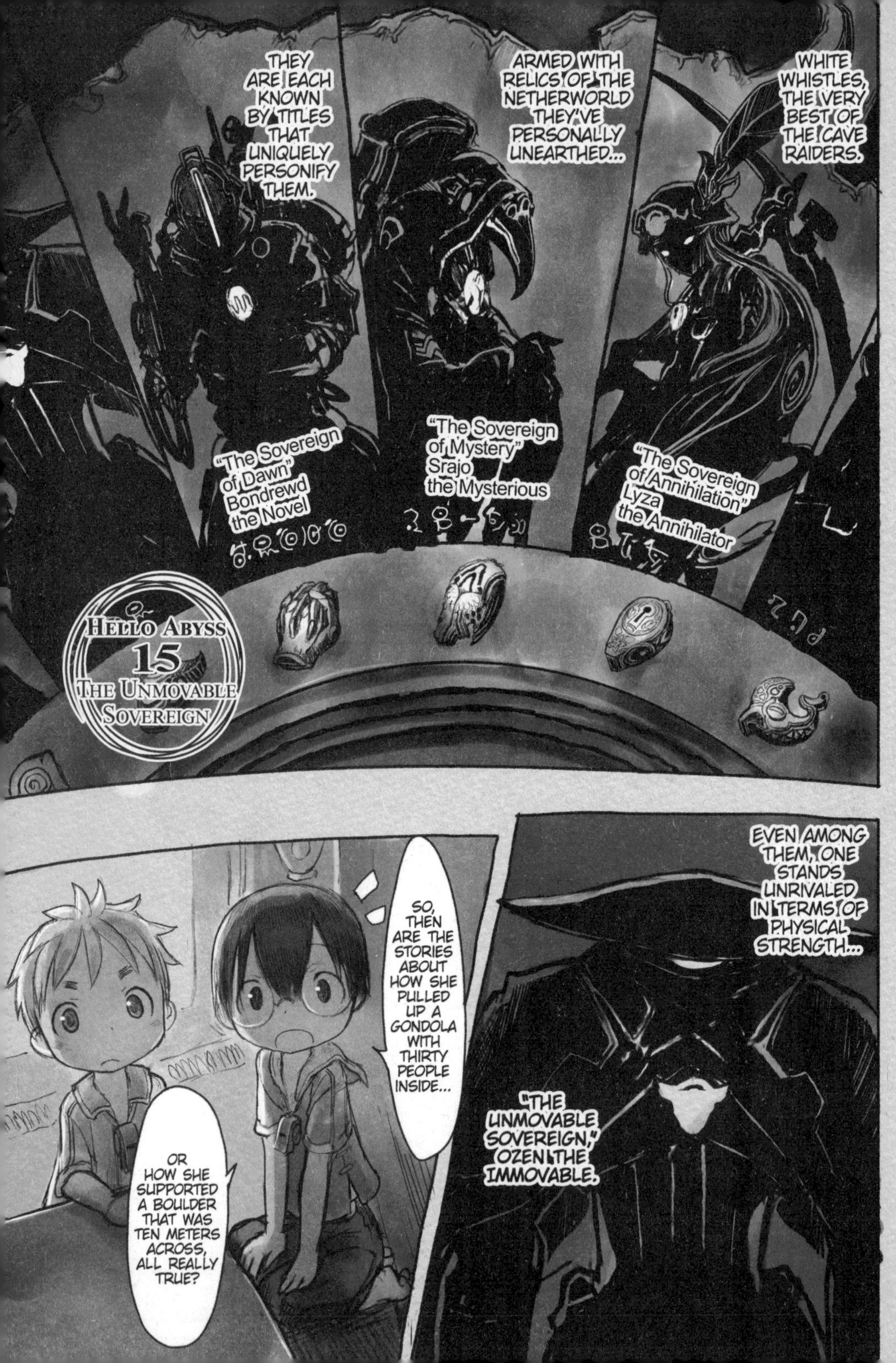
WHITE WHISTLES, THE VERY BEST OF THE CAVE RAIDERS.
ARMED WITH RELICS OF THE NETHERWORLD THEY'VE PERSONALLY UNEARTHED...
THEY ARE EACH KNOWN BY TITLES THAT UNIQUELY PERSONIFY THEM.
"The Sovereign of Annihilation" Lyza the Annihilator
"The Sovereign of Mystery" Srajo the Mysterious
"The Sovereign of Dawn" Bondrewd the Novel
Hello Abyss 15 The Unmovable Sovereign
EVEN AMONG THEM, ONE STANDS UNRIVALED IN TERMS OF PHYSICAL STRENGTH...
"THE UNMOVABLE SOVEREIGN," OZEN THE IMMOVABLE.
SO, THEN ARE THE STORIES ABOUT HOW SHE PULLED UP A GONDOLA WITH THIRTY PEOPLE INSIDE...
OR HOW SHE SUPPORTED A BOULDER THAT WAS TEN METERS ACROSS, ALL REALLY TRUE?

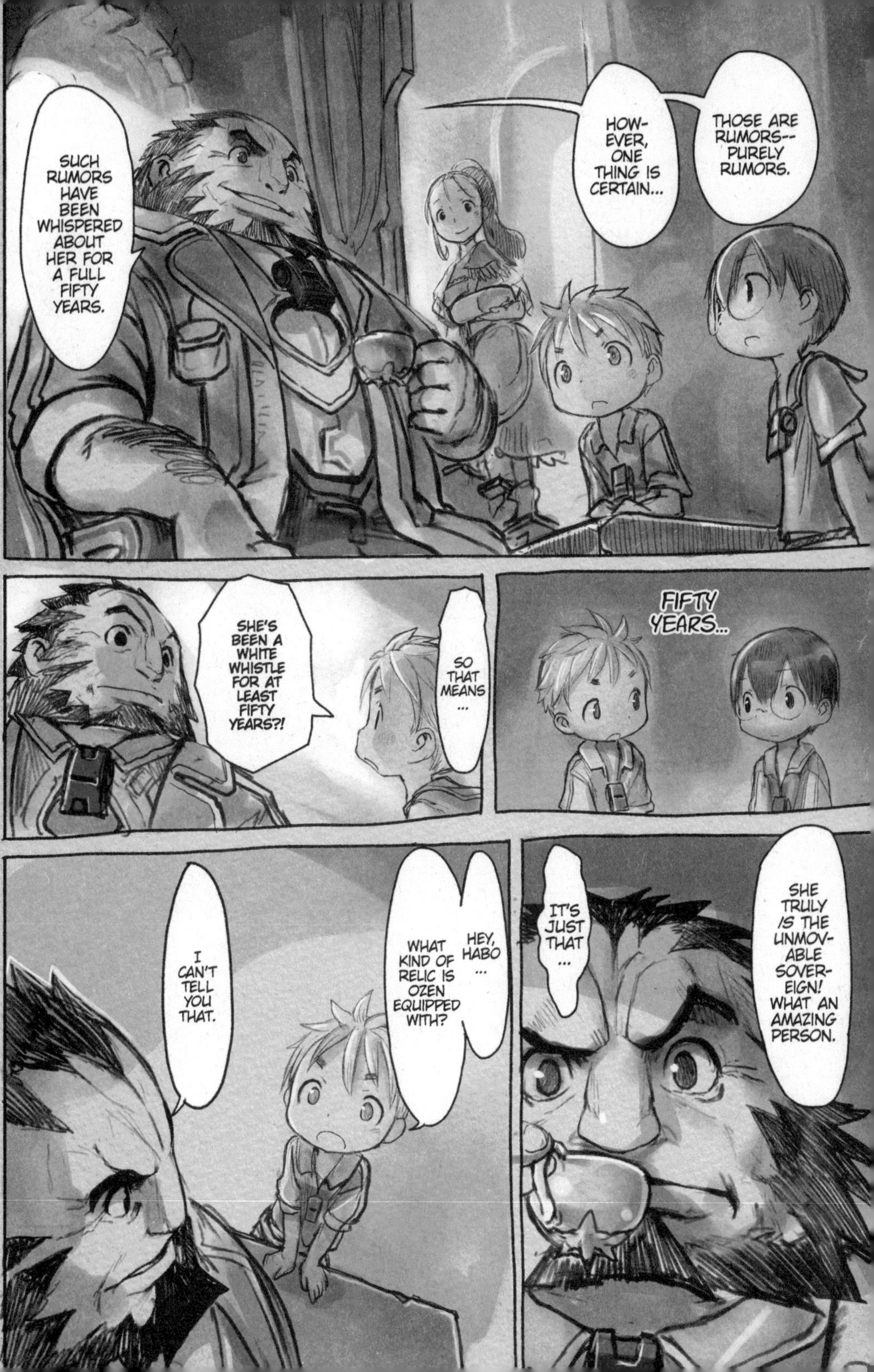
THOSE ARE RUMORS-- PURELY RUMORS.
HOW-EVER, ONE THING IS CERTAIN...
SUCH RUMORS HAVE BEEN WHISPERED ABOUT HER FOR A FULL FIFTY YEARS.
FIFTY YEARS...
SO THAT MEANS ...
SHE'S BEEN A WHITE WHISTLE FOR AT LEAST FIFTY YEARS?!
SHE TRULY IS THE UNMOVABLE SOVEREIGN! WHAT AN AMAZING PERSON.
IT'S JUST THAT ...
HEY, HABO ...
WHAT KIND OF RELIC IS OZEN EQUIPPED WITH?
I CAN'T TELL YOU THAT.

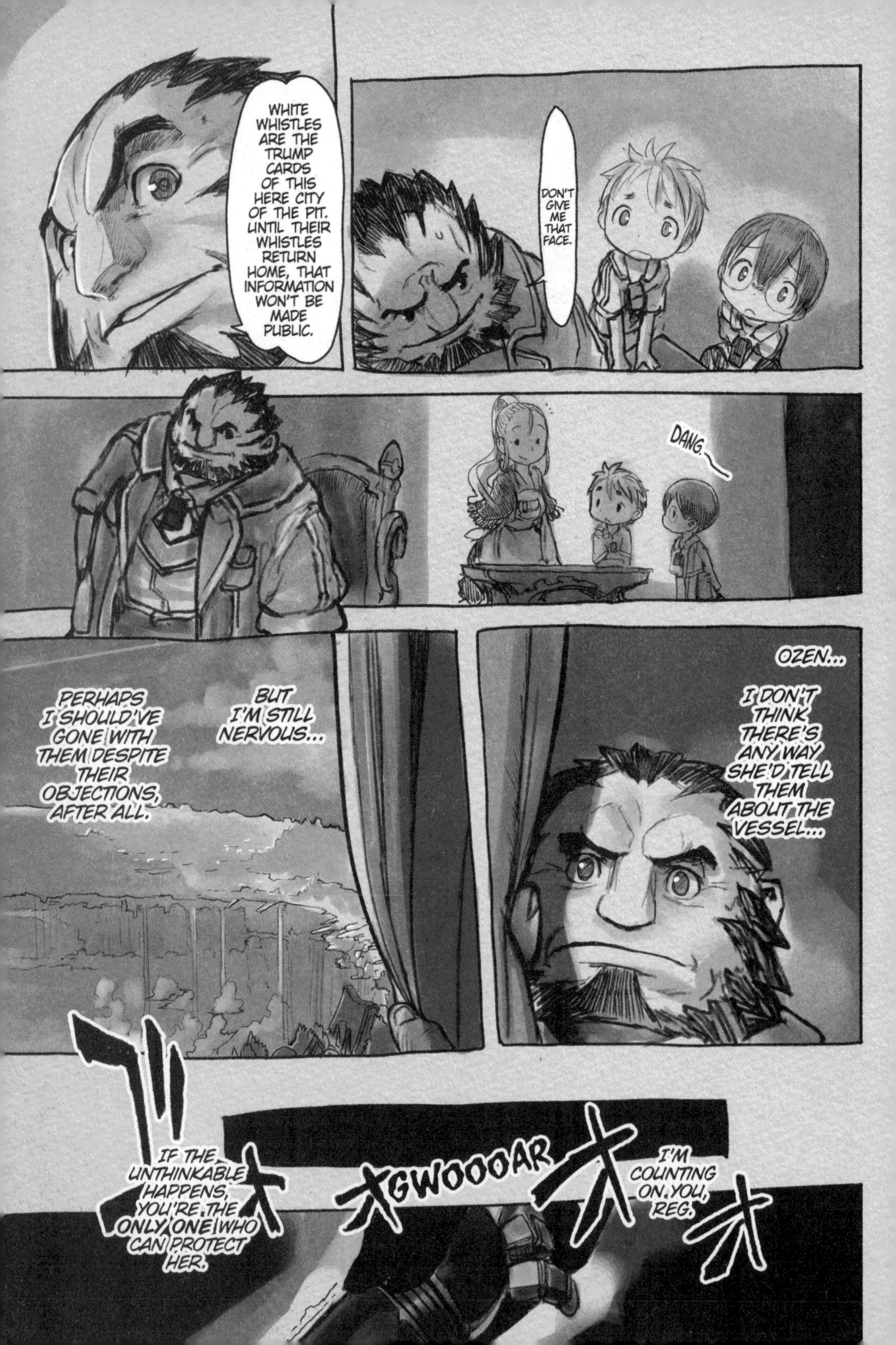
DON'T GIVE ME THAT FACE.
WHITE WHISTLES ARE THE TRUMP CARDS OF THIS HERE CITY OF THE PIT. UNTIL THEIR WHISTLES RETURN HOME, THAT INFORMATION WON'T BE MADE PUBLIC.
DANG.
OZEN...
I DON'T THINK THERE'S ANY WAY SHE'D TELL THEM ABOUT THE VESSEL...
BUT I'M STILL NERVOUS...
PERHAPS I SHOULD'VE GONE WITH THEM DESPITE THEIR OBJECTIONS, AFTER ALL.
I'M COUNTING ON YOU, REG.
GWOOOAR
IF THE UNTHINKABLE HAPPENS, YOU'RE THE ONLY ONE WHO CAN PROTECT HER.

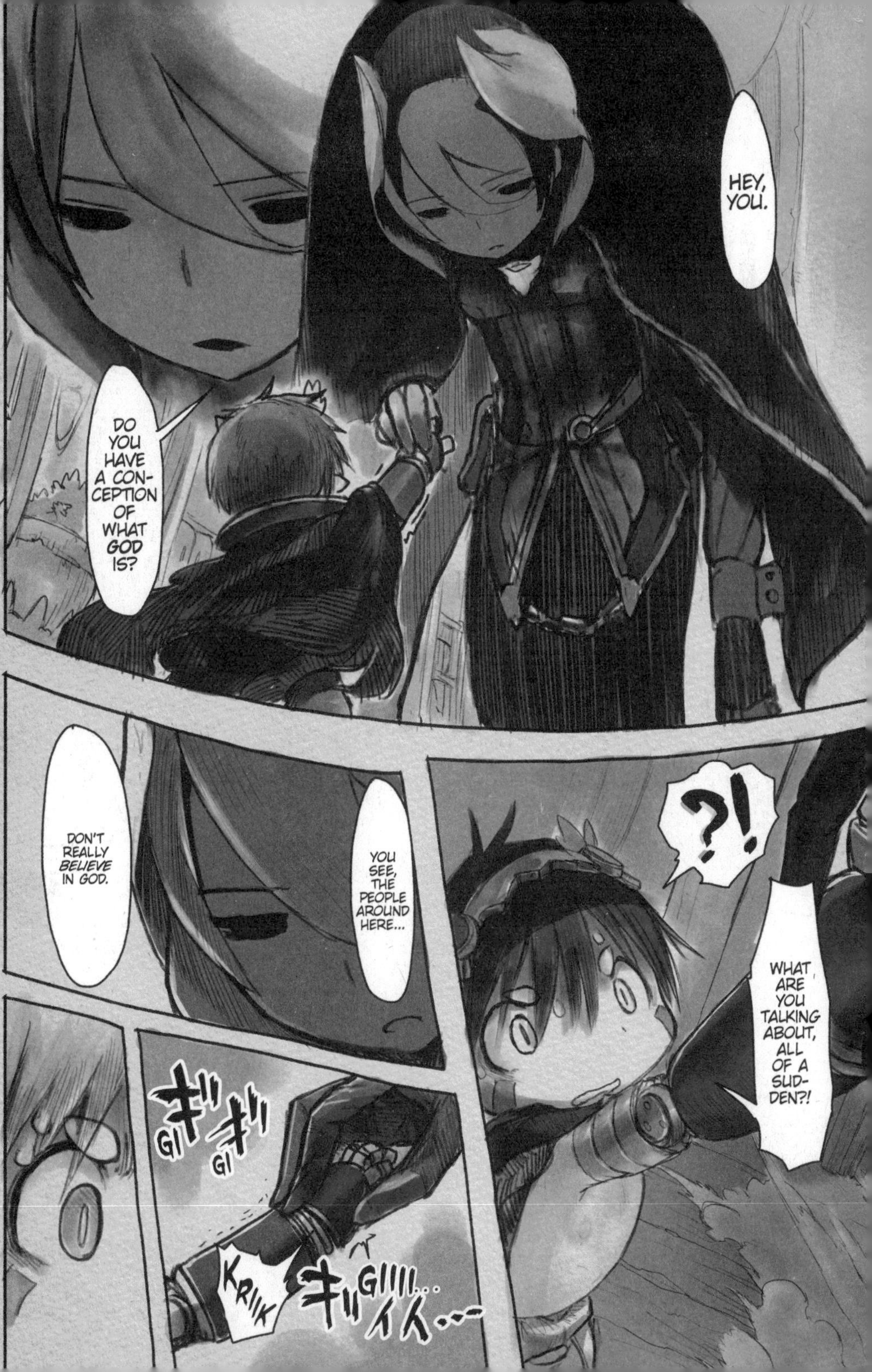
HEY, YOU.
DO YOU HAVE A CONCEPTION OF WHAT GOD IS?
?!
WHAT ARE YOU TALKING ABOUT, ALL OF A SUDDEN?!
YOU SEE, THE PEOPLE AROUND HERE...
DON'T REALLY BELIEVE IN GOD.
GI GI
KRIIK
GIIIII...

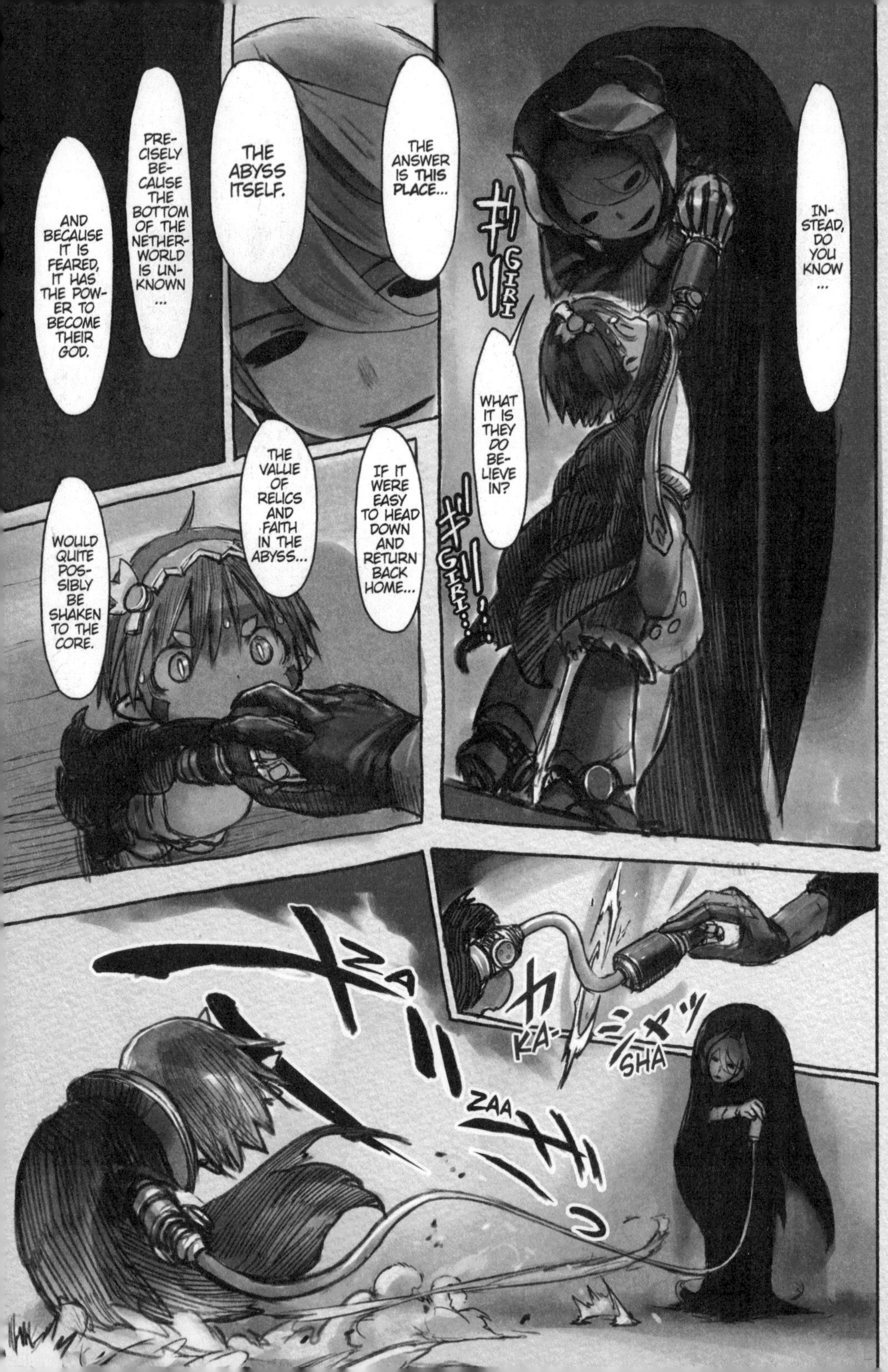
INSTEAD, DO YOU KNOW...
GIRI
WHAT IT IS THEY *DO* BELIEVE IN?
GIRI...
THE ANSWER IS THIS PLACE...
THE ABYSS ITSELF.
PRECISELY BECAUSE THE BOTTOM OF THE NETHERWORLD IS UNKNOWN...
AND BECAUSE IT IS FEARED, IT HAS THE POWER TO BECOME THEIR GOD.
IF IT WERE EASY TO HEAD DOWN AND RETURN BACK HOME...
THE VALUE OF RELICS AND FAITH IN THE ABYSS...
WOULD QUITE POSSIBLY BE SHAKEN TO THE CORE.
KA-SHA
ZAA
ZAA

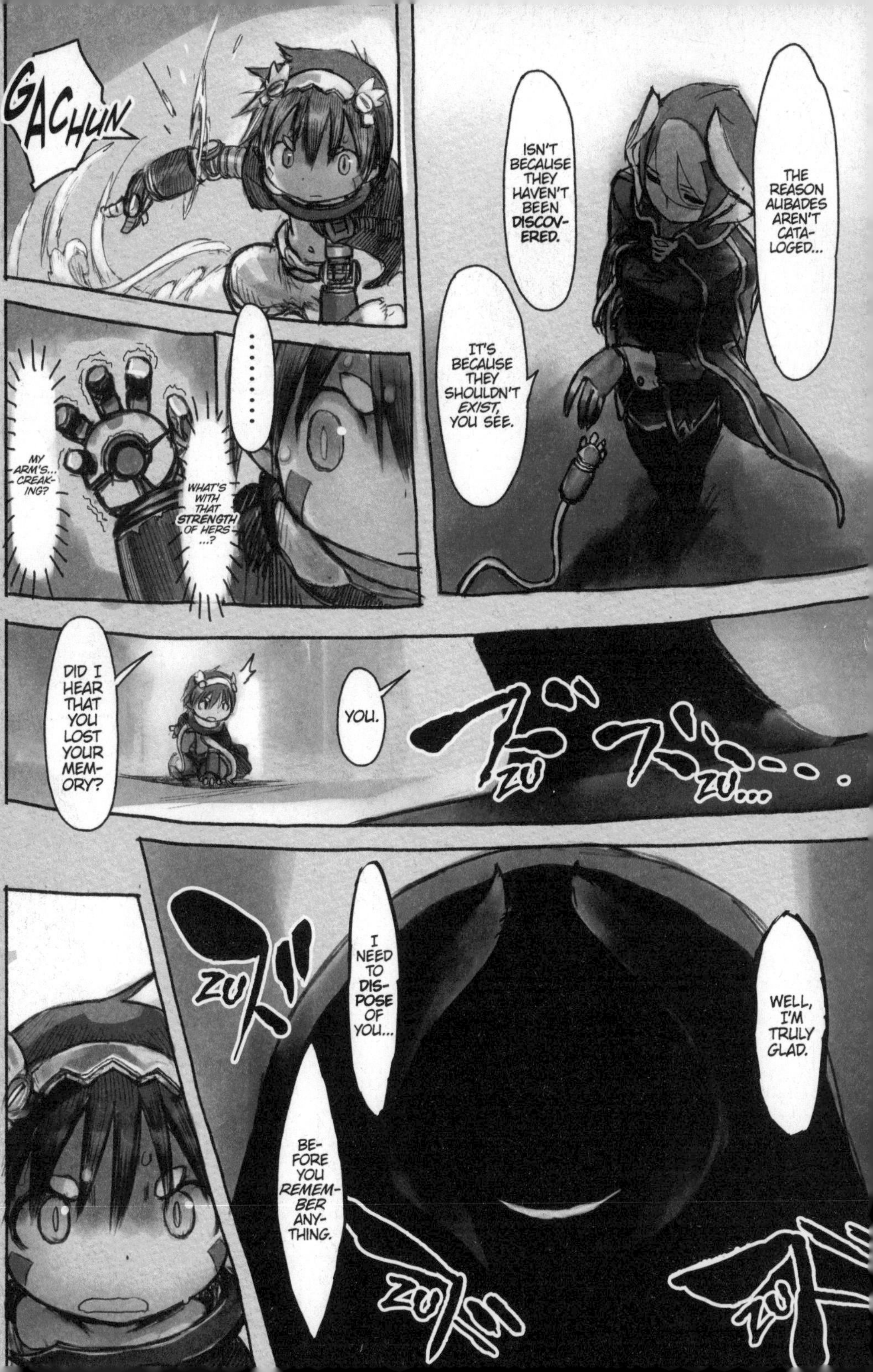
THE REASON AUBADES AREN'T CATALOGED...
ISN'T BECAUSE THEY HAVEN'T BEEN DISCOVERED.
IT'S BECAUSE THEY SHOULDN'T *EXIST*, YOU SEE.
GACHUN
......
WHAT'S WITH THAT STRENGTH OF HERS...?
MY ARM'S... CREAKING?
ZU ZU...
YOU.
DID I HEAR THAT YOU LOST YOUR MEMORY?
WELL, I'M TRULY GLAD.
I NEED TO DISPOSE OF YOU...
BEFORE YOU REMEMBER ANYTHING.
ZU
ZU
ZU

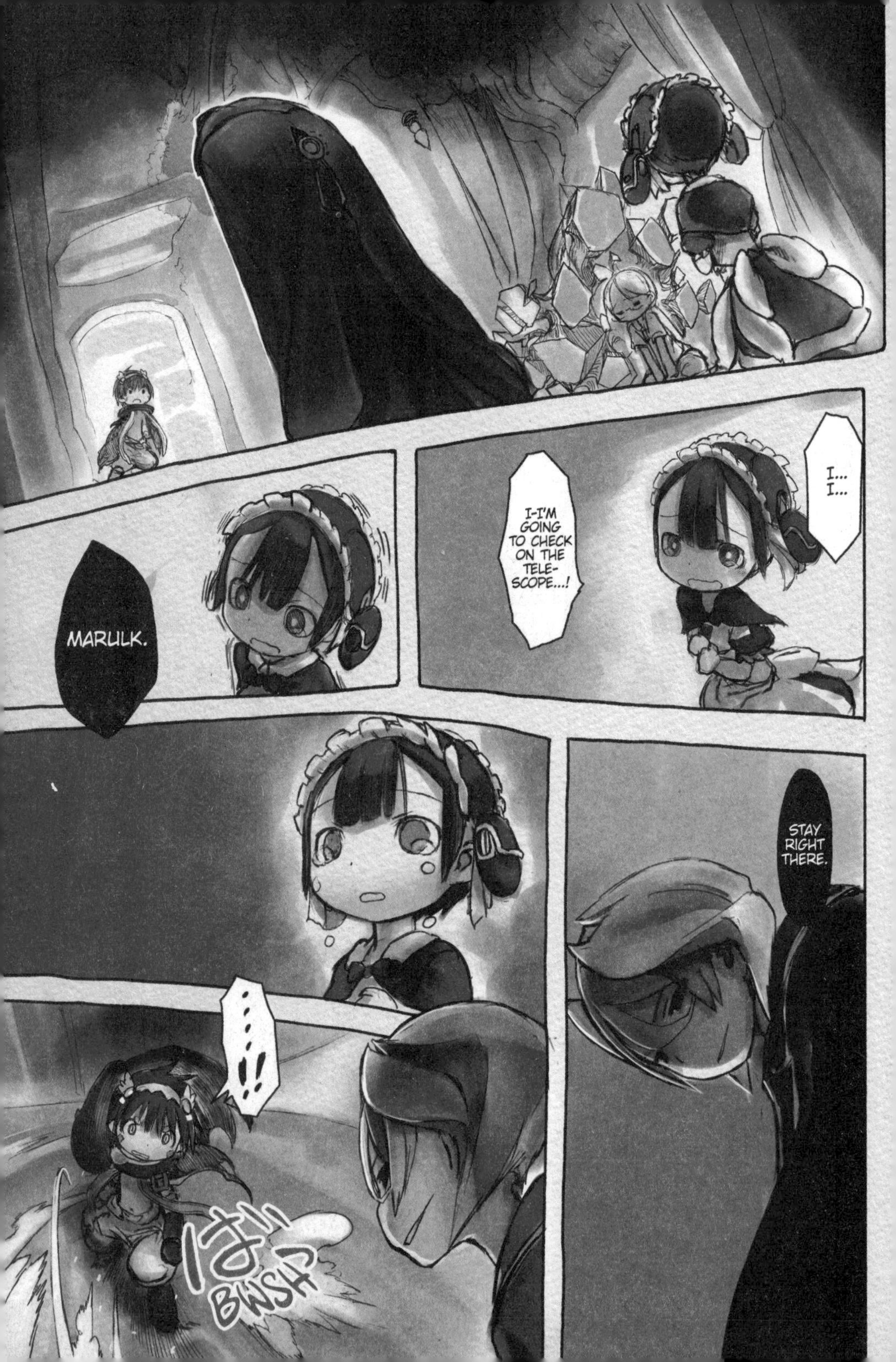

I... I...
I-I'M GOING TO CHECK ON THE TELE-SCOPE...!
MARULK.
STAY RIGHT THERE.
......!!
BWSH

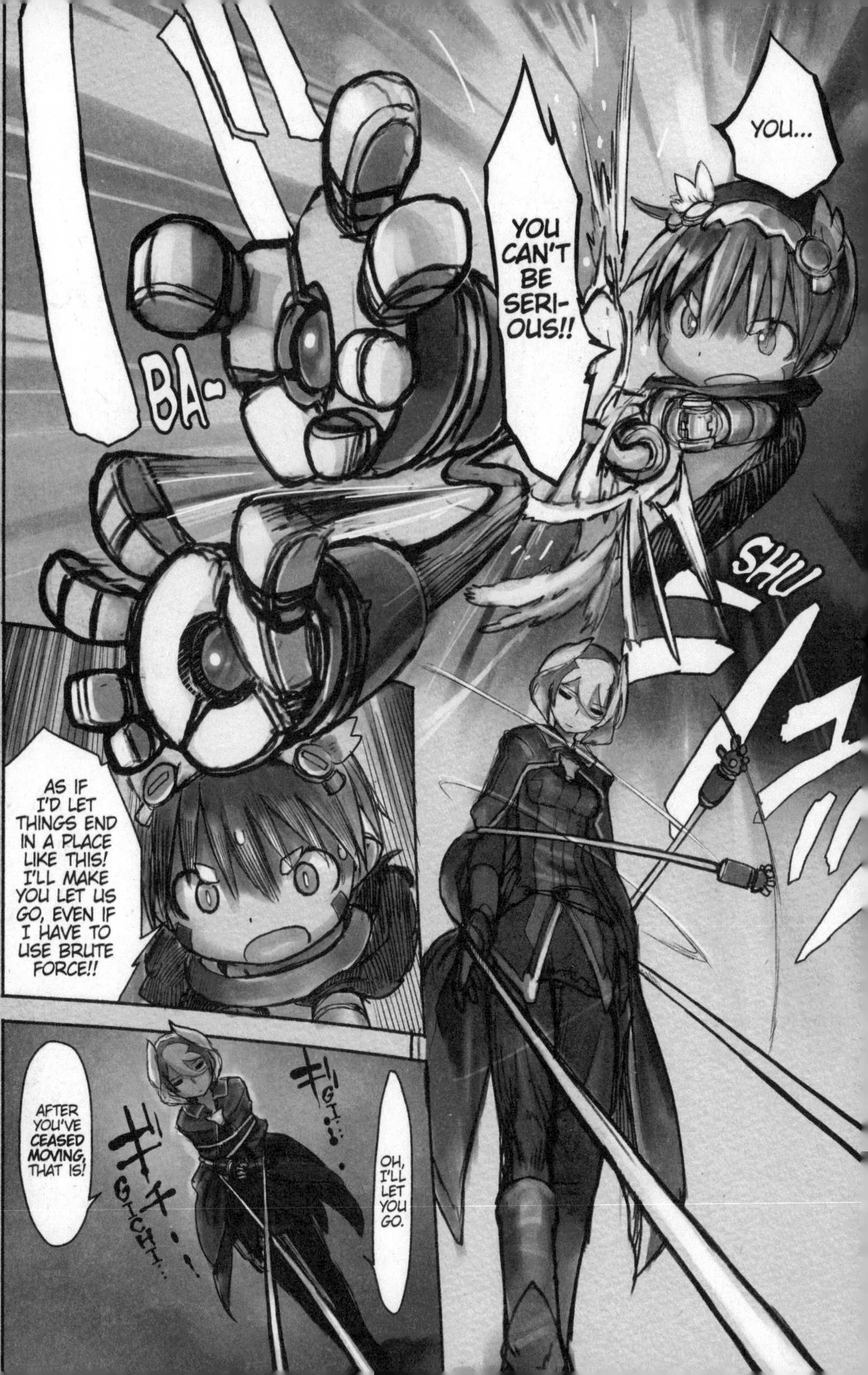

YOU...
YOU CAN'T BE SERI-OUS!!
BA-
SHU
AS IF I'D LET THINGS END IN A PLACE LIKE THIS! I'LL MAKE YOU LET US GO, EVEN IF I HAVE TO USE BRUTE FORCE!!
OH, I'LL LET YOU GO.
GI...
AFTER YOU'VE CEASED MOVING, THAT IS!
GICHI...

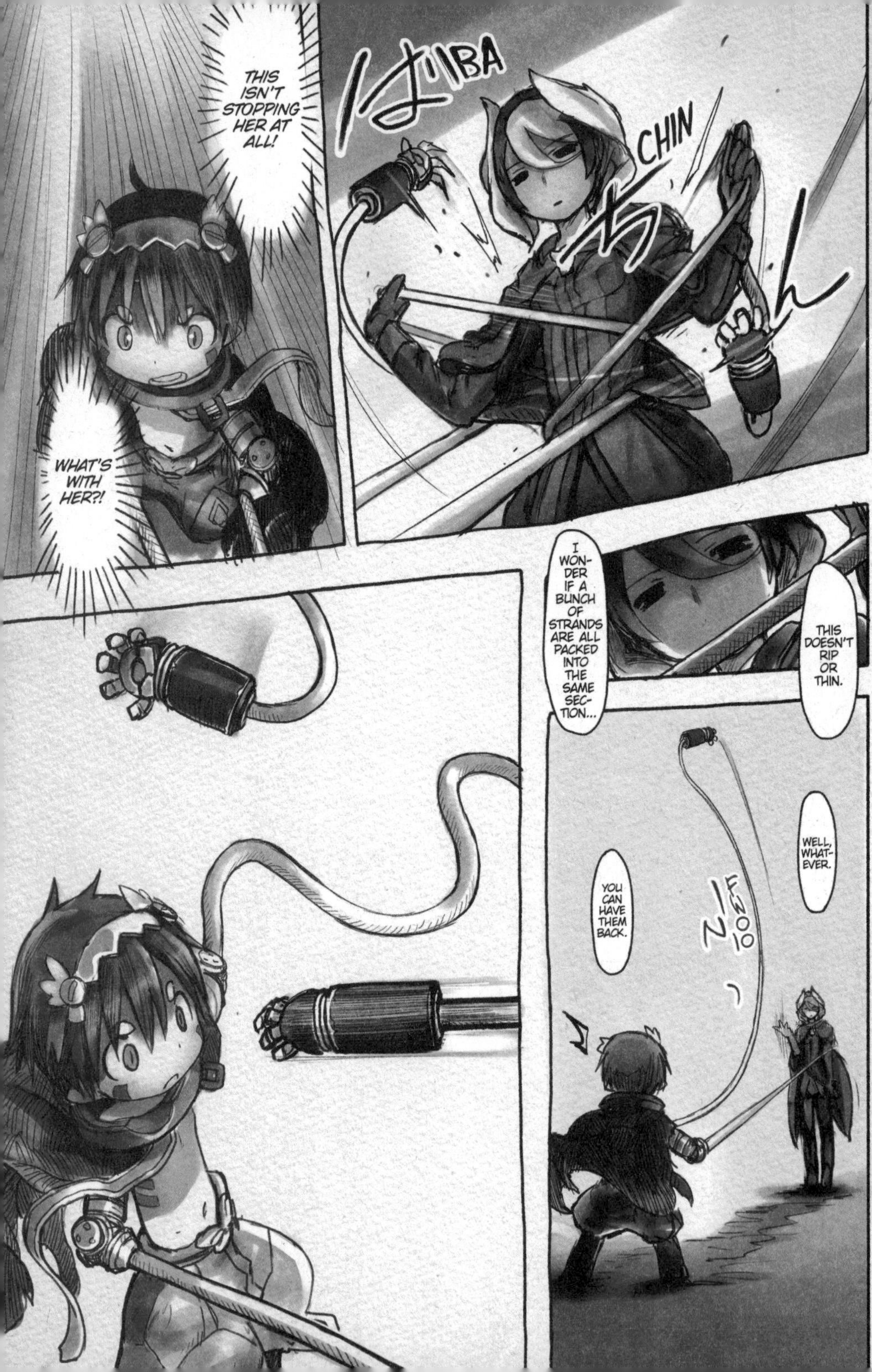
IBA
CHIN
THIS ISN'T STOPPING HER AT ALL!
WHAT'S WITH HER?!
THIS DOESN'T RIP OR THIN.
I WONDER IF A BUNCH OF STRANDS ARE ALL PACKED INTO THE SAME SECTION...
WELL, WHATEVER.
YOU CAN HAVE THEM BACK.
FWOO

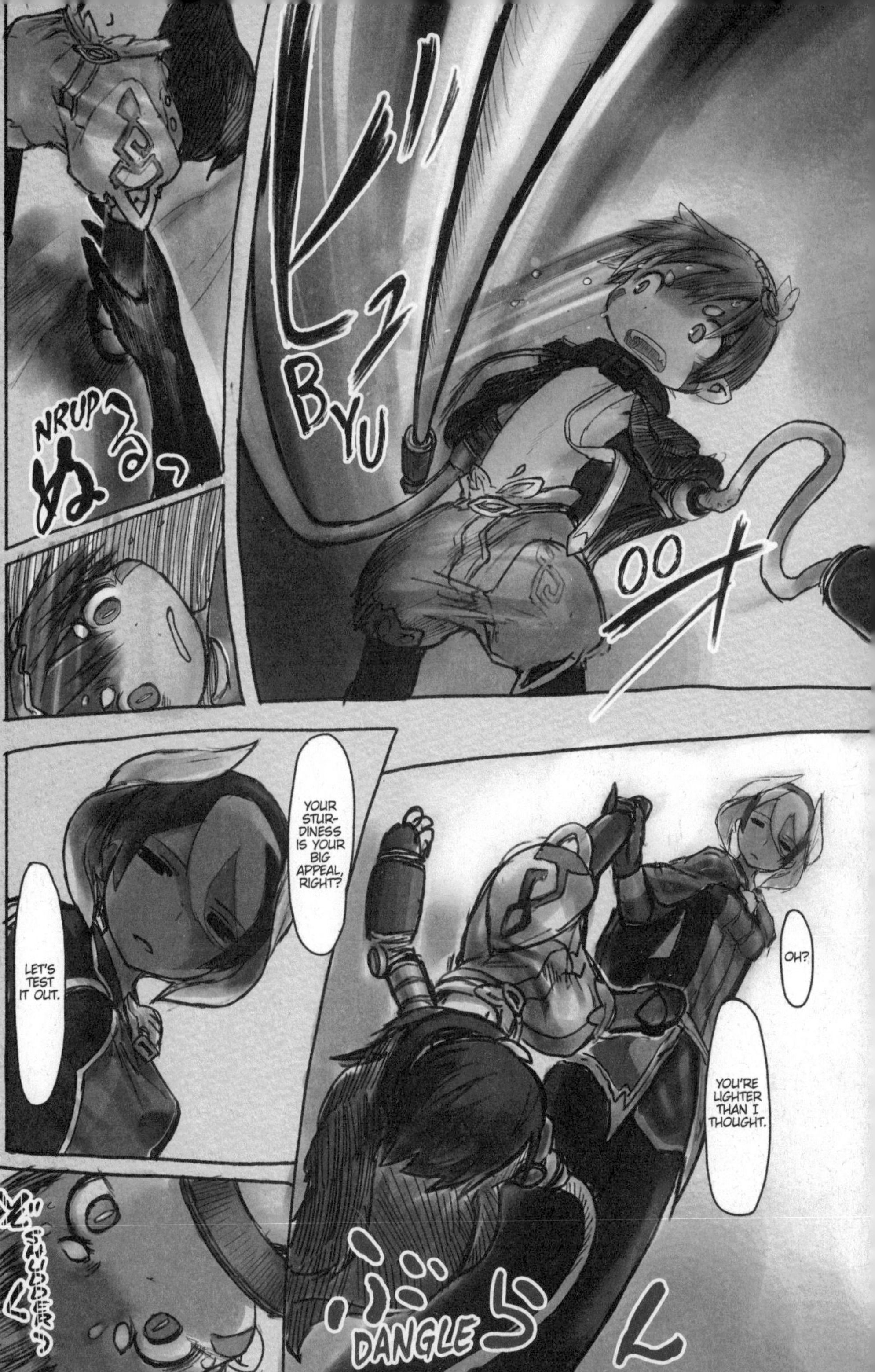
BYU
OOF
NRUP
OH?
YOU'RE LIGHTER THAN I THOUGHT.
DANGLE
YOUR STURDINESS IS YOUR BIG APPEAL, RIGHT?
LET'S TEST IT OUT.
SHUDDER

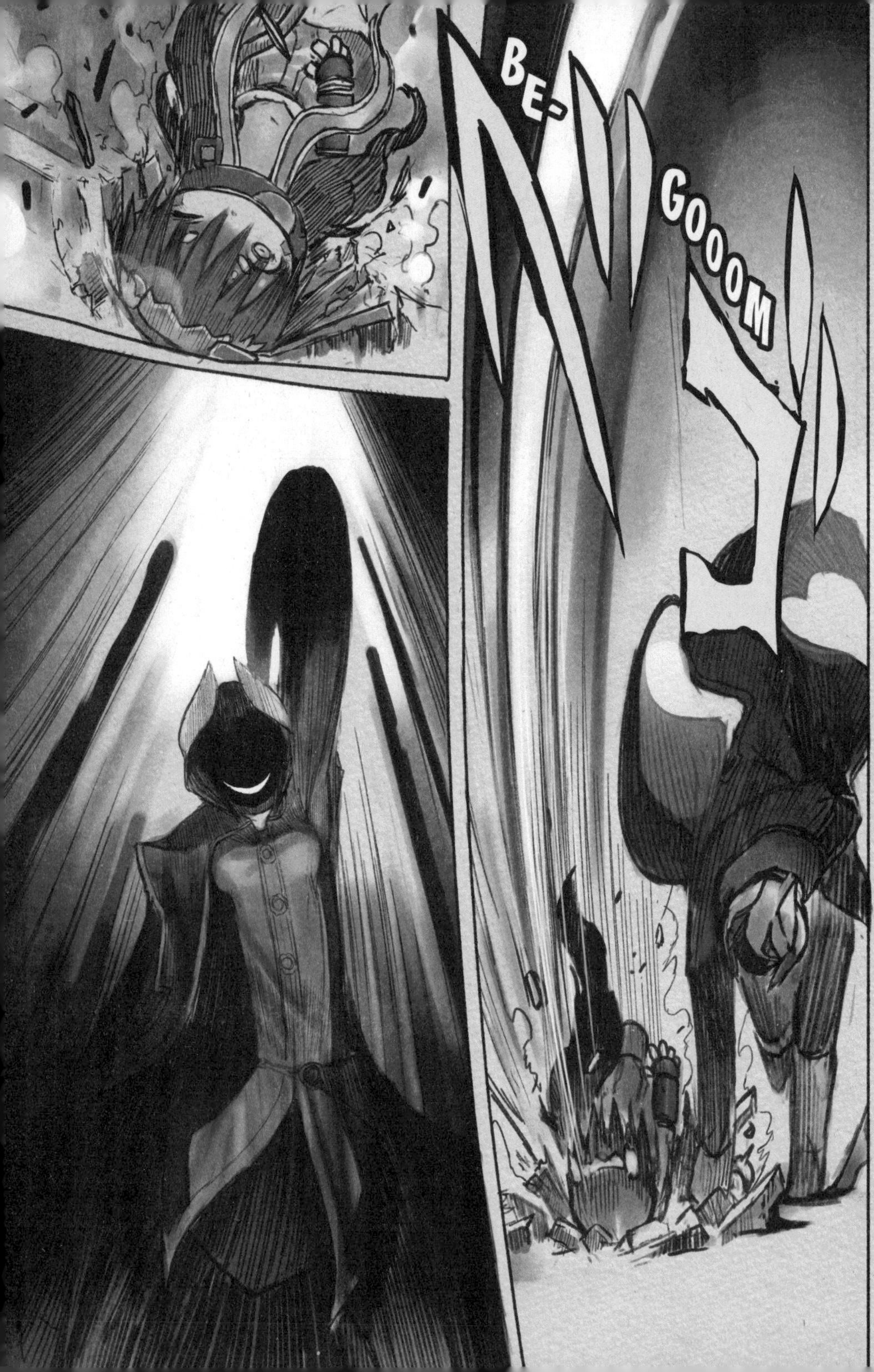
BE-GOOOM

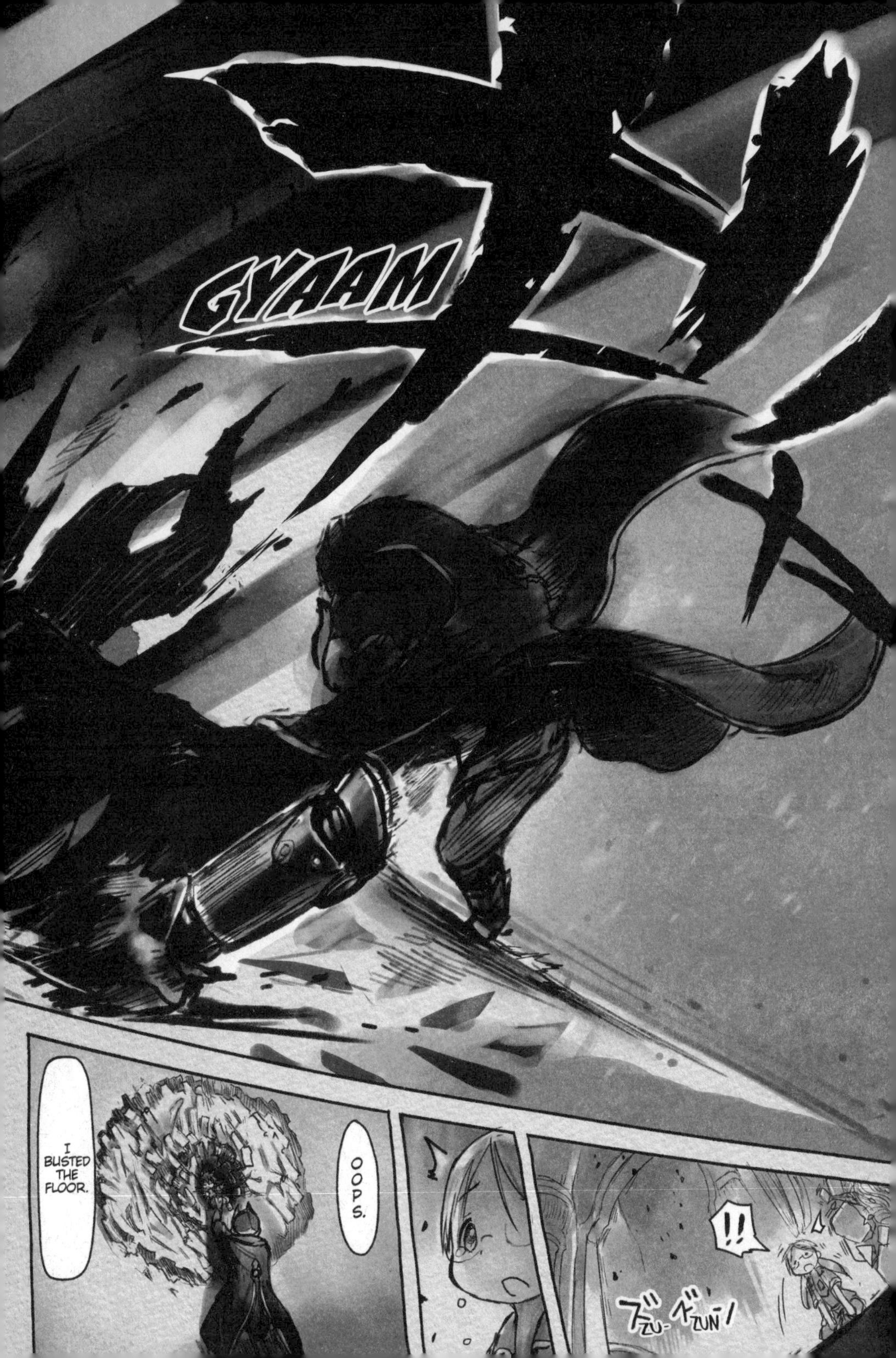
GYAAM
!!
ZU- ZUN!
OOPS.
I BUSTED THE FLOOR.

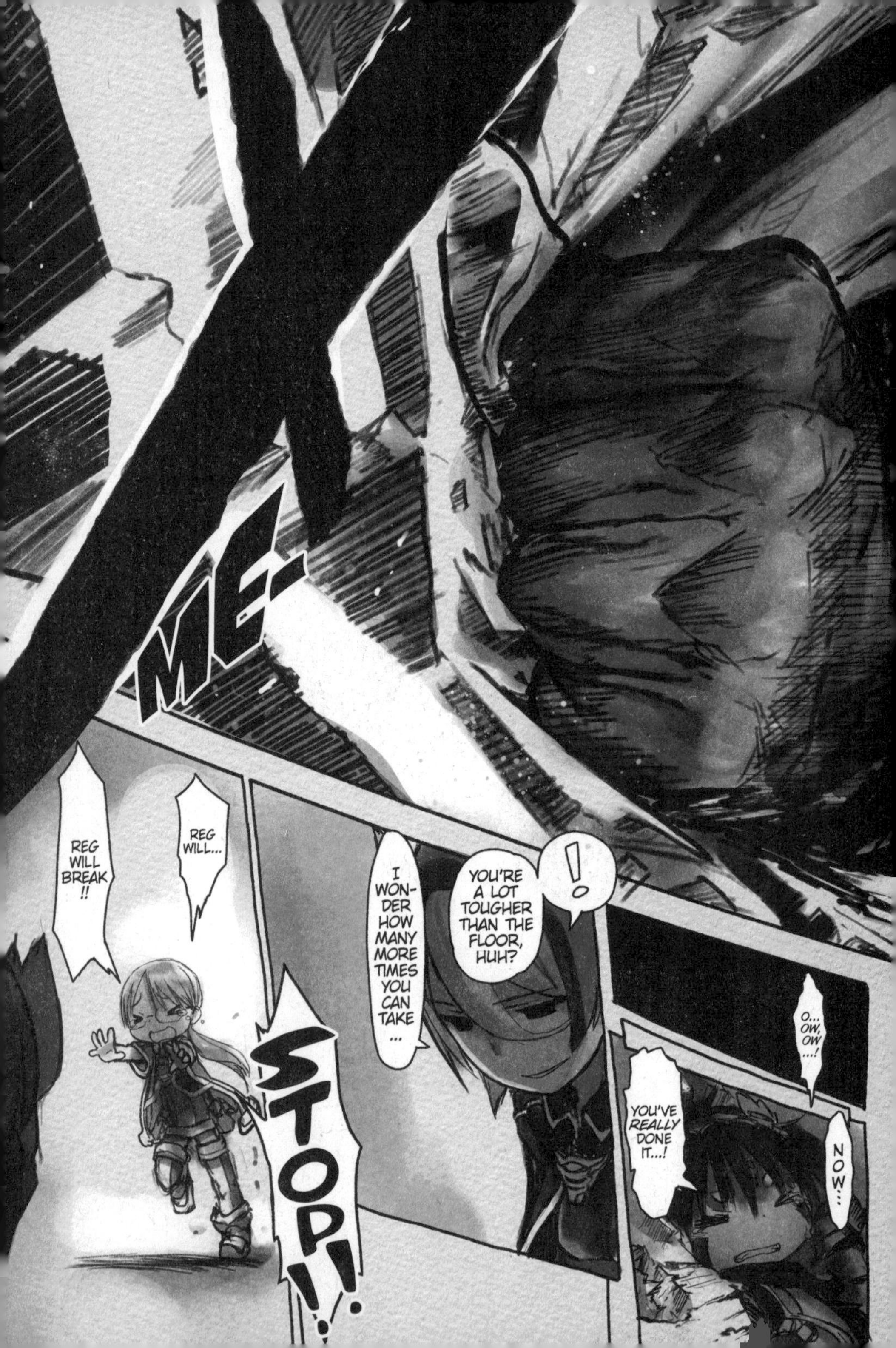
ME-
O... OW, OW...!
NOW...
YOU'VE REALLY DONE IT...!
!
YOU'RE A LOT TOUGHER THAN THE FLOOR, HUH?
I WONDER HOW MANY MORE TIMES YOU CAN TAKE...
REG WILL...
REG WILL BREAK!!
STOP!!

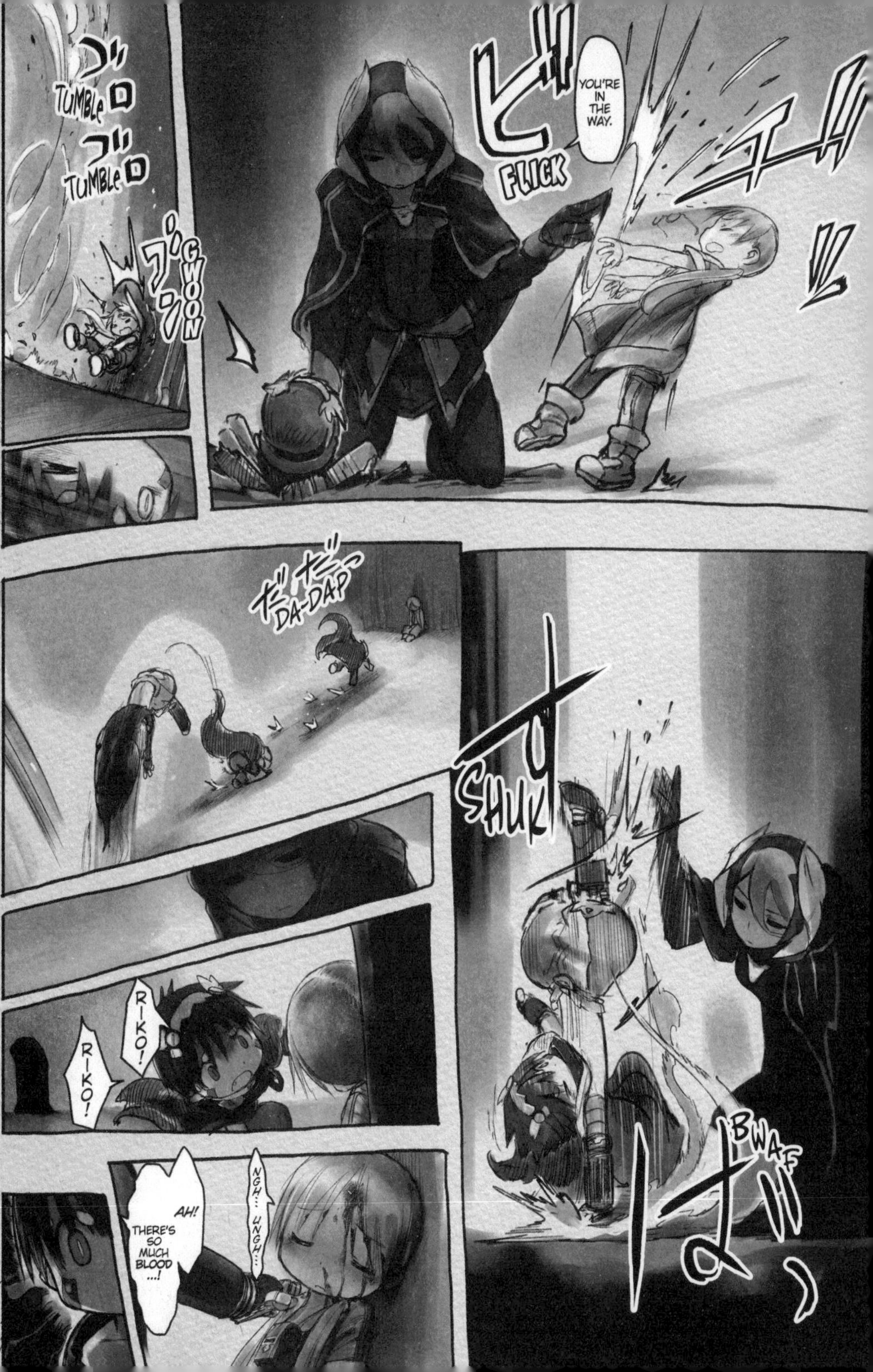
FLICK
YOU'RE IN THE WAY.
TUMBLE
TUMBLE
GWOON
SHUK
BWAF
DA-DAP
RIKO!
RIKO!
NGH... UNGH...
AH! THERE'S SO MUCH BLOOD ...!

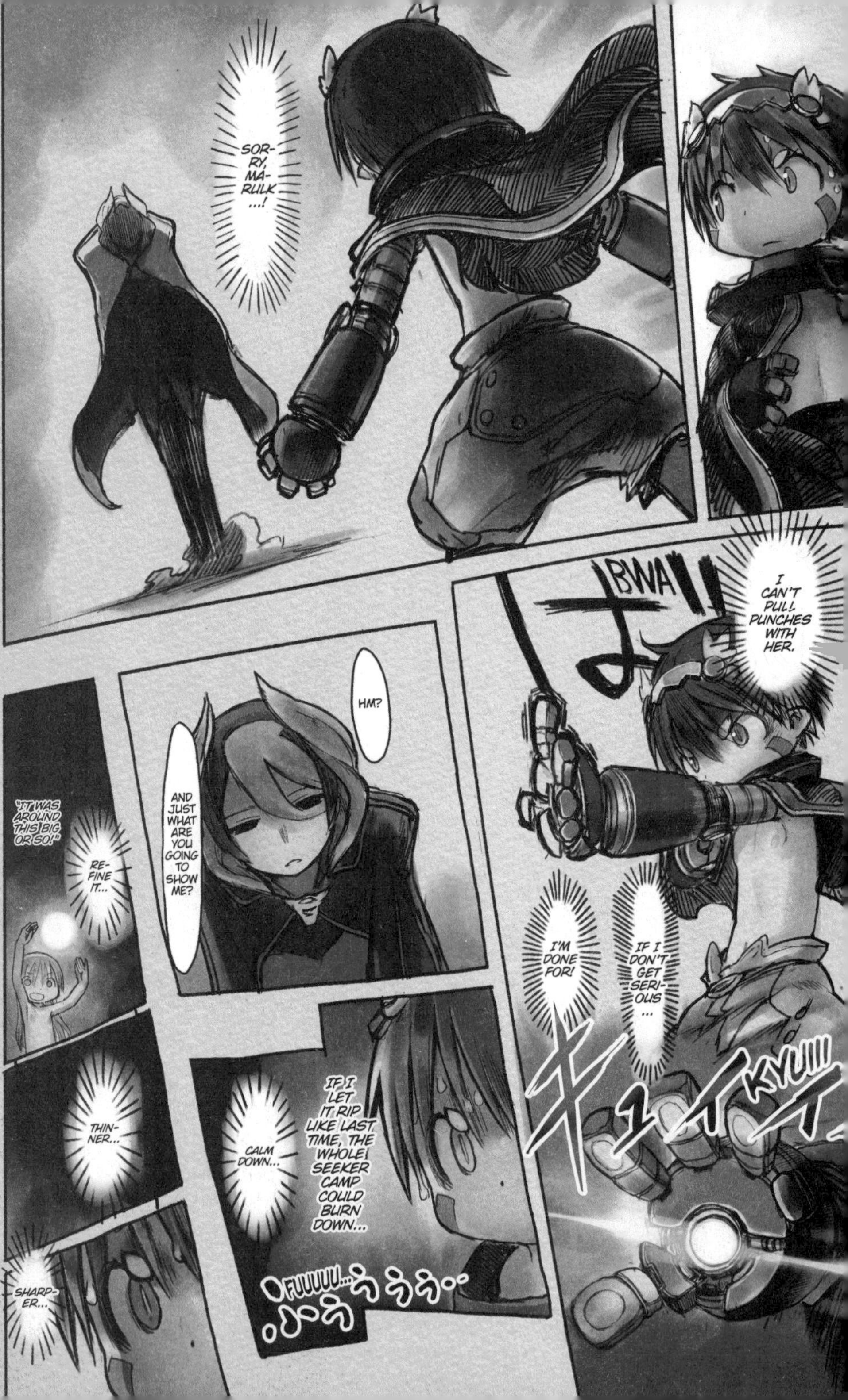

SORRY, MARULK...!
BWA
I CAN'T PULL PUNCHES WITH HER.
IF I DON'T GET SERIOUS...
I'M DONE FOR!
KYUIII
HM?
AND JUST WHAT ARE YOU GOING TO SHOW ME?
IF I LET IT RIP LIKE LAST TIME, THE WHOLE SEEKER CAMP COULD BURN DOWN...
CALM DOWN...
FUUUUU...
"IT WAS AROUND THIS BIG OR SO!"
REFINE IT...
THINNER...
SHARPER...

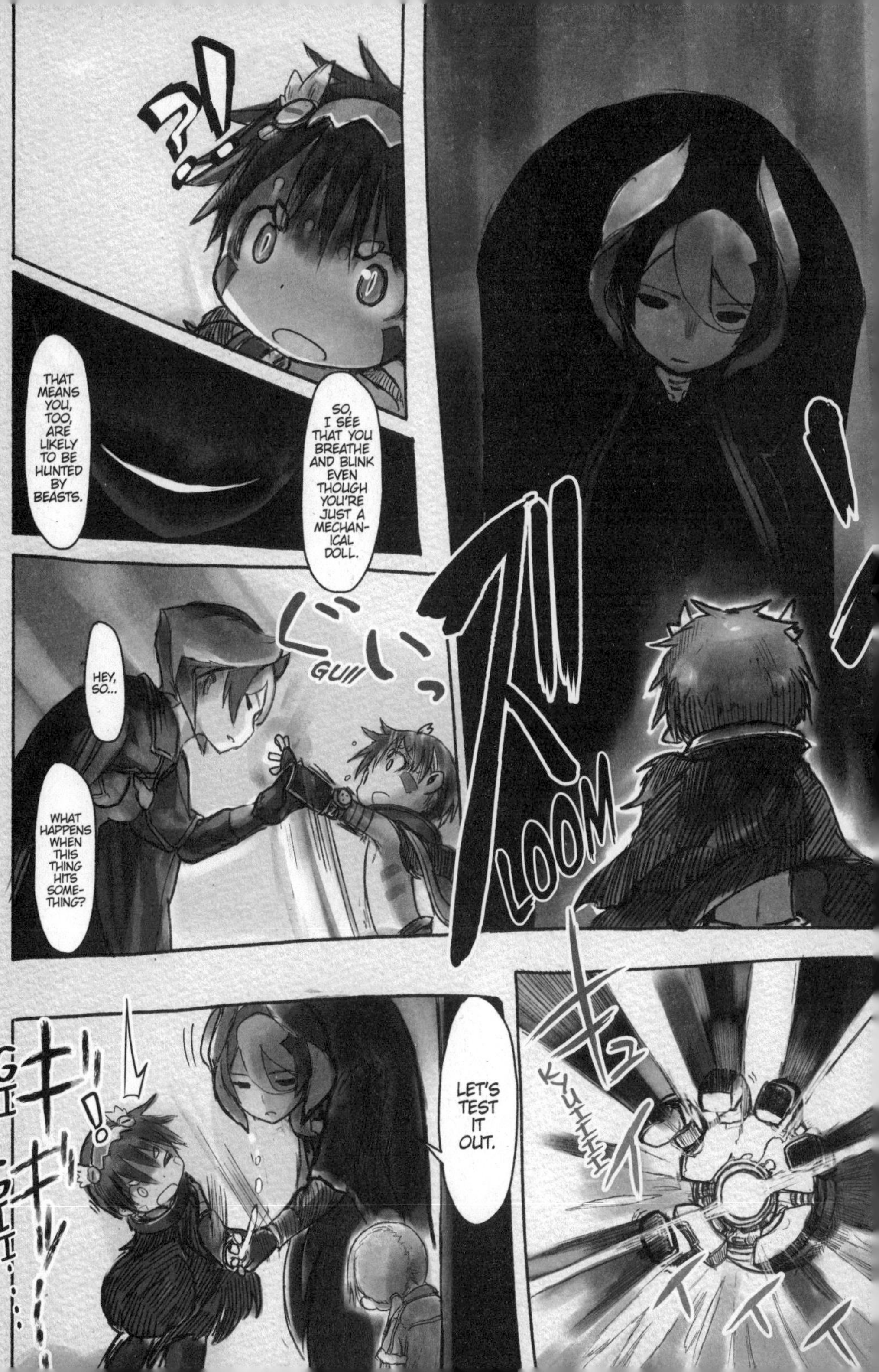

LOOM
?!
SO, I SEE THAT YOU BREATHE AND BLINK EVEN THOUGH YOU'RE JUST A MECHANICAL DOLL.
THAT MEANS YOU, TOO, ARE LIKELY TO BE HUNTED BY BEASTS.
GUII
HEY, SO...
WHAT HAPPENS WHEN THIS THING HITS SOMETHING?
KYUIIII
LET'S TEST IT OUT.
!
GI GII...

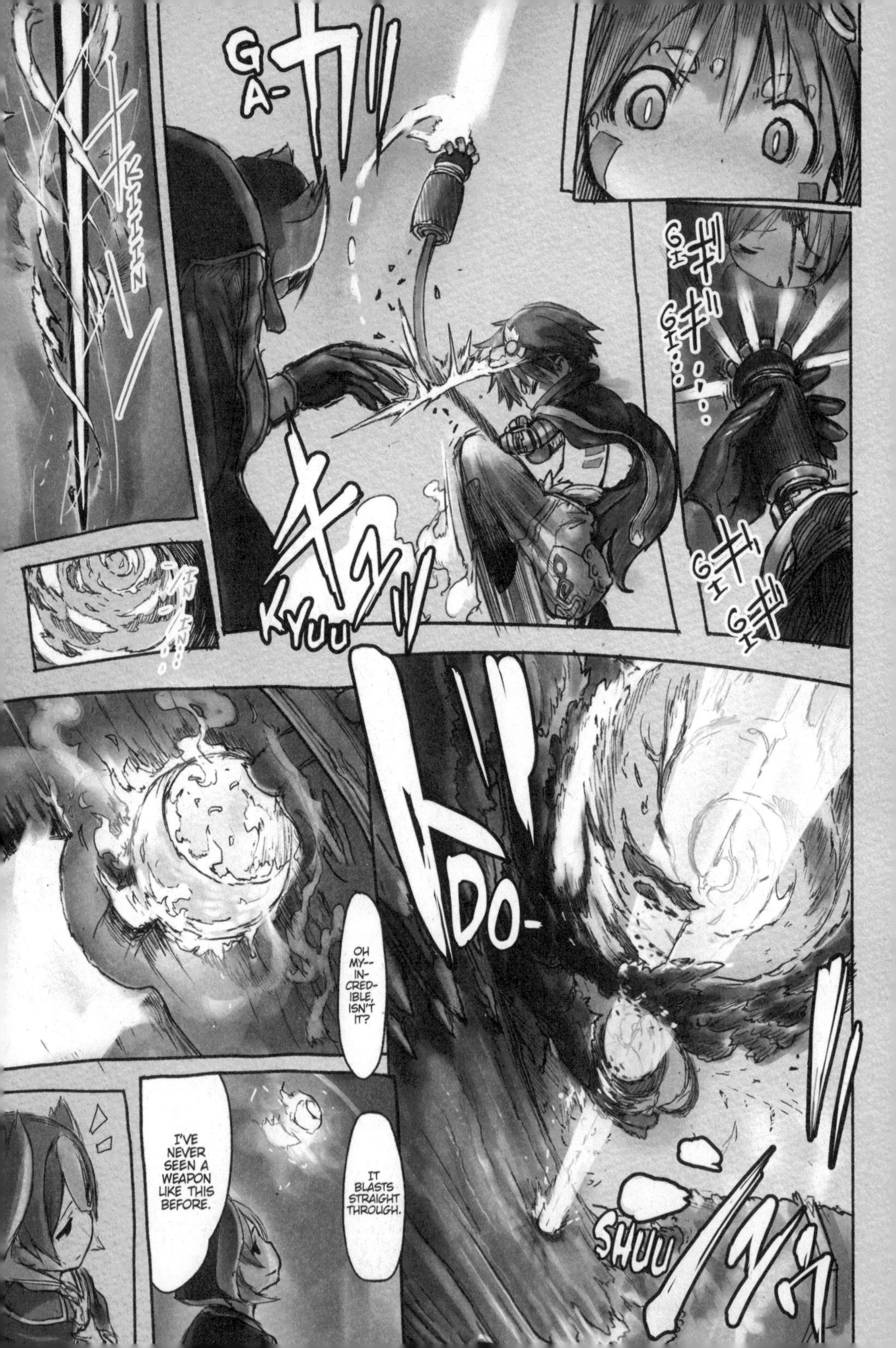
GI GI...
GI GI
GA-
KYUU
KIIIIN
IN IN...
DO-
OH MY-- INCREDIBLE, ISN'T IT?
SHUU
IT BLASTS STRAIGHT THROUGH.
I'VE NEVER SEEN A WEAPON LIKE THIS BEFORE.

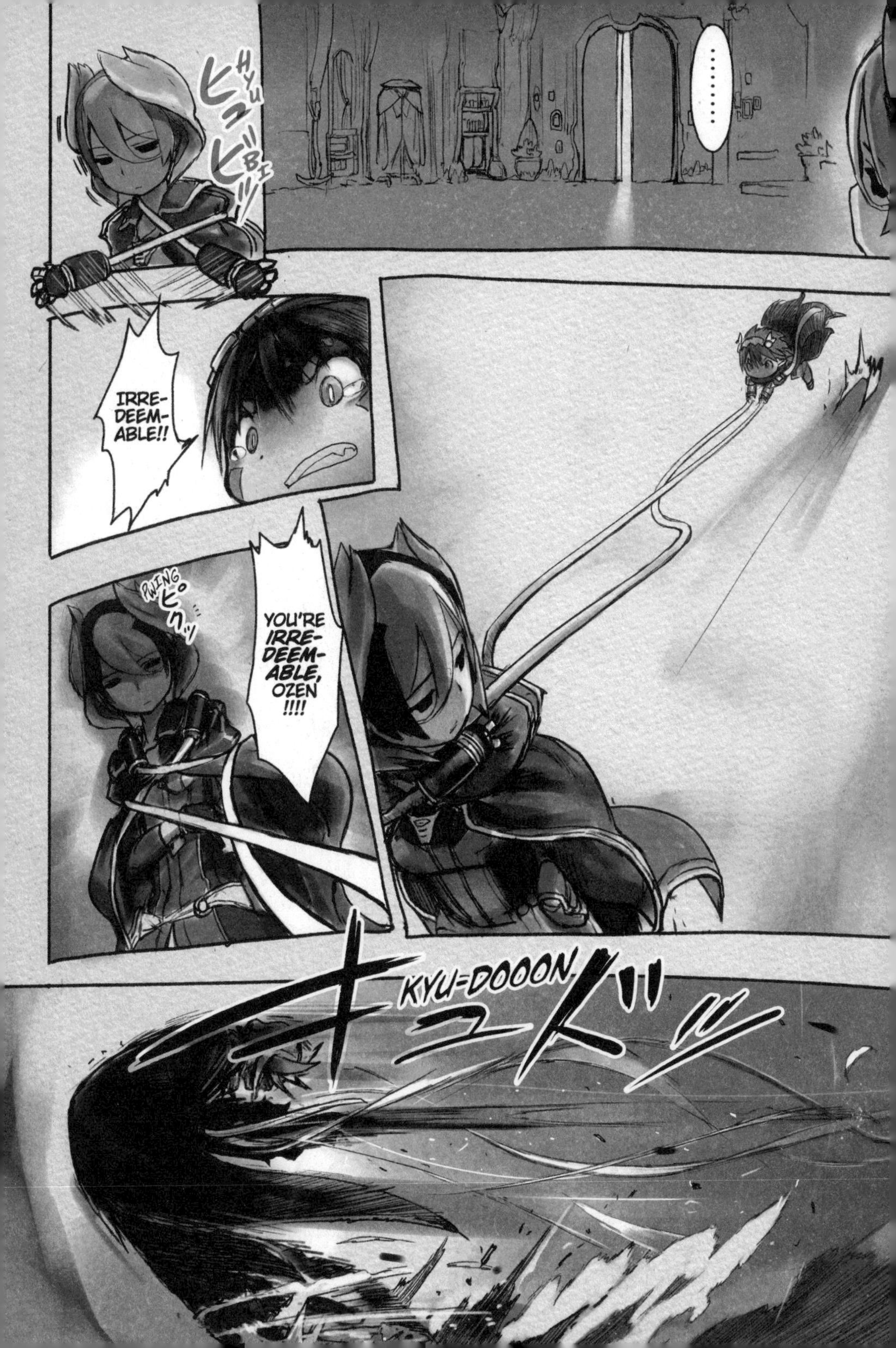
......
HYU BI
IRRE-DEEM-ABLE!!
YOU'RE IRRE-DEEM-ABLE, OZEN!!!!
PWING
KYU-DOOON

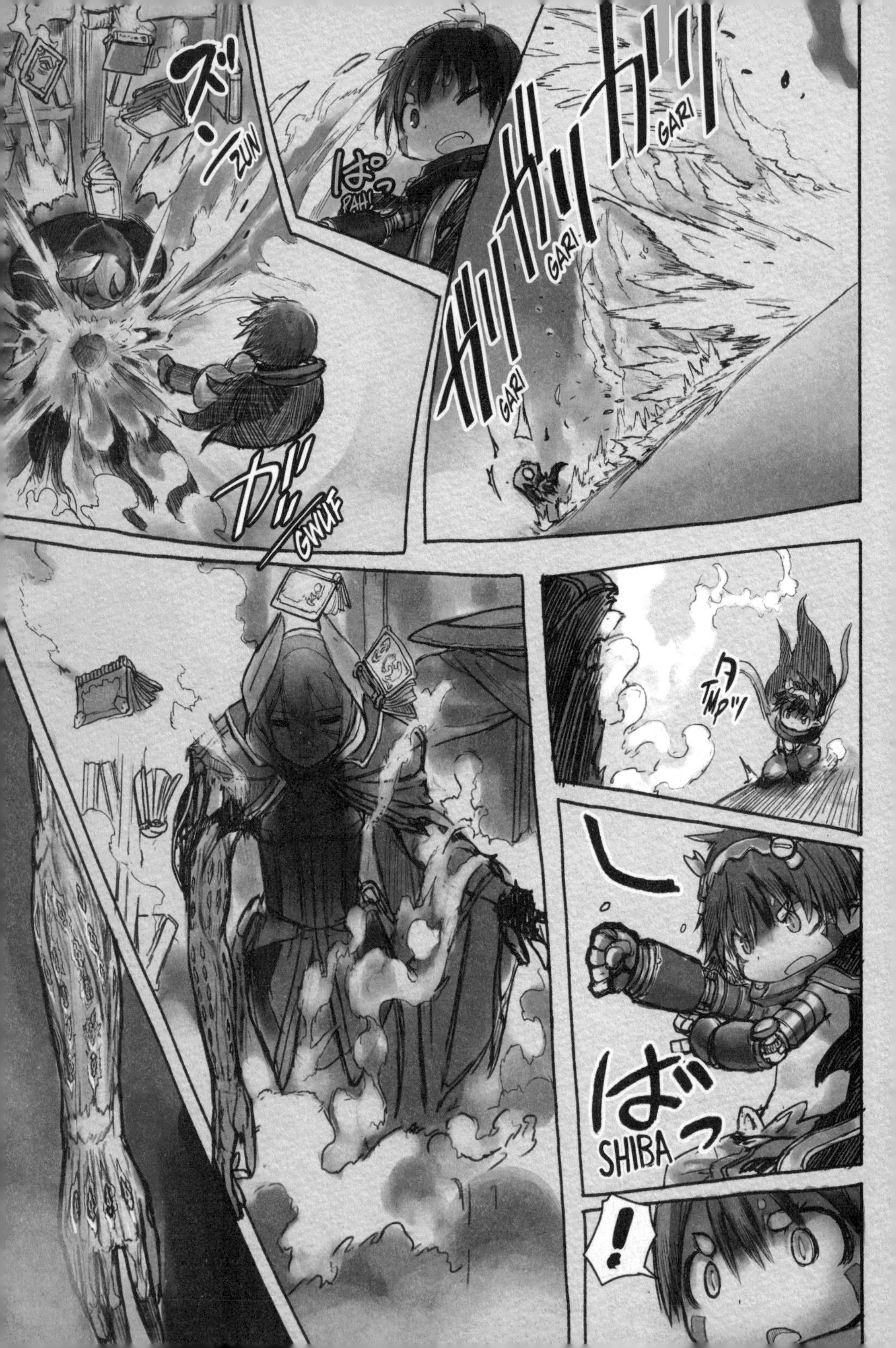
ガリガリガリ
GARI GARI GARI
ぱっ
PAH!
ズン
ZUN
ガッ
GWUF
タッ
TMP
しばっ
SHIBA
!

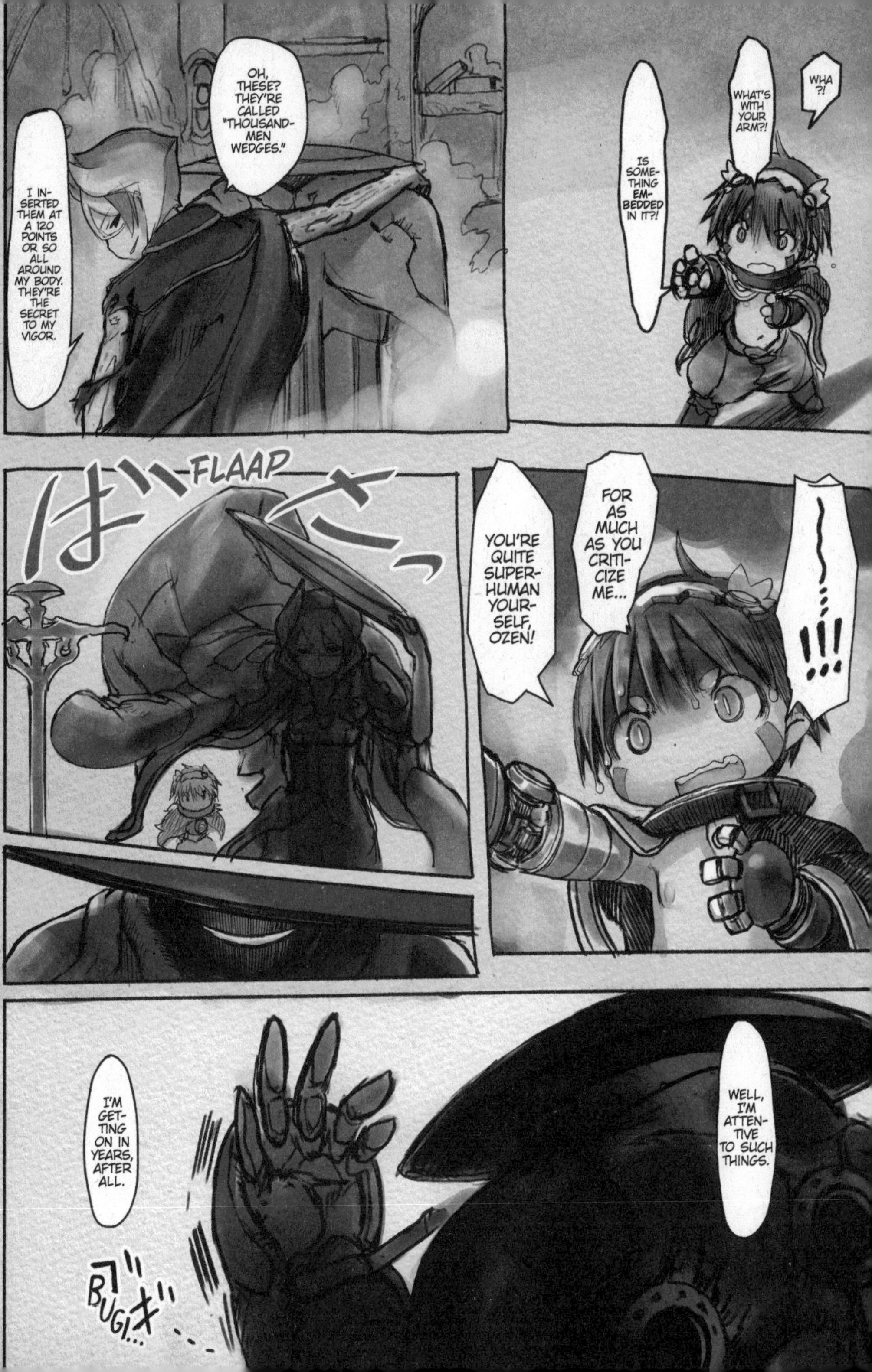
WHA?!
WHAT'S WITH YOUR ARM?!
IS SOMETHING EMBEDDED IN IT?!
OH, THESE? THEY'RE CALLED "THOUSAND-MEN WEDGES."
I INSERTED THEM AT A 120 POINTS OR SO ALL AROUND MY BODY. THEY'RE THE SECRET TO MY VIGOR.
—...!!!
FOR AS MUCH AS YOU CRITICIZE ME...
YOU'RE QUITE SUPERHUMAN YOURSELF, OZEN!
FLAAP
WELL, I'M ATTENTIVE TO SUCH THINGS.
I'M GETTING ON IN YEARS, AFTER ALL.
BUGI...

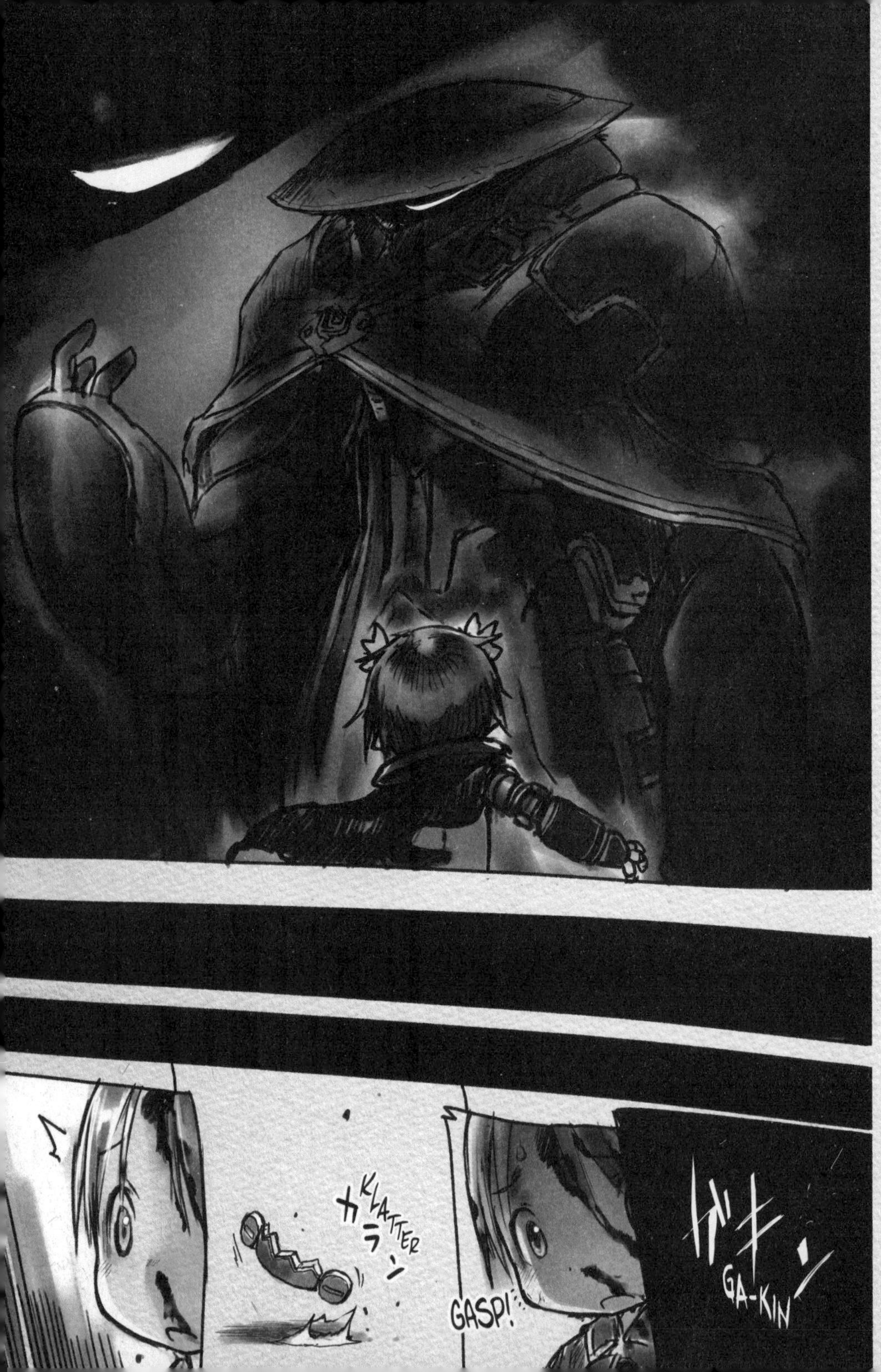
GA-KIN
GASP!
KLATTER

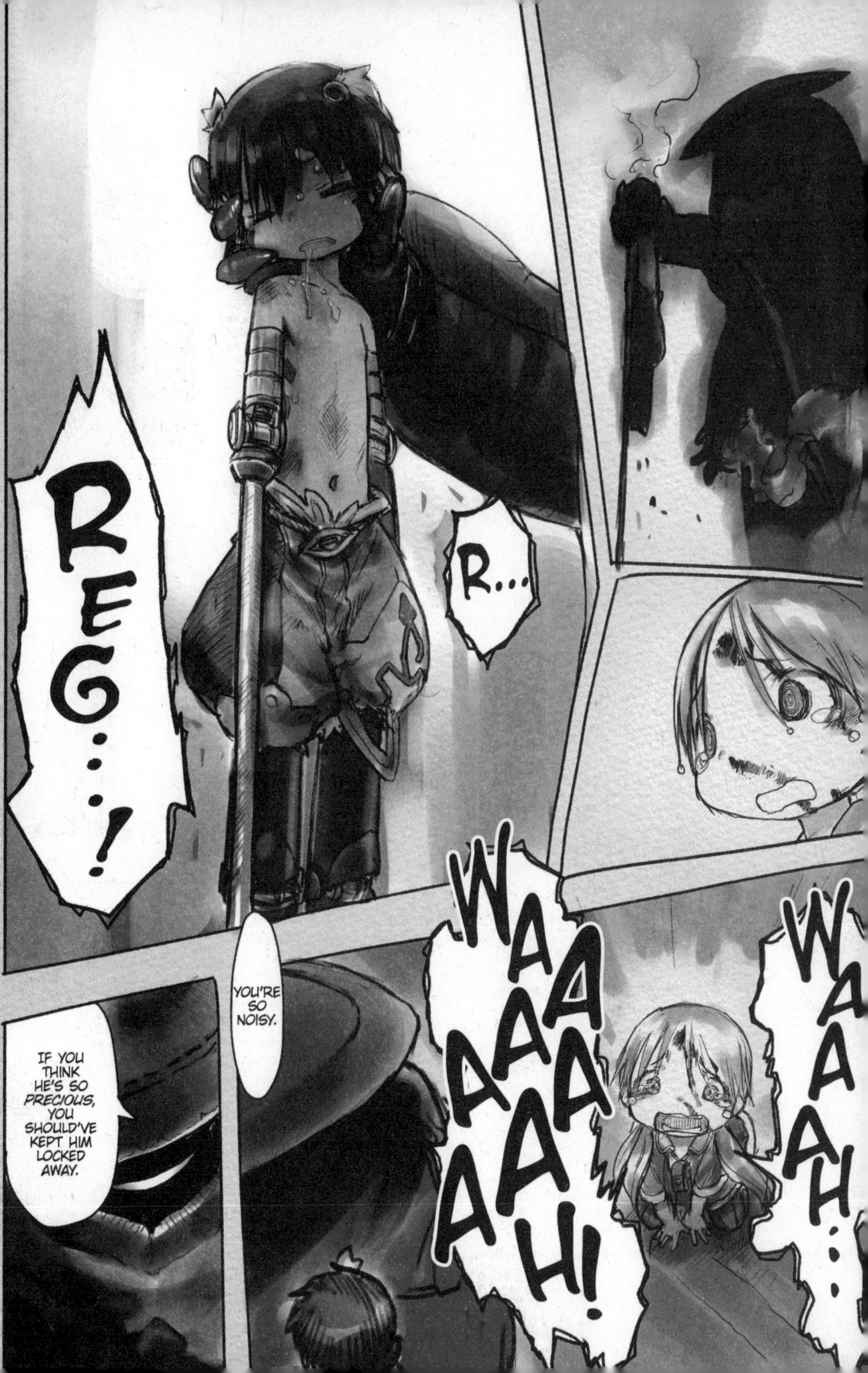
R...
REG...!
WAAAH...
WAAAAAAAAH!
YOU'RE SO NOISY.
IF YOU THINK HE'S SO *PRECIOUS*, YOU SHOULD'VE KEPT HIM LOCKED AWAY.

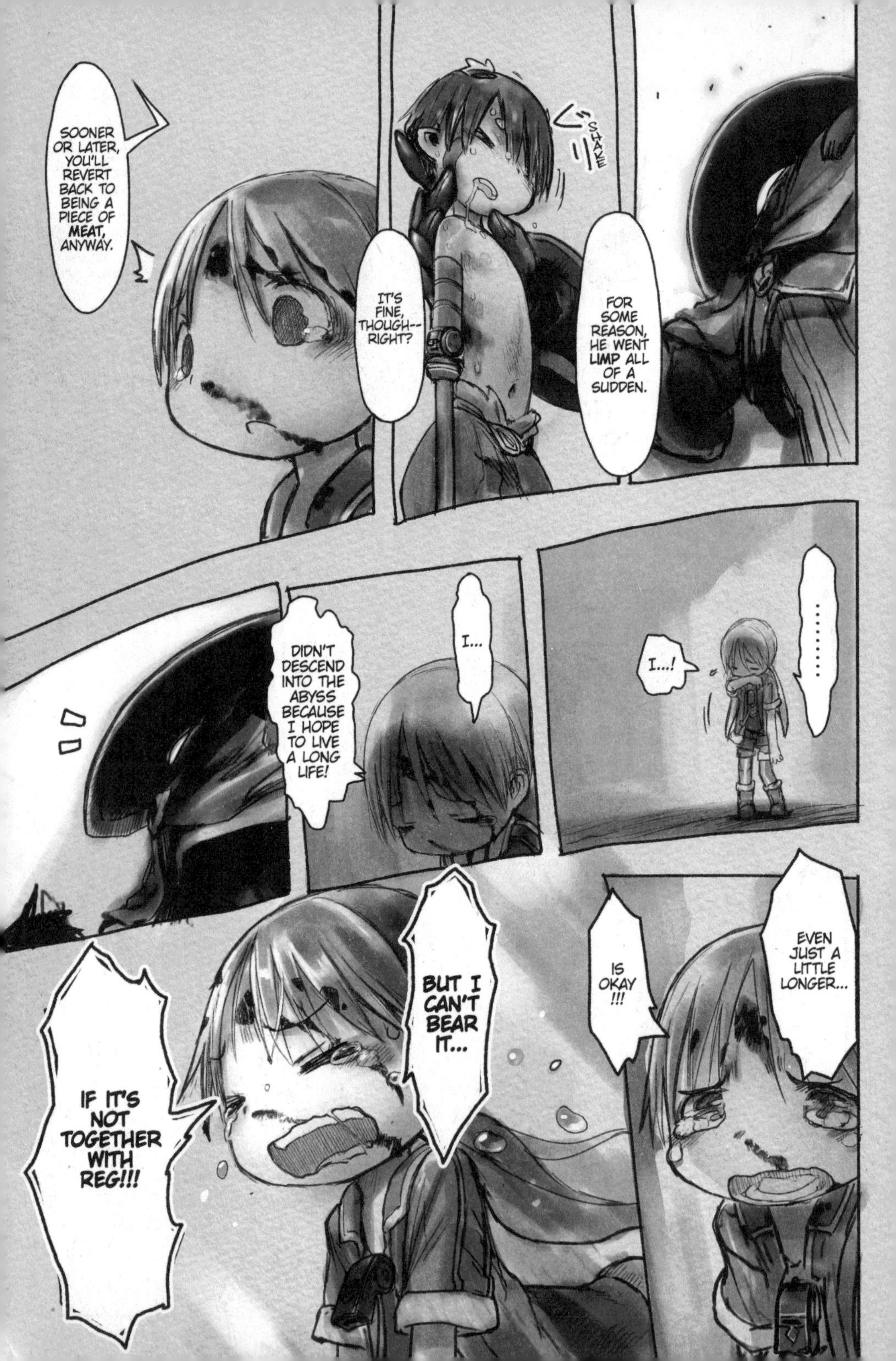
FOR SOME REASON, HE WENT LIMP ALL OF A SUDDEN.
SHAKE
IT'S FINE, THOUGH--RIGHT?
SOONER OR LATER, YOU'LL REVERT BACK TO BEING A PIECE OF MEAT, ANYWAY.
....
I...!
I...
DIDN'T DESCEND INTO THE ABYSS BECAUSE I HOPE TO LIVE A LONG LIFE!
EVEN JUST A LITTLE LONGER...
IS OKAY!!!
BUT I CAN'T BEAR IT...
IF IT'S NOT TOGETHER WITH REG!!!

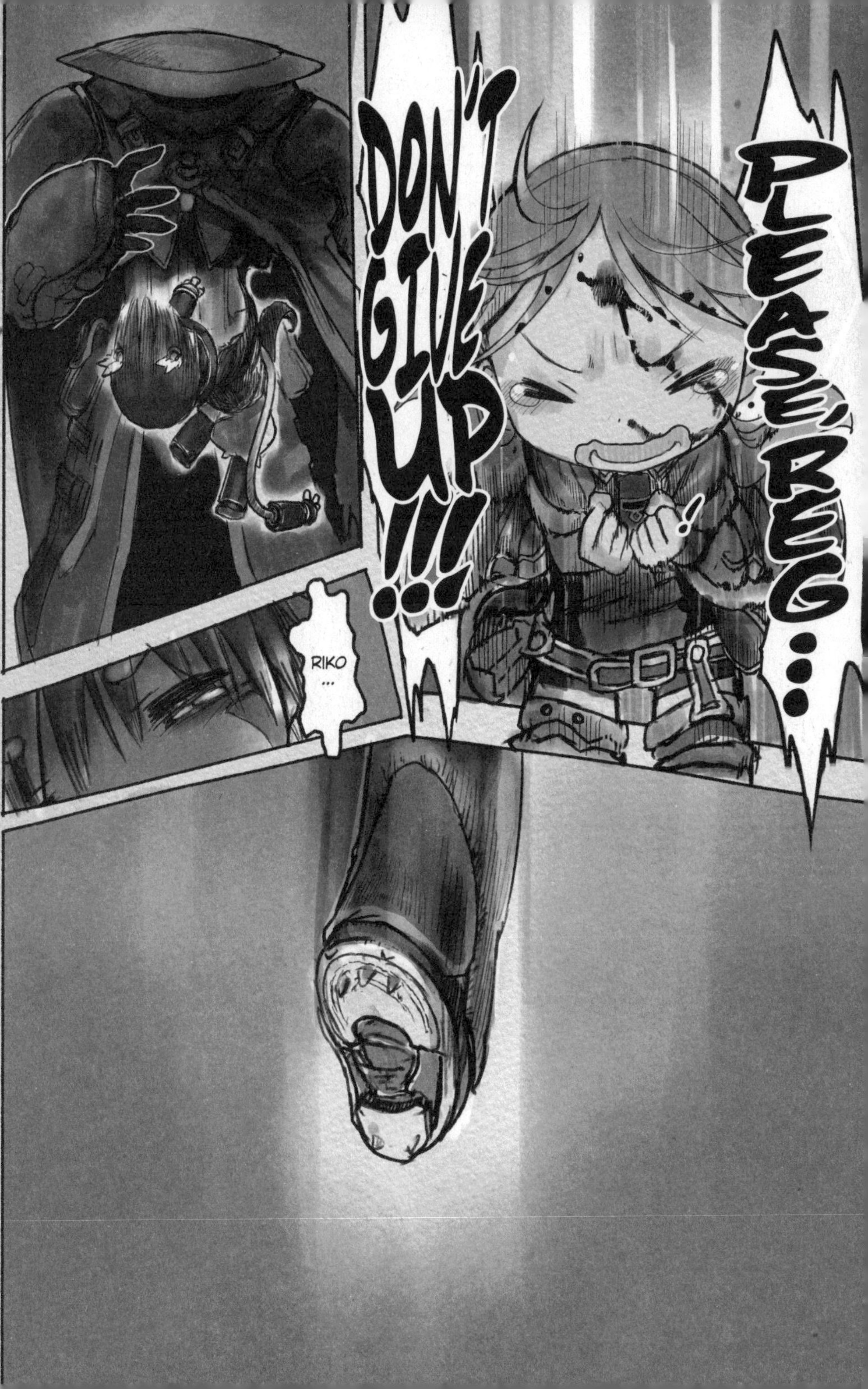
PLEASE, REG...
DON'T GIVE UP!!!
!
RIKO...

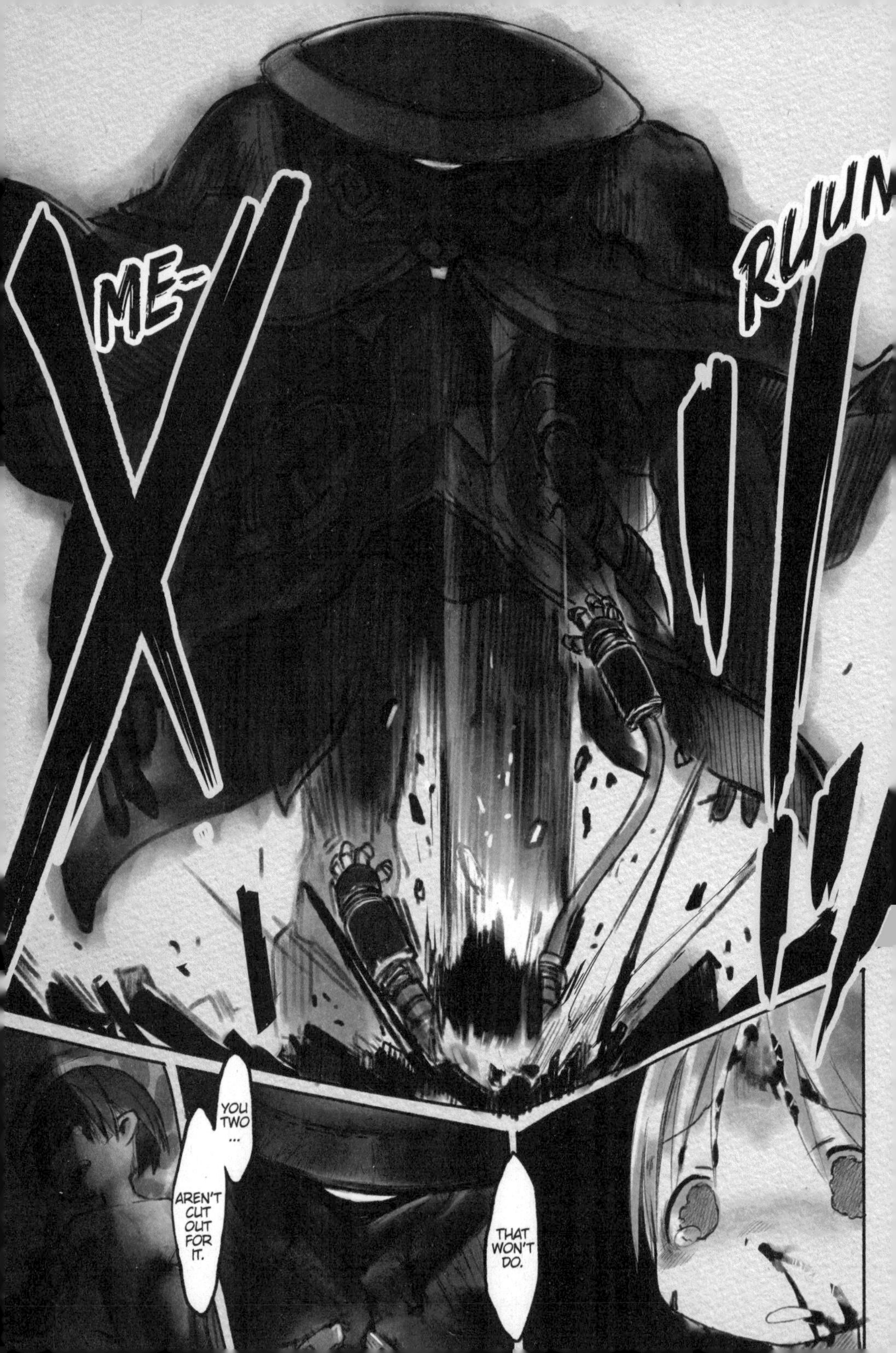
ME-
RYUN
YOU TWO...
AREN'T CUT OUT FOR IT.
THAT WON'T DO.

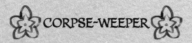

CORPSE-WEEPER

THIS LARGE SPECIES OF BIRD GENERALLY LIVES IN THE DEPTHS' SECOND LAYER. LARGE FLOCKS OF THEM FORM COLONIES, WHERE THEY RAISE THEIR YOUNG COLLECTIVELY. DESPITE THEIR LOOKS, THEY ARE QUITE AFFECTIONATE CREATURES. THEY CAN EVEN BE TAMED IF THEY'RE RAISED BY PEOPLE FROM THE TIME THEY'RE CHICKS.

THEY ARE KNOWN AS BIRDS THAT EXHIBIT AN EXTRAORDINARY CAPACITY FOR VOCAL MIMICRY. THEY WILL BRING HOME HIGHLY SOCIAL PREY, SUCH AS HAMMERBEAKS, SO THAT THE ENTIRE COLONY CAN LEARN ITS CRIES AND USE THEM WHEN HUNTING. DURING BREEDING SEASON, THEY WILL SOMETIMES ENTICE WHOLE GROUPS OF PREY INTO THEIR COLONIES, WHERE THEY PROCEED TO HUNT THEM ALL IN ONE FELL SWOOP.

THE DIFFERING SIZES OF THEIR LEFT AND RIGHT EYES GIVE THEM SUPERB SPATIAL AWARENESS AND ALLOW THEM TO REACT VERY QUICKLY TO ENEMIES IN THE SKIES ABOVE THEM.

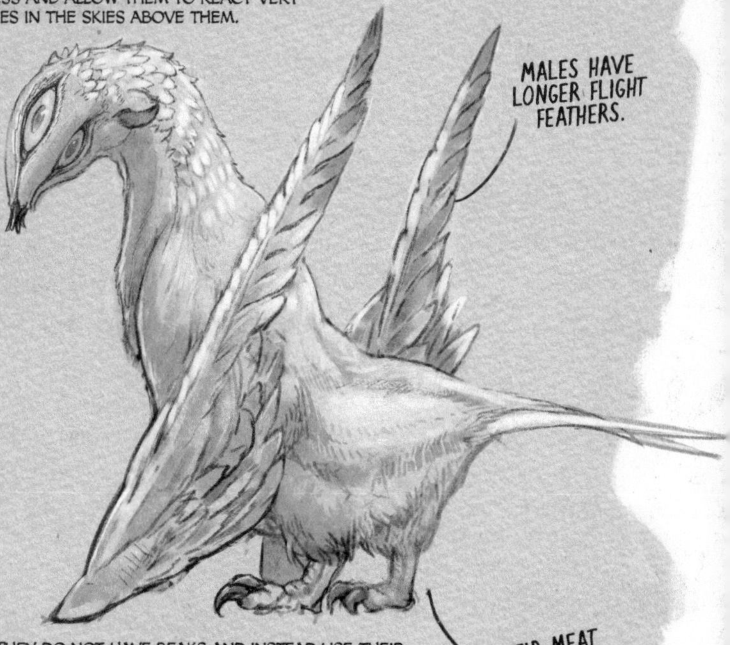

MALES HAVE LONGER FLIGHT FEATHERS.
THEIR MEAT SMELLS BAD, BUT IT'S QUITE SAVORY.

THEY DO NOT HAVE BEAKS AND INSTEAD USE THEIR WELL-DEVELOPED TONGUES TO SLURP UP THE MEAT AND ORGANS OF THEIR PREY. SOME SPECIMENS GROW TO HAVE WINGSPANS OF OVER TEN METERS AND ARE STRONG ENOUGH TO EASILY FLY OFF WITH A HUMAN ADULT.

PLEASE TAKE SPECIAL CARE NOT TO ACCIDENTALLY ENTER THEIR COLONIES.

DANGER LEVEL: ★★★ (SERIOUS)

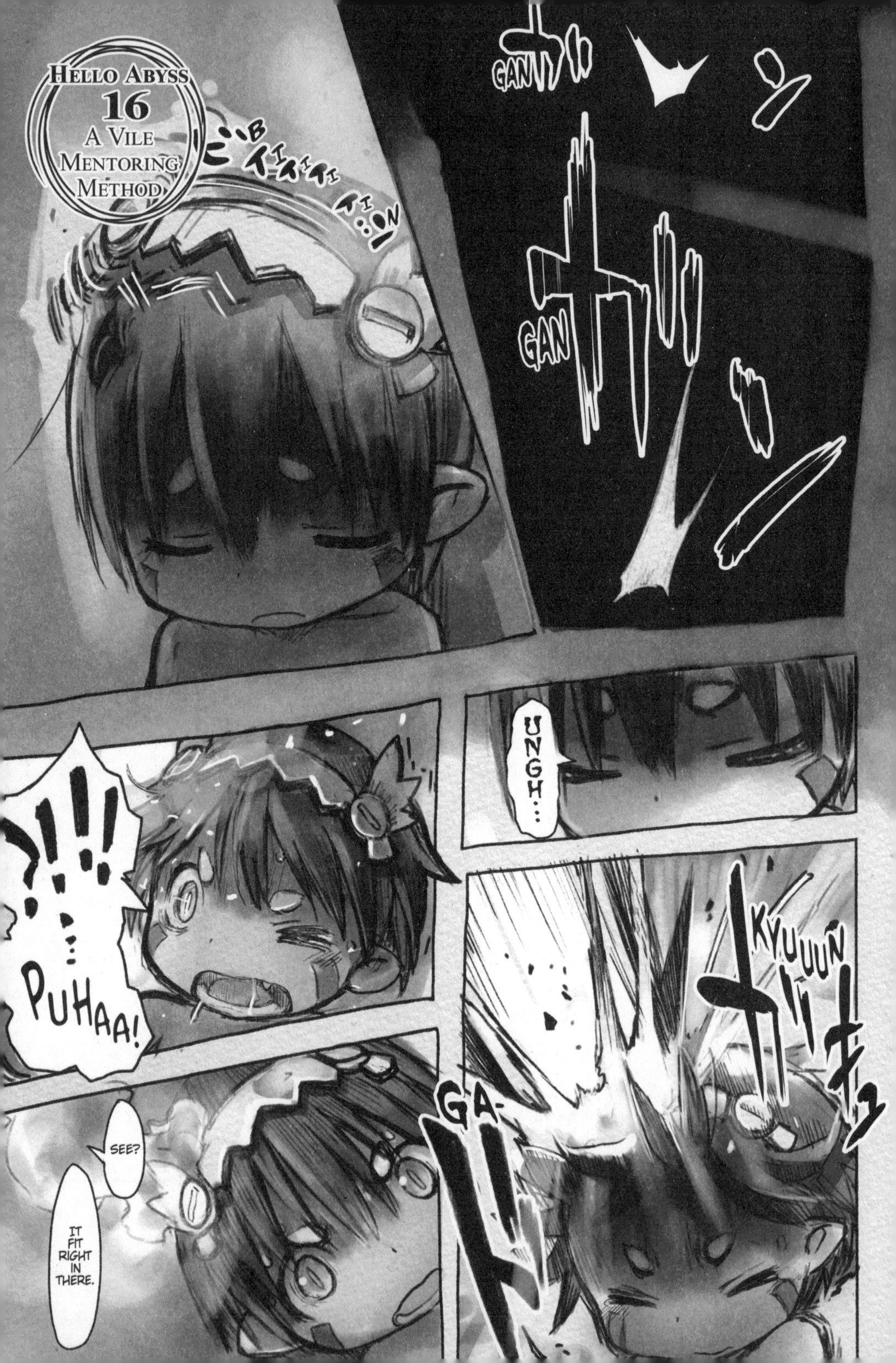
GAN
GAN
Hello Abyss
16
A Vile Mentoring Method
UNGH...
PUHAA!
KYUUUN
GA-
SEE?
IT FIT RIGHT IN THERE.

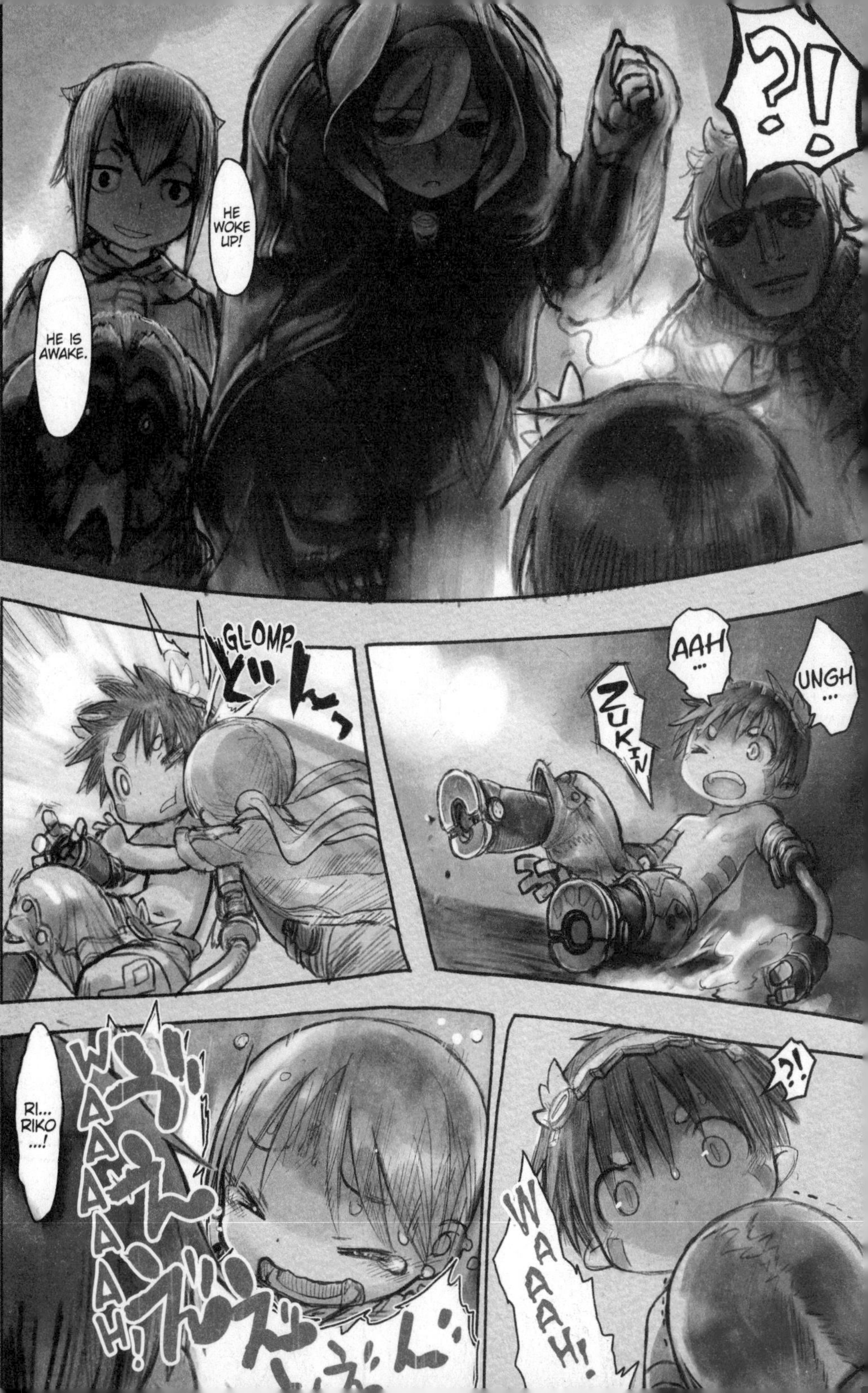
?!
HE WOKE UP!
HE IS AWAKE.
UNGH ...
AAH ...
ZUKIN
GLOMP
?!
WAAAH!
WAAAAAH!
RI... RIKO ...!

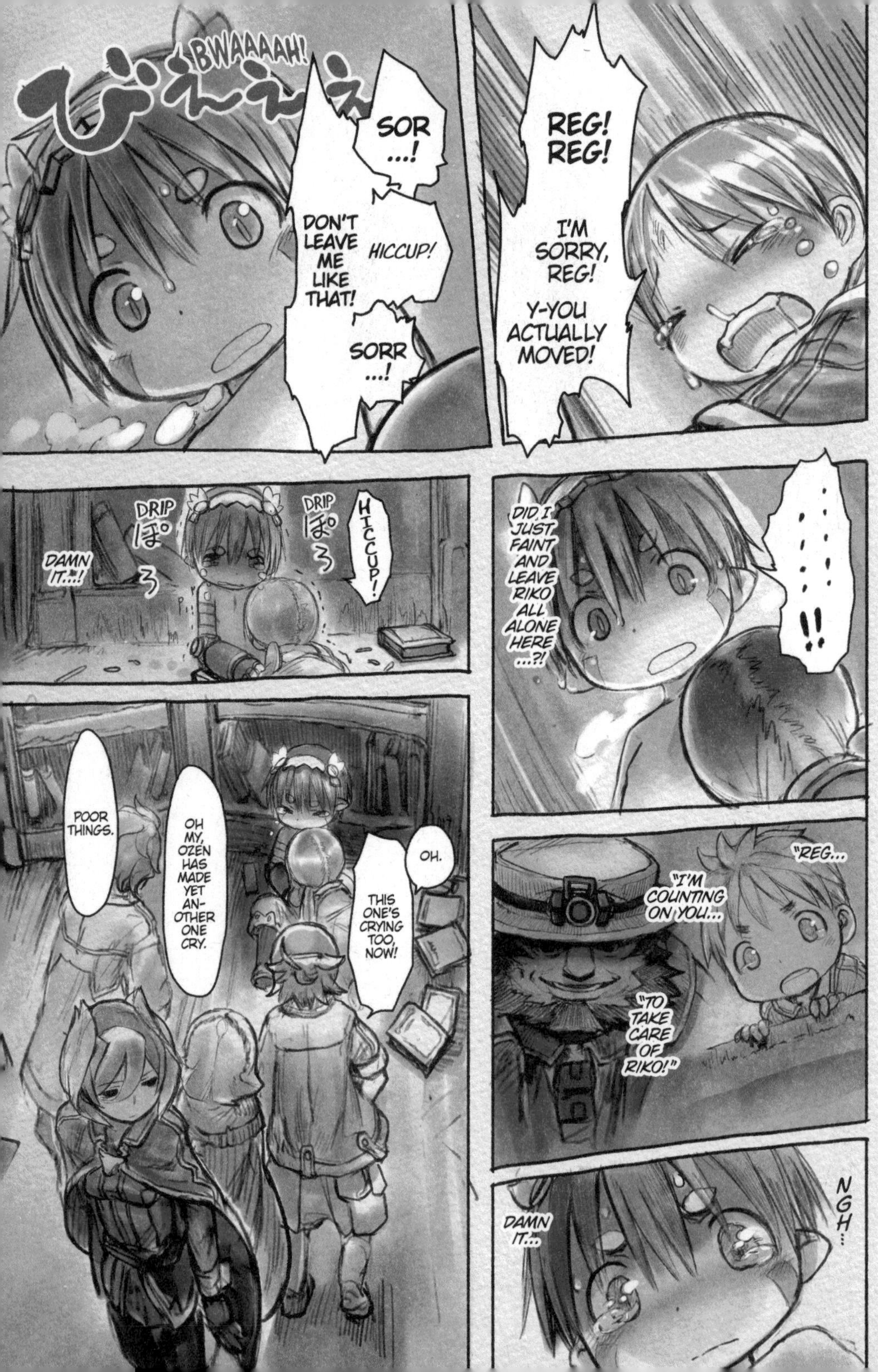
REG! REG!
I'M SORRY, REG!
Y-YOU ACTUALLY MOVED!
びえええ
BWAAAAH!
SOR ...!
HICCUP!
DON'T LEAVE ME LIKE THAT!
SORR ...!
...!!
DID I JUST FAINT AND LEAVE RIKO ALL ALONE HERE ...?!
HICCUP!
ぽろ
DRIP
ぽろ
DRIP
DAMN IT...!
"REG...
"I'M COUNTING ON YOU...
"TO TAKE CARE OF RIKO!"
NGH...
DAMN IT...
OH.
THIS ONE'S CRYING TOO, NOW!
OH MY, OZEN HAS MADE YET AN-OTHER ONE CRY.
POOR THINGS.

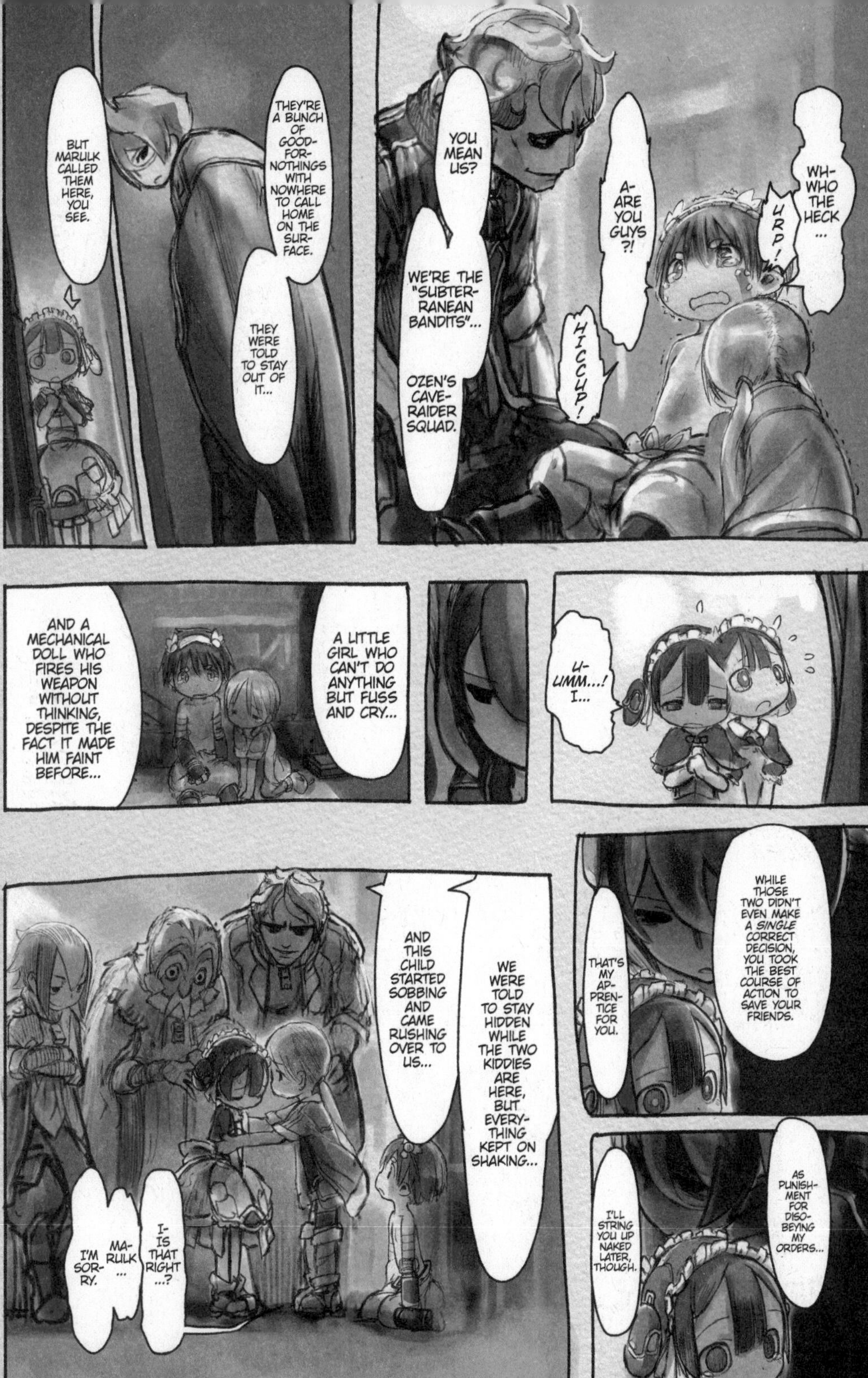
WH-WHO THE HECK...
URP!
A-ARE YOU GUYS?!
HICCUP!
YOU MEAN US?
WE'RE THE "SUBTERRANEAN BANDITS"...
OZEN'S CAVE-RAIDER SQUAD.
THEY'RE A BUNCH OF GOOD-FOR-NOTHINGS WITH NOWHERE TO CALL HOME ON THE SURFACE.
THEY WERE TOLD TO STAY OUT OF IT...
BUT MARULK CALLED THEM HERE, YOU SEE.
U-UMM...! I...
A LITTLE GIRL WHO CAN'T DO ANYTHING BUT FUSS AND CRY...
AND A MECHANICAL DOLL WHO FIRES HIS WEAPON WITHOUT THINKING, DESPITE THE FACT IT MADE HIM FAINT BEFORE...
WHILE THOSE TWO DIDN'T EVEN MAKE A *SINGLE* CORRECT DECISION, YOU TOOK THE BEST COURSE OF ACTION TO SAVE YOUR FRIENDS.
THAT'S MY APPRENTICE FOR YOU.
AS PUNISHMENT FOR DISOBEYING MY ORDERS...
I'LL STRING YOU UP NAKED LATER, THOUGH.
WE WERE TOLD TO STAY HIDDEN WHILE THE TWO KIDDIES ARE HERE, BUT EVERYTHING KEPT ON SHAKING...
AND THIS CHILD STARTED SOBBING AND CAME RUSHING OVER TO US...
I-IS THAT RIGHT...?
MARULK...
I'M SORRY.

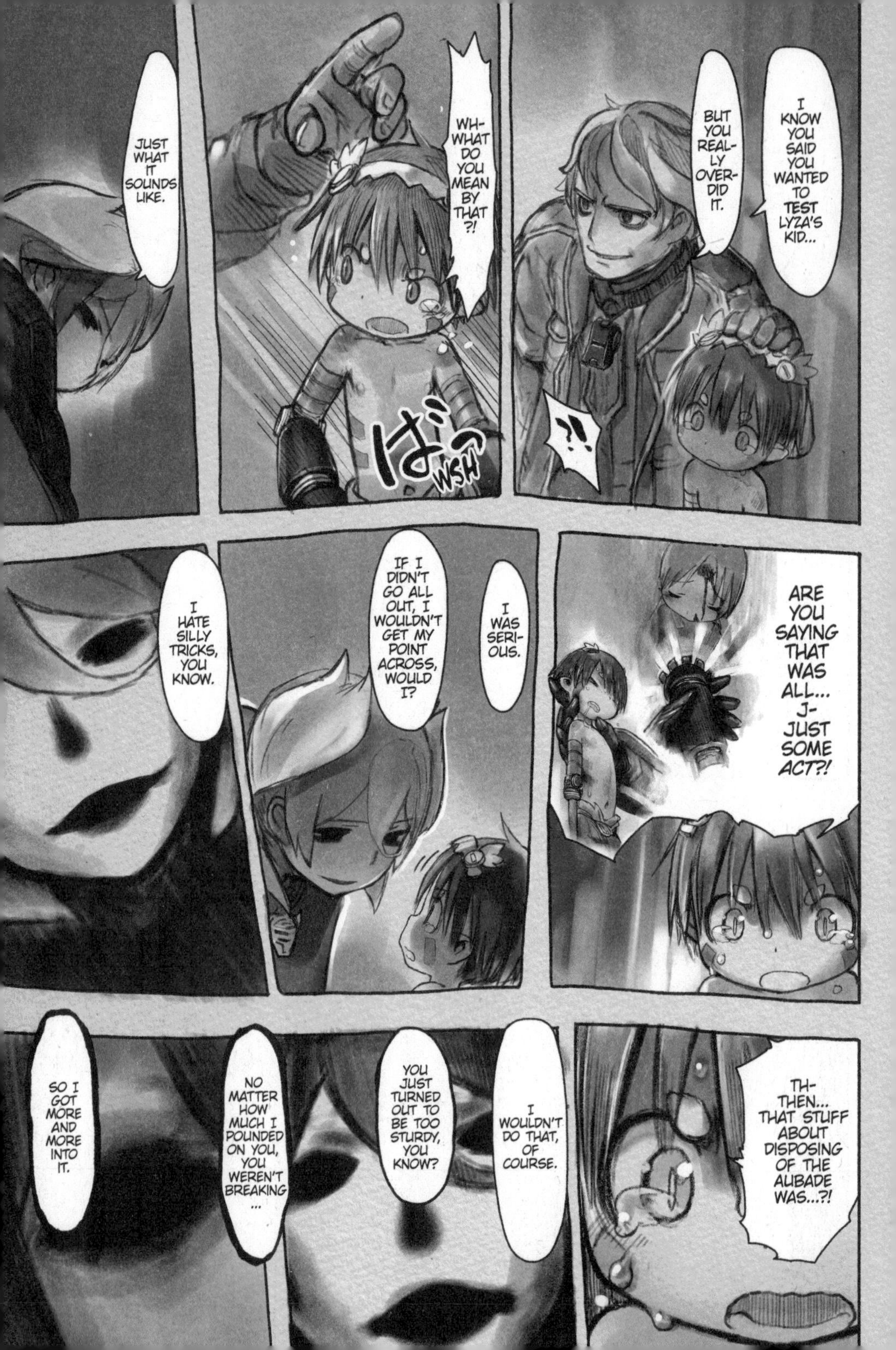
I KNOW YOU SAID YOU WANTED TO TEST LYZA'S KID...
BUT YOU REALLY OVER-DID IT.
?!
WH-WHAT DO YOU MEAN BY THAT?!
はっ
WSH
JUST WHAT IT SOUNDS LIKE.
ARE YOU SAYING THAT WAS ALL... J-JUST SOME ACT?!
I WAS SERI-OUS.
IF I DIDN'T GO ALL OUT, I WOULDN'T GET MY POINT ACROSS, WOULD I?
I HATE SILLY TRICKS, YOU KNOW.
TH-THEN... THAT STUFF ABOUT DISPOSING OF THE AUBADE WAS...?!
I WOULDN'T DO THAT, OF COURSE.
YOU JUST TURNED OUT TO BE TOO STURDY, YOU KNOW?
NO MATTER HOW MUCH I POUNDED ON YOU, YOU WEREN'T BREAKING...
SO I GOT MORE AND MORE INTO IT.

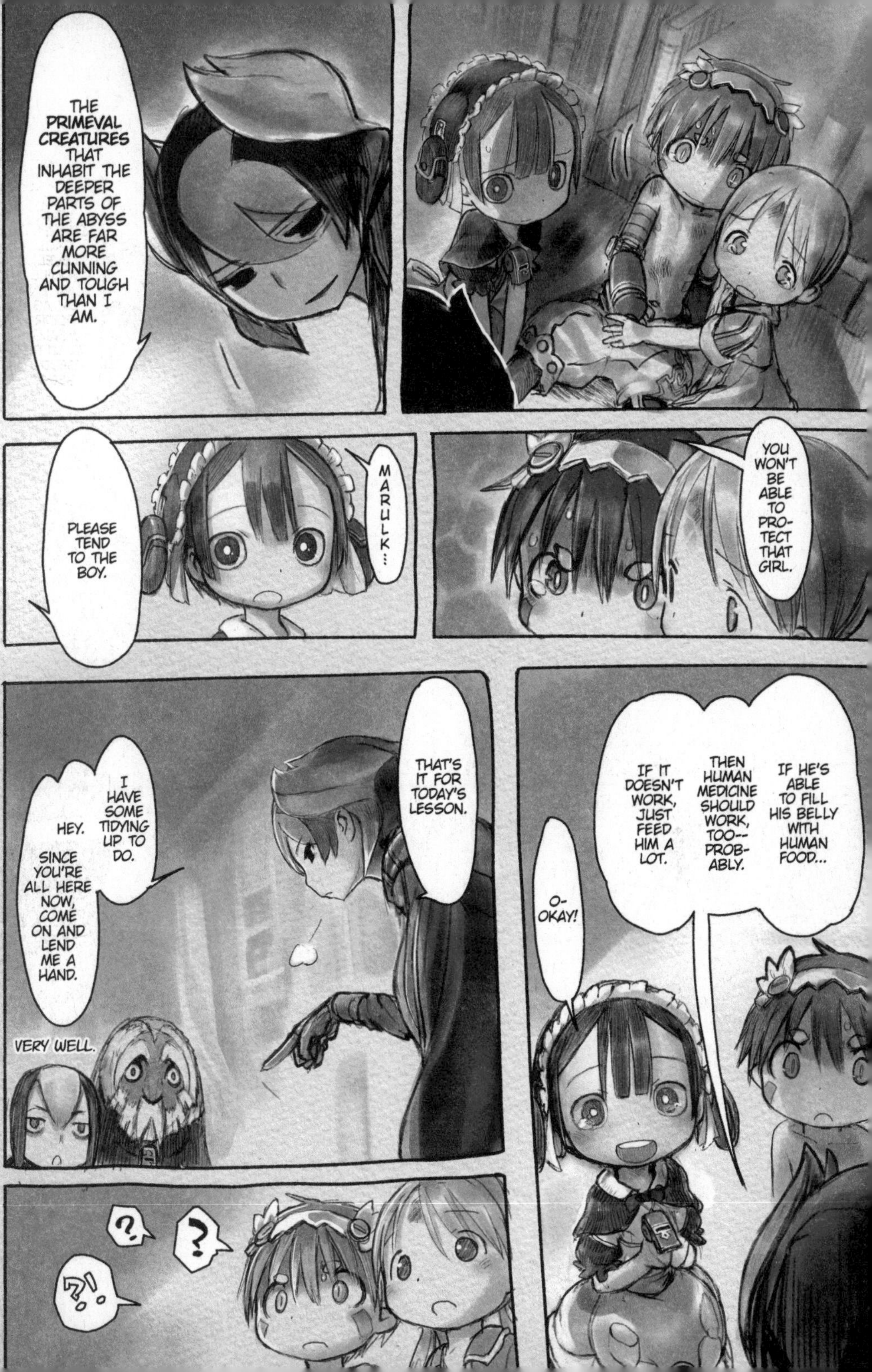
THE PRIMEVAL CREATURES THAT INHABIT THE DEEPER PARTS OF THE ABYSS ARE FAR MORE CUNNING AND TOUGH THAN I AM.
YOU WON'T BE ABLE TO PROTECT THAT GIRL.
MARULK...
PLEASE TEND TO THE BOY.
IF HE'S ABLE TO FILL HIS BELLY WITH HUMAN FOOD...
THEN HUMAN MEDICINE SHOULD WORK, TOO--PROBABLY.
IF IT DOESN'T WORK, JUST FEED HIM A LOT.
O-OKAY!
THAT'S IT FOR TODAY'S LESSON.
I HAVE SOME TIDYING UP TO DO.
HEY. SINCE YOU'RE ALL HERE NOW, COME ON AND LEND ME A HAND.
VERY WELL.
?
?
?!

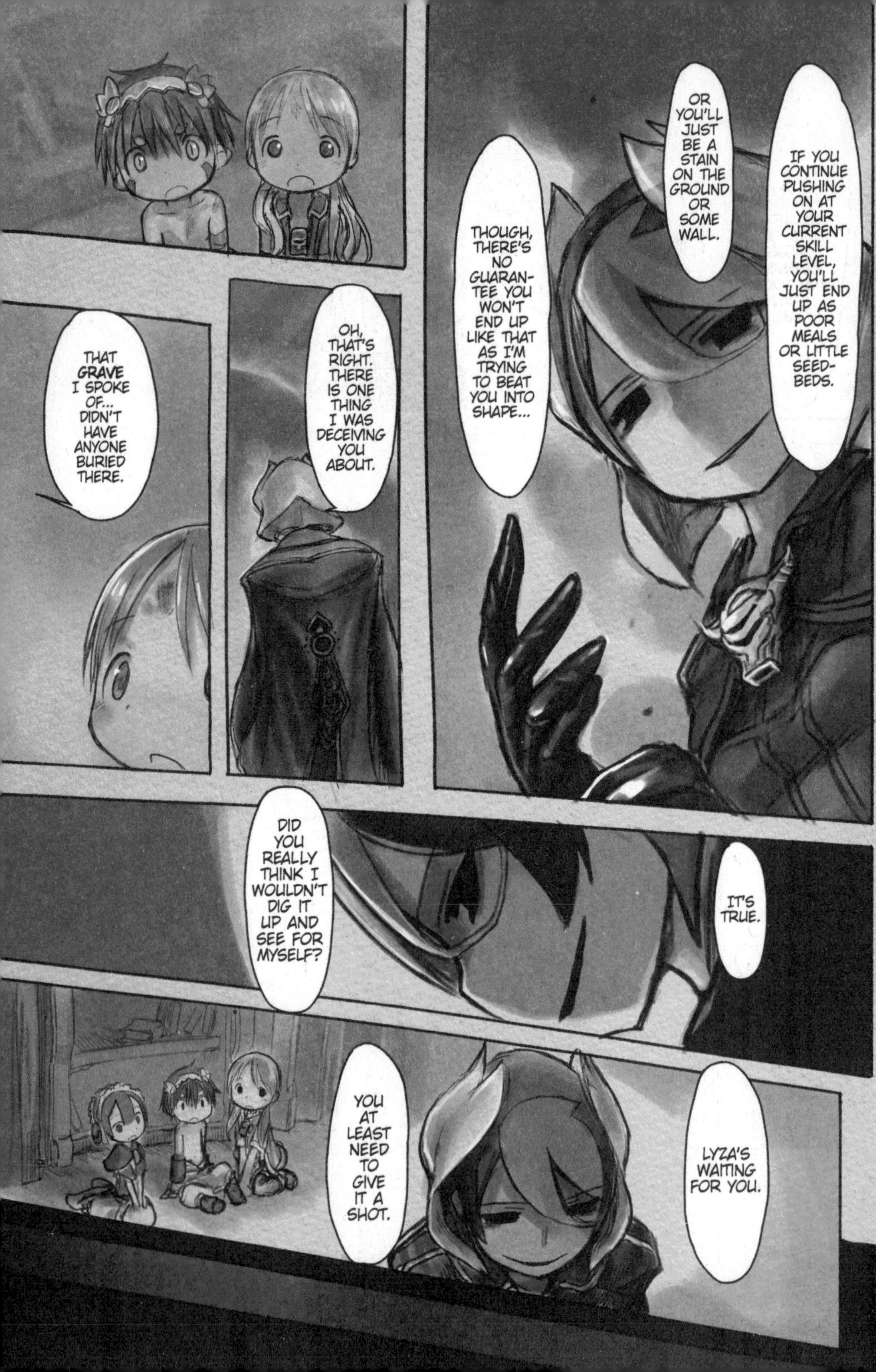
IF YOU CONTINUE PUSHING ON AT YOUR CURRENT SKILL LEVEL, YOU'LL JUST END UP AS POOR MEALS OR LITTLE SEED-BEDS.
OR YOU'LL JUST BE A STAIN ON THE GROUND OR SOME WALL.
THOUGH, THERE'S NO GUARANTEE YOU WON'T END UP LIKE THAT AS I'M TRYING TO BEAT YOU INTO SHAPE...
OH, THAT'S RIGHT. THERE IS ONE THING I WAS DECEIVING YOU ABOUT.
THAT **GRAVE** I SPOKE OF... DIDN'T HAVE ANYONE BURIED THERE.
IT'S TRUE.
DID YOU REALLY THINK I WOULDN'T DIG IT UP AND SEE FOR MYSELF?
LYZA'S WAITING FOR YOU.
YOU AT LEAST NEED TO GIVE IT A SHOT.

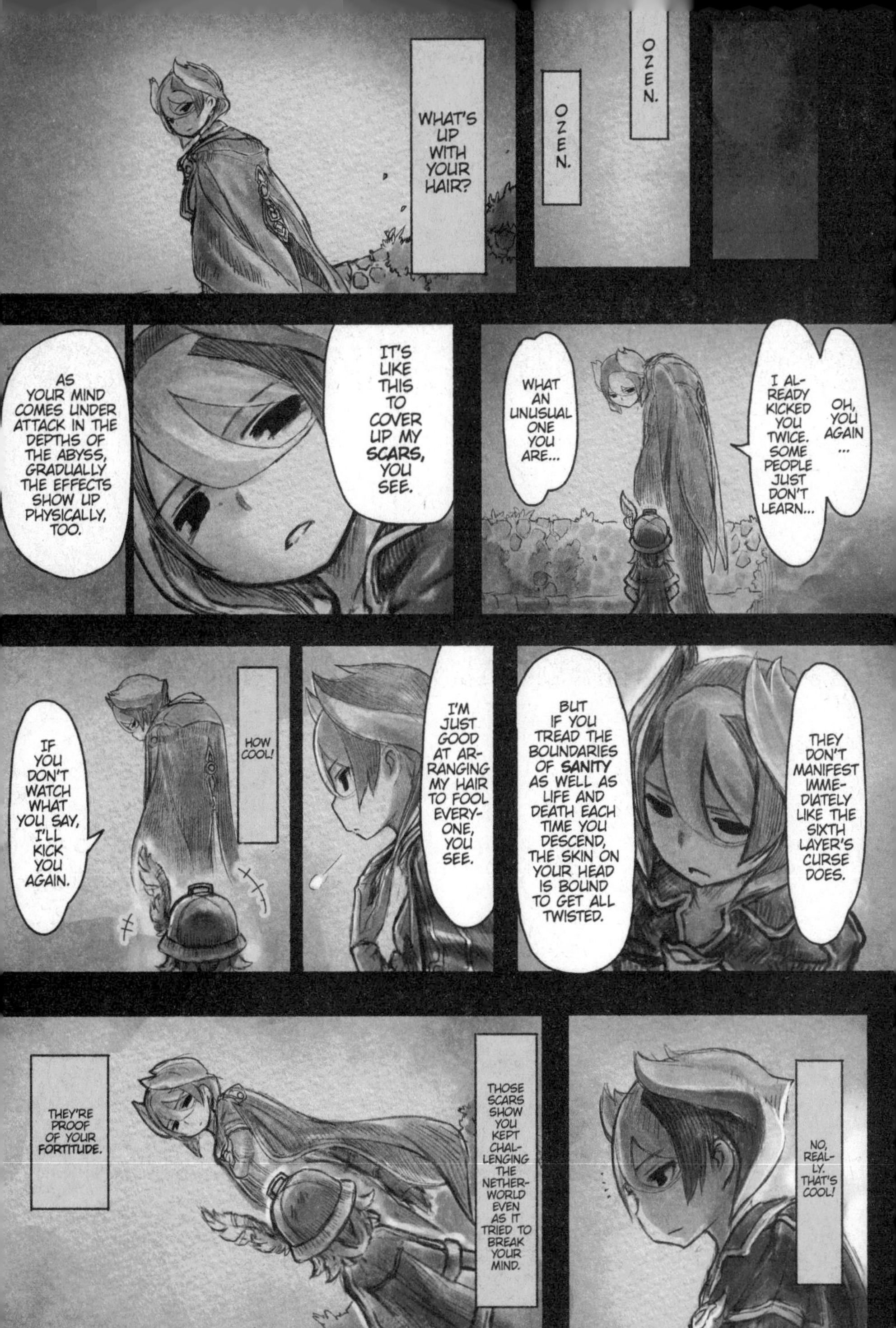
OZEN.
OZEN.
WHAT'S UP WITH YOUR HAIR?
OH, YOU AGAIN...
I ALREADY KICKED YOU TWICE. SOME PEOPLE JUST DON'T LEARN...
WHAT AN UNUSUAL ONE YOU ARE...
IT'S LIKE THIS TO COVER UP MY **SCARS,** YOU SEE.
AS YOUR MIND COMES UNDER ATTACK IN THE DEPTHS OF THE ABYSS, GRADUALLY THE EFFECTS SHOW UP PHYSICALLY, TOO.
THEY DON'T MANIFEST IMMEDIATELY LIKE THE SIXTH LAYER'S CURSE DOES.
BUT IF YOU TREAD THE BOUNDARIES OF **SANITY** AS WELL AS LIFE AND DEATH EACH TIME YOU DESCEND, THE SKIN ON YOUR HEAD IS BOUND TO GET ALL TWISTED.
I'M JUST GOOD AT ARRANGING MY HAIR TO FOOL EVERYONE, YOU SEE.
HOW COOL!
IF YOU DON'T WATCH WHAT YOU SAY, I'LL KICK YOU AGAIN.
NO, REALLY. THAT'S COOL!
THOSE SCARS SHOW YOU KEPT CHALLENGING THE NETHERWORLD EVEN AS IT TRIED TO BREAK YOUR MIND.
THEY'RE PROOF OF YOUR **FORTITUDE.**

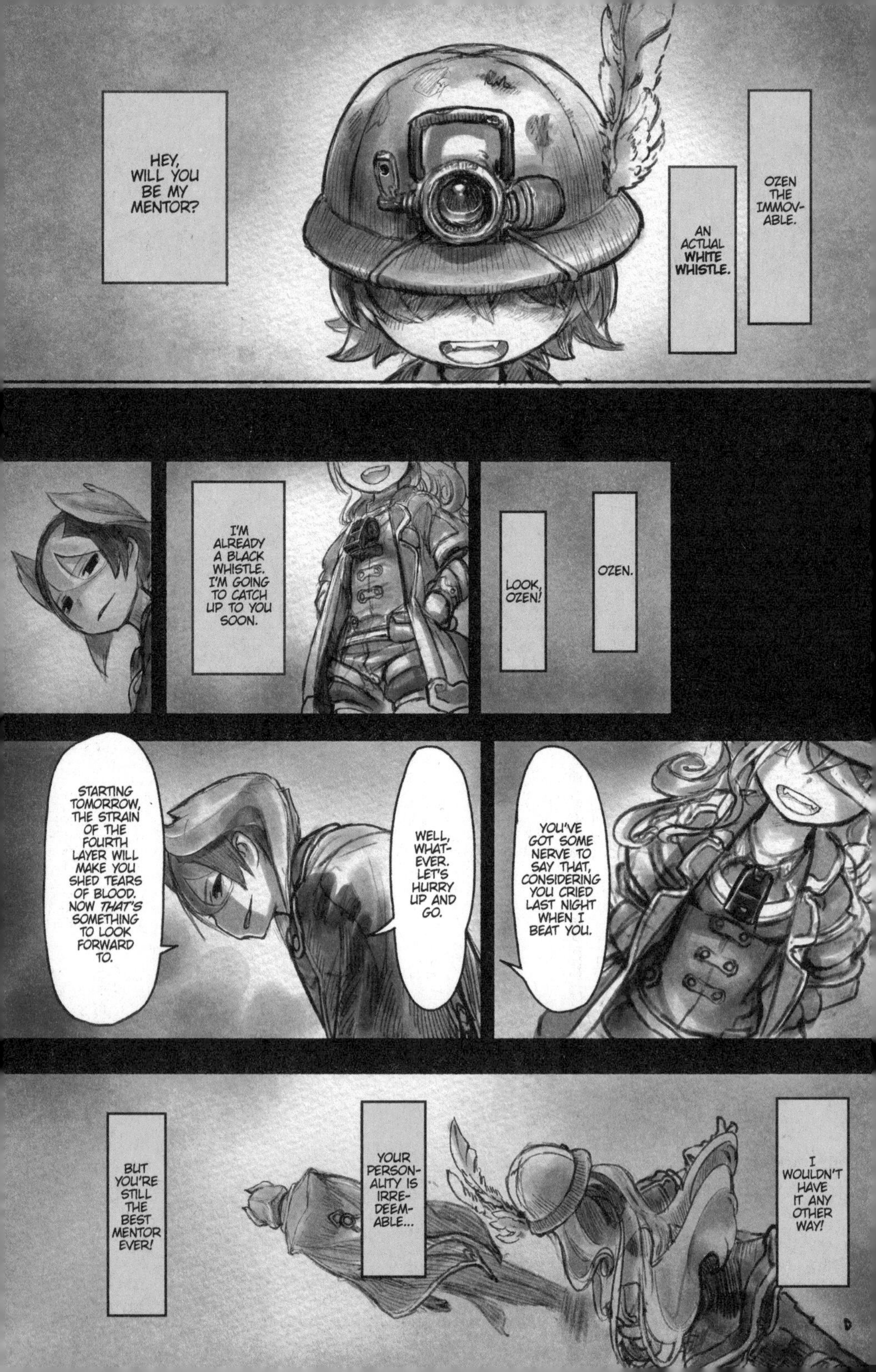
OZEN THE IMMOVABLE.
AN ACTUAL WHITE WHISTLE.
HEY, WILL YOU BE MY MENTOR?
OZEN.
LOOK, OZEN!
I'M ALREADY A BLACK WHISTLE. I'M GOING TO CATCH UP TO YOU SOON.
YOU'VE GOT SOME NERVE TO SAY THAT, CONSIDERING YOU CRIED LAST NIGHT WHEN I BEAT YOU.
WELL, WHATEVER. LET'S HURRY UP AND GO.
STARTING TOMORROW, THE STRAIN OF THE FOURTH LAYER WILL MAKE YOU SHED TEARS OF BLOOD. NOW *THAT'S* SOMETHING TO LOOK FORWARD TO.
I WOULDN'T HAVE IT ANY OTHER WAY!
YOUR PERSONALITY IS IRREDEEMABLE...
BUT YOU'RE STILL THE BEST MENTOR EVER!

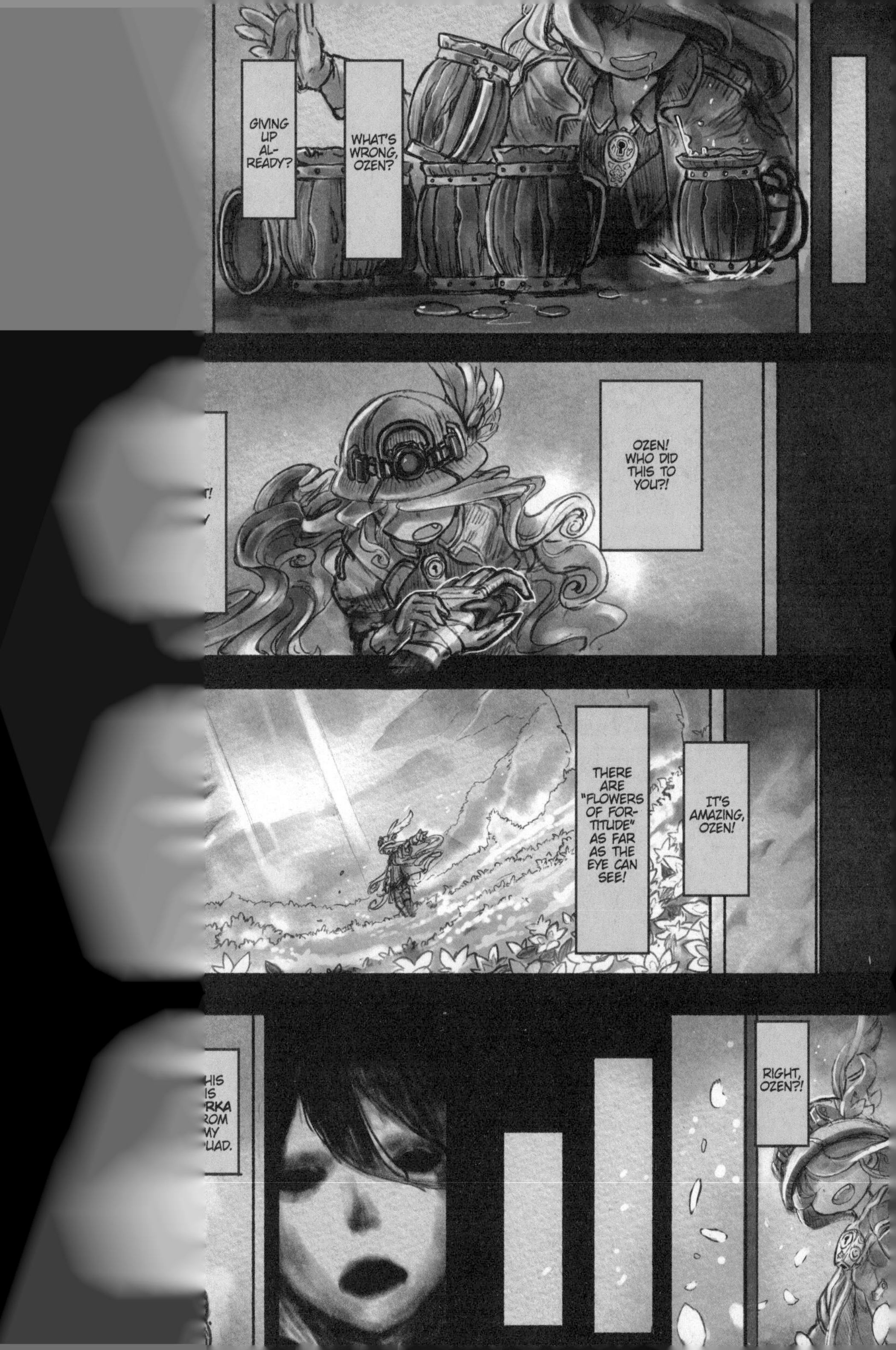
WHAT'S WRONG, OZEN?
GIVING UP AL-READY?
OZEN! WHO DID THIS TO YOU?!
IT'S AMAZING, OZEN!
THERE ARE "FLOWERS OF FOR-TITUDE" AS FAR AS THE EYE CAN SEE!
RIGHT, OZEN?!

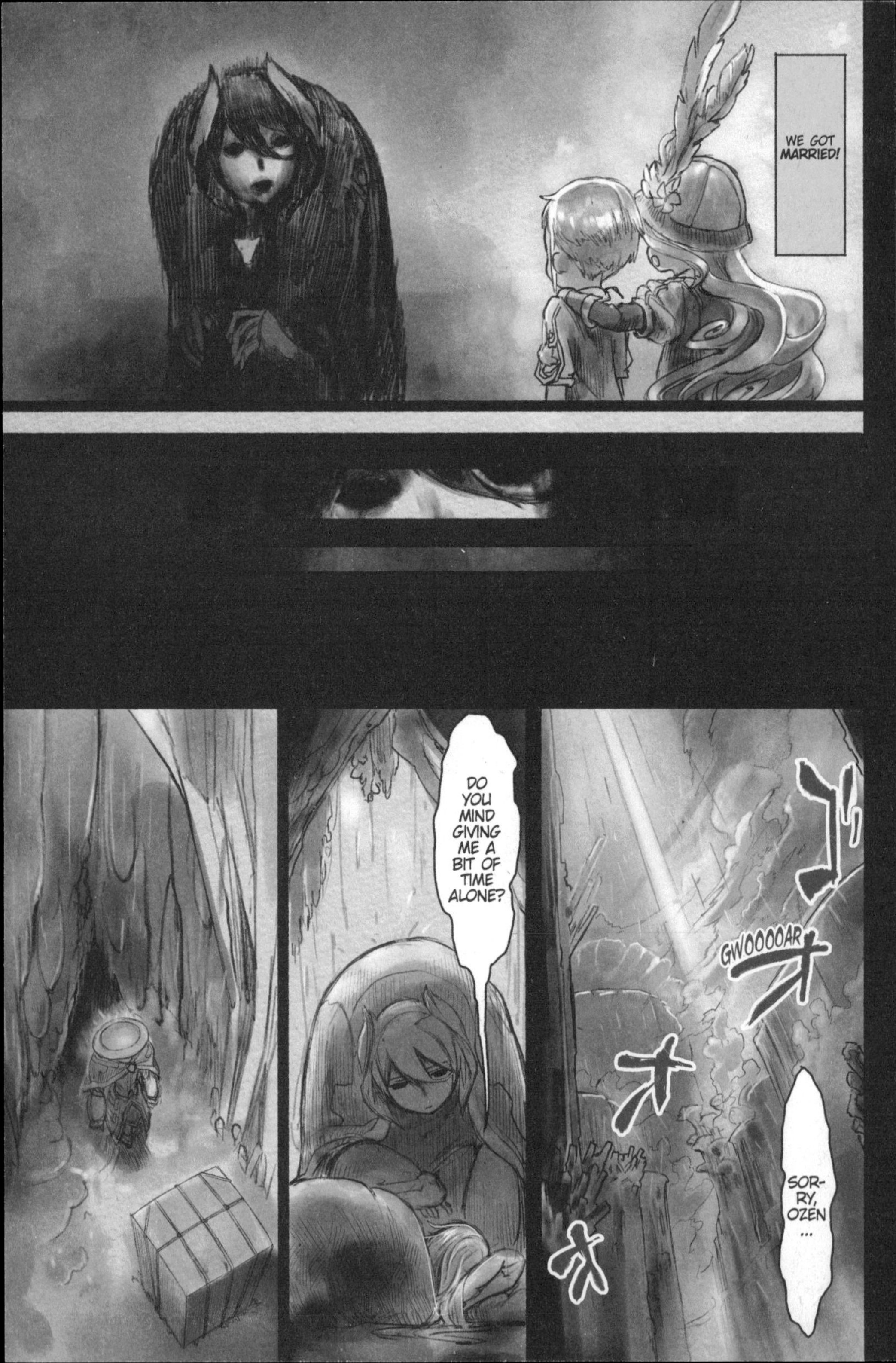
WE GOT MARRIED!
GWOOOOAR
SORRY, OZEN ...
DO YOU MIND GIVING ME A BIT OF TIME ALONE?

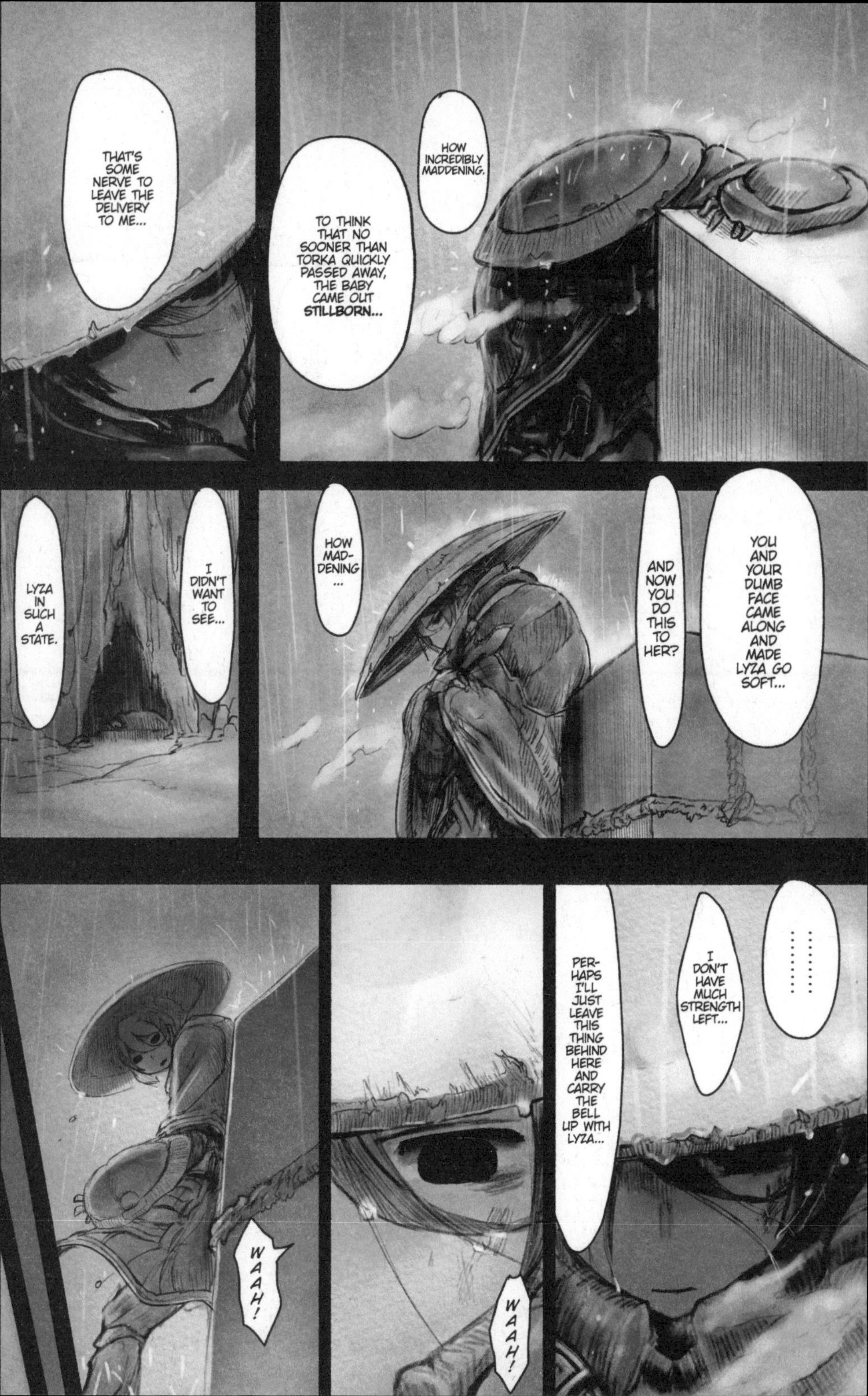

HOW INCREDIBLY MADDENING.
TO THINK THAT NO SOONER THAN TORKA QUICKLY PASSED AWAY, THE BABY CAME OUT **STILLBORN...**
THAT'S SOME NERVE TO LEAVE THE DELIVERY TO ME...
YOU AND YOUR DUMB FACE CAME ALONG AND MADE LYZA GO SOFT...
AND NOW YOU DO THIS TO HER?
HOW MAD-DENING...
I DIDN'T WANT TO SEE...
LYZA IN SUCH A STATE.
......
I DON'T HAVE MUCH STRENGTH LEFT...
PER-HAPS I'LL JUST LEAVE THIS THING BEHIND HERE AND CARRY THE BELL UP WITH LYZA...
WAAH!
WAAH!

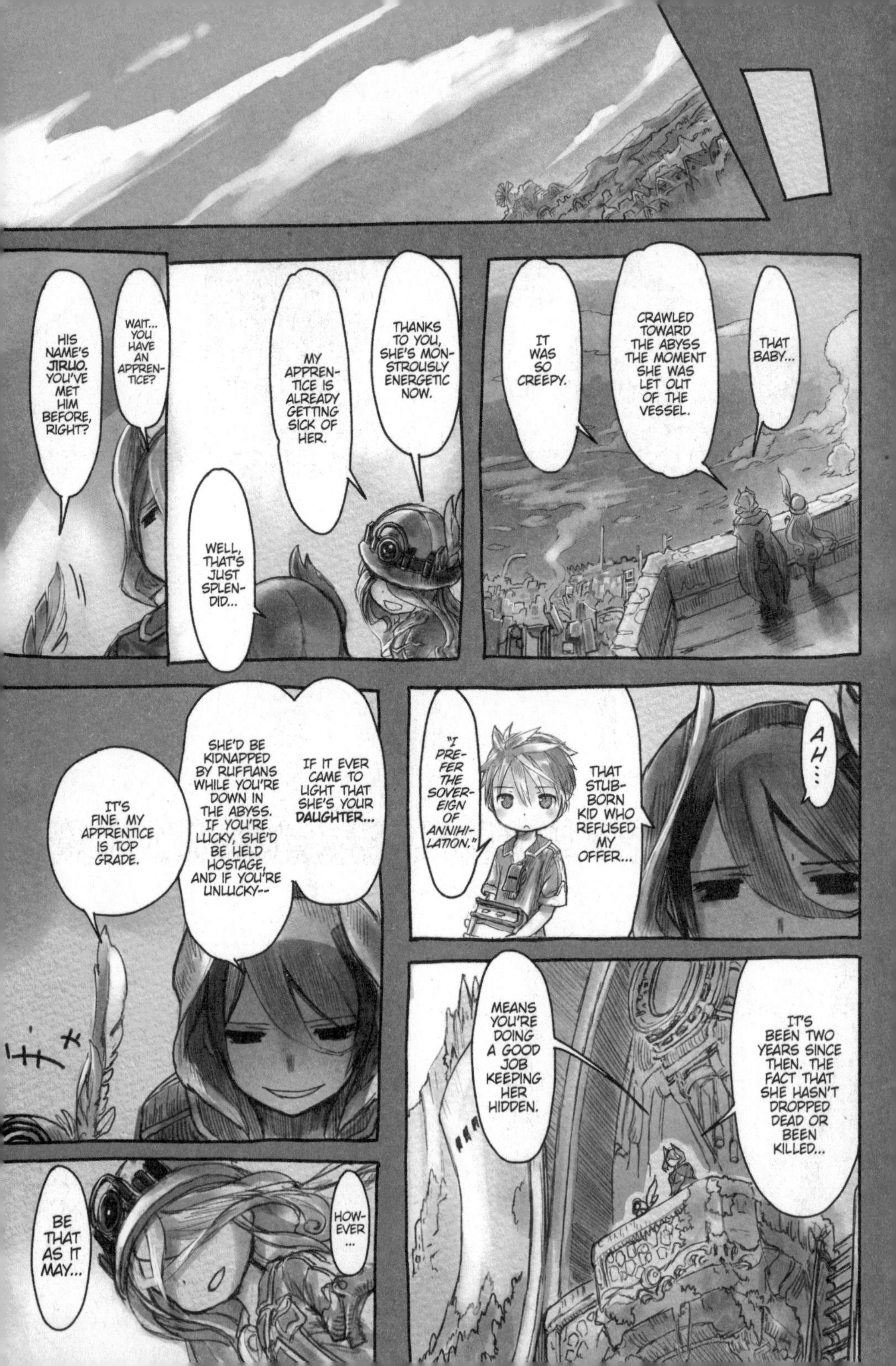
THAT BABY...
CRAWLED TOWARD THE ABYSS THE MOMENT SHE WAS LET OUT OF THE VESSEL.
IT WAS SO CREEPY.
THANKS TO YOU, SHE'S MONSTROUSLY ENERGETIC NOW.
MY APPRENTICE IS ALREADY GETTING SICK OF HER.
WELL, THAT'S JUST SPLENDID...
WAIT... YOU HAVE AN APPRENTICE?
HIS NAME'S JIRUO. YOU'VE MET HIM BEFORE, RIGHT?
AH...
THAT STUBBORN KID WHO REFUSED MY OFFER...
"I PREFER THE SOVEREIGN OF ANNIHILATION."
IT'S BEEN TWO YEARS SINCE THEN. THE FACT THAT SHE HASN'T DROPPED DEAD OR BEEN KILLED...
MEANS YOU'RE DOING A GOOD JOB KEEPING HER HIDDEN.
IF IT EVER CAME TO LIGHT THAT SHE'S YOUR DAUGHTER...
SHE'D BE KIDNAPPED BY RUFFIANS WHILE YOU'RE DOWN IN THE ABYSS. IF YOU'RE LUCKY, SHE'D BE HELD HOSTAGE, AND IF YOU'RE UNLUCKY--
IT'S FINE. MY APPRENTICE IS TOP GRADE.
HOWEVER...
BE THAT AS IT MAY...

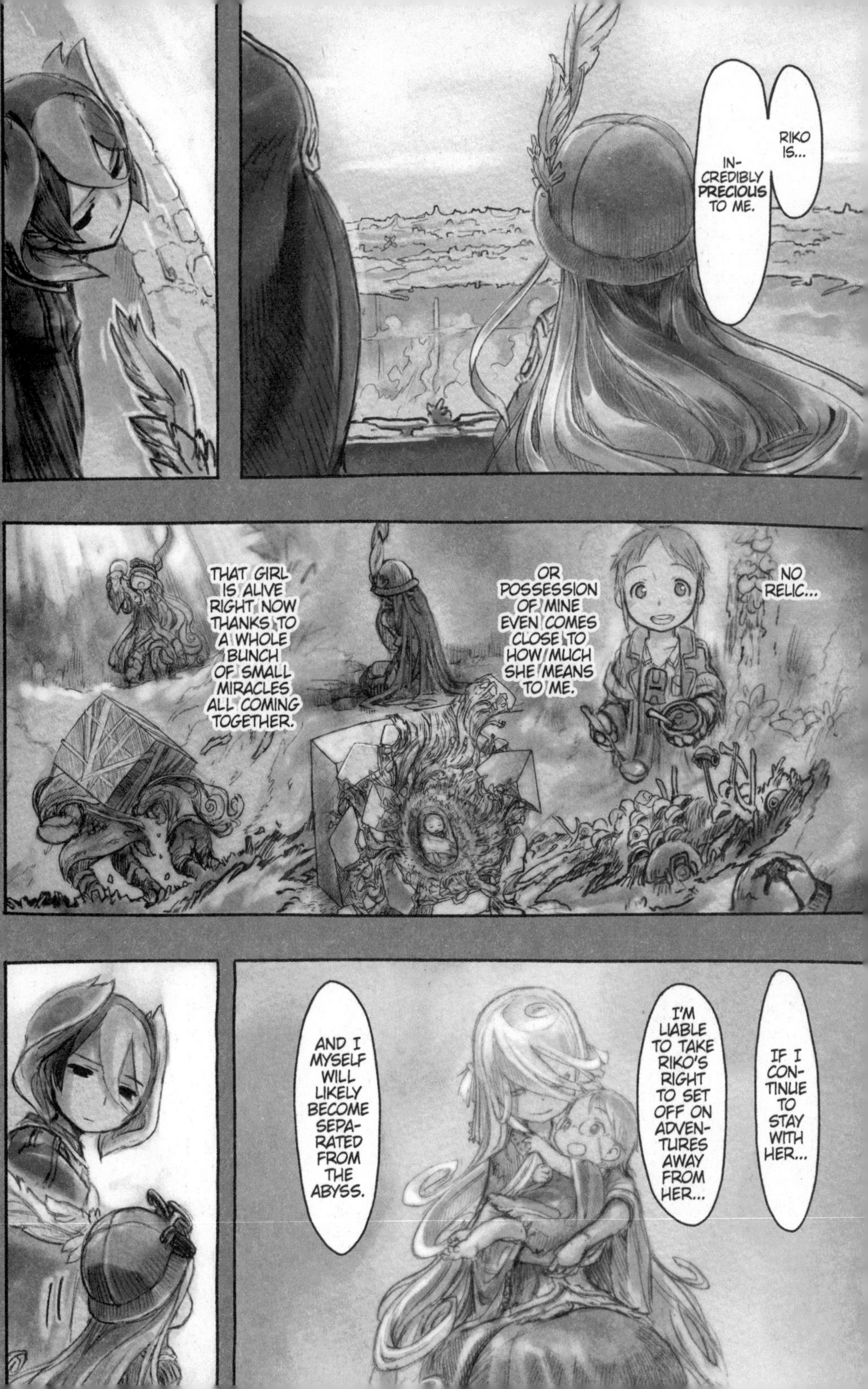

RIKO IS...
INCREDIBLY PRECIOUS TO ME.
NO RELIC...
OR POSSESSION OF MINE EVEN COMES CLOSE TO HOW MUCH SHE MEANS TO ME.
THAT GIRL IS ALIVE RIGHT NOW THANKS TO A WHOLE BUNCH OF SMALL MIRACLES ALL COMING TOGETHER.
IF I CONTINUE TO STAY WITH HER...
I'M LIABLE TO TAKE RIKO'S RIGHT TO SET OFF ON ADVENTURES AWAY FROM HER...
AND I MYSELF WILL LIKELY BECOME SEPARATED FROM THE ABYSS.

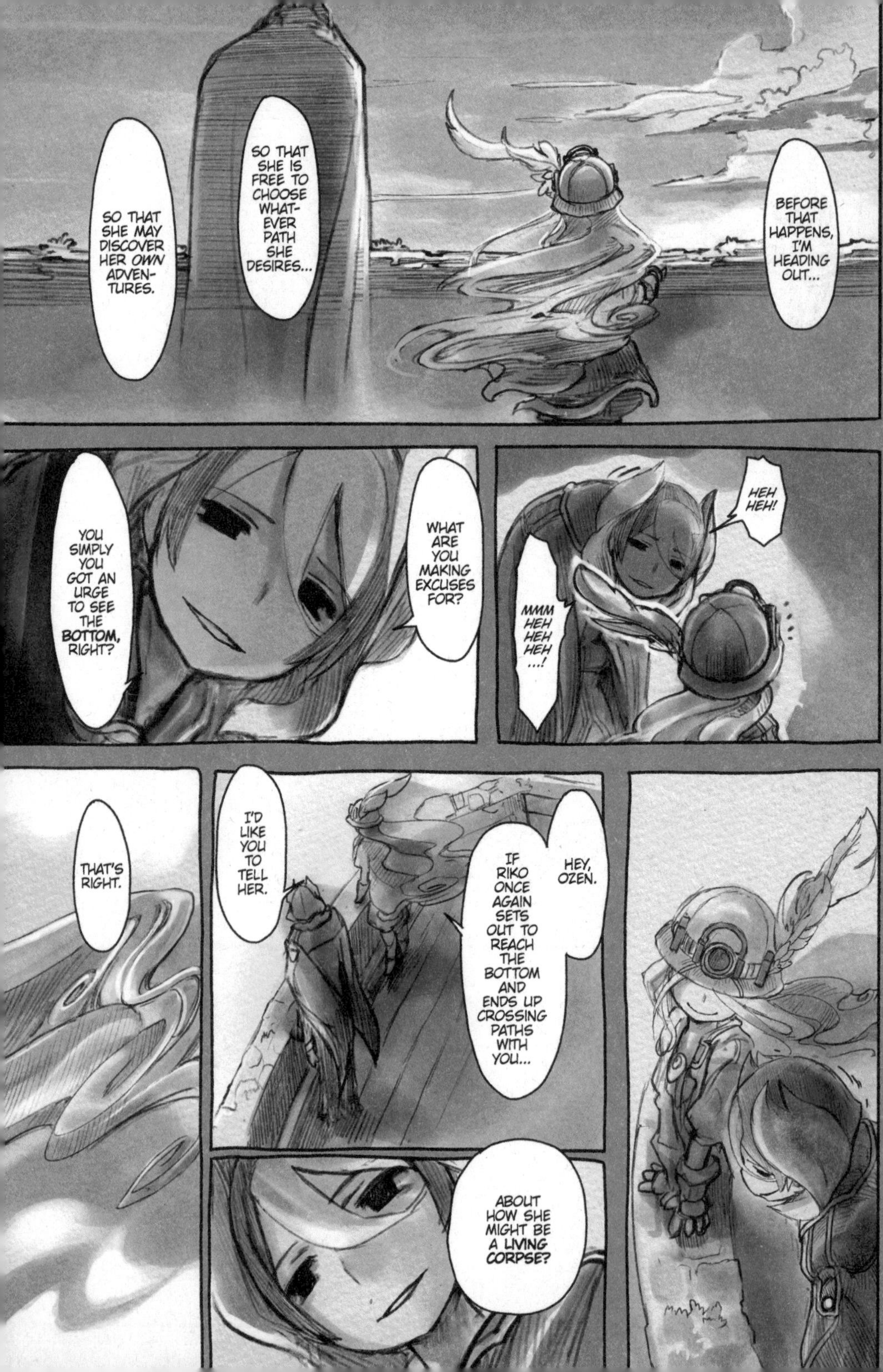
BEFORE THAT HAPPENS, I'M HEADING OUT...
SO THAT SHE IS FREE TO CHOOSE WHAT-EVER PATH SHE DESIRES...
SO THAT SHE MAY DISCOVER HER *OWN* ADVEN-TURES.
HEH HEH!
MMM HEH HEH HEH ...!
WHAT ARE YOU MAKING EXCUSES FOR?
YOU SIMPLY YOU GOT AN URGE TO SEE THE **BOTTOM**, RIGHT?
HEY, OZEN.
IF RIKO ONCE AGAIN SETS OUT TO REACH THE BOTTOM AND ENDS UP CROSSING PATHS WITH YOU...
I'D LIKE YOU TO TELL HER.
ABOUT HOW SHE MIGHT BE **A LIVING CORPSE?**
THAT'S RIGHT.

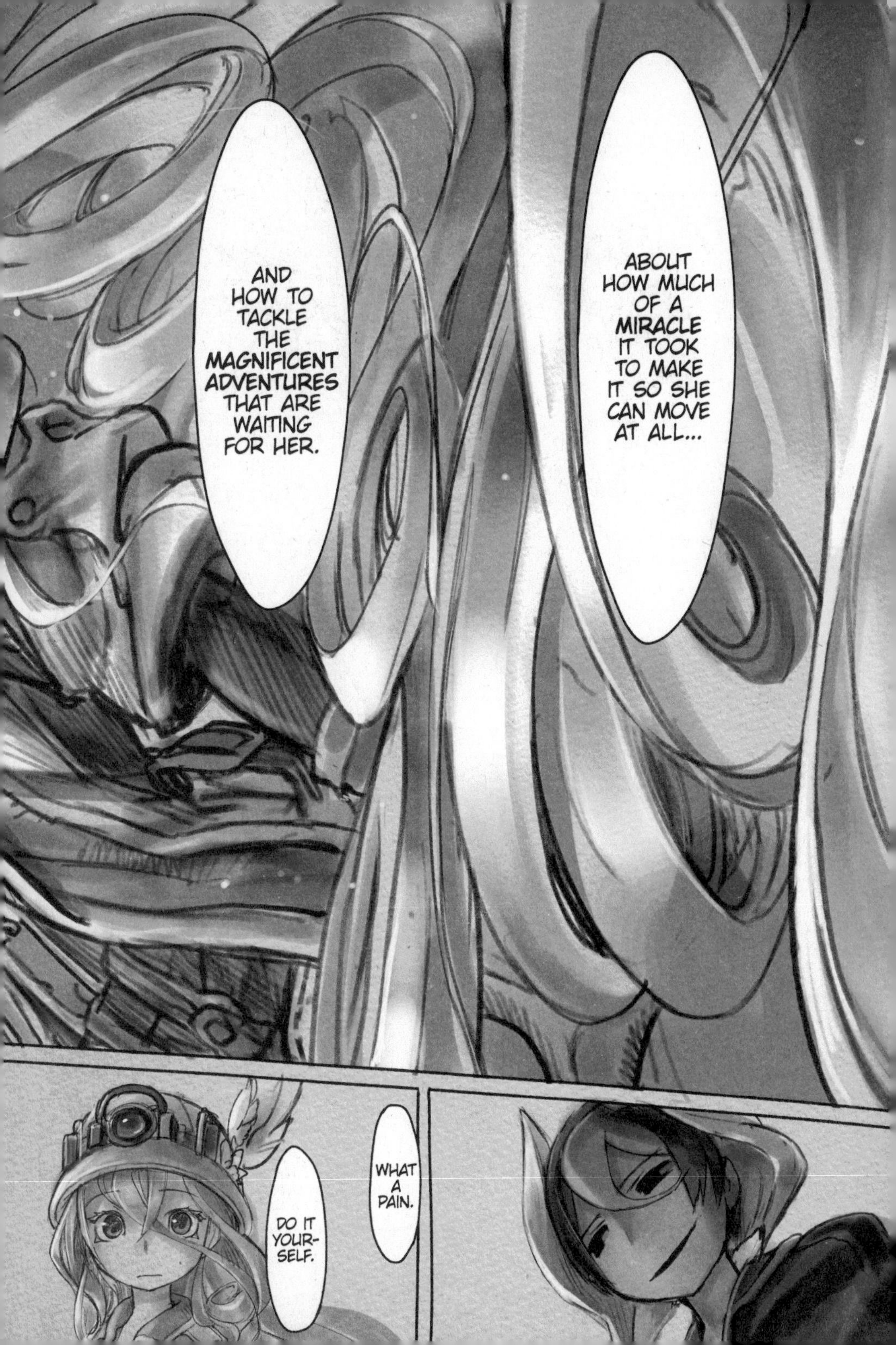
ABOUT HOW MUCH OF A MIRACLE IT TOOK TO MAKE IT SO SHE CAN MOVE AT ALL...
AND HOW TO TACKLE THE MAGNIFICENT ADVENTURES THAT ARE WAITING FOR HER.
WHAT A PAIN.
DO IT YOUR-SELF.

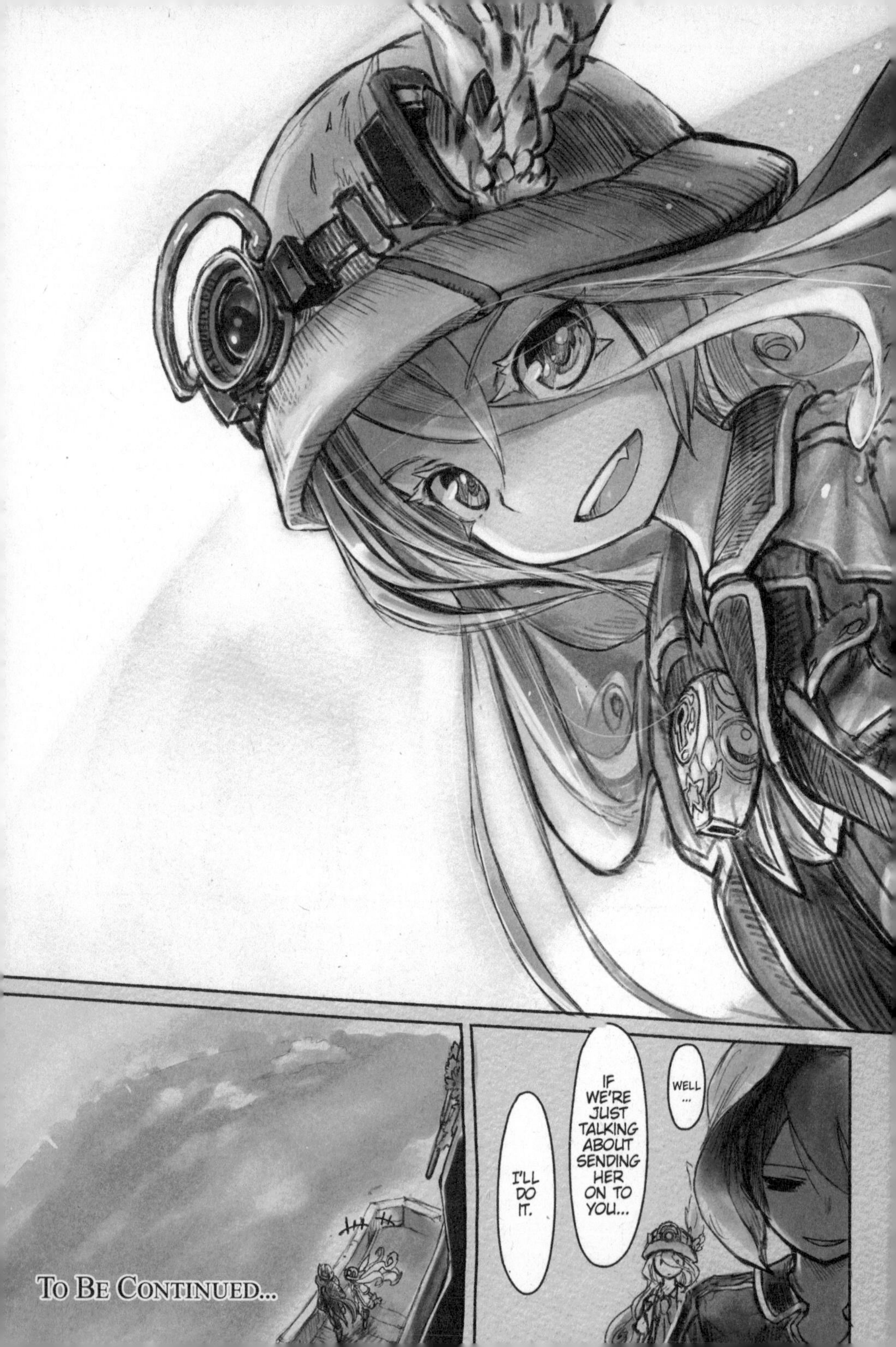
WELL...
IF WE'RE JUST TALKING ABOUT SENDING HER ON TO YOU...
I'LL DO IT.
TO BE CONTINUED...

SEVEN SEAS ENTERTAINMENT PRESENTS

MADE IN ABYSS

story and art by AKIHITO TSUKUSHI   VOLUME 2

TRANSLATION
Beni Axia Conrad

ADAPTATION
Jake Jung

LETTERING AND RETOUCH
James Gaubatz

LOGO DESIGN
Andrea Rodriguez

COVER DESIGN
Nicky Lim

PROOFREADER
Brett Hallahan
Dayna Abel

EDITOR
Jenn Grunigen

PRODUCTION ASSISTANT
CK Russell

PRODUCTION MANAGER
Lissa Pattillo

EDITOR-IN-CHIEF
Adam Arnold

PUBLISHER
Jason DeAngelis

MADE IN ABYSS VOLUME 2
©Akihito Tsukushi/TAKE SHOBO
Originally published in Japan in 2014 by Takeshobo Co. LTD., Tokyo.
English translation rights arranged with Takeshobo Co. LTD., Tokyo,
through TOHAN CORPORATION, Tokyo.

Seven Seas books may be purchased in bulk for promotional, educational, or
business use. Please contact your local bookseller or the Macmillan Corporate
and Premium Sales Department at 1-800-221-7945, extension 5442, or by
e-mail at MacmillanSpecialMarkets@macmillan.com.

Seven Seas and the Seven Seas logo are trademarks of
Seven Seas Entertainment, LLC. All rights reserved.

ISBN: 978-1-626927-74-2

Printed in Canada

First Printing: April 2018

10 9 8 7 6 5 4 3 2 1

FOLLOW US ONLINE: *www.sevenseasentertainment.com*

READING DIRECTIONS

This book reads from *right to left*, Japanese style. If
this is your first time reading manga, you start
reading from the top right panel on each page and
take it from there. If you get lost, just follow the
numbered diagram here. It may seem backwards at
first, but you'll get the hang of it! Have fun!!

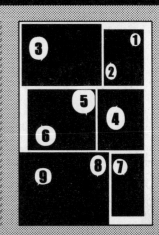

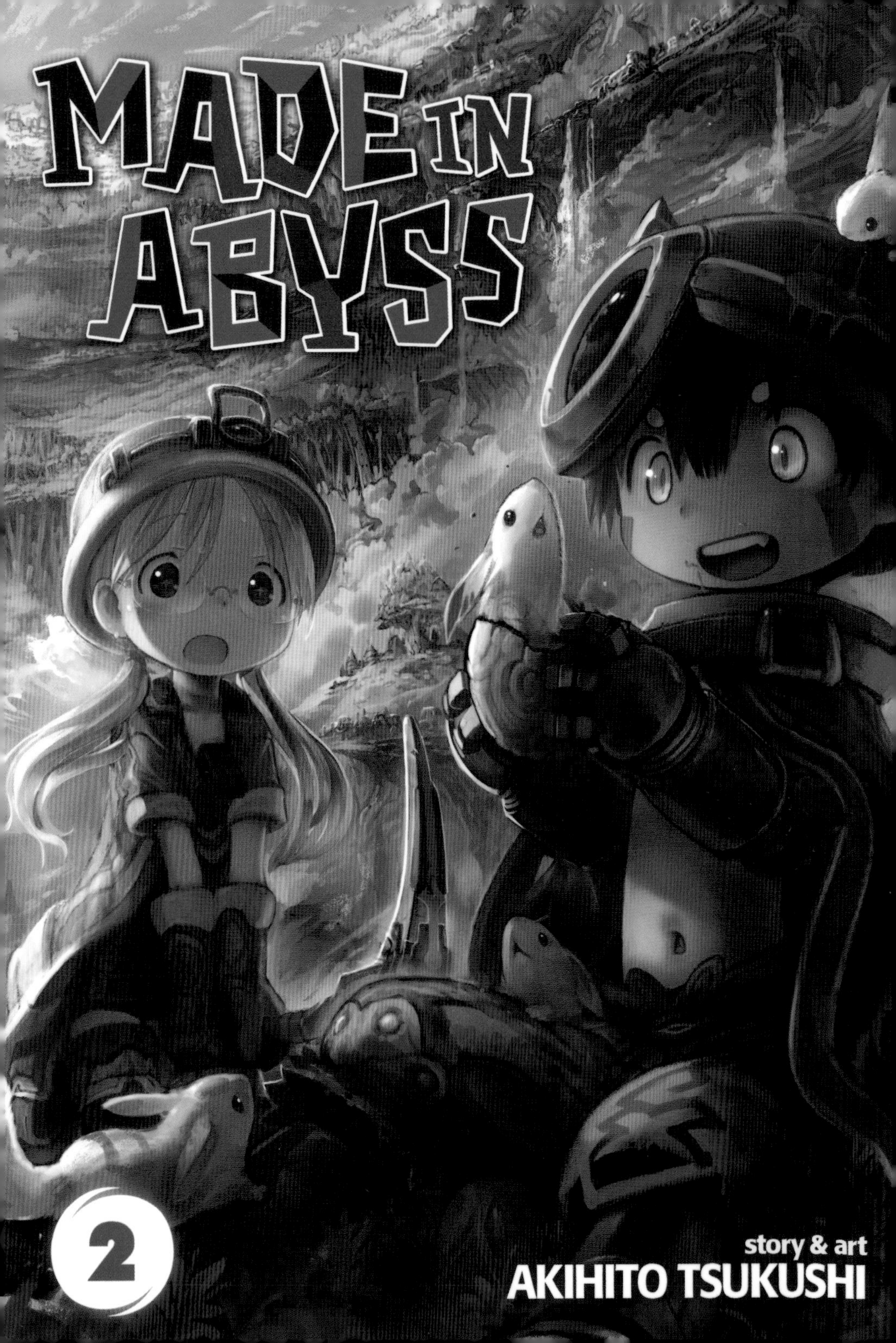
MADE IN ABYSS
2
story & art
AKIHITO TSUKUSHI

NETHER GLYPHS

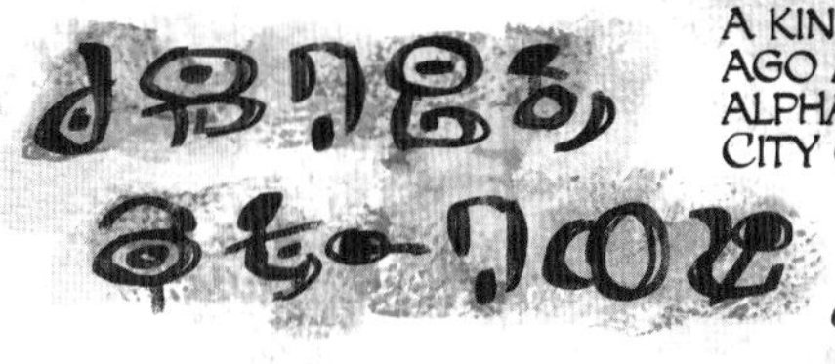

THESE ANCIENT CHARACTERS ARE FOUND ONLY WITHIN THE ABYSS. THEY CAN BE SEEN, EVEN NOW, ON THE RELICS THAT ARE SCATTERED ABOUT THERE.

THEY HAVE BEEN USED BY CAVE RAIDERS AS A KIND OF CODED LANGUAGE SINCE LONG AGO AND ARE NOW THE OFFICIAL ALPHABET OF ORTH, THE CITY OF THE GREAT PIT.

- HOWEVER, RELICS THAT ARE PUT UP FOR AUCTION OR DISPLAYED OVERSEAS ARE ALSO GIVEN NAMES IN FOREIGN LANGUAGES.

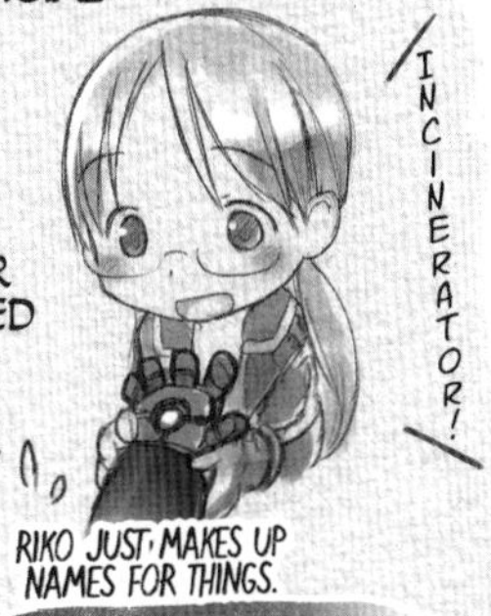
INCINERATOR!

RIKO JUST MAKES UP NAMES FOR THINGS.

COOKING UTENSILS THAT RIKO BROUGHT ALONG

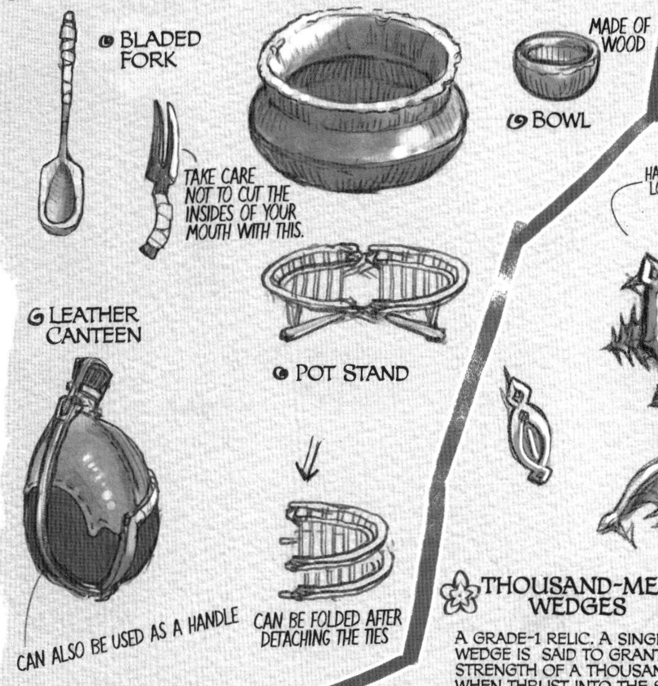
SPATULA SPOON
BLADED FORK
TAKE CARE NOT TO CUT THE INSIDES OF YOUR MOUTH WITH THIS.
POT
MADE OF WOOD
BOWL
LEATHER CANTEEN
POT STAND
CAN ALSO BE USED AS A HANDLE
CAN BE FOLDED AFTER DETACHING THE TIES

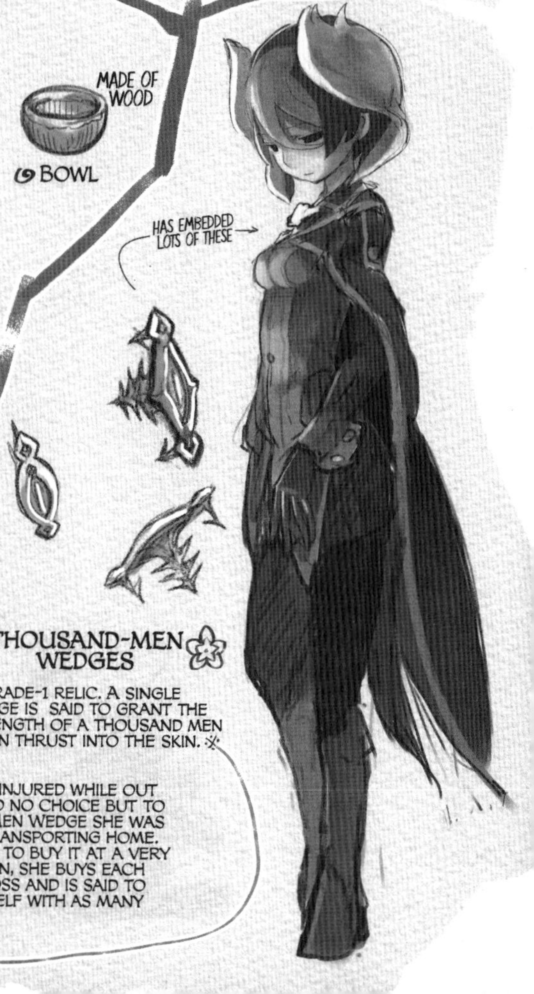
HAS EMBEDDED LOTS OF THESE

THOUSAND-MEN WEDGES

A GRADE-1 RELIC. A SINGLE WEDGE IS SAID TO GRANT THE STRENGTH OF A THOUSAND MEN WHEN THRUST INTO THE SKIN. ※

OZEN WAS SERIOUSLY INJURED WHILE OUT CAVE RAIDING AND HAD NO CHOICE BUT TO USE THE THOUSAND-MEN WEDGE SHE WAS IN THE PROCESS OF TRANSPORTING HOME. SHE ENDED UP HAVING TO BUY IT AT A VERY HIGH PRICE. SINCE THEN, SHE BUYS EACH ONE SHE COMES ACROSS AND IS SAID TO HAVE EMBEDDED HERSELF WITH AS MANY AS 120 OF THEM.

GRADE-1 RELIC:

① OBJECTS THAT CAN CHANGE THE BALANCE OF POWER BETWEEN COUNTRIES.

② OBJECTS THAT ARE EXTREMELY USEFUL WHEN CAVE RAIDING IN THE DEEPER LAYERS.